Learn, Teach...

Succeed...

With **REA's GACE Mathematics Assessment (022, 023)**
test prep, you'll be in a class all your own.

We'd like to hear from you!

Visit **www.rea.com** to send us your comments
or email us at **info@rea.com**

GACE® MATHEMATICS ASSESSMENT (022, 023)

GEORGIA ASSESSMENTS FOR THE CERTIFICATION OF EDUCATORS®

 TestWare® Edition

Greg Chamblee, Ph.D.
Georgia Southern University
Statesboro, Georgia

 Research & Education Association
Visit our Educator Support Center: www.rea.com/teacher
Updates to the test and this book: www.rea.com/gace.htm

Planet Friendly Publishing
GREEN EDITION
✓ Made in the United States
✓ Printed on Recycled Paper
Text: 10%   Cover: 10%
Learn more: www.greenedition.org

At REA we're committed to producing books in an Earth-friendly manner and to helping our customers make greener choices.

Manufacturing books in the United States ensures compliance with strict environmental laws and eliminates the need for international freight shipping, a major contributor to global air pollution.

And printing on recycled paper helps minimize our consumption of trees, water and fossil fuels. This book was printed on paper made with **10% post-consumer waste**. According to Environmental Defense's Paper Calculator, by using this innovative paper instead of conventional papers, we achieved the following environmental benefits:

Trees Saved: 4 • Air Emissions Eliminated: 776 pounds
Water Saved: 726 gallons • Solid Waste Eliminated: 229 pounds

For more information on our environmental practices, please visit us online at **www.rea.com/green**

Research & Education Association
61 Ethel Road West
Piscataway, New Jersey 08854
E-mail: info@rea.com

Georgia GACE® Mathematics Assesment (022, 023) With TestWare® on CD-ROM

Printed in the United States of America

Library of Congress Control Number 20100928192

ISBN-13: 978-0-7386-0703-0
ISBN-10: 0-7386-0703-7

For all references in this book, Georgia Assessments for the Certification of Educators and GACE® are trademarks, in the U.S. and/or other countries, of the Georgia Professional Standards Commission and Pearson Education, Inc., or its affiliates.

Windows® is a registered trademark of Microsoft Corporation.

The Mathematics Test Objectives presented in this book were created and implemented by the Georgia Professional Standards Commission and Pearson Education, Inc. For further information visit the GACE website at www.gace.nesinc.com.

REA® and TestWare® are registered trademarks of Research & Education Association, Inc.

F10-0101

About the Author

Dr. Greg Chamblee has taught mathematics on both the high school and university levels. He is currently a full professor at Georgia Southern University in the Department of Middle Grades and Secondary Education. He specializes in the area of middle grades and secondary mathematics education. His research emphasis is on the impact of technology on the teaching and learning process. Dr. Chamblee completed his doctorate at the University of North Carolina at Chapel Hill.

Acknowledgments

We would like to thank REA's Larry B. Kling, Vice President, Editorial, for supervising development; Pam Weston, Vice President, Publishing, for setting the quality standards for production integrity and managing the publication to completion; John Paul Cording, Vice President, Technology, for coordinating the design, development, and testing of REA's TestWare®; Alice Leonard, Senior Editor, for project management and preflight editorial review; Diane Goldschmidt, Senior Editor, for post-production quality assurance; Heena Patel, software project manager, for her software testing efforts; and Christine Saul, Senior Graphic Artist, for cover design.

We gratefully acknowledge Mel Friedman, Senior Math Editor for ensuring the integrity of the mathematics in this publication.

We also gratefully acknowledge Ashwath Narayana C and Jay G of Transcend Creative Services (TCS Publishing) for managing the page composition and typesetting, Laura Hoffman for technical editing, Wendell Anderson for copyediting, and Stephanie Reymann for creating the index.

Number Concepts and Operations

Real Number System and Its Components

The majority of solutions to algebra-related problems are located within the set of real numbers (R). Real numbers can be classified as either rational (Q) or irrational (S). The real number system is the union of these two sets, $R = Q \cup S$.

There are three important subsets of Q:

1. The set of all natural numbers, N, which is also called the counting numbers. $N = \{1, 2, 3, \ldots\}$

2. The set of whole numbers, W, where $W = \{0, 1, 2, 3, \ldots\}$.

3. The set of integers, I, where $I = \{\ldots, -3, -2, -1, 0, 1, 2, 3, \ldots\}$.

Rational numbers (set Q) are numbers that can be written in the form of $\frac{a}{b}$ where a and b are both integers and $b \neq 0$. Thus, we can write $Q = \{\frac{a}{b} \mid a, b \in I \text{ and } b \neq 0\}$. The decimal names for elements of Q are (1) terminating or (2) nonterminating with a repeating block.

S represents the set of real numbers that cannot be written as a repeating or terminating decimal.

Examples of rational numbers are 2, -3, $\frac{1}{2}$, $\sqrt{16}$, 0.25, and $1.\overline{35}$.

Examples of irrational numbers are

$\sqrt{5}$, $0.323223222\ldots$ π, and $-\sqrt[3]{7}$.

Real numbers are graphed on a real number line. Each real number has a one-to-one correspondence to its location on the number line. Here is an example of a real number line.

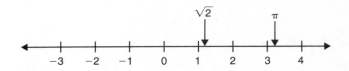

Figure 2.1

Real Number Properties of Equality

The standard properties of equality are as follows. We assume that a, b, and c are real numbers.

1. Reflexive Property of Equality: $a = a$.

2. Symmetric Property of Equality: If $a = b$, then $b = a$.

3. Transitive Property of Equality: If $a = b$, and $b = c$, then $a = c$

Real Number Operations and Their Properties

The operations of addition and multiplication have the majority of the properties. Here is a list of the most important of these properties. As stated above, we assume that a, b, and c are real numbers.

1. Closure Property of Addition: $a + b$ is a real number.

2. Closure Property of Multiplication: ab is a real number.

3. Commutative Property of Addition: $a + b = b + a$.

4. Commutative Property of Multiplication $ab = ba$.

5. Associative Property of Addition: $(a + b) + c = a + (b + c)$.

6. Associative Property of Multiplication: $(ab)c = a(bc)$.

7. Identity Property of Addition: $a + 0 = 0 + a = a$.

8. Identity Property of Multiplication: $a \times 1 = 1 \times a = a$.

9. Inverse Property of Addition: There is a real number $-a$ such that $a + -a = -a + a = 0$

10. Inverse Property of Multiplication: For each $a \neq 0$, there is a real number $\frac{1}{a}$ such that $a \times \frac{1}{a} = \frac{1}{a} \times a = 1$. The number $\frac{1}{a}$ can be written as a^{-1}.

11. Distributive Property: $a(b + c) = ab + ac$.

The operations of subtraction and division are also important. Here are the definitions of these operations. (a, b, and c are assumed to be real numbers.) Definition of Subtraction: $a - b = c$ if and only if $b + c = a$.

Many times subtraction is defined in terms of addition. $a - b = a + (-b)$

Definition of Division: $a \div b = c$ if and only if c is a unique real number such that $bc = a$.

The definition of division eliminates division by 0. Thus, for example, $5 \div 0$ as well as $0 \div 0$ have undefined solutions, but $0 \div 4 = 0$.

Many times division is defined in terms of multiplication. $a \div b = a \times b^{-1} = a \times \frac{1}{b}$.

Absolute Value

The distance that a number a is from 0 is known as its absolute value. The absolute value of a, $|a|$, is evaluated as follows:

$|a| = a$ when $a > 0$

$|a| = -a$ when $a < 0$

$|a| = 0$ when $a = 0$

EXAMPLE 1

Find the absolute value of $|-7|$

SOLUTION

$|-7| = 7$

EXAMPLE 2

Find the absolute value of $-|4|$

SOLUTION

$-|4| = -(4) = -4.$

Number Theory

Factors of an integer n are integers greater than or equal to 1 that are divisors of n.

For example, the factors of 16 are 1, 2, 4, 8, and 16.

The Fundamental Theorem of Arithmetic states that any integer greater than 1 can be written as a unique product of prime numbers. A prime number is a number whose factors are only 1 and itself. Integers that are not prime numbers are composite. The numbers 2, 7, and 23 are examples of prime numbers. The numbers 4, 15, and 100 are examples of composite numbers. The only exception is the number 1, which is neither prime nor composite.

EXAMPLE 3

What is the prime factorization of 24?

SOLUTION

Figure 2.2

Thus, $24 = 2^3 \cdot 3$

Greatest Common Divisor

The greatest common divisor of two numbers, a and b, written as GCD(a,b), is the largest positive integer that divides the number without a remainder. GCD is used when simplifying expressions. GCD(a,b) is determined by either multiplying the common prime factors between a and b or listing all the factors of a and b in increasing order with GCD(a,b) equaling the largest common factor.

EXAMPLE 4

Find the GCD of 24 and 36.

SOLUTION

$24 = 2^3 \cdot 3$ and $36 = 2^2 \cdot 3^2$. Thus, GCD (24,26) $= 2^2 \cdot 3 = 12$.

EXAMPLE 5

Find the GCD of $5xy^4$ and $20x^4y^3$.

SOLUTION

$5xy^4 = 5 \cdot x \cdot y \cdot y \cdot y \cdot y$ and $20x^4y^3 = 2^2 \cdot 5 \cdot x \cdot x \cdot x \cdot x \cdot y \cdot y \cdot y$ Thus, GCD $(20x^4y^3, 5xy^4) = 5xy^3$

Least Common Multiple

The least common multiple (LCM) of two numbers a and b, written as LCM(a,b), is the smallest positive number that is a multiple both of a and of b. Since it is a multiple, it can be divided by a and b without a remainder. LCM is used when finding the least common denominator (LCD). The LCM(a,b) is determined by either multiplying the highest prime factor powers between a and b or listing the multples of a and b with LCM(a,b) equaling the first multiple a and b have in common.

EXAMPLE 6

Find LCM of 24 and 36.

SOLUTION

$24 = 2^3 \cdot 3$ and $36 = 2^2 \cdot 3^2$. Thus, LCM (24,36) $= 2^3 \cdot 3^2 = 72$

EXAMPLE 7

Find the LCD of $2s - 4$ and $s^2 + 2s - 1$.

SOLUTION

$2s - 4 = 2(s - 2)$ and $s^2 + 2s - 8 = (s - 2)(s + 4)$. Thus, LCM $(2s - 4, s^2 + 2s - 8) = 2(s - 2)(s + 4)$

Number of Factors of a Given Integer

By the Fundamental Theorem of Arithmetic, we recall that each number can be written uniquely as a product of prime factors (except for the order of the factors).

The total number of factors of any number can be found by adding 1 to the exponent of each prime factor, and then multiplying these results.

EXAMPLE 8

What is the total number of factors for the number 120?

SOLUTION

Below is the prime factorization for 120.

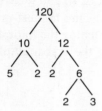

Thus, $120 = 2^3 \cdot 3^1 \cdot 5^1$. (We used the exponent of 1 on the bases 3 and 5 for clarification.) Add 1 to each exponent and multiply the results, to get $(4)(2)(2) = 16$. Thus, there are a total of 16 factors for the number 120. Remember that this total <u>includes</u> the number 1 and the number 120.

As a check for Example 8, here are the 16 factors: 1, 2, 3, 4, 5, 6, 8, 10, 12, 15, 20, 24, 30, 40, 60, and 120. If a number has only one base in its prime factorization, then simply add 1 to its exponent to determine the total number of factors. For example, $81 = 3^4$. Thus, there are five factors for 81.

Real Numbers and Integer Exponents

Integer exponents and their properties are used to solve many problems in the real number system. For each real number a, and for each positive integer n, then a^n represents a as a factor n times. The number a is called the base and n is called the exponent. Thus, a^5 is the equivalent expression for $a \times a \times a \times a \times a$.

Basic Properties of Exponents

For real numbers $a, b \neq 0$, and for each integer n:

1. $a^0 = 1$

2. $a^{-n} = \dfrac{1}{a^n}$

3. $(\dfrac{a}{b})^{-n} = (\dfrac{b}{a})^n$

For each real number $a \neq 0$, for each integer m, and for each integer n:

4. $a^m \cdot a^n = a^{m+n}$

5. $\dfrac{a^m}{a^n} = a^{m-n}$

6. $(ab)^m = a^m \cdot b^m$

7. $(\dfrac{a}{b})^m = \dfrac{a^m}{b^m}$

8. $(a^m)^n = a^{mn}$

EXAMPLE 9

What is the value of $(\dfrac{3}{4})^3$?

SOLUTION

$(\dfrac{3}{4})^3 = \dfrac{3^3}{4^3} = \dfrac{27}{64}.$

EXAMPLE 10

What is the value of $\dfrac{12^{20}}{12^{18}}$?

SOLUTION

$\dfrac{12^{20}}{12^{18}} = 12^{20-18} = 12^2 = 144.$

EXAMPLE 11

What is the simplified expression for $(6^4 x^3 y^5)^4$?

SOLUTION

$(6^4 x^3 y^5)^4 = 6^{4 \cdot 4} x^{3 \cdot 4} y^{5 \cdot 4} = 6^{16} x^{12} y^{20}.$

EXAMPLE 12

What is the simplified expression for $\dfrac{s^3 t^5}{st^2}$?

SOLUTION

$$\frac{s^3 t^5}{st^2} = s^{3-1}t^{5-2} = s^2 t^3.$$

EXAMPLE 13

What is the simplified expression for
$$\frac{(-2x^2 y^{-2})^3}{x^{-1}y^3}?$$

SOLUTION

$$\frac{(-2x^2 y^{-2})^3}{x^{-1}y^3} = \frac{(-2)^3 x^{2\cdot3} y^{(-2)(3)}}{x^{-1}y^3} = \frac{-8x^6 y^{-6}}{x^{-1}y^3}$$

$$= \frac{-8x^6 \cdot x}{y^3 \cdot y^6} = \frac{-8x^7}{y^9}.$$

Scientific Notation

Scientific notation is used to write very large and small numbers. Scientific numbers are written in the form $N \times 10^m$, where N and m are integers and $1 \le N < 10$.

In order to change a number from standard notation to scientific notation, count the number of places that the decimal point moves. This will correspond to the value of m. If the decimal point moves from left to right, m will be negative. If the decimal point moves from right to left, m will be positive.

EXAMPLE 14

Write 0.00000456 in scientific notation.

SOLUTION

In moving from 0.00000456 to 4.56, the decimal point moves six places to the right. Thus, 0.00000456 $= 4.56 \times 10^{-6}$.

EXAMPLE 15

Write 790,000 in scientific notation.

SOLUTION

The (invisible) decimal point is located to the right of the right-most zero. In moving from 790,000 to 7.9, the decimal point moves five places to the left. Thus, $790,000 = 7.9 \times 10^5$.

EXAMPLE 16

Simplify and write the answer in scientific notation: $(3.2 \times 10^3)(5.4 \times 10^{-8})$

SOLUTION

$(3.2 \times 10^3)(5.4 \times 10^{-8}) = 17.28 \; 10^{-5}$. However, 17.28 is not in scientific notation. In changing 17.28 to 1.728, the decimal point moves one place to the left. Since $17.28 = 1.728 \times 10^1$ the final answer becomes $1.728 \times 10^1 \times 10^{-5} = 1.728 \times 10^{-4}$.

In order to change a number from scientific notation to standard notation, look at the exponent for the base 10. This exponent represents the number of places that the decimal point must be moved. If this exponent is positive, move the decimal point to the right; if it is negative, move the decimal point to the left.

EXAMPLE 17

Write 2.34×10^7 in standard notation.

SOLUTION

The decimal point will move seven places to the right. Thus, the answer is 23,400,000.

EXAMPLE 18

Write 6.2×10^{-3} in standard notation.

SOLUTION

The decimal point will move three places to the left. Thus, the answer is 0.0062.

Algebra

Algebraic Terms

A **variable** is defined as symbol that represents an unknown quantity. A **constant** is defined as a symbol that represents only one value. A **term** is a constant, a variable, or a combination of constants and variables that only uses multiplication or division. If a term contains both constants and variables, the constant is known as the **coefficient** of the variable. A variable written without a coefficient is assumed to have a coefficient of 1. As examples, x is a variable with a coefficient of 1 and $5y^2$ is a term where y is a variable with a coefficient of 5.

An **algebraic expression,** often shortened to an **expression**, is a collection of one or more terms. If the number of terms is greater than 1, the expression is said to be the sum of the terms. Thus, 12, $7 + 4y,$ and $9w - 7 + z$ are examples of expressions.

A **monomial** is an expression that consists of one term. A **binomial** is an expression that consists of two terms. A **trinomial** is an expression that consists of three terms. In general, an expression that consists of two or more terms is called a **polynomial**. If two monomials are the same, or differ only by their coefficients, they are called **like terms**. As examples, $9x$ is a monomial, $9x + 2$ is a binomial, and $12x^2 + 9x + 2$ is a trinomial.

Furthermore, $7\ x^2y^2$ and $8\ x^2y^2$ are like terms. However, $6x^2y$ and $6xy^2$ are <u>not</u> like terms. Also, polynomials must have nonnegative integer exponents on their variables. The **degree** of a polynomial is the highest sum of the exponents on any single term. Thus the polynomial $12x^2 + 9x + 2$ is of degree 2. But the polynomial $2x^4y - 5x^3y^4$ is of degree 7, due to the sum of the exponents in the term $5x^3y^4$.

Addition of Polynomials

To add polynomials, combine like terms by adding just their coefficients. Note that parentheses are used to separate the polynomials.

EXAMPLE 1

Express $(2x^2 + 4x + 6) + (7x^2 + 3)$ as a single polynomial.

SOLUTION

$(2x^2 + 4x + 6) + (7x^2 + 3) = (2x^2 + 7x^2) + 4x + (6 + 3) = (2 + 7)x^2 + 4x + (6 + 3) = 9x^2 + 4x + 9.$

Subtraction of Polynomials

To subtract polynomials, change the sign of all of the terms being subtracted and then add like terms.

EXAMPLE 2

Express $(7xy^2 + 8y^2 + 8) - (5xy^2 + 5y^2)$ as a single polynomial.

SOLUTION

$(7xy^2 + 8y^2 + 8) - (5xy^2 + 5y^2) = 7xy^2 + 8y^2 + 8 - 5xy^2 - 5y^2 = (7xy^2 - 5xy^2) + (8y^2 - 5y^2) + 8 = (7 - 5)xy^2 + (8 - 5)y^2 + 8 = 2xy^2 + 3y^2 + 8.$

Multiplication of a Polynomial by a Monomial

In multiplying expressions in which at least one of them is not a monomial, we use the Distributive Property. To multiply a polynomial by a monomial, use the laws of exponents and combine like terms.

EXAMPLE 3

Express $(8a^2b^2)(7a^2 + 2)$ as a single polynomial.

SOLUTION

$(8a^2b^2)(7a^2 + 2) = (8a^2b^2)(7a^2) + (8a^2b^2)(2) = 56a^4b^2 + 16a^2b^2$

Multiplication of Two Binomials

To multiple two binomials, multiply each of the terms in the first binomial by the terms in the second binomial and combine like terms.

EXAMPLE 4

Express $(a + b)(a + b)$ as a single polynomial.

SOLUTION

$(a + b)(a + b) = a^2 + ab + ba + b^2 = a^2 + 2ab + b^2$

Multiplication of Two Polynomials

To multiple two polynomials multiply each of the terms in the first polynomial by the terms in the second polynomial and combine like terms.

EXAMPLE 5

Express $(5a^2 + b + 3)(a^3 + 3x)$ as a single polynomial.

SOLUTION

$5a^2 + b + 3)(a^3 + 3x) = (5a^2 + b + 3)(a^3) + (5a^2 + b + 3)(3x) = (5a^2)(a^3) + (b)(a^3) + (3)(a^3) + (5a^2)(3x) + (b)(3x) + (3)(3x) = 5a^5 + a^3b + 3a^3 + 15a^2x + 3bx + 9x^2$

Division of a Monomial by a Monomial

To divide a monomial by a monomial, divide the constant coefficients and the variable factors separately and then simplify.

EXAMPLE 6

Express $4xy^2z^3 \div 2yz^4$ in simplest form.

SOLUTION

$4xy^2z^3 \div 2yz^4 = \dfrac{4xy^2z^3}{2yz^4} = 2xyz^{-1} = \dfrac{2xy}{z}$. Note that the answer is not a polynomial because it has a variable in the denominator.

Division of a Polynomial by a Polynomial

In dividing one polynomial by a second polynomial, the following method is used. (Note that division by zero is not allowed.)

Step 1: The terms of both the polynomials are arranged in order of ascending or descending powers of one variable.

Step 2: The first term of the dividend is divided by the first term of the divisor, which gives the first term of the quotient.

Step 3: This first term of the quotient is multiplied by the entire divisor and the result is subtracted from the dividend.

Step 4: Using the remainder obtained in Step 3 as the new dividend, Steps 2 and 3 are repeated until the remainder is zero or the degree of the remainder is less than the degree of the divisor.

Step 5: The result is written in the form:

$$\frac{\textit{dividend}}{\textit{divisor}} = \text{quotient} + \frac{\textit{remainder}}{\textit{divisor}}.$$

EXAMPLE 7

Express $(2x^2 + x + 12) \div (x + 1)$ as a quotient with a remainder.

SOLUTION

$$\begin{array}{r l}
 & 2x - 1 \\
x + 1 \,\big) & 2x^2 + x + 12 \\
 & 2x^2 + 2x \\
\hline
 & -x + 12 \\
 & -x - 1 \\
\hline
 & 13
\end{array}$$

Figure 3.1

Thus, the answer is $2x - 1 + \dfrac{13}{x+1}$.

EXAMPLE 8

Express $(3x^3 - 6x + 4) \div (x - 2)$ as a quotient with a remainder.

SOLUTION

Whenever the successive terms of the dividend are "gapped," we fill in the gaps with zeros. This means that the dividend becomes $3x^3 + 0x^2 - 6x + 4$.

$$\begin{array}{r l}
 & 3x^2 + 6x + 6 \\
x - 2 \,\big) & 3x^3 + 0x^2 - 6x + 4 \\
 & 3x^3 - 6x^2 \\
\hline
 & 6x^2 - 6x \\
 & 6x^2 - 12x \\
\hline
 & 6x + 4 \\
 & 6x - 12 \\
\hline
 & 16
\end{array}$$

Figure 3.2

Thus, the answer is $3x^2 + 6x + 6 + \dfrac{16}{x-2}$.

Binomial Theorem

The binomial theorem is used to determine the coefficients of $(a + b)^n$ where a and b are not 0. The first term is always a^n with a coefficient of 1 and the last term is always b^n with a coefficient of 1. The terms between the first and last terms are found by subtracting 1 from exponent of the previous a^n and adding one to b term each time until the b term equals b^n. Here is how this pattern works.

From row 1, $(a + b)^0 = 1a^0b^0 = 1$

From row 2, $(a + b)^1 = 1a^1b^0 + 1a^0b^1 = a + b$

From row 3, $(a + b)^2 = 1a^2b^0 + 2a^1b^1 + 1a^0b^2 = a^2 + 2ab + b^2$

The coefficients of $(a + b)^n$ form a pattern, as shown below.

Row 1	1	$(a + b)^0$
Row 2	1 1	$(a + b)^1$
Row 3	1 2 1	$(a + b)^2$
Row 4	1 3 3 1	$(a + b)^3$
Row 5	1 4 6 4 1	$(a + b)^4$
Row 6	1 5 10 10 5 1	$(a + b)^5$

Figure 3.3

Each digit not equal to 1 can be determined from the sum of the two nearest numbers of the previous row. For example, the third number in row 5 (6) is found by adding the two closest numbers in row 4 (3 + 3). Similarly, the fourth number in row 6 (10) is the sum of the two closest numbers in row 5 (6 + 4). So, we can find the expansion for $(a + b)^5$ by using the coefficients in the sixth row. This means that $(a + b)^5 = a^5 + 5a^4b + 10a^3b^2 + 10a^2b^3 + 5ab^4 + b^5$.

There is a way to express $(a + b)^n$ in an expanded form. However, we need to define factorials and combinations. The factorial symbol (!) can be applied to any non zero integer. The number $n!$ is the product of all positive integers less than or equal to n. Thus, $n! = (n)(n-1)(n-2)(...)(1)$. As an example, $8! = (8)(7)(6)(...)(1) = 40,320$. The symbol $_nC_r$, where $r \leq n$, means the number of different combinations of r items taken from a total of n items. The associated formula is $_nC_r = \dfrac{n!}{[(n-r)!][r!]}$. As an example, $_{10}C_4 = \dfrac{10!}{(6!)(4!)} = \dfrac{3,628,800}{(720)(24)} = 210$.

The expanded form for $(a + b)^n$ becomes $a^n + (_nC_1)(a^{n-1})(b) + (_nC_2)(a^{n-2})(b^2) + (_nC_3)(a^{n-3})(b^3) + ... b^n$.

EXAMPLE 9

What is the fourth term of the expanded form for $(m + n)^7$?

SOLUTION

We are replacing a and b with m and n, respectively. Then the fourth term is $(_7C_3)(m^4)(n^3) = \dfrac{7!}{(4!)(3!)}(m^4)(n^3) = \dfrac{5040}{(24)(6)}(m^4)(n^3) = 35m^4n^3$.

EXAMPLE 10

What is the sixth term of the expanded form for $(x + y)^{12}$?

SOLUTION

We are replacing a and b with x and y, respectively. Then the sixth term is given by $(_{12}C_5)(x^7)(y^5)$.

We calculate $_{12}C_5 = \dfrac{12!}{(7!)(5!)} = \dfrac{479,001,600}{(5040)(120)} = 792$. The final answer is $792x^7y^5$.

Direct and Inverse Variation

Direct variation between x and y means that both variables either increase or decrease at the same time. So, y varies directly as x if there is a constant k such that $y = kx$. Inverse variation between x and y means that one variable increases while the other variable decreases at the same time. So, y varies inversely as x if there is a constant k such that $xy = k$.

An example of direct variation is the amount paid (y) to purchase tickets compared to the number of tickets (t) purchased for a given cost per ticket. If the cost of a ticket is \$5, then $y = 5t$. An example of inverse variation scenario is the amount of hours (k) to clean a yard compared to the number of individuals (x) cleaning the yard, given that all individuals clean at the same pace. If one person working alone would need 12 hours, then $xy = 12$.

EXAMPLE 11

If y varies directly as x, and $y = 12$ when $x = 20$, find x when $y = 30$.

SOLUTION

Since y varies directly as x, we can write $y = kx$. This equation can also be written as $\dfrac{y_1}{x_1} = \dfrac{y_2}{x_2} = k$. Let's substitute 12 for y_1, 20 for x_1, and 30 for y_2. Then $\dfrac{12}{20} = \dfrac{30}{x_2}$. Cross-multiplying, we get $12x_2 = 600$. Thus, $x_2 = \dfrac{600}{12} = 50$.

EXAMPLE 12

If y varies inversely as x, and $y = 12$ when $x = 20$, find x when $y = 30$.

SOLUTION

Since y varies inversely as x, we can write $xy = k$. This equation can also be written as $x_1y_1 = x_2y_2 = k$. As in Example 11, $x_1 = 20$, $y_1 = 12$, and $y_2 = 30$. Then $(20)(12) = (x_2)(30)$, which becomes $240 = 30x_2$. Thus, $x_2 = \dfrac{240}{30} = 8$.

Relations and Functions

A **relation** is any set of ordered pairs of values. The set of first elements of a relation is called a **domain**, whereas the set of second elements of a relation is called a **range**. Consider the following examples.

$B = \{(2, 3), (5, 6), (9, 8)\}$. The domain is $\{2, 5, 9\}$ and the range is $\{3, 6, 8\}$.

$C = \{(4, 6), (6, 1), (8, 1), (0, 7)\}$. The domain is $\{4, 6, 8, 0\}$ and the range is $\{6, 1, 7\}$.

$D = \{(5, 2), (9, 3), (5, 3)\}$. The domain is $\{5, 9\}$ and the range is $\{2, 3\}$.

Note that since the domain and range represent sets, they must contain only unique elements.

A **function** is a set of ordered pairs of numbers (x, y) in which a single value of y is assigned to each value of x. Sets B and C would be functions. (Range values may be repeated for different domain values.) However, set D is _not_ a function because the element 5 in the domain is assigned to both 2 and 3 in the range.

Since the value of x determines the value of y, y is called the **dependent variable** and x is called the **independent variable**. The set of all x values for which the function is defined is called the **domain** of the function. The set of corresponding values of y is called the **range** of the function. Because a **relation** is any set of ordered pairs of numbers (x, y), a function is a specific type of relation. The comparison of relations that are functions to those that are not functions is shown graphically in Figures 3.4 and 3.5 below.

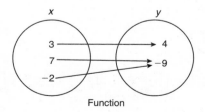

Function

Figure 3.4

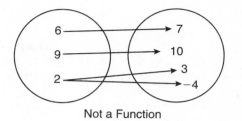

Not a Function

Figure 3.5

In Figure 3.4, the set of circles on the left illustrates the set $\{(3, 4), (7, -9), (-2, -9)\}$, where each x value is assigned to a single y value. (Note that y values may be repeated.) The set of circles on the right illustrates the set $\{(6, 7), (9, 10), (2, 3), (2, -4)\}$. This is not a function because the x value of 2 is assigned to both y values of 3 and -4.

EXAMPLE 12

What are the domain and range of the function whose equation is given by $y = 5x + 2$?

SOLUTION

We first determine if there are x-values (domain) for which the function is undefined (i.e., dividing by zero). Since there are none, the **domain** for this function is the set of real numbers. The range is determined by looking at the outcomes of all the domain values. The substitution of any real number for x results in a real number for y. So, the **range** of this function is the set of real numbers.

EXAMPLE 13

What are the domain and range of the function whose equation is given by $y = \sqrt{4x - 2}$?

SOLUTION

Any quantity inside a square root symbol must be non-negative, so $4x - 2 \geq 0$. The solution to this inequality is $x \geq \dfrac{1}{2}$. Thus, the domain is all values greater than or equal to $\dfrac{1}{2}$. Since the value of a square root must be non-negative, the range must be all non-negative values.

EXAMPLE 14

What are the domain and range for the function whose equation is given by

$$y = \frac{1}{(x-4)(x+1)}?$$

SOLUTION

A fraction may never contain a zero value in the denominator. Thus, neither $x - 4$ nor $x + 1$ may have a value of zero. Symbolically, $x - 4 \neq 0$ and $x + 1 \neq 0$. Thus, the domain is all real numbers except 4 and -1. In order to find the range, we note that if 1 is divided by any real number except zero, the result is a real number. Thus, the range is all real numbers except zero.

Operations with Functions

Functions can be added, subtracted, multiplied, or divided to form new functions.

Here are four basic identities:

(a) $(f + g)(x) = f(x) + g(x)$

(b) $(f - g)(x) = f(x) - g(x)$

(c) $(f \cdot g)(x) = f(x) \cdot g(x)$

(d) $(f/g)(x) = f(x)/g(x)$

EXAMPLE 15

If $f(x) = 2x + 3$ and $g(x) = x^2$, what are the simplified expressions for $(f + g)(x)$, $(f - g)(x)$, $(f \cdot g)(x)$, and $(f \cdot g)(x)$?

SOLUTION

$(f + g)(x) = f(x) + g(x) = 2x + 3 + x^2 = x^2 + 2x + 3$.

$(f - g)(x) = f(x) - g(x) = 2x + 3 - x^2 = -x^2 + 2x + 3$

$(f \cdot g)(x) = f(x) \cdot g(x) = (2x + 3)(x^2) = 2x^3 + 3x^2$

$(f/g)(x) = f(x)/g(x) = \dfrac{2x + 3}{x^2}$

The **composition** function $f \circ g$ is defined $(f \circ g)(x) = f(g(x))$. We first express $g(x)$ explicitly in terms of x. Then the function rule for $f(x)$ is applied to the expression for $g(x)$.

Note that $(f \circ g)(x)$ does <u>not</u> mean the same as $f(x) \cdot g(x)$.

EXAMPLE 16

If $f(x) = 2x + 3$ and $g(x) = x^2$, what are the simplified expressions for $(f \circ g)(x)$ and $(g \circ f)(x)$?

SOLUTION

$(f \circ g)(x) = f(g(x)) = 2(x^2) + 3 = 2x^2 + 3$

$(g \circ f)(x) = g(f(x)) = (2x + 3)^2 = 4x^2 + 12x + 9$

EXAMPLE 17

If $f(x) = \sqrt{x + 5}$ and $g(x) = \dfrac{2}{x}$, what are the simplified expressions for $(f \circ g)(x)$ and $(g \circ f)(x)$?

SOLUTION

$(f \circ g)(x) = f(\dfrac{2}{x}) = \sqrt{\dfrac{2}{x} + 5}$, and

$(g \circ f)(x) = g(\sqrt{x + 5}) = \dfrac{2}{\sqrt{x + 5}}$.

Note that, in general, $(f \circ g)(x) \neq (g \circ f)(x)$.

The **inverse** of a function, f^{-1}, is obtained by interchanging the x and y then solving for y. Two functions f and g are inverses of one another if $g \circ f = x$ and $f \circ g = x$.

EXAMPLE 18

What is the inverse of $f(x) = 4x + 3$?

SOLUTION

We start with $y = 4x + 3$. Then, by interchanging x and y, $x = 4y + 3$. Now subtract 3 and divide by 4 to get $y = \dfrac{x-3}{4}$. Thus, $f^{-1}(x) = \dfrac{x-3}{4}$.

EXAMPLE 19

What is the inverse of $f(x) = \sqrt{2x-1}$?

SOLUTION

We start with $y = \sqrt{2x-1}$. Then interchange the variables so that $x = \sqrt{2y-1}$. By squaring both sides, we get $x^2 = 2y - 1$. Now add 1 and divide by 2, so that $y = \dfrac{x^2+1}{2}$. Thus, $f^{-1}(x) = \dfrac{x^2+1}{2}$.

Note that our recent claim that $f(f^{-1}(x)) = f^{-1}(f(x)) = x$ can be readily verified with both Examples 18 and 19. Let's check this result for Example 18. $f(f^{-1}(x)) = f(\dfrac{x-3}{4}) = 4(\dfrac{x-3}{4}) + 3 = x - 3 + 3 = x$. Also, $f^{-1}(f(x)) = f^{-1}(4x + 3) = \dfrac{(4x+3)-3}{4} = \dfrac{4x}{4} = x$. The reader is encouraged to verify this identity for Example 19.

Linear Equations

Equations of the form $ax + by = c$, where a, b, and c are constants and a, $b \neq 0$, are called **linear equations** in two variables. Linear equations can be written in three forms: slope-intercept, standard form, and point-slope form.

Slope-intercept form is $y = mx + b$, where m is the slope and b is the y-intercept of the line. The slope of the line containing two points (x_1, y_1) and (x_2, y_2) is given by the fraction $\dfrac{y_2 - y_1}{x_2 - x_1}$. The y-intercept is the point $(0, b)$.

Standard form is $ax + by = c$, where a and b cannot both be zero. For example, $y = 2x + 3$ written in standard form is $-2x + y = 3$.

Point-slope form is $y - y_0 = m(x - x_0)$, where m is the slope and (x_0, y_0) is a point on the line.

EXAMPLE 20

Determine the slope of the line that goes through the two points $(2, 4)$ and $(-1, 2)$.

SOLUTION

Slope $= m = \dfrac{2-4}{-1-2} = \dfrac{-2}{-3} = \dfrac{2}{3}$.

EXAMPLE 21

Find the slope, y-intercept, and x-intercept of the equation $8x + 4y - 12 = 0$.

SOLUTION

In order to write $8x + 4y - 12 = 0$ in slope-intercept form, add $-8x + 12$ to both sides to get $4y = -8x + 12$. Then divide by 2 so that $y = -2x + 3$. The slope is -2. The y-intercept is $(0, 3)$. The x-intercept is found by solving for x when $y = 0$. By substitution, $0 = -2x + 3$. Solving, $x = \dfrac{3}{2}$. Thus, the x-intercept is $(\dfrac{3}{2}, 0)$.

EXAMPLE 22

Write the point-slope form of the equation whose line contains the point $(-6, 5)$ and whose slope is 3.

SOLUTION

The answer is $y - 5 = 3(x + 6)$.

Graphing a Linear function

Horizontal lines have a slope of zero and are written in the form $y = k$. Vertical lines have an undefined slope and are written in the form $x = k$. In both cases, k is a constant.

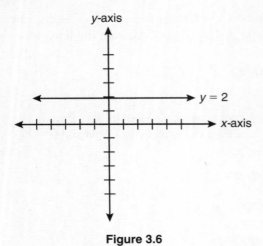

Figure 3.6

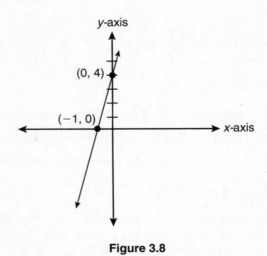

Figure 3.7

Figures 3.6 and 3.7 illustrate a horizontal line and a vertical line, respectively.

The process for graphing non-horizontal and non-vertical lines follows.

Step One: Write linear equation in slope-intercept form, if needed.

Step Two: Determine two points on the graph. The typical points to plot are the x-intercept and the y-intercept.

Step Three: Graph the points and draw a line through the two points.

EXAMPLE 23

Graph: $y = 4x + 4$.

SOLUTION

The y-intercept is found when $x = 0$. Then $y = 4(0) + 4 = 4$. So, the y-intercept is $(0, 4)$. Similarly, the x-intercept is found when $y = 0$. Then $0 = 4x + 4$, so $x = -1$. So, the x-intercept is $(-1, 0)$. Now, plot $(0, 4)$ $(-1, 0)$ and draw the line through these two points. Figure 3.8 shows the desired graph.

Figure 3.8

Determining the Equation of a Line Given a Table

Step One: Plot the points on a graph to determine if all the points are collinear (i.e., lie on a straight line). If the points do not lie on a straight line the graph is not linear.

Step Two: Choose 2 points from the table. Calculate the slope of the line.

Step Three. Determine the y-intercept using one of the points from the table. [Note: Check the table to see if $(0, y)$ is given in the table, since $(0, y)$ is the y-intercept.]

EXAMPLE 24

Determine the line through which all of the points in the table lie written in slope-intercept form.

x	-2	0	2
y	-2	4	10

SOLUTION

Step One: Insert Figure 3.9, which shows that all the points are contained in a straight line.

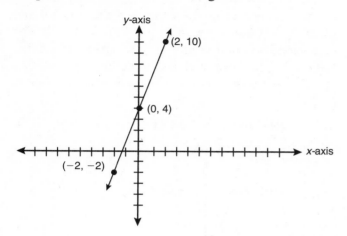

Figure 3.9

Step Two: Calculate the slope using the two points $(-2, -2)$ and $(0, 4)$. Then $m = \dfrac{y_2 - y_1}{x_2 - x_1} = \dfrac{4 + 2}{0 + 2} = 3$.

Step Three: The point $(0, 4)$ is in the table. The y-intercept (b) is 4. The equation of the line is of the form: $y = mx + b$, where $m = 3$ and $b = 4$. Thus, the answer is $y = 3x + 4$.

Determining the Equation of a Line Given a Graph

Step One: Choose two points on the line.

Step Two: Calculate the slope of the line.

Step Three: Calculate the y-intercept using a point on the line and the calculated slope. [Note: Check the table to see if $(0, y)$ is given in the table, since $(0, y)$ is the y-intercept.]

EXAMPLE 25

Determine the equation, in slope intercept form, of the line containing the points in the following graph.

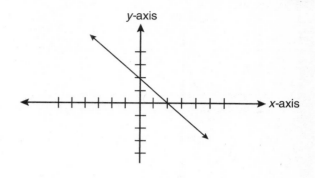

Figure 3.10

SOLUTION

Step One: Choose 2 points on the graph. [x-intercept and y-intercept if possible]

The x-intercept is $(2, 0)$. The y-intercept is $(0, 2)$.

Step Two: Determine the line using the 2 points. The b value must be 2, so we know that $y = mx + 2$. Now solve for m using the point, $(2, 0)$.

$0 = (m)(2) + 2$. Then $m = -1$. Thus, the equation of the line is $y = -x + 2$.

Quadratic Functions

A **quadratic function** (or function of second degree) is defined as $f(x) = ax^2 + bx + c$, where a, b, and c are real numbers and $a \neq 0$. (If $a = 0$, the quadratic is reduced to a linear function whose graph is a straight line.)

The graph of $y = ax^2 + bx + c$ is a U-shaped curve known as a parabola. A minimum of three points are needed to graph a parabola, preferably the vertex and a point on each side of the vertex. The graph of a parabola opens up when $a > 0$ (Figure 3.11) and downward when $a < 0$ (Figure 3.12).

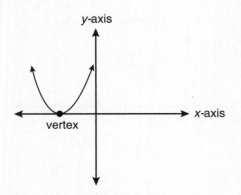

Figures 3.11

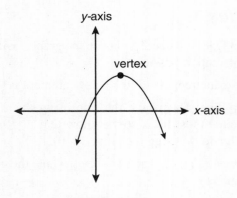

Figures 3.12

The vertex of a parabola is the point $(-\frac{b}{2a}, f(-\frac{b}{2a})) = (\frac{-b}{2a}, \frac{4ac-b^2}{4a})$. A parabola's axis (line of symmetry) is the line $x = \frac{-b}{2a}$.

NOTE:

Instead of memorizing vertex coordinates as $(\frac{-b}{2a}, \frac{4ac-b^2}{4a})$, it will be easier to simply memorize the vertex's x coordinate as $\frac{-b}{2a}$, then substitute this value of x into the formula for $f(x)$.

EXAMPLE 26

Graph $y = x^2 + 3$, by choosing the vertex and two other points.

SOLUTION

The vertex is $(\frac{-b}{2a}, \frac{4ac-b^2}{4a}) = (\frac{-0}{2(1)}, \frac{4(1)(3)-0^2}{4(1)}) = (0, 3)$

Substitute a value for x that is greater than 0 and solve for y. Choosing $x = 2$, $y = (2)^2 + 3 = 7$. The corresponding point is $(2, 7)$. Now substitute a value for x that is less than zero and solve for y. Choosing $x = -2$, $y = (-2)^2 + 3 = 7$. The corresponding point is $(-2, 7)$.

Plot and connect the points $(0, 3)$, $(2, 7)$, and $(-2, 7)$.

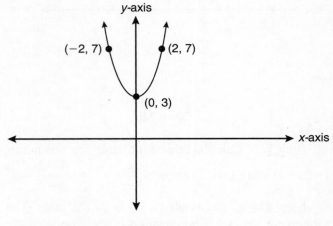

Figure 3.13

EXAMPLE 27

Determine the vertex, line of symmetry, domain, and range of $y = 2x^2 - 5x + 4$.

SOLUTION

The vertex is $(\frac{-b}{2a}, \frac{4ac-b^2}{4a}) = (\frac{-(-5)}{2(2)}, \frac{4(2)(4)-(-5)^2}{4(2)}) = (\frac{5}{4}, \frac{7}{8})$.

The line of symmetry is $x = \frac{-b}{2a} = \frac{-(-5)}{2(2)} = \frac{5}{4}$.

The domain is all real numbers. Since $a > 0$, the parabola opens up. The smallest y-value is located at $\frac{7}{8}$, which is the y-coordinate of the vertex. Thus, the range is the interval $[\frac{7}{8}, +\infty)$.

(Note: ∞ means infinity.) Another way to state the range is all real numbers greater than or equal to $\frac{7}{8}$.

EXAMPLE 28

Graph $y = 2x^2 - 5x + 4$.

SOLUTION

We already have the vertex, which is $(\frac{5}{4}, \frac{7}{8})$. Let's select two x values, one greater than $\frac{5}{4}$ and one less than $\frac{5}{4}$. If $x = 3$, then $y = (2)(3^2) - (5)(3) + 4 = 7$. The corresponding point is $(3, 7)$.

If $x = 0$, $y = (2)(0^2) - (5)(0) + 4 = 4$. The corresponding point is $(0, 4)$. Using the three points $(\frac{5}{4}, \frac{7}{8})$, $(3, 7)$, and $(0, 4)$, the graph appears as Figure 3.14.

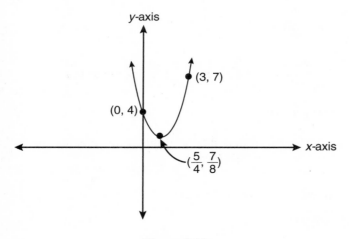

Figure 3.14

Function Transformations

Function transformations involve moving [shifting] a function up or down the y-axis, moving [shifting] a function left or right along the x-axis, and/or expanding or narrowing a function. All movements are

in relation to the parent function and the origin. The parent linear function is $y = x$. For a linear function, $y = mx + b$, a positive b value moves the y-intercept up the y-axis and a negative b value moves the y-intercept down the y-axis.

EXAMPLE 29

The graph of $y = -3x - 7$ represents what type of vertical shift relative to the graph of $y = x$?

SOLUTION

Since $b = -7$, the graph is shifted seven units down from the origin. (Note that the value of m does not affect this shift.)

The parent quadratic function is $y = x^2$, which is a parabola. (The vertex is at the origin.) To determine horizontal and/or vertical shifts for any parabola in the form $y = ax^2$ (with vertex at the origin), use the form $y = a(x - h)^2 + k$. In this formula, a represents how the function expands or narrows, h represents the movement along the x-axis and k represents the movement along the y-axis. The line $x = h$ is the axis of symmetry and (h, k) is the vertex.

EXAMPLE 30

The graph of $y = -2x^2 - 8x - 1$ represents what horizontal and/or vertical shifts from the graph of $y = x^2$?

SOLUTION

Write the given equation in the form $y = a(x - h)^2 + k$ by completing the square.

First, factor out -2 from x^2 and x terms to get $y = -2(x^2 + 4x) - 1$. Second, complete the square for $x^2 + 4x$. Then, $y = -2(x^2 + 4x + 4) - 1 - (-2)(4)$, which simplifies to $y = -2(x + 2)^2 + 7$.

Then, $h = -2$ and $k = 7$. The graph of this function is moved two units to the left and seven units up from $y = -2x^2$.

NOTE

As a check to the solution of Example 30, select any point on the graph of $y = -2x^2$. Let's select $(3, -18)$. Moving the graph of $y = -2x^2$ two units to the left and seven units up means that the point $(3, -18)$ becomes $(1, -11)$. By substitution, it can be readily observed that $(1, -11)$ lies on the graph of $y = -2(x + 2)^2 + 7$.

Quadratic Equations

A quadratic equation is a second-degree equation in x of the type $ax^2 + bx + c = 0$, with a, b, and c are real numbers and $a \neq 0$.

To solve a quadratic equation, we need to find the x value(s) which satisfy $ax^2 + bx + c = 0$. These values of x are called the solutions or roots of the equation.

A quadratic equation has a maximum of two roots. Methods for solving quadratic equations include (a) using direct solution, (b) factoring, (c) completing the square, and (d) using the quadratic formula. Two helpful hints to remember when factoring, where r_1 and r_2 are the roots, are:

(a) $r_1 \cdot r_2 = \dfrac{c}{a}$ and (b) $r_1 + r_2 = \dfrac{-b}{a}$.

The quadratic formula states that $x = \dfrac{-b \pm \sqrt{b^2 - 4ac}}{2a}$. The value under the square root sign $(b^2 - 4ac)$ is called the discriminant. If the discriminant is less than 0 then there are no real roots (only imaginary roots). If the discriminant equals 0 then there is exactly one real solution. If the discriminant is greater than 0 then there are exactly two real roots.

EXAMPLE 31

If $x^2 - 16 = 0$, find the value(s) of x.

SOLUTION

Rewrite as $x^2 = 16$. Then $x = \pm\sqrt{16} = \pm 4$. (Direct solution)

The roots are $\{-4, 4\}$.

EXAMPLE 32

If $x^2 - 6x + 5 = 0$, find the value(s) of x.

SOLUTION

Since $r_1 + r_2 = \dfrac{-b}{a} = \dfrac{-(-6)}{1} = 6$, the possible non-negative integer solutions are $\{0, 6\}$, $\{1, 5\}$, $\{2, 4\}$, and $\{3, 3\}$. Also, $r_1 \cdot r_2 = \dfrac{c}{a} = \dfrac{5}{1} = 5$; this equation is satisfied only by the second pair $\{1, 5\}$, so $r_1 = 1$ and $r_2 = 5$. The factored form is $(x - 1)(x - 5) = 0$. Either $(x - 1) = 0$ or $(x - 5) = 0$ for the equation to be true. The roots are $\{1, 5\}$ since $x = 1$ or $x = 5$.

EXAMPLE 33

If $x^2 - 12x + 8 = 0$, find the value(s) of x.

SOLUTION

The two roots when multiplied together should be 8 since $r_1 \cdot r_2 = \dfrac{c}{a} = \dfrac{8}{1} = 8$. The possible non-negative integer roots are $(1, 8)$ and $(2, 4)$. Neither of these pairs satisfies $r_1 + r_2 = \dfrac{-b}{a} = \dfrac{-(-12)}{1} = 12$. One method to solve this equation is to complete the square.

Step One: Isolate the constant term and if $a \neq 1$ then divide each side by a. Then $x^2 - 12x = -8$.

Step Two: Take half the coefficient of x, square it and add to both sides. This means that $x^2 - 12x + \left(\dfrac{-12}{2}\right)^2 = -8 + \left(\dfrac{-12}{2}\right)^2$, which becomes $x^2 - 12x + 36 = 28$.

We can factor the left side so that the equation becomes $(x - 6)^2 = 28$. Taking the square root of both sides, $x - 6 = \pm\sqrt{28} = \pm 2\sqrt{7}$. Thus, $x = 6 \pm 2\sqrt{7}$.

The roots are $x = 6 + 2\sqrt{7}$ and $x = 6 - 2\sqrt{7}$.

EXAMPLE 34

If $2x^2 + 2x + 7 = 0$, find the value(s) of x using the quadratic formula.

SOLUTION

Since $b^2 - 4ac = 2^2 - (4)(2)(7) = -52$, there are no real roots. (only complex roots). By the quadratic formula, $x = \dfrac{-b \pm \sqrt{b^2 - 4ac}}{2a} = \dfrac{-2 \pm i\sqrt{52}}{4} = \dfrac{-2 \pm 2i\sqrt{13}}{4} = \dfrac{-1 \pm i\sqrt{13}}{2}$. The two complex roots are $\left\{ \dfrac{-1 \pm i\sqrt{13}}{2} \right\}$.

Systems of Linear Equations

Linear equations with two or more variables are called a system of linear equations. There are several ways to solve systems of linear equations with two variables.

Method One: **Addition or Subtraction** − If the signs of the coefficients of the same variable are additive inverses, add the equations; otherwise, subtract. If necessary, use multiplication to make the coefficients of the same variable equal to each other, then either add or subtract the equations.

The result is one equation with one unknown; solve it and substitute the value into the other equation to find the unknown that we first eliminated.

Method Two: **Substitution** − Find the value of one variable in terms of the other. Substitute this value in the other equation and solve.

Method Three − **Graph** − Graph both equations. The point of intersection is the solution to the system of equations.

In the third last method, parallel lines have the same slope but different y-intercepts. The system of equations is called **inconsistent** and it does not have a solution. Systems that have one solution are called **consistent**. Their graph is two intersecting lines. Systems that represent the same line have infinite solutions and are called **dependent**.

EXAMPLE 35

Using the method of substitution, solve the following system of equations:

$x + y = 3$ (Equation 1)

$4x - 2y = 8$ (Equation 2)

SOLUTION

Solve the first equation for x, to get $x = 3 - y$. Substitute this expression into the second equation and solve for y. Then $(4)(3 - y) - 2y = 8$, which simplifies to $12 - 6y = 8$. By Subtracting 12, then dividing by -6, $y = \dfrac{-4}{-6} = \dfrac{2}{3}$. Substitute the y-value into the Equation 1 and solve for x. So, $x + \dfrac{2}{3} = 3$, which means that $x = \dfrac{7}{3}$.

NOTE:

In graphing this system, the point of intersection is $\left(\dfrac{7}{3}, \dfrac{2}{3} \right)$. The system has one solution, so it is classified as **consistent**.

EXAMPLE 36

Using the method of addition and subtraction, solve the following system of equations:

$2x + 5y = 28$ (Equation 1)

$3x - y = -9$ (Equations 2)

SOLUTION

If we multiply the second equation by 5, the coefficients of y will be additive inverses. Here is how the system will appear:

$2x + 5y = 28$ (Equation 1)

$15x - 5y = -45$ (Equation 3)

Now add Equations 1 and 3 to get $17x = -17$. So, $x = -1$.

Substitute this value of x into Equation 2 (any equation would work) so that $(3)(-1) - y = -9$. This equation simplifies to $-3 - y = -9$, so $y = 6$. In graphing this system, the point of intersection would be $(-1, 6)$.

EXAMPLE 37

Using the method of addition and subtraction, solve the following system of equations:

$x - 4y = 5$ (Equation 1)

$4x - 16y = 20$ (Equation 2)

SOLUTION

By multiplying the first equation by 4, we get an exact duplicate of the second equation. Both equations will read as $4x - 16y = 20$. Now, by subtraction, the result is $0 = 0$. This means that the graph of these two equations is simply one line. Therefore, there are an infinite number of solutions.

EXAMPLE 38

Using the method of addition and subtraction, solve the following system of equations:

$3x + 4y = 7$ (Equation 1)

$6x + 8y = 11$ (Equation 2)

SOLUTION

Doubling Equation 1 leads to $6x + 8y = 14$. (Equation 3). By subtracting Equation 2 from Equation 3, the result is $0 = 3$. This means that there is no solution. The graph of Equations 1 and 2 are parallel lines.

General Systems of Equations

EXAMPLE 38

Using the method of substitution, solve the following system of equations:

$y = x^2 + 7x - 5$ (Equation 1)

$y - 2x = 1$ (Equation 2)

SOLUTION

Rewrite Equation 2 as $y = 2x + 1$, and substitute this expression for y into Equation 1. Then $2x + 1 = x^2 + 7x - 5$, which can be written as $x^2 + 5x - 6 = 0$. Using factoring, $(x - 1)(x + 6) = 0$. This means that there are x values of 1 and -6. Substituting $x = 1$ into the first equation, $y = 1^2 + (7)(1) - 5 = 3$. Substituting $x = -6$ into the first equation, $y = (-6)^2 + (7)(-6) - 5 = -11$. The two solutions are the ordered pairs $(1, 3)$ and $(-6. -11)$.

Inequalities

An inequality is a statement where the value of one quantity or expression is greater than ($>$), less than ($<$), greater than or equal to ($\geq$), less than or equal to ($\leq$), or not equal to ($\neq$) that of another.

If x and y are real numbers, then one and only one of the following statements is true (trichotomy property).

$x > y, x = y$, or $x < y$.

Note that the statement $x \geq y$ is a combination of two statements, namely $x > y$ or $x = y$. Similarly, $x \leq y$ means that $x < y$ or $x = y$.

If a, b, and c are real numbers, the following statements are true (transitive property).

a) If $a < b$ and $b < c$ then $a < c$.

b) If $a > b$ and $b > c$ then $a > c$.

If a, b, and c are real numbers, the following statements are true (addition and subtraction properties of inequalities).

c) If $a > b$, then $a + c > b + c$ and $a - c > b - c$.

d) If $a < b$, then $a + c < b + c$ and $a - c < b - c$.

Two inequalities are said to have the same **sense** if their signs of inequality point in the same direction. The sense of an inequality remains the same if both sides are multiplied or divided by the same positive real number. Inequalities that have the same solution set are called equivalent inequalities.

The solution of a given inequality in one variable x consists of all x values for which the inequality is true. The graph of an inequality in one variable is represented by either a line segment or ray on a real number line. The endpoint is not considered a solution for less than ($<$), greater ($>$), or not equal to ($\neq$) and is represented by an open circle around the endpoint. The endpoint is considered a solution for greater than or equal to ($\geq$) or less than or equal to ($\leq$) and is represented by a closed circle around the endpoint.

EXAMPLE 39

Graph the solution set of $x > 4$.

SOLUTION

The number 4 is not a solution and should be represented using an open circle. The inequality is true for all values larger than 4.

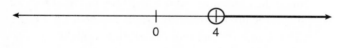

Figure 3.15

EXAMPLE 40

Graph the solution set for $-4 < x \leq 2$.

SOLUTION

The number -4 is not a solution and should be represented using an open circle. The number 2 is a solution and should be represented using a closed circle. The inequality is true for all values between -4 and 2 (not including -4).

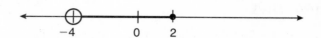

Figure 3.16

EXAMPLE 41

Write and graph the solution set for $-2x + 7 < 5$.

SOLUTION

Add -7 to both sides $-2x + 7 - 7 < 5 - 7$. Next, combine terms: $-2x < -2$. Finally, divide both sides by -2: $\dfrac{-2x}{-2} > \dfrac{-2}{-2}$, which becomes $x > 1$. The solution set is $\{x \mid x > 1\}$.

Note dividing by a **negative** x coefficient changes the inequality sign. The graph appears below in Figure 3.17.

Figure 3.17

Inequalities that involve two variables are graphed on the xy-coordinate plane. The variable y will be written as a function of x. The function itself is not considered a solution for less than ($<$), greater ($>$), or not equal to ($\neq$) and is represented by dashed line. The function is considered a solution for greater than or equal to ($\geq$) or less than or equal to ($\leq$) and is represented by a solid line.

EXAMPLE 42

Write and graph the solution set for $2x + 3y - 6 > 0$.

SOLUTION

Add $-2x + 6$ to both sides of the inequality: $3y > -2x + 6$. Then divide both sides by 3 to yield the solution set: $y > -\frac{2}{3}x + 2$. An alternative way to write this solution set is $\{(x, y)| \ y > -\frac{2}{3}x + 2\}$. The graph will consist of all points that lie above (but not including) the line that represents $y = -\frac{2}{3}x + 2$. In order to show the graph, we need to select two points that lie on this line. If $x = 0$, $y = -\frac{2}{3}(0) + 2 = 2$. If $x = 3$, $y = -\frac{2}{3}(3) + 2 = 0$. The two points that we are plotting are $(0, 2)$ and $(3, 0)$. The solution is shown by the shaded area in Figure 3.18.

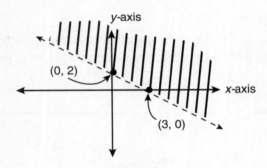

Figure 3.18

EXAMPLE 43

Graph and find the solution set for $y \leq x^2 + 9x + 20$.

SOLUTION

The parabola opens up since $a > 0$. The vertex of a parabola is the point $(\frac{-b}{2a}, \frac{4ac - b^2}{4a}) =$

$(\frac{-(9)}{2(1)}, \frac{4(1)(20) - (9)^2}{4(1)}) = (\frac{-9}{2}, \frac{-1}{4})$.

Use the discriminant to determine the number of roots:

$b^2 - 4ac = (-9)^2 - 4(1)(20) = 81 - 80 = 1$ so there are 2 real roots.

$x^2 + 9x + 20$ can be factored: $(x + 4)(x + 5)$. The roots are $\{-5, -4\}$.

Since the roots are the x-intercepts, the points $(-5, 0)$ and $(-4, 0)$ are on the graph of $y = x^2 + 9x + 20$. Using the three points $(\frac{-9}{2}, \frac{-1}{4})$, $(-5, 0)$, and $(-4, 0)$, we can sketch the parabola as shown in Figure 3.19.

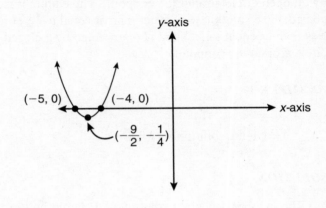

Figure 3.19

Since the inequality reads "less than or equal to," we will shade the area below this graph, as shown in Figure 3.20. (Note that the parabola is solid, not dashed.)

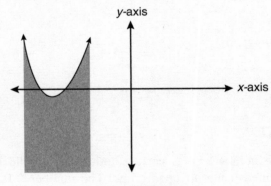

Figure 3.20

Linear Programming

Linear programming is the mathematical process of first determining a region defined by a series of linear inequalities in two variables (usually x and y). The second step is to either find the maximum or minimum value of a linear function in x and y (called the **objective function**). Without a formal proof, we claim that this objective function will have a maximum value at one of the vertices that represents the intersection of two of the linear inequalities. The same statement will hold for a minimum value of the objective function. Our discussion will be limited to objective functions for which there is exactly one minimum or one maximum value.

EXAMPLE 44

Given the linear inequalities $x \geq 0$, $y \geq 0$, $2x + y \leq 6$, and $y \geq 4x$, find the maximum value of the function $C = x + 3y$ over the region defined by these inequalities.

SOLUTION

We use the x, y axes to represent $y = 0$ and $x = 0$, respectively. We then graph $2x + y = 6$ by using the points $(0, 6)$ and $(3, 0)$. Next, graph $y = 4x$ by using the points $(0, 0)$ and $(1, 4)$. In order to identify the appropriate region, we shade above the line $y = 4x$ and below the line $y = 2x + 6$. Since x, $y \geq 0$, we are only concerned with the first quadrant.

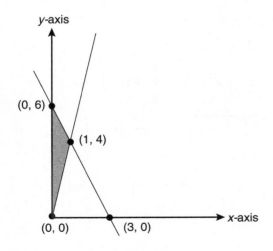

Figure 3.21

Figure 3.21 illustrates the desired region. The vertices are found by determining the intersection of each pair of the lines $x = 0$, $y = 0$, $y = 4x$, and $y = 2x + 6$.

The three vertices of the triangular region that is shaded are $(0, 0)$, $(0, 6)$, and $(1, 4)$. Note that the vertex $(3, 0)$ is not part of this region. The last step is to evaluate $C = x + 3y$ for each of these vertices. For $(0, 0)$, $C = 0$. For $(0, 6)$, $C = 0 + (3)(6) = 18$. For $(1, 4)$, $C = 1 + (3)(4) = 13$. Thus, the maximum value of C is 18.

EXAMPLE 45

Given the inequalities $x \geq 0$, $y \geq 0$, $y \geq -\dfrac{3}{8}x + 3$, $y \leq 2x$, and $x \leq 3$, find the minimum value of the function $C = 3x + 5y$.

SOLUTION

Begin by graphing the five lines $x = 0$, $y = 0$, $y = -\dfrac{3}{8}x + 3$, $y = 2x$, and $x = 3$. As before, we note that $x = 0$ and $y = 0$ are simply the axes. For the line $y = -\dfrac{3}{8}x + 3$, we can use the points $(8, 0)$ and $(0, 3)$. For $y = 2x$, we can use the points $(0, 0)$ and $(1, 2)$. The line $x = 3$ is a vertical line through $(3, 0)$. Now we need to shade the region that lies above $y = -\dfrac{3}{8}x + 3$, below $y = 2x$, and to the left of $x = 3$. Figure 3.22 illustrates the desired region.

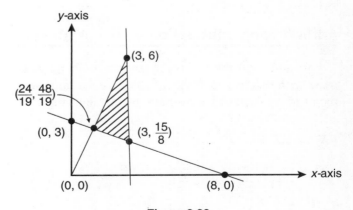

Figure 3.22

We identify the vertices of the shaded triangular region as follows: The intersection of $y = 2x$ and $y = -\frac{3}{8}x + 3$ is $(\frac{24}{19}, \frac{48}{19})$. The intersection of $y = 2x$ and $x = 3$ is $(3, 6)$. The intersection of $y = -\frac{3}{8}x + 3$ and $x = 3$ is $(3, \frac{15}{8})$. Note that $(8, 0)$ is not part of the intersection of the given inequalities. The last step is to evaluate C for the coordinates that represent the three vertices that comprise the shaded region. For $(\frac{24}{19}, \frac{48}{19})$, $C = (3)(\frac{24}{19}) + (5)(\frac{48}{19}) \approx 16.42$. For $(3, 6)$, $C = (3)(3) + (5)(6) = 39$. For $(3, \frac{15}{8})$, $C = (3)(3) + (5)(\frac{15}{8}) = 18.375$. Thus, the minimum value of C is approximately 16.42.

Matrices

A matrix is a system of rows and columns, with each value called an **element** of the matrix. The **dimension (size)** of a matrix is the number of rows and columns in the matrix written in this order. $A_{2 \times 3}$ is a matrix that consists of 2 rows and 3 columns. A matrix with n rows and n columns is called a square matrix. Two matrices are equal if and only if they have the same dimension and all the corresponding elements are equal.

NOTE:

Rows are horizontal and columns are vertical.

Addition and Subtraction of Two Matrices

To add (or subtract) two matrices, both matrices must be the same size. If the matrices are the same size, then add (or subtract) corresponding elements together.

EXAMPLE 46

$$\begin{bmatrix} -2 & 4 \\ 3 & 7 \end{bmatrix} + \begin{bmatrix} 1 & 4 \\ -3 & 2 \end{bmatrix} = \underline{\hspace{2cm}}.$$

SOLUTION

By adding corresponding elements, we get

$$\begin{bmatrix} -2+1 & 4+4 \\ 3-3 & 7+2 \end{bmatrix} = \begin{bmatrix} -1 & 8 \\ 0 & 9 \end{bmatrix}.$$

EXAMPLE 47

$$\begin{bmatrix} 5 & 4 & -2 \\ 0 & 4 & 6 \\ 2 & 4 & -7 \end{bmatrix} - \begin{bmatrix} 1 & 2 & 3 \\ 7 & 6 & 5 \\ -4 & 0 & 0 \end{bmatrix} = \underline{\hspace{1.5cm}}.$$

SOLUTION

$$\begin{bmatrix} 5 & 4 & -2 \\ 0 & 4 & 6 \\ 2 & 4 & -7 \end{bmatrix} - \begin{bmatrix} 1 & 2 & 3 \\ 7 & 6 & 5 \\ -4 & 0 & 0 \end{bmatrix} =$$

$$\begin{bmatrix} 5-1 & 4-2 & -2-3 \\ 0-7 & 4-6 & 6-5 \\ 2+4 & 4-0 & -7-0 \end{bmatrix} = \begin{bmatrix} 4 & 2 & -5 \\ -7 & -2 & 1 \\ 6 & 4 & -7 \end{bmatrix}.$$

Multiplication of a Matrix by a Scalar

The product of a matrix by a scalar k is obtained by multiplying the scalar k by every element in the matrix. The product is often written in the form kA.

EXAMPLE 48

If $A = \begin{bmatrix} 1 & -5 \\ 3 & 2 \end{bmatrix}$, what is the matrix that represents $4A$?

SOLUTION

$$4A = \begin{bmatrix} 4 \cdot 1 & 4 \cdot -5 \\ 4 \cdot 3 & 4 \cdot 2 \end{bmatrix} = \begin{bmatrix} 4 & -20 \\ 12 & 8 \end{bmatrix}.$$

Multiplication of Two Matrices

To multiply two matrices A and B, the number of columns in matrix $A_{m \times n}$ must equal the number of rows in matrix $B_{n \times p}$. To calculate each element of AB, multiply the elements in row i of matrix A by the corresponding elements in column j of matrix B. Add up the resulting products; this sum is the $(ij)^{th}$ entry of AB. If $AB = C$ then C has dimension $m \times p$.

SPECIAL NOTE

Given that the matrix AB exists, in general, $AB \neq BA$. In fact, unless A and B are square matrices of the same dimensions, the matrix BA will not exist.

EXAMPLE 49

If $A = \begin{bmatrix} 2 & 1 \\ -1 & 3 \\ 3 & 4 \end{bmatrix}$ and $B = \begin{bmatrix} 1 & 4 & 3 \\ 0 & 2 & 2 \end{bmatrix}$, what is the matrix that represents AB?

SOLUTION

$$AB = \begin{bmatrix} (2 \cdot 1)+(1 \cdot 0) & (2 \cdot 4)+(1 \cdot 2) & (2 \cdot 3)+(1 \cdot 2) \\ (-1 \cdot 1)+(3 \cdot 0) & (-1 \cdot 4)+(3 \cdot 2) & (-1 \cdot 3)+(3 \cdot 2) \\ (3 \cdot 1)+(4 \cdot 0) & (3 \cdot 4)+(4 \cdot 2) & (3 \cdot 3)+(4 \cdot 2) \end{bmatrix}$$

$$= \begin{bmatrix} 2 & 10 & 8 \\ -1 & 2 & 3 \\ 3 & 20 & 17 \end{bmatrix}.$$

Properties of Matrix Arithmetic

For these properties, A, B, and C are matrices, whereas a, b, and k are scalars.

(1) $A + B = B + A$ (Commutative Law of Addition)

(2) $A + (B + C) = (A + B) + C$ (Associative Law of Addition)

(3) $A(BC) = (AB)C$ (Associative Law of Multiplication)

(4) $A(B \pm C) = AB \pm AC$ (Distributive Law)

(5) $k(B + C) = kB + kC$

(6) $(a \pm b)C = aC \pm bC$

(7) $(ab)C = a(bC)$

(8) $k(BC) = (kB)C = B(kC)$

A matrix whose entries are all zero is called a zero matrix, **0**. Examples of zero matrices are $\begin{bmatrix} 0 \\ 0 \end{bmatrix}$, $\begin{bmatrix} 0 & 0 \\ 0 & 0 \end{bmatrix}$ and $\begin{bmatrix} 0 & 0 & 0 \end{bmatrix}$.

With respect to the zero matrix, the following properties are also valid.

(9) $A + \mathbf{0} = \mathbf{0} + A = A$

(10) $A - A = \mathbf{0}$

(11) $\mathbf{0} - A = -A$

(12) $(A)(\mathbf{0}) = \mathbf{0}$

An identity matrix (I) is a square matrix with ones on the main diagonal and zeros everywhere else. The main diagonal of a matrix begins at the top left corner of the matrix and ends at the bottom right of the matrix.

Examples of identity matrices are $\begin{bmatrix} 1 & 0 \\ 0 & 1 \end{bmatrix}$ and $\begin{bmatrix} 1 & 0 & 0 \\ 0 & 1 & 0 \\ 0 & 0 & 1 \end{bmatrix}$.

Determinant of a Matrix

Only square matrices have determinants. The determinant of a matrix A has the same dimensions as the matrix A but is written using vertical bars $|A|$ instead of brackets $[A]$. The determinant of a 2×2 matrix is written as $\det \begin{bmatrix} a & b \\ c & d \end{bmatrix} = \begin{vmatrix} a & b \\ c & d \end{vmatrix} = ad - bc$. The determinant of a 3×3 matrix is found through a process called expansion of minors. The process is $\det \begin{bmatrix} a & b & c \\ d & e & f \\ g & h & i \end{bmatrix} = a \begin{vmatrix} e & f \\ h & i \end{vmatrix} - b \begin{vmatrix} d & f \\ g & i \end{vmatrix} + c \begin{vmatrix} d & e \\ g & h \end{vmatrix}$.

EXAMPLE 48

Find the determinant of $\begin{bmatrix} 3 & 4 \\ -3 & 5 \end{bmatrix}$.

SOLUTION

$\det \begin{bmatrix} 3 & 4 \\ -3 & 5 \end{bmatrix} = \begin{vmatrix} 3 & 4 \\ -3 & 5 \end{vmatrix} = (3)(5) - (4)(-3)$
$= 15 + 12 = 27$.

EXAMPLE 49

Find the determinant of $\begin{bmatrix} -1 & 1 & 2 \\ 3 & 0 & 5 \\ 4 & 1 & 2 \end{bmatrix}$

SOLUTION

$\det \begin{bmatrix} -1 & 1 & 2 \\ 3 & 0 & 5 \\ 4 & 1 & 2 \end{bmatrix} = (-1)\begin{vmatrix} 0 & 5 \\ 1 & 2 \end{vmatrix} - 1\begin{vmatrix} 3 & 5 \\ 4 & 2 \end{vmatrix} + 2\begin{vmatrix} 3 & 0 \\ 4 & 1 \end{vmatrix}$

$= (-1)(0 - 5) - (1)(6 - 20) + (2)(3 - 0) = 5 + 14$
$+ 6 = 25$.

Inverse of a Matrix

Any square matrix A has an inverse A^{-1} if and only if the determinant of matrix $A \neq 0$. If matrix A has an inverse A^{-1} then $A \cdot A^{-1} = A^{-1} \cdot A = I$.

For a 2×2 matrix $A = \begin{bmatrix} a & b \\ c & d \end{bmatrix}$, $A^{-1} =$

$\dfrac{1}{ad - bc} \begin{bmatrix} d & -b \\ -c & a \end{bmatrix}$.

EXAMPLE 50

Find A^{-1} if $A = \begin{bmatrix} 2 & 3 \\ 4 & 5 \end{bmatrix}$.

SOLUTION

First, find the determinant of A, which is $\begin{vmatrix} 2 & 3 \\ 4 & 5 \end{vmatrix} =$
$10 - 12 = -2$. Since the determinate of matrix $A \neq 0$, A^{-1} exists.

$A^{-1} = \dfrac{1}{(2)(5) - (3)(4)} \begin{bmatrix} 5 & -3 \\ -4 & 2 \end{bmatrix} = -\dfrac{1}{2} \begin{bmatrix} 5 & -3 \\ -4 & 2 \end{bmatrix}$

$= \begin{bmatrix} -\dfrac{5}{2} & \dfrac{3}{2} \\ 2 & -1 \end{bmatrix}$.

Inverse matrices are often used to solve systems of linear equations. A matrix equation is used to solve the system of linear equations. A matrix equation consists of a coefficient matrix, variable matrix, and constant matrix.

EXAMPLE 51

Using matrices, solve the following system of equations:

$x + 4y = 6$

$2x + 6y = 4$

SOLUTION

The matrix equation is $\begin{bmatrix} 1 & 4 \\ 2 & 6 \end{bmatrix} \cdot \begin{bmatrix} x \\ y \end{bmatrix} = \begin{bmatrix} 6 \\ 4 \end{bmatrix}$. Second,

we find the determinant of $\begin{bmatrix} 1 & 4 \\ 2 & 6 \end{bmatrix}$, which is $(1)(6)$
$- (4)(2) = 6 - 8 = -2$.

Third, we identify the inverse of $\begin{bmatrix} 1 & 4 \\ 2 & 6 \end{bmatrix}$ as

$-\dfrac{1}{2} \begin{bmatrix} 6 & -4 \\ -2 & 1 \end{bmatrix}$.

Fourth, we solve $\begin{bmatrix} x \\ y \end{bmatrix} = -\dfrac{1}{2} \begin{bmatrix} 6 & -4 \\ -2 & 1 \end{bmatrix} \cdot \begin{bmatrix} 6 \\ 4 \end{bmatrix}$.

The right side of this equation simplifies to

$\begin{bmatrix} -3 & 2 \\ 1 & -\dfrac{1}{2} \end{bmatrix} \cdot \begin{bmatrix} 6 \\ 4 \end{bmatrix}$

$$= \begin{bmatrix} (-3)(6)+(2)(4) \\ (1)(6)-(\frac{1}{2})(4) \end{bmatrix} = \begin{bmatrix} -10 \\ 4 \end{bmatrix}. \text{ Thus, } x = -10 \text{ and}$$

$y = 4$.

NOTE:

The inverse matrix times the coefficient matrix must always equal the identity matrix. That is,

$$-\frac{1}{2}\begin{bmatrix} 6 & -4 \\ -2 & 1 \end{bmatrix} \cdot \begin{bmatrix} 1 & 4 \\ 2 & 6 \end{bmatrix} \underline{\text{must}} \text{ equal } \begin{bmatrix} 1 & 0 \\ 0 & 1 \end{bmatrix}.$$

If not, the calculated identity matrix is incorrect and must be recalculated before completing the solution.

Augmented Matrices

An augmented matrix is used to solve a system of three or more linear equations. (Our focus will be on three linear equations in three variables.) An augmented matrix consists of the coefficient matrix plus a column containing equation constants. Elementary row operations are used on rows of the augmented matrix to solve for the solutions of the system of linear equations. Valid operations are:

a) Multiply a row by a non-zero constant.

b) Interchange two rows.

c) Replace any row with the sum of that row and a multiple of another row.

Our objective is to transform the given augmented matrix into the following form:

$$\begin{bmatrix} 1 & 0 & 0 & a \\ 0 & 1 & 0 & b \\ 0 & 0 & 1 & c \end{bmatrix}, \text{ so that the solution will be}$$

$x = a$, $y = b$, and $z = c$. As an alternative, we look for a single row that matches any of the three rows of this augmented matrix. For example, if we get the first row,

then we conclude that $x = a$. In similar fashion, the middle row implies that $y = b$, and the last row implies that $z = c$.

EXAMPLE 52

Using an augmented matrix, solve the following system of linear equations.

$2x - y + 3z = 4$

$3x + 2z = 5$

$-2x + y + 4z = 6$

SOLUTION

We start with the augmented matrix

$$\begin{bmatrix} 2 & -1 & 3 & 4 \\ 3 & 0 & 2 & 5 \\ -2 & 1 & 4 & 6 \end{bmatrix}.$$

Change the third row to the sum of the first and

third rows to get $\begin{bmatrix} 2 & -1 & 3 & 4 \\ 3 & 0 & 2 & 5 \\ 0 & 0 & 7 & 10 \end{bmatrix}$. Next, divide the

third row by 7 to get $\begin{bmatrix} 2 & -1 & 3 & 4 \\ 3 & 0 & 2 & 5 \\ 0 & 0 & 1 & \frac{10}{7} \end{bmatrix}$.

From the last equation $z = \frac{10}{7}$. Substituting $z =$

$\frac{10}{7}$ into the second equation and solving for x gives

$x = \frac{5}{7}$. Substituting $z = \frac{10}{7}$ and $x = \frac{5}{7}$ into the first

equation and solving for y gives $y = \frac{12}{7}$. The solution

to the system is $x = \frac{5}{7}$, $y = \frac{12}{7}$, and $z = \frac{10}{7}$.

Sequences

A sequence is a function whose domain is the set of all natural numbers. The range of all the sequences in this section will be a subset in the set of all real numbers. It is common to let a_n represent the nth term of a sequence. For example, if $a_n = 5n$ then

Term (n)	Notation (a_n)	Value ($5n$)
1	a_1	$5(1) = 5$
2	a_2	$5(2) = 10$
3	a_3	$5(3) = 15$

Arithmetic Sequences and Series

For a fixed number a_1 and a fixed number d, the sequence $a_1, a_1 + d, a_1 + 2d, a_1 + 3d, \ldots$ is called an arithmetic sequence, and the nth term of this sequence is given by the formula $a_n = a_1 + (n - 1)d$. The number a_1 represents the first term and the number d represents the common difference.

EXAMPLE 53

Find the next three terms of sequence 16, 48, 80, . . .

SOLUTION

Find the common difference d between the first two terms (consecutive terms), which is $48 - 16 = 32$. Add 32 to the next term of the given sequence, and continue until the next three terms are determined. Then $80 + 32 = 112$, $112 + 32 = 144$, and $144 + 32 = 176$. Thus, the next three terms are 112, 144, and 176.

EXAMPLE 54

Determine the formula for 16, 48, 80, . . .

SOLUTION

We need to find a_1 and d then substitute in $a_n = a_1 + (n - 1)d$. a_1 equals the first term of the sequence, which

is 16. d represents the common difference between the successive terms. Using the first and second terms, $d = 48 - 16 = 32$. Then $a_n = 16 + (n - 1)(32)$.

An arithmetic series is a specific sum of the terms of an arithmetic sequence. For example, the symbol $\sum_{i=1}^{n} i$ represents a series that is used to represent the sum of the corresponding finite sequence of the first n counting numbers. As a second example, $\sum_{i=1}^{3} 2i$ means the summation of $2i$ from 1 to 3. This sum becomes $(2)(1) + (2)(2) + (2)(3) = 2 + 4 + 6 = 12$. The symbol S_n represents a series of n terms, and can be used to denote the sum of the first n terms of any sequence.

For an arithmetic series, $S_n = a_1 + (a_1 + d) + (a_1 + 2d) + (a_1 + 3d) + \ldots + [a_1 + (n - 1)d] = \sum_{i=1}^{n} [a_1 + (i - 1)d] = \dfrac{n(a_1 + a_n)}{2}$ or $S_n = \dfrac{n(a_1 + a_n)}{2}$. If the last term ($n$) of a sequence is not known, $S_n = \dfrac{n(2a_1 + (n - 1)d)}{2}$.

EXAMPLE 55

Find the sum of the first 50 positive integers.

SOLUTION

$$S_{50} = \frac{50(1 + 50)}{2} = \frac{50(51)}{2} = \frac{2550}{2} = 1275.$$

EXAMPLE 56

If $a_1 = 12$, $d = -1$ find the sum of the first 12 terms.

SOLUTION

Since $n = 12$ and the last term is not known, use the formula $S_n = \dfrac{n(2a_1 + (n - 1)d)}{2}$. Then

$$S_{12} = \frac{12(2(12) + 11(-1))}{2} = \frac{12(24 - 11)}{2} = \frac{12(13)}{2}$$

$$= \frac{156}{2} = 78.$$

Geometric Sequences and Series

A sequence of the form a_1, a_1r, a_1r^2, a_1r^3, . . . is called an infinite geometric sequence, where a_1 is the first term and r is the common ratio. The nth term of the sequence is $a_n = a_1 r^{n-1}$.

The symbol S_n can be used to represent a geometric series (sum of the corresponding finite geometric sequence of n terms). For a geometric series $S_n = a_1 + a_1 r + a_1 r^2 + \ldots + ar^{n-1} = \sum_{i=1}^{n} a_1 r^{i-1} = \dfrac{a_1 - a_n r}{1 - r}$.

EXAMPLE 57

If $a_1 = 3$ and $r = 4$, find the first four terms of the geometric sequence.

SOLUTION

$a_1 = 3$, $a_2 = 3 \cdot 4 = 12$, $a_3 = 3 \cdot 4^2 = 48$, and $a_4 = 3 \cdot 4^3 = 192$. Thus, the terms are 3, 12, 48, 192.

EXAMPLE 58

If $a_1 = 3$, $a_n = 24$, and $r = 2$, find the sum of the first n terms of the geometric sequence.

SOLUTION

$$S_n = \frac{a_1 - a_n r}{1 - r} = \frac{3 - (24)(2)}{1 - 2} = \frac{3 - 48}{-1} = \frac{-45}{-1} = 45.$$

EXAMPLE 59

Express $1 + 2 + 4 + 8 + 16$ using sigma notation.

SOLUTION

We can recognize that each term of this series is in the form $a_n = ar^{n-1}$, where $r = 2$ and $a_1 = 1$. Note that $a_1 = (1)(2^0)$, $a_2 = (1)(2^1)$, $a_3 = (1)(2^2)$, and so forth. So, $a_n = 2^{n-1}$.

Since there are 5 terms, the sigma notation is

$$\sum_{i=1}^{5} (1)(2^{i-1}) = \sum_{i=1}^{5} 2^{i-1}.$$

If the absolute value of the ratio of a geometric sequence is less than 1, then the infinite series $a_1 + a_1 r + a_1 r^2 + a_1 r^{n-1} + \ldots$ has a finite sum. The formula is

$$S_\infty = \frac{a_1}{1 - r}, \text{ where } \infty \text{ means infinity.}$$

EXAMPLE 60

Find the value of $90 + 30 + 10 + \dfrac{10}{3} + \ldots$.

SOLUTION

By inspection, we can determine that this is a geometric series in which $a_1 = 90$ and $r = \dfrac{1}{3}$. Thus,

$$S_\infty = \frac{90}{1 - \frac{1}{3}} = \frac{90}{\frac{2}{3}} = 135.$$

Chapter 3 Quiz

1. What is the simplified form of $\dfrac{a^3 b^{-2} c^4}{c^{-5} b^2 a^4}$?

   (A) $a^7 c^{-1}$

   (B) $\dfrac{c^9}{ab^4}$

   (C) $\dfrac{a^8 c^8}{b^4}$

   (D) $\dfrac{c^9}{a}$

2. Which of the following is equivalent to $(2x^2 - 6x - 4) \div (x + 1)$?

   (A) $2x + 8 - \dfrac{4}{x+1}$

   (B) $2x - 4 + \dfrac{8}{x+1}$

   (C) $2x + 4 - \dfrac{8}{x+1}$

   (D) $2x - 8 + \dfrac{4}{x+1}$

3. Let $f(x) = 2x + 3$ and $g(x) = x^2 + 4$. Which expression is equivalent to $g(f(x))$?

   (A) $4x^2 + 13$

   (B) $x^2 + 2x + 7$

   (C) $4x^2 + 12x + 13$

   (D) $2x^2 + 19$

4. Which equation contains all the points in the table below?

x	-2	-1	1	2
y	-1	-4	-10	-13

   (A) $x - 3y = 13$

   (B) $x + 3y = -13$

   (C) $3x + y = -7$

   (D) $3x - y = 7$

5. What is the line of symmetry for the graph of $y = -2x^2 + 6x - 9$?

   (A) $x = \dfrac{3}{2}$

   (B) $y = -\dfrac{9}{2}$

   (C) $y = \dfrac{3}{2}$

   (D) $x = -\dfrac{3}{2}$

6. Which of the following parabolas has a vertex at $(-3, 2)$.

   (A) $y = -2(x + 2)^2 - 3$

   (B) $y = (x + 3)^2 - 2$

   (C) $y = 4(x - 3)^2 + 2$

   (D) $y = -2(x + 3)^2 + 2$

7. What are the roots of $0 = 2x^2 + 8x + 3$?

   (A) $x = -2 \pm \dfrac{\sqrt{10}}{2}$

   (B) $x = -4 \pm \sqrt{10}$

   (C) $x = -2 \pm \dfrac{\sqrt{22}}{2}$

   (D) $x = -3$ or $-\dfrac{1}{2}$

8. Which of the following describes the solution set for the graph of $3x - y \geq 15$?

   (A) All points below but not including the line described by $y = 3x - 15$.

   (B) All points below and including the line described by $y = 3x - 15$.

   (C) All points above but not including the line described by $y = 3x - 15$.

   (D) All points above and including the line described by $y = 3x - 15$.

9. Let $A = 2\begin{bmatrix} -1 & 3 & 0 \\ 4 & 6 & 1 \end{bmatrix}$.

Let $B = \begin{bmatrix} 2 & 2 \\ -2 & 2 \end{bmatrix}\begin{bmatrix} 3 & 4 & -5 \\ 2 & -1 & 7 \end{bmatrix}$.

Find $A + B$.

(A) $\begin{bmatrix} 22 & 10 & -140 \\ 6 & 28 & 142 \end{bmatrix}$

(B) $\begin{bmatrix} 8 & 12 & 4 \\ 6 & 2 & 26 \end{bmatrix}$

(C) $\begin{bmatrix} 0 & 12 & -24 \\ 18 & 18 & 6 \end{bmatrix}$

(D) No Solution

10. What is the sum of the first 100 positive integers?

   (A) 5151

   (B) 4950

   (C) 5050

   (D) 5100

Chapter 3 Quiz Solutions

1. **(B)**

$$\frac{a^3b^{-2}c^4}{c^{-5}b^2a^4} = \frac{a^3b^{-2}c^4}{a^4b^2c^{-5}} = a^{3-4}b^{-2-2}c^{4+5}$$
$$= a^{-1}b^{-4}c^9 = \frac{c^9}{ab^4}$$

2. **(D)**

$$
\begin{array}{r}
2x - 8 \\
x + 1 \overline{) 2x^2 - 6x - 4} \\
\underline{2x^2 + 2x} \\
-8x - 4 \\
\underline{-8x - 8} \\
4
\end{array}
$$

3. **(C)**

$g(f(x)) = (2x + 3)^2 + 4 = 4x^2 + 12x + 9 + 4 = 4x^2 + 12x + 13$

4. **(C)**

By plotting the points on a graph, we can see that the points are collinear.

Choose two consecutive points and determine the slope of the line. Two consecutive points are $(-2, -1)$ and $(-1, -4)$. Then $m = \frac{-4+1}{-1+2} = \frac{-3}{1} = -3$.

Choose one of the two points to determine the y-intercept (b) using the slope-intercept form. Using the point $(-1, -4)$, $-4 = (-3)(-1) + b$.

So, $-4 = 3 + b$, which means that $b = -7$.

The slope-intercept form of the line is $y = -3x - 7$. Thus, the standard form of the line is $3x + y = -7$.

5. **(A)**

Line of symmetry is represented as $x = \frac{-b}{2a}$. Since $a = -2$ and $b = 6$, $x = \frac{-b}{2a} = \frac{-6}{2(-2)} = \frac{-6}{-4} = \frac{3}{2}$.

SOLUTION

The amplitude $= |A| = \left|\dfrac{1}{2}\right| = \dfrac{1}{2}$. The period $= \dfrac{2\pi}{B}$ $= \dfrac{2\pi}{2} = \pi$.

The phase shift $= \dfrac{C}{B} = \dfrac{-\dfrac{\pi}{4}}{2} = -\dfrac{\pi}{8}$. Since $C < 0$, the phase shift is to the right. One period of the graph is shown in Figure 4.19. Note that we can write $y = \dfrac{1}{2}$ $\cos\left(2x - \left(-\dfrac{\pi}{4}\right)\right)$

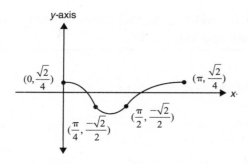

Figure 4.19

EXAMPLE 16

Find the amplitude, period, and phase shift for $y = -5\sin(3x + \pi) + 2$. Graph this function.

SOLUTION

The amplitude $= |-5| = 5$. The period $= \dfrac{2\pi}{3}$. The phase shift is $\dfrac{\pi}{3}$ units to the left. One period of the graph is shown in Figure 4.20. Note: $3x + \pi = 3x - (-\pi)$, so $C = -\pi$

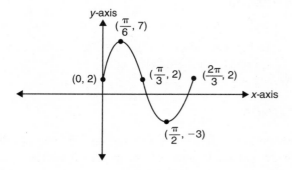

Figure 4.20

Inverse Trigonometric Functions

An inverse trigonometric function is an angle whose trigonometric ratio is known. As an example, if $y = \sin x$, then $x = \sin^{-1} y$. Another commonly used notation is $x = \arcsin y$. Every trigonometric function has an inverse. However, the range of each inverse must be limited in order for each trigonometric inverse to be denoted as a function. Following is a table of each inverse trigonometric function, along with its domain and range.

Function	Domain	Range
$y = \arcsin x$ or $y = \sin^{-1} x$	$-1 \leq x \leq 1$	$-\dfrac{\pi}{2} \leq y \leq \dfrac{\pi}{2}$
$y = \operatorname{arccsc} x$ or $y = \csc^{-1} x$	$x > 1$ or $x < -1$	$-\dfrac{\pi}{2} \leq y \leq \dfrac{\pi}{2}$, $y \neq 0$
$y = \arctan x$ or $y = \tan^{-1} x$	All reals	$-\dfrac{\pi}{2} < y < \dfrac{\pi}{2}$
$y = \arccos x$ or $y = \cos^{-1} x$	$-1 \leq x \leq 1$	$0 \leq y \leq \pi$
$y = \operatorname{arcsec} x$ or $y = \sec^{-1} x$	$x > 1$ or $x < -1$	$0 \leq y \leq \pi$, $y \neq \dfrac{\pi}{2}$
$y = \operatorname{arccot} x$ or $y = \cot^{-1} x$	All reals	$-\dfrac{\pi}{2} \leq y \leq \dfrac{\pi}{2}$ $y \neq 0$

EXAMPLE 17

Find $\sin^{-1}\left(\dfrac{\sqrt{2}}{2}\right)$

SOLUTION

Arcsin $\left(\dfrac{\sqrt{2}}{2}\right)$ means to find an angle whose sine is $\dfrac{\sqrt{2}}{2}$. The arcsin range is $-\dfrac{\pi}{2} \leq y \leq \dfrac{\pi}{2}$, and the only angle in this range whose sine is $\dfrac{\sqrt{2}}{2}$ is $\dfrac{\pi}{4}$. Thus, $\sin^{-1}\left(\dfrac{\sqrt{2}}{2}\right) = \dfrac{\pi}{4}$.

EXAMPLE 18

Find arccos $(\sin \frac{\pi}{2})$.

SOLUTION

Since $\sin \frac{\pi}{2} = 1$, we need to determine arccos (1). So, arccos (1) means to find an angle whose cosine is 1. We know that the arccos range is $0 \leq y \leq \pi$. The only angle in this range whose cosine has a value of 1 is 0. Thus, arccos $(\sin \frac{\pi}{2}) = 0$.

Trigonometric Identities - Basic

$$\tan \theta = \frac{y}{x} = \frac{\sin \theta}{\cos \theta}$$

$$\cot \theta = \frac{1}{\tan \theta} = \frac{\cos \theta}{\sin \theta}$$

$$\sec \theta = \frac{1}{\cos \theta}$$

$$\csc \theta = \frac{1}{\sin \theta}$$

$$\cos^2 \theta + \sin^2 \theta = 1$$

$$1 + \tan^2 \theta = \sec^2 \theta$$

$$1 + \cot^2 \theta = \csc^2 \theta$$

Trigonometric Identities — Angle Addition and Subtraction Formulas

$$\sin (A \pm B) = \sin A \cos B \pm \cos A \sin B$$

$$\cos (A \pm B) = \cos A \cos B \mp \sin A \sin B$$

$$\tan (A \pm B) = \frac{\tan A \pm \tan B}{1 \mp \tan A \tan B}$$

Trigonometric Identities — Double-Angle Formulas

$$\sin 2\theta = 2 \sin \theta \cos \theta$$

$$\cos 2\theta = 2 \cos^2 \theta - 1$$

$$= 1 - 2 \sin^2 \theta$$

$$= \cos^2 \theta - \sin^2 \theta$$

$$\tan 2\theta = \frac{2 \tan \theta}{1 - \tan^2 \theta}$$

Trigonometric Identities — Half-Angle Formulas

$$\sin \frac{1}{2}\theta = \pm \sqrt{\frac{1 - \cos \theta}{2}}$$

$$\cos \frac{1}{2}\theta = \pm \sqrt{\frac{1 + \cos \theta}{2}}$$

$$\tan \frac{1}{2}\theta = \pm \sqrt{\frac{1 - \cos \theta}{1 + \cos \theta}} = \frac{1 - \cos \theta}{\sin \theta} = \frac{\sin \theta}{1 + \cos \theta}$$

Trigonometric Identities — Sum and Difference Formulas

$$\sin A + \sin B = 2 \sin \left(\frac{A+B}{2}\right) \cos \left(\frac{A-B}{2}\right)$$

$$\sin A - \sin B = 2 \cos \left(\frac{A+B}{2}\right) \sin \left(\frac{A-B}{2}\right)$$

$$\cos A + \cos B = 2 \cos \left(\frac{A+B}{2}\right) \cos \left(\frac{A-B}{2}\right)$$

$$\cos A - \cos B = -2 \sin \left(\frac{A+B}{2}\right) \sin \left(\frac{A-B}{2}\right)$$

EXAMPLE 19

Simplify completely: $\dfrac{1 - \cos^2 \theta}{\sin^2 \theta}$.

SOLUTION

$$\frac{1 - \cos^2 \theta}{\sin^2 \theta} = \frac{\sin^2 \theta}{\sin^2 \theta} = 1$$

EXAMPLE 20

Using the angle addition and subtraction formulas, find the value of cos 15°.

SOLUTION

Note $(45 - 30) = 15$, and that cos 45° and cos 30° are exact values. Use the cosine angle subtraction identity to find cos 15°.

$\cos (A - B) = \cos A \cos B + \sin A \sin B$

$\cos (45° - 30°) = \cos 45° \cos 30° + \sin 45° \sin 30°$

$= \dfrac{\sqrt{2}}{2} \cdot \dfrac{\sqrt{3}}{2} + \dfrac{\sqrt{2}}{2} \cdot \dfrac{1}{2} = \dfrac{\sqrt{6}}{4} + \dfrac{\sqrt{2}}{4} = \dfrac{\sqrt{6} + \sqrt{2}}{4}.$

EXAMPLE 21

Solve for all values of x: $\sin^2 x - 1 = \cos^2 x$ for $0 \le x < 2\pi$

SOLUTION

Using one of our basic identities, we can write $\cos^2 x = 1 - \sin^2 x$. Then, rewrite the given equation as $\sin^2 x - 1 = 1 - \sin^2 x$, which simplifies to $2 \sin^2 x = 2$.

Then $\sin^2 x = 1$, which leads to $\sin x = \pm 1$. Thus, $x = 90°$ or $270°$.

EXAMPLE 22

Solve for all values of x:

$\cos 2x + \sin^2 x = 0.5$ for $0° \le x < 360°$

SOLUTION

Use the identity $\cos 2x = \cos^2 x - \sin^2 x$. Then the left side of this equation simplifies to $\cos^2 x = 0.5$. Then $\cos x = \pm\sqrt{0.5}$, so $x = 45°, 135°, 225°,$ or $315°$.

Law of Sines

Let $\triangle ABC$ be any triangle with a, b, c representing the measures of sides opposite angles with measurements A, B, and C, respectively. Then, the Law of Sines states that the ratio of any side to the sine of its opposite angle must be constant. Mathematically, $\dfrac{a}{\sin A} = \dfrac{b}{\sin B} = \dfrac{c}{\sin C}.$

Given the measures of any two angles of a triangle and the length of any side, we can determine the measure of the third angle and the lengths of the other two sides.

EXAMPLE 23

If $a = 8$, $m\angle A = 50°$, and $m\angle B = 60°$, determine the values of $m\angle C$, b, and c.

SOLUTION

Draw the appropriate triangle, as shown in Figure 4.21.

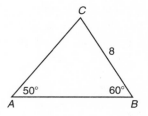

Figure 4.21

$m\angle C = 180° - 50° - 60° = 70°.$

Using $\dfrac{a}{\sin A} = \dfrac{b}{\sin B}$, we get $\dfrac{8}{\sin 50°} = \dfrac{b}{\sin 60°}$. Then

$b = \dfrac{8 \sin 60°}{\sin 50°} = \dfrac{8(0.8660)}{0.7660} \approx 9.044.$

Finally, using $\dfrac{a}{\sin A} = \dfrac{c}{\sin C}$, we get $\dfrac{8}{\sin 50°} = \dfrac{c}{\sin 70°}.$

Then $c = \dfrac{8 \sin 70°}{\sin 50°} = \dfrac{8(0.9397)}{0.7660} \approx 9.814.$

A special case of the Law of Sines exists. When the measurement of two sides of the triangle and the angle opposite one of them is given there may be no triangle, one triangle, or two possible triangles. Consider $\triangle ABC$ with sides a, b, and c. Given the values of a, b, $\angle A$, here are the various situations and the associated number of triangles that are possible.

Case 1: $m\angle A \ge 90°$

If $a > b$, then there is only one triangle.

If $a \le b$, then there is no triangle.

Case 2: $m\angle A < 90°$

If $a > b$ or if $a = b \sin\angle A$, then there is only one triangle.

If $a < b \sin\angle A$, then there is no triangle.

If $b \sin A < a < b$, then there are two possible triangles.

EXAMPLE 24

> A triangular garden has one angle of 45°, the side opposite is 30 yards, and another side is 20 yards. What is the perimeter of the garden.

SOLUTION

Let $m\angle A = 45°$, $a = 30$, and $b = 20$. Since $a > b$, Case 2 mentioned above tells us that there is only one possible triangle. Figure 4.22 illustrates this triangle.

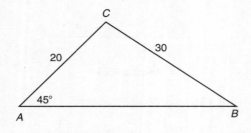

Figure 4.22

Using $\dfrac{a}{\sin A} = \dfrac{b}{\sin B}$, we have $\dfrac{30}{\sin 45°} = \dfrac{20}{\sin B}$. Then $\sin B = \dfrac{20 \sin 45°}{30} \approx 0.4714$.

Now there are two angles whose sine value is about 0.4714, namely 28° and 152°. We recall the rule that within one triangle, the larger the value of a side, the larger the value of the opposite angle. Since $a > b$, the only admissible value of the measure of $\angle B$ is 28°. Then the measure of $\angle C$ is $180° - 45° - 28° = 107°$. Now we can use the proportion $\dfrac{a}{\sin A} = \dfrac{c}{\sin C}$. By substitution, $\dfrac{30}{\sin 45°} = \dfrac{c}{\sin 107°}$. Since $\sin 45° \approx 0.7071$ and $\sin 107° \approx 0.9563$, $c = \dfrac{(30)(0.9563)}{0.7071} \approx 40.57$. Thus, the perimeter is $30 + 20 + 40.57 = 90.57$ yards.

Law of Cosines

Let ΔABC be any triangle with a, b, c representing the measures of sides opposite angles with measurements A, B, and C respectively. Then,

$a^2 = b^2 + c^2 - 2bc \cos A$

$b^2 = a^2 + c^2 - 2ac \cos B$

$c^2 = a^2 + b^2 - 2ab \cos C$

The Law of Cosines is used when either all three sides or two sides and the included angle are given.

EXAMPLE 25

> Given that $m\angle A = 50°$, $b = 10$ ft , and $c = 12$ ft, find the value of a.

SOLUTION

Figure 4.23 shows an appropriate triangle.

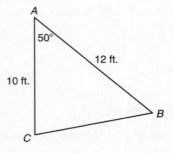

Figure 4.23

$a^2 = b^2 + c^2 - 2bc \cos A$

$a^2 = 10^2 + 12^2 - 2(10)(12) \cos 50°$

$a^2 = 100 + 144 - 2(10)(12)(0.6428)$

$a^2 = 100 + 144 - 154.27 = 89.73$

$a = \sqrt{89.73} \approx 9.47$ ft

EXAMPLE 26

> A triangular garden has these lengths: 10 yards, 14 yards and 20 yards. What is the measure of the largest angle?

SOLUTION

Draw a diagram of the problem, as shown in Figure 4.24.

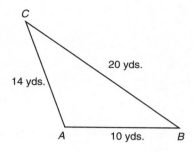

Figure 4.24

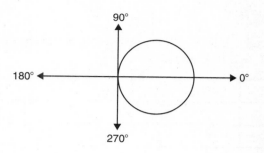

Figure 4.25

The largest angle is opposite the longest side. Let $a = 20$, $b = 14$, and $c = 10$. $a^2 = b^2 + c^2 - 2bc \cos A$. Then $\cos A = \dfrac{b^2 + c^2 - a^2}{2bc} = \dfrac{14^2 + 10^2 - 20^2}{(2)(14)(10)} = -\dfrac{104}{280} \approx -0.3714$. Thus, $m\angle A = \cos^{-1}(-0.3714) \approx 112°$.

Polar Graphs and Equations

Polar graphs are plotted using either rectangular or polar coordinates. Rectangular coordinates are plotted using (x, y). Polar coordinates are plotted using (r, θ).

EXAMPLE 27

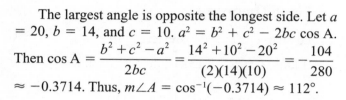

Graph $r = 2\cos\theta$

SOLUTION

Create a table of values to plot using the form $r, \theta)$.

θ (degrees)	$\cos\theta$	$2\cos\theta$	(r, θ)
0°	1	2	$(2, 0)$
90°	0	0	$(0, 90°)$
180°	−1	−2	$(-2, 180°)$
270°	0	0	$(0, 270°)$
360°	1	2	$(2, 270°)$

Plot the coordinates and graph as shown in Figure 4.25.

Special Polar Equations

Several polar graphs have special names. The sketches and their corresponding equations are noted below:

1. Cardioid $r = a + a\cos\theta$

                   $r = a + a\sin\theta$

2. Limacon $r = a + b\cos\theta$

                   $r = a + b\sin\theta$

3. Lemniscate $r^2 = a^2\cos 2\theta$

                   $r^2 = a^2\sin 2\theta$

4. Rose $r = a\cos n\theta$

                   $r = a\sin n\theta$

5. Spiral of Archimedes $r = a\theta$

Parametric Graphs and Equations

A parametric equation is a curve where the coordinates (x, y) is defined by the functions $x = f(t)$ and $y = f(t)$. t is defined as the **parameter**.

EXAMPLE 28

Graph the equation defined by $x = 4t$ and $y = 2 + t$ where t is all real numbers.

SOLUTION

Create a table of (x, y) values, using given t values of $-2, -1, 0, 1$, and 2.

t	-2	-1	0	1	2
x	-8	-4	0	4	8
y	0	1	2	3	4

Plot the coordinates. Note that the result is a line, as shown in Figure 4.26.

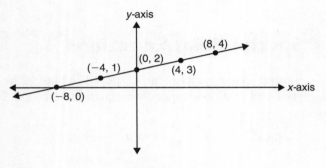

Figure 4.26

Calculus

The generally accepted definition of calculus is that it is the study of the rate of change of a quantity.

Limits

Let f be a function that is defined on an open interval containing a, but possibly not defined at a itself. The statement $\lim_{x \to a} f(x) = L$ defines the limit of the function $f(x)$ at the point a, where L is a real number. L is the value of $f(x)$ as it approaches a, even though it is possible that $f(a)$ does not exist.

EXAMPLE 29

If $f(x) = 3(x + 3)$, evaluate $\lim_{x \to 2} f(x)$.

SOLUTION

As x approaches 2, the value of L approaches $3(2 + 3) = 15$.

EXAMPLE 30

If $f(x) = \dfrac{x^2 - 5}{x - 2}$, evaluate $\lim_{x \to 3} f(x)$.

SOLUTION

As x approaches 3, the value of L approaches $\dfrac{3^2 - 5}{3 - 2} = 4$.

Limit Theorems

Let $\lim_{x \to a} f(x) = L$ and $\lim_{x \to a} g(x) = K$.

1. If $\lim_{x \to a} f(x) = L$ exists, then it is unique.

2. $\lim_{x \to a} [f(x) + g(x)] = \lim_{x \to a} f(x) + \lim_{x \to a} g(x) = L + K$

3. $\lim_{x \to a} [f(x) - g(x)] = \lim_{x \to a} f(x) - \lim_{x \to a} g(x) = L - K$

4. $\lim_{x \to a} [f(x) \times g(x)] = [\lim_{x \to a} f(x)] \times [[\lim_{x \to a} g(x)] = LK$.

5. $\lim_{x \to a} \left[\dfrac{f(x)}{g(x)} \right] = \dfrac{\lim_{x \to a} f(x)}{\lim_{x \to a} g(x)} = \dfrac{L}{K}$, provided that $K \neq 0$.

6. $\lim_{x \to a} \left[\dfrac{1}{f(x)} \right] = \dfrac{1}{L}$, provided that $L \neq 0$.

7. $\lim_{x \to a} \left[f(x) \right]^n = [\lim_{x \to a} f(x)]^n = L^n$.

8. $\lim_{x \to a} \left[cf(x) \right] = c[\lim_{x \to a} f(x)] = cL$, for all real c.

9. $\lim_{x \to a} \sqrt[n]{f(x)} = \sqrt[n]{\lim_{x \to a} f(x)}$, provided that $n > 1$.

10. If $f(x)$ is a polynomial function then $\lim_{x \to a} f(x) = f(a)$

EXAMPLE 31

What is the value of $\lim_{x \to 2} \dfrac{x^2 + x + 2}{x^2}$?

SOLUTION

By substitution, the limit is $\dfrac{4 + 2 + 2}{4} = 2$.

EXAMPLE 32

What is the value of $\lim_{x \to 3}(2x^2 - x + 5)^4$

SOLUTION

By the seventh rule mentioned above, we just need to evaluate $[\lim_{x \to 3}(2x^2 - x + 5)]^4$. So, $\lim_{x \to 3}(2x^2 - x + 5) = 2(3^2) - 3 + 5 = 20$. Thus, the answer becomes $20^4 = 160,000$.

One-sided Limits

Not all functions are defined for all values of x. Therefore, the direction in which the limit approaches the function might impact the limit value. The notation $\lim_{x \to a+} f(x)$ and $\lim_{x \to a-} f(x)$ are used for one-sided limits. This notation means to find the limit as x approaches a from positive infinity $(+\infty)$ or from negative infinity $(-\infty)$, respectively. A piecewise function is shown below for which the limits would differ depending on the direction.

EXAMPLE 33

You are given the function
$$f(x) = \begin{cases} x^2 + 2, x \leq 1 \\ 2x, x > 1 \end{cases}$$
What are the values of $\lim_{x \to 1^-} f(x)$ and $\lim_{x \to 1^+} f(x)$?

SOLUTION

We look at the graph of this function, as shown in Figure 4.27

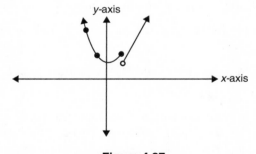

Figure 4.27

$\lim_{x \to 1^-} f(x)$ means to find the limit of $f(x)$ as x approaches 1 from the left (negative infinity). The point $(1, 3)$ lies on the portion of the graph defined by $f(x) = x^2 + 2$, so our answer would be 3. This answer can also be verified by substitution, that is $1^2 + 2 = 3$.

$\lim_{x \to 1^+} f(x)$ means to find the limit of $f(x)$ as x approaches 1 from the right (positive infinity). Although $f(x) = 2x$ is defined for all values of x greater than 1, it is not defined at 1. However, as x approaches 1 from the right, the value of $f(x)$ approaches $(2)(1) = 2$. Thus, $\lim_{x \to 1^+} f(x) = 2$.

Note that since $\lim_{x \to 1^-} f(x) \neq \lim_{x \to 1^+} f(x)$, we conclude that $\lim_{x \to 1} f(x)$ does not exist for the function in Example 33.

Special Limits

Certain limits occur with ample frequency that they merit special attention. Here are the most common.

1. $\lim_{x \to 0} \dfrac{\sin x}{x} = 1$

2. $\lim_{x \to 0} \dfrac{1 - \cos x}{x} = 0$

3. $\lim_{x \to 0}(1 + x)^{\frac{1}{x}} = \lim_{x \to \infty}(1 + \frac{1}{x})^x = e$

4. For $a > 1$, $\lim_{x \to +\infty} a^x = +\infty$ and $\lim_{x \to -\infty} a^x = 0$

5. For $a > 1$, $\lim_{x \to +\infty} \log_a x = +\infty$ and $\lim_{x \to 0} \log_a x = -\infty$

6. For $0 < a < 1$, $\lim_{x \to +\infty} a^x = 0$ and $\lim_{x \to -\infty} a^x = +\infty$

7. For $0 < a < 1$, $\lim_{x \to +\infty} \log_a x = -\infty$ and $\lim_{x \to 0} \log_a x = +\infty$

It should be noted that when the limit "value" is listed as $+\infty$ or as $-\infty$, these are really descriptions of limits that do not exist as real numbers. In reality, the statement $\lim_{x \to a} f(x) = \pm \infty$ means that the function has no limit as x approaches a.

Many limits have "values" of $+\infty$ or $-\infty$. Several possible scenarios are: division by 0, or function values that continue to get larger and larger in the direction of $+\infty$ or $-\infty$.

EXAMPLE 34

What is the value of $\lim_{x \to -\infty}(x^2 + 2)$?

SOLUTION

Consider negative x-values that get larger and larger [approach $-\infty$]. Note that $x^2 + 2$ gets larger and larger in the positive direction since x^2 is always positive [approach $+\infty$]. Therefore, this limit is $+\infty$, which means that the limit does not exist.

Limits for Rational Functions when x approaches infinity (plus or minus)

If $f(x)$ is a polynomial function, the value of the limit as x approaches infinity will be $+\infty$ or $-\infty$, depending on the leading coefficient. Thus, the limit does not exist.

If $f(x)$ is a rational function in the form $\dfrac{p(x)}{q(x)}$, then there are three basic rules to follow:

Rule 1: If the degree of $p(x)$ is less than that of $q(x)$, then $\lim_{x \to \infty} f(x) = 0$.

Rule 2: If the degree of $p(x)$ is equal to that of $q(x)$, then $\lim_{x \to \infty} f(x) = k$, where k is the ratio of the leading coefficients of $p(x)$ and $q(x)$.

Rule 3: If the degree of $p(x)$ is greater than that of $q(x)$, then $\lim_{x \to \infty} f(x) = \infty$. This is equivalent to stating that $\lim_{x \to \infty} f(x)$ does not exist.

EXAMPLE 35

What is the value of $\lim_{x \to \infty}(3x^5 - 10x^3 + 40)$?

SOLUTION

The leading term is $3x^5$. As x increases without bound, the value of $3x^5$ also increases without bound. Thus, the limit does not exist.

EXAMPLE 36

What is the value of $\lim_{x \to \infty} \dfrac{-3x^4 + 7x - 4}{6x^4 + 91}$?

SOLUTION

Since the degrees of the numerator and denominator are equal, the limit is the ratio of the leading coefficients, which is $-\dfrac{1}{2}$.

EXAMPLE 37

What is the value of $\lim_{x \to -\infty} \dfrac{10x^3 + 5}{8x^5 + x + 9}$?

SOLUTION

The same rules apply whether x approaches ∞ or $-\infty$. Since the degree of the numerator is smaller than that of the denominator, the answer is 0.

EXAMPLE 38

What is the value of $\lim_{x \to \infty} \dfrac{-9x^6 + 5x + 2}{10x^4 - 3x}$?

SOLUTION

The degree of the numerator is larger than that of the denominator. Thus, the limit does not exist.

Continuity

A function f is continuous at $x = a$ if and only if

1. $f(a)$ exists and
2. $\lim_{x \to a} f(x) = f(a)$

There are several main rules that govern continuity for functions.

1. If f and g are continuous functions at a, then so are the functions $f + g, f - g, fg$, and $\dfrac{f}{g}$ where $g(a) \neq 0$.

2. If $\lim_{x \to a} g(x) = L$ and $f(x)$ is continuous at L, then $\lim_{x \to a} f(g(x)) = f(L) = f \lim_{x \to a}(g(x))$.

3. If f is continuous on a closed interval $[a, b]$ and of $f(a) \neq f(b)$, then f takes on every value between $f(a)$ and $f(a)$ in the interval $[a, b]$. This is known as the **Intermediate Value Theorem**.

4. $f(x) = k$, where k is a real number, is continuous everywhere.

5. $f(x) = x$, the identity function is continuous everywhere.

6. If f is continuous at a, then $\lim\limits_{x \to \infty} f(a + \frac{1}{x}) = f(a)$.

7. If f is continuous on an interval containing a and b, $a < b$, and if $f(a) \cdot f(b) < 0$ then there exists at least one point, c, $a < c < b$, such that $f(c) = 0$.

EXAMPLE 39

Determine if $f(x) = 3x + 2$ is continuous at $x = 3$.

SOLUTION

$f(3) = 3x + 2 = 3(3) + 2 = 11$. Also, $\lim\limits_{x \to 3}(3x + 2) = 11$. Therefore, $f(x)$ is continuous at 3.

EXAMPLE 40

Determine if $f(x) = \dfrac{x^2 - 2x + 1}{x - 1}$ is continuous at $x = 1$.

SOLUTION

$f(1) = \dfrac{1 - 2 + 1}{1 - 1} = \dfrac{0}{0}$ = undefined (division by 0)

$\lim\limits_{x \to 1} \dfrac{x^2 - 2x + 1}{x - 1} = \dfrac{(x-1)(x-1)}{x - 1} = x - 1 = 1 - 1 = 0$

$\lim\limits_{x \to 1} \dfrac{x^2 - 2x + 1}{x - 1} \neq f(1)$ so the function is not continuous.

If $f(x)$ is continuous in the interval $[a, b]$, the **average rate of change** of the function over this interval is the slope of the line segment connecting the points $(a, f(a))$ and $(b, f(b))$.

Thus, the average rate of change equals $\dfrac{f(b) - f(a)}{b - a}$.

EXAMPLE 41

What is the average rate of change for $f(x) = 2x^2 + 5$ over the interval [2, 5]?

SOLUTION

$f(2) = (2)(2^2) + 5 = 13$ and $f(5) = (2)(5^2) + 5 = 55$. Thus, the average rate of change is $\dfrac{55 - 13}{5 - 2} = 14$.

Differentiation

The first derivative of a function expresses the instantaneous rate of change with respect to the independent variable (usually x). The first derivative is also the limit of the slope of the secant line to the curve that joins two points, as the distance between these points approaches zero. In effect, this value is the slope of the tangent line to the curve as these two points become one point. This is illustrated in Figure 4.28

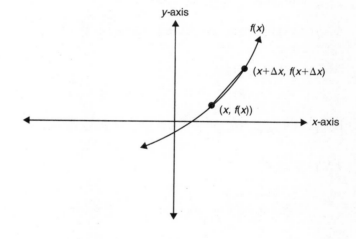

Figure 4.28

In Figure 4.28, the two given points are $(x, f(x))$ and $(x + \Delta x, f(x + \Delta x))$. We construct the secant line that contains these two points. The average rate of change for $f(x)$ over the interval $[(x, x + \Delta x)]$ can be expressed as $\dfrac{f(x + \Delta x) - f(x)}{(x + \Delta x) - x} = \dfrac{\Delta y}{\Delta x}$. The term Δy represents the change in y, whereas Δx (which is also written as h) represents the corresponding change in x. Then the first derivative, commonly written as $f'(x)$, is equal to

$$\lim_{\Delta x \to 0} \frac{f(x+\Delta x)-f(x)}{\Delta x} \text{ or } \lim_{h \to 0} \frac{f(x+h)-f(x)}{h}.$$

If $f(x)$ is defined on an open interval containing a

value a, then $f'(a) = \lim_{x \to a} \frac{f(x)-f(a)}{x-a}$, provided the limit exists.

There are several other notations for the first derivative, including y', $\frac{dy}{dx}$, and $D_x y$.

Rules of First Derivatives

1. If $f(x)$ is a constant function, then $f(x) = c$, and $f'(x) = 0$.

2. If $f(x) = x$, then $f'(x) = 1$.

3. If $f(x)$ is differentiable, then $(cf(x))' = cf'(x)$.

4. Power Rule: If $f(x) = x^n$ and $n \neq 0$, then $f'(x) = nx^{n-1}$.

5. Chain Rule: Suppose that y is a function of u, and u is a function of x. Then $\frac{dy}{dx} = \frac{dy}{du} \times \frac{du}{dx}$.

6. If $f(x)$ and $g(x)$ are differentiable on the interval (a, b) then

   a) $(f+g)'(x) = f'(x) + g'(x)$

   b) Product Rule: $(fg)'(x) = f(x)g'(x) + g(x)f'(x)$

   c) Quotient Rule: $\left(\frac{f}{g}\right)'(x) = \frac{g(x)f'(x)-f(x)g'(x)}{[g(x)]^2}$

EXAMPLE 42

What is the first derivative of $y = x^2 + (4x+1)$?

SOLUTION

Use the $(f+g)'(x) = f'(x) + g'(x)$ rule. Let $f(x) = x^2$ and $g(x) = 4x + 1$.

Then $y' = (f+g)'(x) = f'(x) + g'(x) = 2x + 4$.

EXAMPLE 43

What is the first derivative of $y = \frac{x^2+2x+1}{x-1}$?

SOLUTION

Use the quotient rule in which $f(x) = x^2 + 2x + 1$, $f'(x) = 2x + 2$, $g(x) = x - 1$ and $g'(x) = -1$. Then

$$\frac{dy}{dx} = \frac{(x-1)(2x+2)-(x^2+2x+1)(-1)}{(x-1)^2}$$

$$= \frac{2x^2-2+x^2+2x+1}{(x-1)^2} = \frac{3x^2+2x-1}{(x-1)^2}.$$

EXAMPLE 44

What is the first derivative of $y = (3x^2 - 7)^3$?

SOLUTION

Instead of expanding the right side of this function, let's use the Chain Rule. Let $u = 3x^2 - 7$. Then $y = u^3$, $\frac{dy}{du} = 3u^2$, and $\frac{du}{dx} = 6x$. Then $\frac{dy}{dx} = \frac{dy}{du} \times \frac{du}{dx} = (3u^2)(6x)$ $= (3)(3x^2 - 7)^2(6x) = (18x)(3x^2 - 7)^2$.

Trigonometric Differentiation

Each of the six trigonometric functions can be differentiated.

$$D_x \sin u = \cos u \, D_x u$$
$$D_x \cos u = -\sin u \, D_x u$$
$$D_x \tan u = \sec^2 u \, D_x u$$
$$D_x \sec u = \tan u \sec u \, D_x u$$
$$D_x \cot u = -\csc^2 u \, D_x u$$
$$D_x \csc u = -\csc u \cot u \, D_x u$$

EXAMPLE 45

What is the first derivative of $y = \sin 3\theta$?

SOLUTION

Let $u = 3\theta$, so that $\frac{dy}{du} = \cos u$ and $\frac{du}{d\theta} = 3$. Using the Chain Rule, $\frac{dy}{d\theta} = \frac{dy}{du} \times \frac{du}{d\theta} = 3 \cos u = 3 \cos 3\theta$.

EXAMPLE 46

What is the first derivative of $y = (\sec x)(4x^3)$?

SOLUTION

Let $f(x) = \sec x$ and $g(x) = 4x^3$. Then $f'(x) = (\sec x)(\tan x)$ and $g'(x) = 12x^2$. Thus, $\frac{dy}{dx} = (\sec x)(12x^2) + (4x^3)(\sec x)(\tan x)$ or $(4x^2 \sec x)(3 + x \tan x)$.

Exponential and Logarithmic Differentiation

The exponential function and logarithmic function can be differentiated.

$D_x e^x = e^x$

$D_x e^u = e^u \dfrac{du}{dx}$

$D_x \ln y = \dfrac{1}{y} \dfrac{dy}{dx}$

$D_x \ln u = \dfrac{1}{u} \dfrac{du}{dx}$

$D_x a^x = a^x \ln a$

$D_x a^u = a^u \ln a \dfrac{du}{dx}$

$D_x (\log_a x) = \dfrac{1}{x \ln a}$

$D_x (\log_a |u|) = \dfrac{1}{u \ln a} \dfrac{du}{dx}$

EXAMPLE 47

What is the first derivative of $y = e^{x^2}$?

SOLUTION

Let $u = x^2$ and $du = 2x$

$D_x e^u = e^u \dfrac{du}{dx} = e^{x^2}(2x) = 2x e^{x^2}$

EXAMPLE 48

What is the first derivative of $y = \ln(2x - 1)^3$

SOLUTION

Rewrite $y = \ln(2x - 1)^3$ as $y = 3\ln(2x - 1)$. Now, let $u = 2x - 1$ and $du = 2$.

Then $(3)(D_x \ln u) = (3) (\dfrac{1}{u} \dfrac{du}{dx}) = (3)(\dfrac{1}{2x-1}) (2) = \dfrac{6}{2x-1}$.

Higher-Order Derivatives

Many functions can be differentiated several times. The second derivative is found by taking the derivative of the first derivative. The third derivative is found by taking the derivative of the second derivative. The most common derivatives used are the first and second derivative. If $y = f(x)$, the second derivative can be symbolized as $\dfrac{d^2 y}{dx^2}$, as y'', or as $f''(x)$.

EXAMPLE 49

What is the second derivative of $y = 3x^3 + 2x^2 + 1$?

SOLUTION

$y' = 9x^2 + 4x$, so $y'' = 18x + 4$.

EXAMPLE 50

What is the second derivative of $f(x) = (x)(4^x)$?

SOLUTION

Recall that the first derivative of 4^x is $4^x \ln 4$. Then $f'(x) = (x)(4^x)(\ln 4) + (4^x)(1) = (4^x)(x \ln 4 + 1)$. Keeping in mind that the first derivative of $x \ln 4$ is $\ln 4$, we calculate $f''(x)$ as $(4^x)(\ln 4) + (x \ln 4 + 1)(4^x)(\ln 4)$ or $(4^x)(\ln 4)(2 + x \ln 4)$.

Implicit Differentiation

An implicit function of x and y is a function in which one of the variables is not directly expressed in terms of the other. Examples are $xy = 12$ and $x^2 - 2xy = 9$. Apply the rules of differentiation that will result in $\dfrac{dy}{dx}$ as part of the differentiation. Then solve for $\dfrac{dy}{dx}$.

EXAMPLE 51

> Using implicit differentiation, what is the first derivative of $xy^2 = 12$?

SOLUTION

We differentiate each term with respect to x. Using the product rule, we get $(x)(2xy)(y') + (y^2)(1) = 0$. Then $(2xy)(y') = -y^2$, so $y' = \dfrac{-y^2}{2xy} = \dfrac{-y}{2x}$.

EXAMPLE 52

> Using implicit differentiation, what is the first derivative of $x^2 + 3y^2 = 6$?

SOLUTION

The first step is $2x + (6y)(\dfrac{dy}{dx}) = 0$. Then $(6y)(\dfrac{dy}{dx}) = -2x$, so $\dfrac{dy}{dx} = \dfrac{-2x}{6y} = \dfrac{-x}{3y}$.

Applications of the First Derivative

Graphically, the first derivative at a particular point represents the slope of the tangent line to the curve at that point. If the first derivative is zero, then the tangent line must be horizontal. In Figure 4.29, the graph of $f(x) = x^2 + 2$ is shown. Note that the slope of the tangent line at $(0, 2)$ is zero.

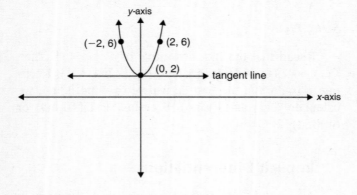

Figure 4.29

Rolle's Theorem states the following: Let $f(x)$ be continuous on a closed interval $[a, b]$. and assume $f'(x)$

exists at each point in the open interval (a, b). If $f(a) = f(b) = 0$, then there is at least one point (c) in (a, b) such that $f'(c) = 0$. Figure 4.30 and Figure 4.31 illustrate this theorem geometrically.

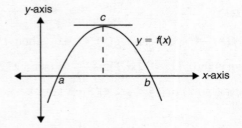

Figure 4.30

Note that Figure 4.30 contains one point (P) that satisfies Rolle's theorem, whereas Figure 4.31 contains two such points $(Q$ and $R)$.

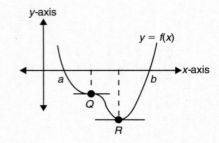

Figure 4.31

The **Mean Value Theorem** is actually an extension of Rolle's Theorem. Let $f(x)$ be continuous on a closed interval $[a, b]$ and assume $f'(x)$ exists at each point in the open interval (a, b). Then there is at least one number c in (a, b) such that $f'(c) = \dfrac{f(b) - f(a)}{b - a}$. Figure 4.32 illustrates this theorem.

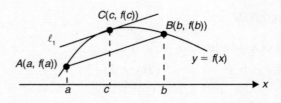

Figure 4.32

Note that the slope of the secant line segment, whose endpoints are A and B, is $\dfrac{f(b) - f(a)}{b - a}$. This value matches the slope of the tangent line l_1 at point C.

As with Rolle's Theorem, there may exist more than one point that satisfies the Mean Value Theorem. Here are two important consequences of the Mean Value Theorem.

1. If $f(x)$ is defined on an interval (a, b) and if $f'(x) = 0$ for each point in the interval, then $f(x)$ is constant over the interval.

2. Let $f(x)$ and $g(x)$ be differentiable on an interval (a, b). If for each point x in the interval, $f'(x)$ and $g'(x)$ are equal, then there is a constant c, such that $f(x) + c = g(x)$ for all x. This result is illustrated in Figure 4.33.

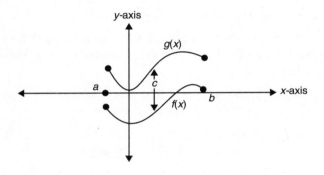

Figure 4.33

Note that the two functions appear to "parallel" each other. For any given value of x in the interval (a, b), the graphs of $f(x)$ and $g(x)$ are c units apart.

EXAMPLE 53

Consider $f(x) = x^3 - 5x^2$ over the interval $(0, 5)$. Determine the c value(s) in $(0, 5)$ for which $f'(c) = 0$.

SOLUTION

We note that $f(0) = 0^3 - (5)(0)^2 = 0$ and that $f(5) = 5^3 - (5)(5)^2 = 0$. By Rolle's Theorem, there must exist at least one c in $(0, 5)$ such that $f'(c) = 0$. Since $f'(x) = 3x^2 - 10x$, we need to solve $3x^2 - 10x = 0$. By factoring the left side of the equation, we get $(x)(3x - 10) = 0$.

The two solutions are $x = 0$ and $x = \dfrac{10}{3}$. Since we are only seeking solutions in the open interval $(0, 5)$, the desired c value is $\dfrac{10}{3}$.

EXAMPLE 54

Consider the function $g(x) = 2x^2 + 5$ over the interval $(2, 5)$. Determine a value of c in this interval for which $g'(c)$ equals the average rate of change of $g(x)$ over $(2, 5)$.

SOLUTION

Since $g(2) = (2)(2^2) + 5 = 13$ and $g(5) = (5)(5^2) + 5 = 55$, the average rate of change of $g(x)$ over $(2, 5)$ is $\dfrac{55 - 13}{5 - 2} = \dfrac{42}{3} = 14$. Next, we find that $g'(x) = 4x$. Using the Mean Value Theorem, we need to solve $g'(c) = 4c = 14$. Thus, $c = 3.5$.

L'Hopital's Rule states that if $\lim_{x \to a} \dfrac{f(x)}{g(x)} = \dfrac{0}{0}$ or $= \dfrac{\infty}{\infty}$, then we differentiate the numerator and the denominator separately. The value of $\lim_{x \to a} \dfrac{f(x)}{g(x)}$ will be given by $\lim_{x \to a} \dfrac{f'(x)}{g'(x)}$.

EXAMPLE 55

What is the value of $\lim_{x \to 2} \dfrac{2x^2 - 4x}{x - 2}$?

SOLUTION

Each of $\lim_{x \to 2}(2x^2 - 4x)$ and $\lim_{x \to 2}(x - 2)$ has a value of zero, so we take the first derivative of the numerator and denominator. Thus, we seek the value of $\lim_{x \to 2} \dfrac{4x - 4}{1} = 4$.

EXAMPLE 56

What is the value of $\lim_{x \to 0} \dfrac{\sin x}{x}$?

SOLUTION

Each of $\lim_{x\to 0} \sin x$ and $\lim_{x\to 0} x$ equals zero, so we use L'Hopital's Rule. Let $f(x) = \sin x$ and $g(x) = x$. We know that $f'(x) = \cos x$ and that $g'(x) = 1$. Thus, $\lim_{x\to 0} \dfrac{\sin x}{x} = \lim_{x\to 0} \dfrac{\cos x}{1} = 1$.

A **critical value** for a function $f(x)$ is defined as any value in the domain for which $f'(x) = 0$ or $f(x)$ is not differentiable. Each of Figures 4.34 and 4.35 illustrates an example of a graph of $f(x)$ for which $f'(x) = 0$ when $x = x_0$. As expected, the slope of the tangent line is zero.

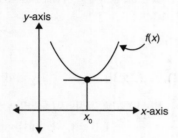

Figure 4.34

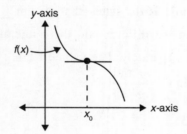

Figure 4.35

Each of Figures 4.36 and 4.37 illustrates an example of a graph of $g(x)$ for which $g'(x)$ does not exist at $x = x_0$.

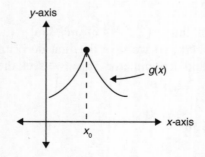

Figure 4.36

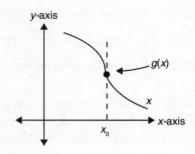

Figure 4.37

In Figure 4.36, there is more than one tangent line at x_0. In Figure 4.37, the tangent line is vertical and thus has an undefined slope.

Differentiation can be used to determine function minimums and maximums and graph the function itself.

First Derivative Test:

Suppose that c is a critical value of a function $f(x)$ in an interval (a, b). Also, $f(x)$ is continuous and differentiable over (a, b).

1. If $f'(x) > 0$ for all $a < x < c$ and $f'(x) < 0$ for all $c < x < b$ then $f(c)$ is a local maximum.

2. If $f'(x) < 0$ for all $a < x < c$ and $f'(x) > 0$ for all $c < x < b$ then $f(c)$ is a local minimum.

3. If $f'(x) > 0$ or $f'(x) < 0$ for all x in (a, b) then $f(c)$ is neither a local maximum nor a local minimum.

Second Derivative Test:

Suppose that c is a critical value of a function $f(x)$ in an interval (a, b) with $f'(c) = 0$ and $f''(x)$ exists in (a, b). Also, $f(x)$ is continuous and differentiable over (a, b).

1. If $f''(c) < 0$, then $f(c)$ is a relative maximum.

2. If $f''(c) > 0$, then $f(c)$ is a relative minimum.

3. If $f''(c) = 0$, then there is no conclusion from the test.

If a function is twice differentiable on an open interval containing c, then the graph at this point is **concave upward** if $f''(c) > 0$, and **concave downward** if $f''(c) < 0$.

If $f(x)$ is continuous and twice differentiable on an open interval, then the **points of inflection** are those at which the concavity of a curve changes sign.

Let's summarize these concepts with Figure 4.38 that shows a continuous function $f(x)$ over (a, b), with points A, B, C, D, E, F, and G.

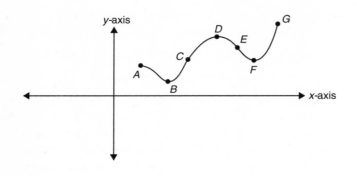

Figure 4.38

The minimum value is located at *A* and the maximum value is located at *G*.

$f'(x) > 0$ between *B* and *D*, and between *F* and *G*.

$f'(x) < 0$ between *A* and *B*, and between *D* and *F*.

$f'(x) = 0$ at *B*, *D*, and *F*.

$f''(x) > 0$ between *A* and *C*, and between *E* and *G*. The curve is concave upward.

$f''(x) < 0$ between *C* and *E*. The curve is concave downward.

$f''(x) = 0$ at *C* and *E*. These are the points of inflection.

EXAMPLE 57

Find the maximum, minimum, concavity, and points of inflection for $f(x) = 2x^2 - 8x + 6$ in the interval $(-\infty, \infty)$. Also, trace the curve.

SOLUTION

First, we'll find $f'(x)$, set the derivative to 0, and solve for *x* to locate the critical points. So, $f'(x) = 4x - 8 = 0$. This means that $x = 2$ is the only critical value.

Next, use the Second Derivative Test to determine whether or not $x = 2$ represents the *x* value of a maximum or minimum point. We find that $f''(x) = 4$. Since $4 > 0$, the value of 2 represents the lowest point of the graph of this function. Therefore, the minimum $f(x)$ value is $(2)(2^2) - (8)(2) + 6 = -2$.

Since $f''(x) > 0$ for all *x* values, the graph is concave upward.

Finally, since there is no point for which $f''(x) = 0$, there are no points of inflection.

Figure 4.39 shows the graph of

$f(x) = 2x^2 - 8x + 6$, with specific coordinates.

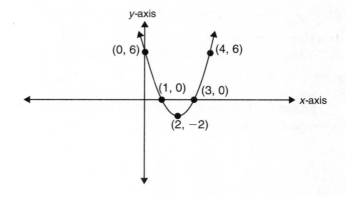

Figure 4.39

EXAMPLE 58

Find the maximum, minimum, concavity, and points of inflection for $f(x) = x^3 + x^2 - x$ in the interval $(-\infty, \infty)$. Also, trace the curve.

SOLUTION

We determine that $f'(x) = 3x^2 + 2x - 1$, which factors as $(3x - 1)(x + 1)$.

Solving $(3x - 1)(x + 1) = 0$, we find the critical *x* values of $\frac{1}{3}$ and -1. By graphing $f(x)$, we can determine that there is no absolute minimum or maximum value. However, when $x = \frac{1}{3}$, the graph shows a <u>local</u> minimum value; the corresponding *y* value is $(\frac{1}{3})^3 + (\frac{1}{3})^2 - \frac{1}{3} = -\frac{5}{27}$. Likewise, when $x = -1$, the graph shows a <u>local</u> maximum value; the corresponding *y* value is $(-1)^3 + (-1)^2 - (-1) = 1$.

To find the inflection point(s), we set $f''(x) = 6x + 2 = 0$. Then $x = -\frac{2}{6} = -\frac{1}{3}$. The corresponding *y* value is $(-\frac{1}{3})^3 + (-\frac{1}{3})^2 - (-\frac{1}{3}) = \frac{11}{27}$. The only inflection point is $(-\frac{1}{3}, \frac{11}{27})$.

Geometry and Measurement

Metric and Customary System

Length, weight and capacity are most often used to describe items. Two systems are used to measure length, weight and capacity: metric system and customary system.

The metric system is base 10. The same prefixes are used for all types of measurements. Each prefix describes a specific amount of the standard measure. Standard measure for length is meter (m), weight is gram (g), and capacity is liter (l). To convert from a larger measure to a smaller measure, **multiply** by the given factor. To convert from a smaller measure to a larger measure, **divide** by the given factor. The metric measurement system follows.

Milli-(m)	Centi-(c)	Deci-(d)	Meter (length) Gram (weight) Liter (capacity)	Deka-(de)	Hecto-(h)	Kilo-(k)
$\frac{1}{1000}$	$\frac{1}{100}$	$\frac{1}{10}$		10	100	1000

EXAMPLE 1

Convert 30 meters to centimeters.

SOLUTION

Since we are converting from a larger unit to a smaller unit, we multiply by the given factor (100). The answer is $30 \times 100 = 3000$ centimeters.

EXAMPLE 2

The weight of a pencil is 5 grams. What is the weight of the pencil in kilograms?

SOLUTION

Since we are converting from a smaller unit to a larger unit, we divide by the given factor (1000). The answer is $5 \div 1000 = 0.005$ kilograms.

The customary system has no standard units for length, weight and capacity. The most common units for length, weight and capacity are described below. The smallest unit typically used to measure length is the inch (in). The smallest unit typically used to measure weight is the ounce (oz). The smallest unit typically used to measure capacity is the fluid ounce (fl oz).

Length	Weight	Capacity
1 foot (ft) = 12 in	1 pound (lb) = 16 oz	1 pint (pt) =16 fl oz
1 yard (yd) = 3 ft	1 ton = 2,000 lbs	1 quart = 2 pts
1 mile (mi) = 1760 yds		1 gallon (gal) = 4 qts

EXAMPLE 3

Convert 7000 yards to miles.

SOLUTION

Use the yards-to-miles conversion factor. Since we are changing from a smaller unit to a larger unit, we divide. Thus, 7000 yards $= \dfrac{7000}{1760} \approx 3.98$ miles.

EXAMPLE 4

How many quarts of water are in a swimming pool that contains 15,000 gallons of water?

SOLUTION

Four quarts are equivalent to one gallon. We are changing from a larger unit to a smaller unit. Thus, we multiply by the conversion factor. The answer is $(15,000)(4) = 60,000$ quarts.

Mathematical Arguments

Many statements are conditional, which means that the occurrence of one event results in the occurrence of a second event. As an example, consider the statement, "If it is sunny today, then I will go to the park." If the first event occurs (weather is sunny), then the second event will also occur (I go to the park).

In mathematics this idea is often written as, "If x, then y." The variable x is called the hypothesis and y

is called the conclusion. As an example, consider the statement, "If the light is red, then cars stop at the intersection." Here, x represents "the light is red" and y represents "cars stop at the intersection." There are several ways to re-write the sentence: converse, contrapositive, and inverse. The contrapositive and original statements are equivalent. Likewise, the converse and inverse statements are equivalent.

Term	Definition	Example
Converse	Switch the hypothesis and conclusion. (If y, then x.)	If cars are stopped at the intersection, then the light is red.
Contrapositive	Switch and negate the hypothesis and conclusion. (If not y, then not x.)	If cars are not stopped at the intersection, then the light is not red.
Inverse	Negate the hypothesis and conclusion. (If not x, then not y.)	If the light is not red, then cars are not stopped at the intersection.

EXAMPLE 5

Write the contrapositive of, "If you are riding a four-wheeler, then you are wearing a helmet."

SOLUTION

Switch and negate the hypothesis and conclusion. The answer is, "If you are not wearing a helmet, then you are not riding a four-wheeler."

EXAMPLE 6

Write the converse of, "If you study, then you will pass the final exam."

SOLUTION

We just switch the hypothesis and conclusion. The answer is, "If you pass the final exam, then you studied."

Note that the converse may not be true, even if the original statement is true. It is possible that you already know the material well enough that you don't have to study.

Geometry Basics

The assumptions upon which geometry is based are called **postulates**. Additionally, the assumptions upon which algebra is based are called **axioms**. **Theorems** are derived from postulates and definitions. Secondary mathematics geometry is the study of Euclidean geometry. There are several other geometries that exist but are beyond the scope of this text. The basic building blocks of geometry are points, lines, and planes.

Term	Definition	Example
Point	a location	$\bullet\, P$
Line	one-dimensional, has no specific length or width, and extends indefinitely	line ℓ, $\overrightarrow{AB}$, or $\overrightarrow{BA}$
Plane	two-dimensional, has no thickness, extends indefinitely in two directions	Plane RST or Plane P
Segment	A finite portion of a line, with two endpoints	$\overline{AB}$ or $\overline{BA}$
Ray	A portion of a line with one endpoint. It extends forever in one direction.	$\overrightarrow{AB}$
Angle	Two rays connected at a single endpoint.	$\angle B$, $\angle ABC$, or $\angle CBA$

Angles that have equal measure and congruent segments equal measure are denoted using tick marks.

Figure 5.1 shows two triangles with pairs of congruent segments.

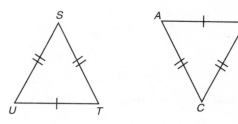

Figure 5.1

$\overline{UT}$ and $\overline{AB}$ have the same length, and each of $\overline{ST}$, $\overline{SU}$, $\overline{AC}$, and $\overline{BC}$ have the same length. The symbol for congruence is $\cong$. Thus, we can write $\overline{UT} \cong \overline{AB}$ and $\overline{ST} \cong \overline{SU} \cong \overline{AC} \cong \overline{BC}$.

Figure 5.2 shows two triangles with pairs of congruent angles.

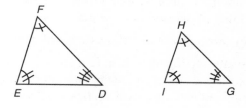

Figure 5.2

Using the congruence symbol, we can write $\angle F \cong \angle H$, $\angle E \cong \angle I$ and $\angle D \cong \angle G$.

Angles

The size of an angle is classified by its measure. The name of an angle is written as a single letter (the vertex) or as three letters with the vertex as the middle letter. Angles are measured using a protractor. The symbol ° is used to denote the measure of an angle. An **acute** angle is one whose measure is between 0° and 90°, including 0° but not including 90°. A **right** angle is one whose measure is exactly 90°. An **obtuse** angle is one whose measure is between 90° and 180°, not including 90° and 180°. A **straight** angle is one whose measure is exactly 180°. Finally, a **reflex** angle is one whose measure is between 180° and 360°, not including 180° and 360°. Figures 5.3, 5.4, 5.5, 5.6, and 5.7, illustrate these five types of angles.

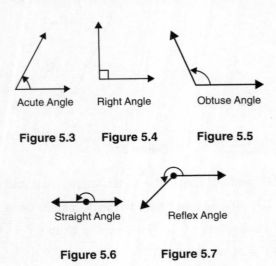

Acute Angle   Right Angle   Obtuse Angle

Figure 5.3   **Figure 5.4**   **Figure 5.5**

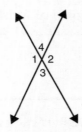

Straight Angle   Reflex Angle

Figure 5.6   **Figure 5.7**

Note the box at the vertex in Figure 5.4. This box symbol means a 90-degree angle. For the other four angles, an arc symbol with an arrow is used to denote the direction of the angle's measure.

There are a few other titles associated with angles.

Two intersecting lines form four angles. Angles that are opposite each other formed by two intersecting lines are **congruent** and are called **vertical** angles, as shown in Figure 5.8. (Note that angles may also be named with numbers, provided that there is no ambiguity.)

Figures 5.8

In this figure, ∠1 ≅ ∠2 and ∠3 ≅ ∠4.

Complementary angles are two angles whose measures sum to 90°, whereas **supplementary** angles are two angles whose measures sum to 180°. These are shown in Figures 5.9 and 5.10.

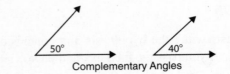

Complementary Angles

Figure 5.9

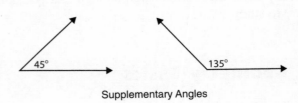

Supplementary Angles

Figure 5.10

An **angle bisector** divides a given angle into two congruent angles. The measure of each of these congruent angles is one half that of the given angle. Figure 5.11 shows the bisector of an angle whose measure is 110°.

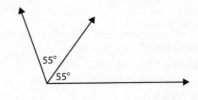

Figure 5.11

Lines

Two lines, $\overrightarrow{AB}$ and $\overrightarrow{CD}$, that intersect at a right angle are called **perpendicular** lines and are written as $\overrightarrow{AB} \perp \overrightarrow{CD}$. Two lines, $\overrightarrow{AB}$ and $\overrightarrow{CD}$, that do not intersect (but lie in the same plane) are called **parallel** and are written as $\overrightarrow{AB} \parallel \overrightarrow{CD}$. **Skew lines** are lines that are neither parallel nor lie in the same plane. Figures 5.12, 5.13, and 5.14 illustrate these concepts.

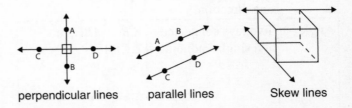

perpendicular lines   parallel lines   Skew lines

Figure 5.12   **Figure 5.13**   **Figure 5.14**

A **perpendicular bisector** is a line or segment that is perpendicular and divides a line segment equally. This concept is shown in Figure 5.15.

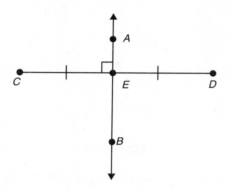

Figure 5.15

In this figure, $\overrightarrow{AB}$ is perpendicular to and bisects $\overline{CD}$ at point E.

A **transversal** is a line that intersects two or more lines and lies in the same plane. Angles formed by parallel lines cut by a transversal have specific names and properties. In Figure 5.16, lines l and m are parallel; line n is a transversal.

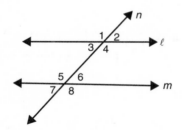

Figure 5.16

Angles 1, 2, 7 & 8 are called **exterior** angles. Angles 3, 4, 5 & 6 are called **interior** angles. Angle pairs 1 & 5, 2 & 6, 3 & 7, and 4 & 8 are called **corresponding** angles and are congruent. Angle pairs 3 & 6 and 4 & 5 are called **alternate interior** angles and are congruent.

Two lines can be determined to be parallel (proven to be parallel) by any of the following.

a) Congruent alternate interior angles

b) Congruent corresponding angles

c) Consecutive interior angles that are supplementary

d) Perpendicular to the same line

EXAMPLE 7

Referring to Figure 5.16, determine the measure of $\angle 8$ if $m \angle 2 = 50°$.

SOLUTION

Angles 2 and 4 form a straight line, and are supplementary. So $m\angle 4 = 180° - 50° = 130°$. Now since angles 4 and 8 are corresponding angles, the measure of $\angle 8$ must also be 130°.

Polygons

A polygon is a closed figure with the same number of sides and angles. There are several special classifications of polygons. Some polygons have specific names.

Number of Sides	Polygon Name
3	Triangle
4	Quadrilateral
5	Pentagon
6	Hexagon
7	Heptagon
8	Octagon
9	Nonagon
10	Decagon
12	Dodecagon
n	n-sided

Equiangular polygon — Polygon where all of the angles have the same measure.

Equilateral polygon — Polygon where all of the lengths of the sides have the same measure.

Regular Polygon — Polygon that is both equiangular and equilateral.

The sum of the interior angles of an n-sided polygon is given by the expression $(n-2)(180°)$. If the polygon is regular, then each interior angle has a measure of $\dfrac{(n-2)(180°)}{n}$ and each exterior angle has a measure of $\dfrac{360°}{n}$.

EXAMPLE 8

Determine the measure of each interior angle of a regular nonagon.

SOLUTION

A nonagon has 9 sides. Thus, the measure of each interior angle is $\dfrac{(n-2)(180°)}{n} = \dfrac{(9-2)(180°)}{9} = \dfrac{(7)(180°)}{9} = \dfrac{1260°}{9} = 140°$.

EXAMPLE 9

The sum of the measures of the interior angles of a regular polygon is known to be 2340°. What is the measure of each exterior angle?

SOLUTION

First, we'll determine the number of sides. We know that $(n - 2)(180°) = 2340$. Then $n-2 = \dfrac{2340°}{180°} = 13$, which means that $n = 15$. Thus, the measure of each exterior angle is $\dfrac{360°}{15} = 24°$.

Perimeter and Area of a Regular Polygon

The perimeter of a regular polygon is the product of the length of a side and the number of sides. The formula is $P = ns$, where n = number of sides and s = length of a side.

The **center** of a regular polygon is the point that is equidistant from each of the vertices. The **apothem** of a regular polygon is the segment from the center to the midpoint of one of the sides. The **radius** is the segment joining any vertex with the center. For a regular polygon all apothems are congruent and all radii are congruent. Furthermore, it can be proven that an apothem is perpendicular to the side to which it is drawn.

Figure 5.17 shows a regular pentagon in which $\overline{PK}$ is an apothem and $\overline{PG}$ is a radius.

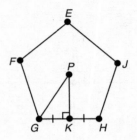

Figure 5.17

The area of a regular polygon equals one-half the product of the length of the apothem and the perimeter. The formula is A $= \dfrac{1}{2}a \cdot p$, where a = length of the apothem and p = perimeter.

EXAMPLE 10

What is the area of a regular decagon with a side of length 6 cm. and an apothem of length 10.2 cm.?

SOLUTION

The perimeter $= ns = (10)(6 \text{ cm}) = 60$ cm. Then the area $= \dfrac{1}{2}a \cdot p = \dfrac{1}{2}(10.2)\text{cm} \cdot 60\text{cm} = 306$ sq. cm.

EXAMPLE 11

The area of a regular octagon is 216 square inches. If each side is 4 inches, what is the length of the apothem?

SOLUTION

The perimeter must be $(8)(4) = 32$ inches. Using the area formula, we get $216 = (\dfrac{1}{2})(a)(32) = 16a$. Thus, $a = \dfrac{216}{16} = 13.5$ inches.

Triangle Properties

A triangle is a closed three-sided geometric figure. The points of intersection of the sides are called the

vertices. The sum of the measures of all three angles equals 180°.

Triangles are classified by their angles and/or their sides. An **acute** triangle is a triangle with all acute angles. A **right** triangle is a triangle with one right angle. An **obtuse** triangle is a triangle with one obtuse angle. A **scalene** triangle is a triangle with no sides of equal measure. An **isosceles** triangle is a triangle with <u>at least two</u> sides of equal measure. Additionally, the angles opposite congruent sides are also congruent. An **equilateral** triangle is a triangle with all three sides of equal measure.

<u>Special Note</u>: An equilateral triangle is a special case of an isosceles triangle. In most cases, though, when an isosceles triangle is presented in a problem, it has exactly two congruent sides (and two congruent angles).

EXAMPLE 12

In $\triangle ABC$, $m\angle A = m\angle B$. If $m\angle A = 50°$, what is the measure of $\angle C$?

SOLUTION

Since this is an isosceles triangle, we know that $m\angle B = 50°$. Thus, $m\angle C = 180° - 50° - 50° = 80°$.

EXAMPLE 13

Consider the triangle shown in Figure 5.18.

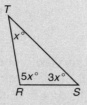

Figure 5.18

What is the measure of the largest angle?

SOLUTION

The sum of all three angles is 180°, so $x + 3x + 5x = 180$. Then $9x = 180$, which means that $x = 20°$.

Finally, $\angle R$ is the largest of the three angles, and its measure is $(5)(20°) = 100°$.

The **Pythagorean theorem** is extremely useful for solving the missing sides of right triangles. The theorem states that the sum of the squares of the two shorter sides (legs) equals the square of the longest side (hypotenuse). Expressed mathematically, $a^2 + b^2 = c^2$, where c must be the hypotenuse.

EXAMPLE 14

Consider $\triangle ABC$, as shown in Figure 5.19.

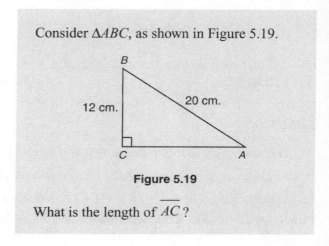

Figure 5.19

What is the length of $\overline{AC}$?

SOLUTION

In this triangle, $a = 12$ cm. and $c = 20$ cm. Then b represents the length of $\overline{AC}$. So, $(12)^2 + b^2 = (20)^2$. Simplifying, we get $b^2 = 400 - 144 = 256$. Thus, $b = \sqrt{256} = 16$ cm.

NOTE:

The letters a, b, and c need not always be used when applying the Pythagorean theorem. If the sides of a triangle are given as x, y, and z, with z representing the hypotenuse, this theorem would be written as $x^2 + y^2 = z^2$.

The perimeter of a triangle is simply the sum of the lengths of the sides. The area formula is given by $A = \frac{1}{2}b \cdot h$, where b represents any side (base) and h represents the altitude drawn to that side.

EXAMPLE 15

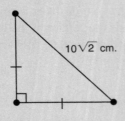

Consider the triangle shown in Figure 5.20.

$10\sqrt{2}$ cm.

Figure 5.20

Determine the perimeter and the area of this triangle.

SOLUTION

The given tick marks indicate that this is an isosceles right triangle, with $c = 10\sqrt{2}$. Let a represent the length of each leg. Then $a^2 + a^2 = (10\sqrt{2})^2$, which simplifies to $2a^2 = 200$. This becomes $a^2 = 100$, which means that $a = 10$. Then the perimeter is $10 + 10 + 10\sqrt{2} = 20 + 10\sqrt{2}$ cm. To find the area, either leg can represent the base and the other leg must represent the height. Thus, the area is $(\frac{1}{2})(10)(10) = 50$ sq. cm.

There are two important relationships that exist among the sides and angles of any one triangle.

1. If two sides of a triangle are congruent, then the angles opposite these sides are congruent. (The converse is also true.)

2. The order of the size of the angles of a triangle is exactly the same as the order of the size of the sides opposite these angles.

The **Triangle Inequality theorem** states that the sum of any two sides of a triangle must exceed the length of the third side.

EXAMPLE 16

Given $\triangle XYZ$ in which $XY = 13$, $XZ = 18$, and $YZ = 15$, which angle is the largest?

SOLUTION

A figure is not needed! Since XZ is the largest side, the largest angle lies opposite *XZ*. The answer is $\angle Y$.

EXAMPLE 17

What type of triangle can be formed with sides of 3, 4, and 10?

SOLUTION

Hopefully you had your thinking cap on! According to the Triangle Inequality theorem, this situation is <u>impossible</u> because $3 + 4 < 10$.

Here are additional definitions of points and line segments that are associated with a triangle.

The **median** of a triangle is a segment that connects the vertex to the midpoint of the opposite side. The intersection point of the three medians is called the **centroid** of the triangle. In Figure 5.21, point P is the centroid of $\triangle ABC$.

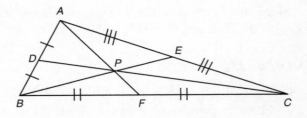

Figure 5.21

An important theorem concerning the centroid is that it divides each median into two parts that are in the ratio of 2:1. The longer of these two segments has a vertex as an endpoint. Referring to Figure 5.21, for example, $AP : PF = 2:1$.

The **altitude** of a triangle is a line segment from a vertex of the triangle perpendicular to the opposite side. The intersection point of the three altitudes is called the **orthocenter** of the triangle. The orthocenter is inside an acute triangle, outside an obtuse triangle, and the vertex of the right angle in a right triangle. In each of Figures 5.22, 5.23, and 5.24, point Q is the orthocenter.

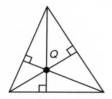

Figure 5.22

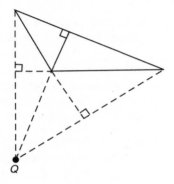

Figure 5.23

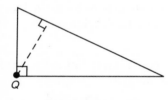

Figure 5.24

The **angle bisector** of a triangle is line segment that divides an angle in half and extends to the opposite side of the triangle. The intersection point of the three angle bisectors is called the **incenter** of the triangle. This point forms the center of a circle, known as an inscribed circle, that touches all the sides of the triangle.

In Figure 5.25, point *R* is the incenter of the triangle.

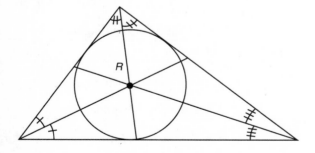

Figure 5.25

The intersection point of the three perpendicular bisectors is called the **circumcenter** of the triangle. This point forms the center of a circle that touches all the vertices of the triangle, thus inscribing the triangle inside the circle. In Figure 5.26, point S is the circumcenter of the triangle.

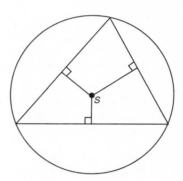

Figure 5.26

The orthocenter, centroid, and circumcenter form a line called an **Euler Line**, named after Leonhard Euler, a Swiss mathematician who discovered this property.

Quadrilateral Properties

A **diagonal** is a line segment that connects non-adjacent vertices. There are several different quadrilaterals. The names, definitions, and special properties of each are shown below.

Name	Definition	Example	Properties
Parallelogram	Quadrilateral with two pairs of parallel lines		• Opposite sides are congruent • Diagonals bisect each other
Rhombus	Parallelogram with all four sides congruent		• Diagonals bisect each other • Diagonals bisect the angles • Diagonals are perpendicular to each other
Rectangle	Parallelogram with all four angles congruent		• Diagonals bisect each other • Diagonals are congruent to each other
Square	Rectangle with all four sides congruent or a rhombus with four right angles		• Diagonals bisect each other • Diagonals are equal to each other • Diagonals bisect the angles at their endpoints • Diagonals are perpendicular to each other
Kite	Quadrilateral with exactly two pairs of adjacent congruent sides		• Diagonals are perpendicular to each other • The longer diagonal is the perpendicular bisector of the shorter diagonal • The longer diagonal bisects the angles at its endpoints
Trapezoid	Quadrilateral with exactly one pair of parallel sides		• Median is parallel to the bases and equal to one-half their sum
Isosceles Trapezoid	Trapezoid with a pair of congruent non-parallel sides		• Median is parallel to the bases and equal to one-half their sum • Base angles are equal • Diagonals are equal • Opposite angles are supplementary

A trapezoid can be isosceles. An **isosceles trapezoid** is a trapezoid whose non-parallel sides are equal. The **median** of the trapezoid is the line joining the midpoints of the non-parallel sides. The **altitude** of the trapezoid is the perpendicular segment connecting any point in the line containing one base of the trapezoid to the line containing the other base. Figure 5.27 shows a trapezoid with its median $\overline{MN}$ and an altitude $\overline{PQ}$.

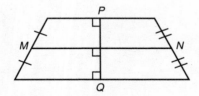

Figure 5.27

Area Formulas

Figure	Area
Parallelogram	$A = bh$
Rhombus	$A = \frac{1}{2}(d_1 \cdot d_2)$ where d_1 and d_2 are the lengths of the diagonal
Rectangle	$A = lw$
Square	$A = s^2$ or $\frac{1}{2}\,d^2$ where d is the length of the diagonal
Trapezoid	$A = \frac{1}{2}h(b_1 + b_2)$

EXAMPLE 18

Trapezoid *ABCD* is isosceles, as shown in Figure 5.28.

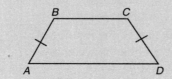

Figure 5.28

If $m\angle A = 74°$ and $m\angle D = (2x - 6)°$, what is the value of x?

SOLUTION

The trapezoid is isosceles so the base angles are equal. Therefore

$2x - 6 = 74$. Then $2x = 80$, so $x = 40$.

EXAMPLE 19

The area of a rectangle is 128 cm². The length of the rectangle is twice its width. What is the length of the rectangle?

SOLUTION

$A = lw$. Since the length is twice the width, we can represent the length by $2w$. Then $128 = w \cdot 2w = 2w^2$. So $w^2 = 64$, which means that $w = 8$ cm. Thus, $l = 16$ cm.

EXAMPLE 20

The area of a rhombus is 45 square units. If one diagonal is nine units more than the other diagonal, what is the length of the shorter diagonal?

SOLUTION

Let d and $d + 9$ represent the lengths of the two diagonals. Then $45 = (\frac{1}{2})(d)(d + 9)$. Then $90 = d^2 + 9d$,

which can be written as $0 = d^2 + 9d - 90$. The right side factors as $(d + 15)(d - 6)$. Note that $d + 15 = 0$ leads to a negative answer, so it is rejected. Thus, the answer is the solution to $d - 6 = 0$, which is $d = 6$ units.

(The longer diagonal is 15 units.)

Circles—Properties

A **circle** is a two-dimensional figure where all points are equidistant from the center. A circle is named using its center. The **diameter** of a circle connects two points on the circle through the center. The **radius** of a circle is one-half the diameter. The formula for the circumference of a circle (distance around the circle) is $C = \pi d$ or $2\pi r$ where d is the diameter and r is the radius. The area of a circle is $A = \pi r^2$. Two circles are congruent if and only if their radii have the same measure (i.e., are congruent).

Figure 5.29 shows circle P with radius $\overline{AP}$ and diameter $\overline{AB}$.

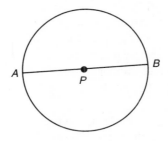

Figure 5.29

EXAMPLE 21

What is the area of a circle whose diameter is 8 cm.?

SOLUTION

The radius is $(\frac{1}{2})(8) = 4$cm. Thus, the area is $\pi(4)^2 = 16\pi$ cm²

EXAMPLE 22

> The circumference of a circle is 100π ft. Determine the radius.

SOLUTION

Use the formula $C = 2\pi r$. Then $100\pi = 2\pi r$, so $r = \dfrac{100\pi}{2\pi} = 50$ ft.

There are a number of terms that are associated with circles, and they are defined below.

Term	Definition	Example
Arc	Portion of a circle	
Minor arc	Arc that is less than half a circle and named by its endpoints	A B $\overset{\frown}{AB}$
Major arc	Arc that is greater than half a circle and named by its endpoints and one other point on the arc	D C E $\overset{\frown}{CDE}$
Secant	Line that intersects a circle in two points	ℓ_1
Chord	Line segment joining two points on a circle	E F
Central Angle	Angle whose vertex is at the center and whose sides are radii	P H G
Inscribed Angle	Angle whose vertex is on the circle	J K L

Tangent	Line that intersects a circle at exactly one point [lengths of tangent segments are equal from same external point].	ℓ_2
Sector	Part of the interior of a circle between two radii	P M N
Semicircle	Arc whose endpoints lie on the diameter	Q R

The measure of an arc that represents a full circle is $360°$. Angle measure depends on how the angles are formed in relation to the circle and their corresponding arcs.

Term	Formula	Example
Central angle	$a° = \text{arc}°$	P $a°$ $\text{arc}°$
Inscribed angle	$a° = \dfrac{1}{2}(\text{arc}°)$	$a°$ $\text{arc}°$
Angle outside circle formed by two secant segments	$a° = \dfrac{{arc_1}° - {arc_2}°}{2}$	$a°$ $arc_2°$ arc_1
Angle inside circle formed by two chords	$a° = \dfrac{{arc_1}° + {arc_2}°}{2}$	$arc_1°$ $a°$ $arc_2°$
Semicircle	$a° = 180°$	$180°$

The measures of central angles can be added to form a larger central angle or arc. There is a relationship between minor arcs, major arcs, and their central angles. Minor arc degree measure is the same as the degree measure of its central angle. Major arc degree measure is 360° degrees minus the measure of its central angle. Two central angles are congruent if and only if their minor arcs are congruent.

EXAMPLE 23

Look at Figure 5.30.

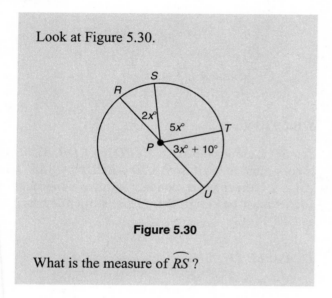

Figure 5.30

What is the measure of $\overarc{RS}$?

SOLUTION

$\overline{RU}$ is a diameter, so $\overarc{RU}$ is a semicircle whose measure is 180°. The measures of each minor arc measure can be added together. Each minor arc measure is equal to the measure of its corresponding central angle. Then $2x + 5x + 3x + 10 = 180$. This equation simplifies to $10x = 170$, so $x = 17$. Thus, $m\overarc{RS} = 2(17) = 34°$.

EXAMPLE 24

Look at Figure 5.31.

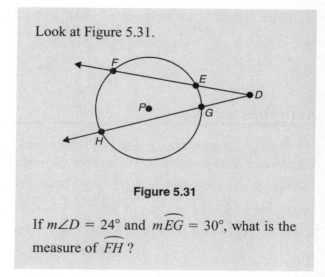

Figure 5.31

If $m\angle D = 24°$ and $m\overarc{EG} = 30°$, what is the measure of $\overarc{FH}$?

SOLUTION

Let x represent the measure of $\overarc{FH}$. Then since $\angle D$ is outside the circle formed by two secant segments, we have $24° = \dfrac{x - 30°}{2}$. Multiply by 2 to get $48° = x - 30°$. Thus, $x = 78°$.

EXAMPLE 25

Look at Figure 5.32.

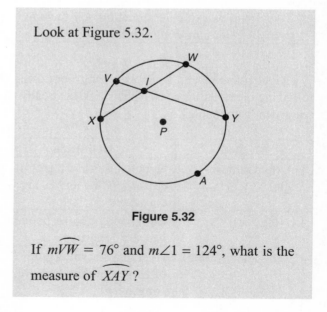

Figure 5.32

If $m\overarc{VW} = 76°$ and $m\angle 1 = 124°$, what is the measure of $\overarc{XAY}$?

SOLUTION

Let x represent the measure of $\overarc{XAY}$. Then $124°$ $= (\frac{1}{2})(76° + x)$, which simplifies to $248° = 76° + x$. Thus, $x = 172°$.

Congruence

Figures that have the same angle measure and side lengths are called **congruent**. The symbol use to denote two figures are congruent is $\cong$. $\Delta ABC \cong \Delta FGH$ means $\angle A \cong \angle F$, $\angle B \cong \angle G$, $\angle C \cong \angle H$, $\overline{AB} \cong \overline{FG}$, $\overline{BC} \cong \overline{GH}$, and $\overline{CA} \cong \overline{HF}$. Triangles can be proven to be congruent by:

Method	Definition
SSS	All pairs of corresponding sides are congruent
SAS	Two pairs of corresponding sides and the pair of included angles are congruent
ASA	Two pairs of corresponding angles and the pair of corresponding included sides are congruent
AAS	Two pairs of corresponding angles and a pair of corresponding non-included sides are congruent

Right triangles can be proven congruent using the following methods, since all right triangles already have congruent right angles.

Method	Definition
HA (hypotenuse-angle)	Hypotenuses and a pair of corresponding angles are congruent
LL (leg-leg)	Both pairs of corresponding legs are congruent
HL (hypotenuse-leg)	Hypotenuses and a pair of corresponding legs are congruent
LA (leg-angle)	A pair of corresponding legs and a pair of corresponding angles are congruent.

EXAMPLE 26

Look at Figure 5.33, in which $\overline{AB} \parallel \overline{CD}$ and $AB = CD$.

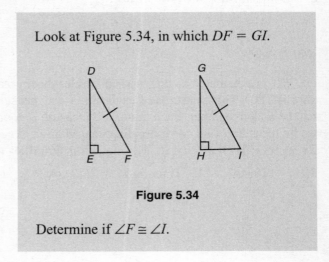

Figure 5.33

Determine if $\angle A \cong \angle C$.

SOLUTION

$\overline{BD}$ is a transversal, so $\angle ABD \cong \angle CDB$. Also, $\overline{BD}$ is congruent to itself, so $\Delta ABD \cong \Delta CDB$ by SAS. Then $\angle A \cong \angle C$ since corresponding parts of congruent triangles must be congruent. (This is often abbreviated as CPCTC.)

EXAMPLE 27

Look at Figure 5.34, in which $DF = GI$.

Figure 5.34

Determine if $\angle F \cong \angle I$.

SOLUTION

We are given two right triangles in which a pair of corresponding hypotenuses is congruent. This is <u>not</u> sufficient information to conclude that the triangles are congruent. Thus, we <u>cannot</u> conclude that $\angle F \cong \angle I$.

Similarity

Figures that have the same shape but differ by size are called **similar**. The symbol use to denote two figures are similar is ~. All the angles in similar figures have the same measure, which means that they are congruent (≅). The corresponding sides are proportional (have the same ratio). The proportion is called the **scale factor** between the two similar figures. Triangles can be determined to be similar via these methods:

Method	Definition
AA/AAA	At least two pairs of corresponding angles are congruent.
SAS	Two pairs of corresponding sides are proportional and the pair of included angles are congruent.
SSS	All pairs of corresponding sides are proportional.

In general, any two figures can be determined to be similar if angles are congruent and/or sides are proportional. The most common use of similarity is indirect measurement.

EXAMPLE 28

Look at Figure 5.35.

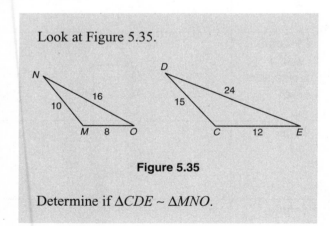

Figure 5.35

Determine if $\triangle CDE \sim \triangle MNO$.

SOLUTION

The lengths of all the sides are given, so use SSS to determine if the triangles are similar.

$$\frac{15}{10} = 1.5; \quad \frac{12}{8} = 1.5; \quad \frac{24}{16} = 1.5$$

The ratios (scale factors) are equal so $\triangle CDE \sim \triangle MNO$.

EXAMPLE 29

In Figure 5.36, $\overline{DE}$ represents a building, $\overline{AE}$ represents its shadow, $\overline{BC}$ represents a person, and $\overline{AC}$ represents the person's shadow.

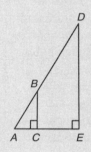

Figure 5.36

The shadow of a building is 100 feet, and the shadow of a 6- foot person is 3 feet. Determine the height of the building.

SOLUTION

$\triangle ABC \sim \triangle ADE$ by AA, since $\angle BAC \cong \angle DAE$ (angle common to both triangles) and $\angle BCA \cong \angle DEA$ (both right angles). The means that $\frac{BC}{AC} = \frac{DE}{AE}$. Let x represent the height of the building. Then $\frac{6}{3} = \frac{x}{100}$. Cross- multiply to get $3x = 600$. Thus, $x = 200$ feet

Three-Dimensional Shapes

Three-dimensional shapes with flat surfaces are called **polyhedrons**. Each flat surface of a polyhedron is a polygon, and is called a **face**. An **edge** is the intersection of two faces. A **vertex** is the intersection of two edges. The polyhedrons that are usually considered are prisms and pyramids. Other common three-dimensional (non-polyhedron) shapes are cones, cylinders, and spheres.

Shape	Definition	Example
Prism	Solid with two parallel, congruent polygon bases. Its lateral faces are parallelograms.	
Rectangular Prism	Prism in which the bases are rectangles and the lateral faces are rectangles.	
Cube	Rectangular prism will all six sides congruent square faces	
Cylinder	Solid with two congruent circular bases in parallel planes that are connected by a curved plane.	
Pyramid	Solid with a polygon base and all faces as triangles that meet at a point called the vertex.	
Cone	Solid with circular base and one vertex.	
Sphere	Solid with all points equidistant from the center.	

The cylinders and cones discussed in the above chart are known as right circular cylinders and right circular cones, respectively. A right circular cylinder is one in which the segment joining the centers is perpendicular to both bases. A right circular cone is one in which the segment from the vertex to the base is perpendicular to the base.

Nets

Each three-dimensional shape has a two-dimensional representation. The two-dimensional representation is called a **net**. Nets are often used in finding surface areas.

Shape	Net
Rectangular Prism	
Cube	
Cylinder	
Pyramid (with a rectangular base)	
Cone	
Sphere	

Volume and surface area are calculated for three-dimensional shapes. **Volume** is the amount of space a figure encloses. **Surface area** is the sum of the areas of the faces.

Shape	Volume Formula	Surface Area Formula
Rectangular Prism	$V = lwh$	$SA = 2lw + 2lh + 2wh$
Cube	$V = e^3$	$SA = 6e^2$
Cylinder	$V = \pi r^2 h$	$SA = 2\pi r^2 + 2\pi rh$
Pyramid	$V = \dfrac{1}{3} Bh$	$SA = B + \dfrac{1}{2} Ps$
Cone	$V = \dfrac{1}{3} \pi r^2 h$	$SA = \pi r^2 + \pi rs$
Sphere	$V = \dfrac{4}{3} \pi r^3$	$SA = 4\pi r^2$

Here is an alphabetical summary of the meaning of each variable in the chart above. B = area of base, e = edge, h = vertical height, l = length, P = perimeter of base, r = radius, s = slant height, and w = width.

EXAMPLE 30

What is the volume of a sphere whose radius is 6 m.?

SOLUTION

$$V = \frac{4}{3} \pi(6)^3 = \frac{4}{3} \pi(216) = 288 \ \pi\text{m}^3$$

EXAMPLE 31

A pyramid has a rectangular base with a length of 12 *m*. and a width of 10 *m*. If the vertical height is 15 *m*., what is the volume?

SOLUTION

Since the base is a rectangle, its area is $(12)(10)$ = $120 \ m^2$. Thus, the volume is $\frac{1}{3} (120)(15) = 600 \ m^3$

EXAMPLE 32

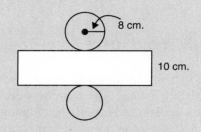

Consider the net shown in Figure 5.37.

8 cm.

10 cm.

Figure 5.37

What is the surface area of this three-dimensional solid?

SOLUTION

The net is a cylinder, so $SA = 2\pi r^2 + 2\pi rh$. The radius is 8 cm and the height is 10 cm. Thus, $SA = 2\pi(8)^2 + 2\pi(8)(10) = 2\pi(64) + 2\pi(80) = 128\pi + 160\pi = 288\pi \ \text{cm}^2$.

EXAMPLE 33

What is the surface area of a cube whose volume is 729 cubic feet?

SOLUTION

First, we must determine the size of each edge. So, $729 = e^3$. Then $e = \sqrt[3]{729} = 9$ feet. Thus, $SA = 6(9)^2 = (6)(81) = 486$ square feet.

EXAMPLE 34

The volume of a cone is 2400 cubic centimeters. If the radius is 12 cm., how large is the perpendicular height, to the nearest hundredth?

SOLUTION

$$2400 = (\frac{1}{3})(\pi)(12^2)(h) = (\frac{1}{3})(\pi)(144)(h) = 48\pi h.$$

Thus, $h = \dfrac{2400}{48\pi} = \dfrac{50}{\pi} \approx 15.92$ cm.

Conic Sections

Conic sections are the curves created when a cone is intercepted with a plane. The conic sections are parabolas, ellipses, circles, and hyperbolas. Figures 5.38, 5.39, 5.40, and 5.41 illustrate these different curves.

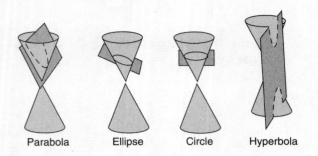

Parabola   Ellipse   Circle   Hyperbola

Figure 5.38   **Figure 5.39**   **Figure 5.40**   **Figure 5.41**

Parabolas

A **parabola** is a set of all points in the plane that are equidistant from a given point called the **focus** and a given line called the **directrix**. The **axis of symmetry** of the parabola is the line that goes through the focus and is perpendicular to the directrix. The **vertex** is the point on the parabola where the axis of symmetry and parabola intersect. The distance between the directrix and the focus is often labeled $2c$. These concepts are shown graphically in Figure 5.42.

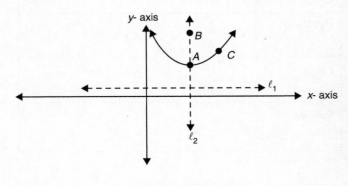

Figure 5.42

The parabola is represented by the curve of $y = f(x)$. Line l_1 is the directrix, line l_2 is the axis of symmetry, point A is the vertex, point B is the focus, and point C lies on the curve. By the definition of a parabola, the distance from C to l_1 must equal BC.

The following table notes the relationships among the standard form, directrix, focus, vertex, and the direction in which the parabola opens.

Standard Form	Directrix	Focus	Vertex	Parabola Opens
$x^2 = 4cy$	$y = -c$	$(0, c)$	$(0,0)$	Up
$y^2 = 4cx$	$x = -c$	$(c, 0)$	$(0,0)$	Right
$x^2 = -4cy$	$y = c$	$(0, -c)$	$(0,0)$	Down
$y^2 = -4cx$	$x = c$	$(-c, 0)$	$(0,0)$	Left
$(x - h)^2 = 4c(y - k)$	$y = -c + k$	$(h, c + k)$	(h, k)	Up
$(y - k)^2 = 4c(x - h)$	$x = -c + h$	$(c + h, k)$	(h, k)	Right
$(x - h)^2 = -4c(y - k)$	$y = c + k$	$(h, -c + k)$	(h, k)	Down
$(y - k)^2 = -4c(x - h)$	$x = c + h$	$(-c + h, k)$	(h, k)	Left

EXAMPLE 35

> What is the directrix, focus and vertex of the graph of $y^2 = -32x$?

SOLUTION

The curve has the form $y^2 = -4cx$, for which $c = 8$. Therefore, the directrix is $x = 8$, the focus is $(-8, 0)$, vertex is $(0, 0)$, and the parabola opens left. (Note that the equation is <u>not</u> a function.)

Here is a sketch of the graph for Example 31, along with a few selected points. (Figure 5.43)

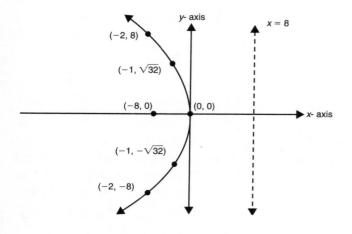

Figure 5.43

EXAMPLE 36

> What is the equation of the directrix for the parabola described by the equation $(x + 5)^2 = -24(y - 1)$?

SOLUTION

The vertex is located at $(-5,1)$, so $k = 1$. Since $-4c = -24$, $c = 6$. The equation of the directrix is given by $y = c + k$. By substitution, $c + k = 7$. Thus, the required equation is $y = 7$.

NOTE:

> An alternative way to solve Example 32, without memorizing the table of formulas, is as follows: We identify the vertex as $(-5,1)$ and we recognize that the parabola opens downward. This means that the directrix must be in the form $y = $ constant. Since $-4c = -24$, $c = 6$. Now, we recall that $2c$ represents the distance between the focus and the directrix. Since the vertex is midway between the focus and the directrix, c must represent the distance from the vertex to either the directrix or to the focus. Then the directrix must be a horizontal line that lies six units above the vertex. Thus, the equation of the directrix is $y = 7$. Figure 5.44 illustrates this example. [The focus is $(-5,-5)$.]

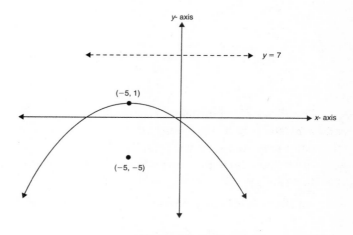

Figure 5.44

Ellipses

An ellipse is the set of all points in the plane where the sum of the distances from two fixed points is constant. This distance is represented by $2a$. Each of the fixed points is called a **focus** (Plural: **foci**). The distance from the center to a focus is c units. The **center** of the ellipse is the midpoint of the segment that connects each focus. There are two axes of symmetry resulting in two line segments whose endpoints are on the ellipse. The major axis is the longer of the segments formed by one of the lines of symmetry. The shorter segment formed by the other line of symmetry is called the minor axis and is perpendicular to major axis at the center of the ellipse. The distance from the center to the endpoint on the major axis is a units, whereas the distance from the center to an endpoint on the minor axis is b units. The lengths a, b, and c are related via a slight variation of the standard Pythagorean theorem. For the ellipse, $a^2 = b^2 + c^2$. This implies that $a > b$ and $a > c$. An ellipse with a major axis parallel to the x-axis and a center at $(0, 0)$ has the form $\frac{x^2}{a^2} + \frac{y^2}{b^2} = 1$. This ellipse is illustrated in Figure 5.45.

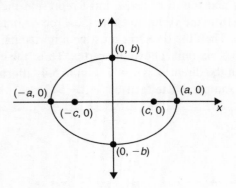

Figure 5.45

The foci have coordinates $(c, 0)$ and $(-c, 0)$. The major axis is $y = 0$. The coordinates of the vertices of the major axis are $(a, 0)$ and $(-a, 0)$. The minor axis is $x = 0$. The coordinates of the vertices of the minor axis are $(0, b)$ and $(0, -b)$.

An ellipse with a major axis parallel to the x-axis and a center at (h, k) has the form $\frac{(x-h)^2}{a^2} + \frac{(y-k)^2}{b^2} = 1$. This ellipse is illustrated in Figure 5.46.

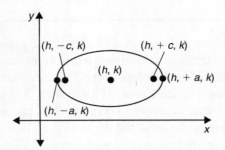

Figure 5.46

The foci have coordinates $(h + c, k)$ and $(h - c, k)$. The major axis is $y = k$. The major axis vertices coor-

dinates are $(h + a, k)$ and $(h - a, k)$. The minor axis is $x = h$. The minor axis vertices coordinates are $(h, k + b)$ and $(h, k - b)$.

An ellipse with a major axis parallel to the y-axis and a center at $(0, 0)$ has the form $\frac{x^2}{b^2} + \frac{y^2}{a^2} = 1$. (Note that the inequalities $a > b$ and $a > c$ still hold.) This ellipse is illustrated in Figure 5.47.

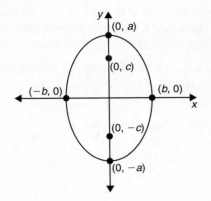

Figure 5.47

The foci have coordinates $(0, c)$ and $(0, -c)$. The major axis is $x = 0$. The major axis vertices coordinates are $(0, a)$ and $(0, -a)$. The minor axis is $y = 0$. The minor axis vertices coordinates are $(b, 0)$ and $(-b, 0)$.

An ellipse with a major axis parallel to the y-axis and a center at (h, k) has the form $\frac{(x-h)^2}{b^2} + \frac{(y-k)^2}{a^2} = 1$. This ellipse is illustrated in Figure 5.48.

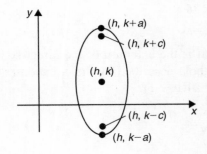

Figure 5.48

The foci have coordinates $(h, k + c)$ and $(h, k - c)$. The major axis is $x = h$. The major axis vertices coordinates are $(h, k + a)$ and $(h, k - a)$. The minor axis is $y = k$. The minor axis vertices coordinates are $(h + b, k)$ and $(h - b, k)$.

If you are already given the equation, the size of the denominators will reveal whether the ellipse's major axis is horizontal or vertical. If the larger denominator is contained in the fraction with x, then the major axis is horizontal. Similarly, if the larger denominator is contained in the fraction with y, then the major axis is vertical.

EXAMPLE 37

In the graph of the equation $\dfrac{x^2}{9} + \dfrac{y^2}{16} = 1$, what are the coordinates of the following?

a) center, b) foci, c) endpoints of the axes.

SOLUTION

The larger denominator is in the fraction with y, which means that the major axis is vertical. Now, $a^2 = 16$ so $a = \pm 4$ and $b^2 = 9$ so $b = \pm 3$. Substituting into the equation $a^2 = b^2 + c^2$, we have $16 = 9 + c^2$. Then $c^2 = 16 - 9 = 7$, which leads to $c = \pm\sqrt{7}$.

a) The numerators can be written as $(x - 0)^2$ and $(y - 0)^2$, respectively, so the center is $(0, 0)$.

b) The coordinates of the foci are $(0, \pm\sqrt{7})$.

c) The coordinates of the endpoints of the major axis are $(0, \pm 4)$, and the coordinates of the endpoints of the minor axis are $(\pm 3, 0)$.

EXAMPLE 38

Given that the equation of an ellipse is $\dfrac{(x-3)^2}{100} + \dfrac{(y+2)^2}{4} = 1$, what are the coordinates of the endpoints of the major axis?

SOLUTION

Since $100 > 4$, the major axis must be horizontal. The center is located at $(3, -2)$, $a = \sqrt{100} = 10$, and $b = \sqrt{4} = 2$. In order to find the endpoints of the major axis, we need to count 10 units to the left and 10 units to the right of $(3, -2)$. Thus, the endpoints of the major are located at $(-7, -2)$ and $(13, -2)$.

Circles — Equations

As a quick review, a circle is the set of all points at a given distance from a given point. This given point is called the center.

The standard form of a circle with a center $(0, 0)$ and a radius r is $x^2 + y^2 = r^2$. The standard form of a circle with a center (h, k) and a radius r is $(x - h)^2 + (y - k)^2 = r^2$, which is shown in Figure 5.49.

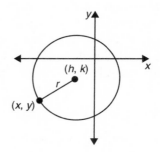

Figure 5.49

EXAMPLE 39

Write the equation of the circle with center $(3, -4)$ and a diameter of 16.

SOLUTION

The radius equals 8, since it is one half the diameter. By direct substitution into the general formula, our answer becomes $(x - 3)^2 + (y + 4)^2 = 64$.

EXAMPLE 40

Determine the equation of the circle with center $(-4, -3)$ and which has the origin as one of its points.

SOLUTION

By direct substitution, we can write $(x + 4)^2 + (y + 3)^2 = r^2$. Determine r^2 by using the distance formula between $(-4, -3)$ and $(0, 0)$. Then $r^2 = (0 - (-4))^2 + (0 - (-3))^2 = 16 + 9 = 25$. Thus, the answer is $(x + 4)^2 + (y + 3)^2 = 25$.

Hyperbolas

A hyperbola is the set of all points where the difference of the distances from two fixed points is a constant. The two fixed points are called **foci** of the hyperbola. The midpoint connecting the foci is the **center** of the hyperbola. Hyperbolas have two branches; the **vertex** of each branch is the point closest to the center. The distance from the center to a vertex is a units and center to a focus is c units. Every hyperbola has two axes of symmetry: **tranverse** axis and **conjugate** axis. The transverse axis has endpoints at the foci and length $2a$. The conjugate axis is a segment that is perpendicular to tranverse axis at the center and has length of $2b$. The lengths a, b, and c are related via the Pythagorean theorem as $a^2 + b^2 = c^2$.

A hyperbola with a transverse axis parallel to the x-axis and a center at the origin has the form $\dfrac{x^2}{a^2} - \dfrac{y^2}{b^2} = 1$. This hyperbola is illustrated in Figure 5.50.

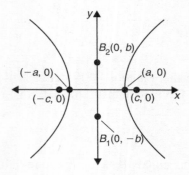

Figure 5.50

The foci have coordinates $(c, 0)$ and $(-c, 0)$. The vertices for each branch have coordinates $(a, 0)$ and $(-a, 0)$. Note that $c > a$ and $c > b$. (Remember that for the hyperbola, $b^2 = c^2 - a^2$.) The transverse axis is the line segment whose endpoints are $(a, 0)$ and $(-a, 0)$. The segment $\overline{B_1 B_2}$ is the conjugate axis.

We now introduce the concept of asymptotes, in connection with hyperbolas. If we solve the equation $\dfrac{x^2}{a^2} - \dfrac{y^2}{b^2} = 1$ for y, the result is $y = \pm \dfrac{b}{a}x\sqrt{1 - \dfrac{a^2}{x^2}}$.

(We have spared the reader the algebraic steps.) As x increases without bound, the value of $\sqrt{1 - \dfrac{a^2}{x^2}}$ approaches 1, so that y approaches the values of $\pm \dfrac{b}{a}x$. The equations $y = \pm \dfrac{b}{a}x$ are called the **asymptotes** for the hyperbola. Figure 5.51 illustrates the graph of $\dfrac{x^2}{a^2} - \dfrac{y^2}{b^2} = 1$, along with the asymptotes.

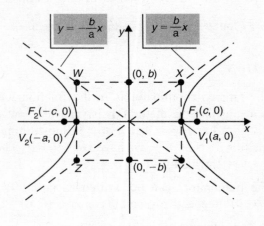

Figure 5.51

WXYZ is called the **asymptotic rectangle**. It has a horizontal length of $2a$ and a vertical length of $2b$. Note that although it appears that $a > b$ in this figure, this need not be true.

As an extension to the above discussion, a hyperbola with a transverse axis parallel to the x-axis and a center at (h, k) has the form $\dfrac{(x-h)^2}{a^2} - \dfrac{(y-k)^2}{b^2} = 1$. The foci have coordinates $(h + c, k)$ and $(h - c, k)$. The vertices have coordinates $(h + a, k)$ and $(h - a, k)$.

The equations of its asymptotes become $y - k = \pm \dfrac{b}{a}(x - h)$. The asymptotic rectangle changes its location, but its dimensions remain the same. Figure 5.52 shows the graph of the hyperbola $\dfrac{(x-h)^2}{a^2} - \dfrac{(y-k)^2}{b^2} = 1$.

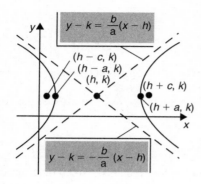

Figure 5.52

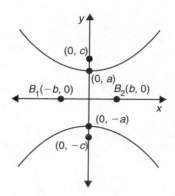

Figure 5.53

EXAMPLE 41

What is the equation of a hyperbola for which the center is located at $(0, 0)$, the horizontal transverse axis length is 18, and the conjugate axis length is 8?

SOLUTION

The general equation must be of the form $\dfrac{x^2}{a^2} - \dfrac{y^2}{b^2} = 1$, since the transverse axis is horizontal. Since $2a = 18$ and $2b = 8$, we know that $a = 9$ and $b = 4$. Thus, the equation is $\dfrac{x^2}{81} - \dfrac{y^2}{16} = 1$.

EXAMPLE 42

If the equation of a hyperbola is $\dfrac{(x-5)^2}{81} - \dfrac{(y+1)^2}{64} = 1$, what are the equations of the asymptotes?

SOLUTION

The center is located at $(5, -1)$, $a = 9$, and $b = 8$. Thus the equations of the asymptotes are $y + 1 = \pm \dfrac{8}{9}(x - 5)$.

A hyperbola with a tranverse axis parallel to the y-axis and a center at $(0, 0)$ has the form $\dfrac{y^2}{a^2} - \dfrac{x^2}{b^2} = 1$. This hyperbola is illustrated in Figure 5.53.

The foci have coordinates $(0, c)$ and $(0, -c)$. The vertices for each branch have coordinates $(0, a)$ and $(0, -a)$. The transverse axis is the line segment whose endpoints are $(0, a)$ and $(0, -a)$. The segment $\overline{B_1 B_2}$ is the conjugate axis.

As you would expect, this hyperbola also has a set of asymptotes. If we solve the equation $\dfrac{y^2}{a^2} - \dfrac{x^2}{b^2} = 1$ for y, we get $y = \pm \dfrac{a}{b}x\sqrt{1 + \dfrac{b^2}{x^2}}$. As x increases without bound, the value of $\sqrt{1 + \dfrac{b^2}{x^2}}$ approaches 1, so that y approaches the values of $\pm \dfrac{a}{b}x$. Thus, the equations of the asymptotes are $y = \pm \dfrac{a}{b}x$.

A hyperbola with a tranverse axis parallel to the y-axis and a center at (h, k) has the form $\dfrac{(y-k)^2}{a^2} - \dfrac{(x-h)^2}{b^2} = 1$. The foci have coordinates $(h, k + c)$ and $(h, k - c)$. The vertices have coordinates $(h, k + a)$ and $(h, k - a)$. The equations of the asymptotes become $y - k = \pm \dfrac{a}{b}(x - h)$. Figure 5.54 shows the graph of $\dfrac{(y-k)^2}{a^2} - \dfrac{(x-h)^2}{b^2} = 1$, along with its asymptotes.

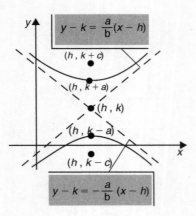

Figure 5.54

It is important to remember is that the size of a or b does not determine whether the graph of a hyperbola has a transverse axis parallel to the x-axis or to the y-axis. In fact, for a hyperbola such as $\frac{x^2}{9} - \frac{y^2}{9} = 1$, a and b each equal 3. Rather, the direction of the hyperbola is determined by which one of x^2 or y^2 is preceded by a positive sign.

EXAMPLE 43

A hyperbola has a vertical transverse axis. If the equations of its asymptotes are $y = \pm\frac{1}{3}x$, what is the equation of the hyperbola?

SOLUTION

The equations of the asymptotes can be written as $y - 0 = \pm\frac{1}{3}(x - 0)$, so we know that the center is located at $(0, 0)$. Furthermore, since the transverse axis is vertical, the general form of the equation of the asymptotes is $y = \pm\frac{a}{b}x$. Then $a = 1$ and $b = 3$. Finally, by substitution of these values into $\frac{y^2}{a^2} - \frac{x^2}{b^2} = 1$, we get the equation $\frac{y^2}{1} - \frac{x^2}{9} = 1$.

EXAMPLE 44

If the equation of a hyperbola is $\frac{(y+6)^2}{16} - \frac{x^2}{49} = 1$, what are the coordinates of the foci?

SOLUTION

The center is located at $(0, -6)$. The equation reveals that $a^2 = 16$ and $b^2 = 49$. Then $c^2 = 16 + 49 = 65$, so $c = \sqrt{65} \approx 8.06$. This number must be added to and subtracted from the y-coordinate of $(0, -6)$. Thus, the foci are located at $(0, 2.06)$ and $(0, -14.06)$.

General Conic Section Equation

The general form of the equation of a conic section is $Ax^2 + Bxy + Cy^2 + Dx + Ey + F = 0$ in which at least one of A, B, C is nonzero. In addition, each variable is an integer, and the greatest common factor of all six variables is 1.

EXAMPLE 45

What are the coordinates of the center of the circle described by the equation $x^2 + y^2 + 6x - 10y = -32$?

SOLUTION

Since the standard form for a circle is $(x - h)^2 + (y - k)^2 = r^2$, we'll proceed as follows: Using the "completing the square" method, $x^2 + y^2 + 6x - 10y + 32 = 0$ can be written as $(x^2 + 6x + 9) + (y^2 - 10y + 25) = -32 + 9 + 25$. This equation can be written in factored form as $(x + 3)^2 + (y - 5)^2 = 2$. Thus, the center is located at $(-3, 5)$.

EXAMPLE 46

What is the length of the major axis of the ellipse described by the equation $6x^2 - 24x + 4y^2 + 32y = -52$?

SOLUTION

Rewrite the equation as: $6x^2 + 4y^2 - 24x + 32y + 52 = 0$, which reduces to $3x^2 + 2y^2 - 12x + 16y + 26 = 0$.

The standard form for an ellipse is either $\dfrac{(x-h)^2}{a^2} + \dfrac{(y-k)^2}{b^2} = 1$ or $\dfrac{(x-h)^2}{b^2} + \dfrac{(y-k)^2}{a^2} = 1$. We will complete the square in order to express $3x^2 + 2y^2 - 12x + 16y + 26 = 0$ in standard form.

By partial factoring, we can write $3(x^2 - 4x) + 2(y^2 + 8y) = -26$. Next, use the process of completing the square. (Remember to add the appropriate terms to the right side of the equation.) Then $3(x^2 - 4x + 4) + 2(y^2 + 8y + 16) = -26 + 12 + 32$, which becomes $3(x - 2)^2 + 2(y + 4)^2 = 18$. Finally, dividing by 18, we get $\dfrac{(x-2)^2}{6} + \dfrac{(y+4)^2}{9} = 1$.

So, $b = \sqrt{6}$ and $a = 3$. The major axis of this ellipse is parallel to the y-axis and has a length of $(2)(3) = 6$.

EXAMPLE 47

What are the coordinates of the vertex of the parabola described by the equation $x^2 + 10x + 3y + 34 = 0$?

SOLUTION

Since the x term is squared, we want to write this equation in the form $(x - h)^2 = 4c(y - k)$ or $(x - h)^2 = -4c(y - k)$. First we will rewrite the equation as $x^2 + 10x = -3y - 34$. Then, by completing the square, the next step is $x^2 + 10x + 25 = -3y - 34 + 25$, which simplifies to $(x + 5)^2 = -3y - 9$. Finally, by using common term factoring on the right side, we rewrite the equation as $(x + 5)^2 = -3(y + 3)$. Thus, the vertex is located at $(-5, -3)$.

Any equation in the form $xy = k$ is a hyperbola for which the vertices and foci lie on the line whose equation is either $y = x$ or $y = -x$. Consider the equation $xy = -4$. Its graph is shown in Figure 5.55, along with a few key sets of coordinates. Note that the transverse axis is the line $y = -x$.

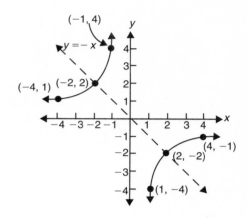

Figure 5.55

Function Transformations on the Coordinate Plane

Figures can be translated, reflected, rotated, and dilated on the coordinate plane. When graphing functions, the following statements apply, given that $a > 0$.

$y = f(x) + a$ translates the graph upwards a units.

$y = f(x) - a$ translates the graph downwards a units.

$y = f(x + a)$ translates the graph to the left a units.

$y = f(x - a)$ translates the graph to the right a units.

$y = -f(x)$ reflects the graph over the x-axis.

$y = f(-x)$ reflects the graph over the y-axis.

$y = af(x)$ dilates the graph (If $0 < a < 1$, the graph widens. If $a > 1$, the graph narrows.)

EXAMPLE 48

Given the graph of $f(x) = x^2$, which transformations take place to create the graph for $y = 2(x + 1)^2 + 3$?

SOLUTION

The graph has been narrowed, moved to the left 1 unit, and up 3 units

EXAMPLE 49

Given the graph of $f(x) = \sqrt{x}$, write a function whose graph is translated down 2 units, moved to the right 5 units, and reflected across the x-axis. Assume no dilation.

SOLUTION

After the translations down 2 units and to the right 5 units, the function becomes $y = \sqrt{x-5} - 2$. A reflection across the x-axis uses the form $-f(x)$. Thus, the answer becomes $y = -(\sqrt{x-5} - 2) = -\sqrt{x-5} + 2$.

EXAMPLE 50

Given the graph of $f(x) = 3x^3$, write a function whose graph is narrowed by a factor of 2, moved to the left 1 unit, and reflected across the y-axis.

SOLUTION

The dilation changes the function to $y = 6x^3$. After moving the graph to the left 1 unit, the function becomes $y = 6(x + 1)^3 = 6x^3 + 18x^2 + 18x + 6$. A reflection across the y-axis means that x is replaced by $-x$. The answer becomes $y = -6x^3 + 18x^2 - 18x + 6$.

Symmetry

Plane figures can have rotational and line symmetry. **Rotational symmetry (point symmetry)** occurs when a figure can be rotated n times around a point so that the resulting figure matches the original figure in size and shape. The figure then has rotational symmetry of order n. The formula is $\dfrac{360}{n}$, where $n > 1$. This determines the number of degrees in one rotation. A figure that has "360 degree rotational symmetry" is defined as having no rotational symmetry. (This would be the case involving $n = 1$.)

The letter "S" has rotational symmetry of order 2; an equilateral triangle has rotational symmetry of order 3, a propeller with four blades has rotational symmetry of order 4; a bronze star has rotational symmetry of order 5. These symmetries are shown below in Figures 5.56, 5.57, 5.58, and 5.59.

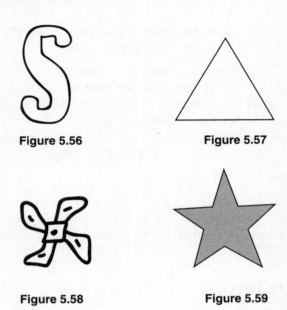

| Figure 5.56 | Figure 5.57 |

Figure 5.58   Figure 5.59

As a special case, a regular polygon with n sides has rotational symmetry of order n.

Thus, a square would have rotational symmetry of order 4. Similarly, a regular hexagon would have rotational symmetry of order 6.

Many figures do not have rotational symmetry. Figures 5.60, 5.61 and 5.62 illustrate three such examples.

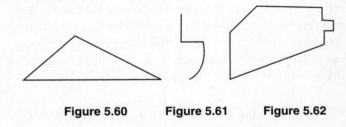

Figure 5.60   Figure 5.61   Figure 5.62

EXAMPLE 51

How many degrees are in one rotation of a regular 20-sided geometric figure?

SOLUTION

This figure has rotational symmetry and one rotation contains $\frac{360}{20} = 18°$.

Line symmetry occurs when a figure can be folded on top of itself so that the figure remains unchanged. A figure can have multiple lines of symmetry. In each of Figures 5.63, 5.64, and 5.65, the dashed line indicates a line of symmetry.

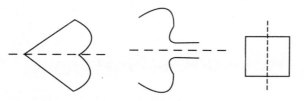

| **Figure 5.63** | **Figure 5.64** | **Figure 5.65** |

You may have realized that in Figure 5.65, we could have drawn other lines of symmetry.

Figures 5.66 and 5.67 illustrate this concept.

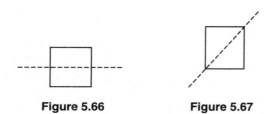

| **Figure 5.66** | **Figure 5.67** |

Note that a circle has an unlimited number of lines of symmetry.

An interesting observation is that for a regular polygon with *n* sides, there are exactly *n* lines of symmetry. Referring back to Figures 5.65, 5.66, and 5.67, we could have drawn a fourth line of symmetry. This line would contain the diagonal of the square that connects the upper left and lower right corners.

EXAMPLE 52

Draw the line of symmetry for the following figure.

SOLUTION

A horizontal line would fit the requirement.

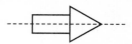

As with the discussion on rotational symmetry, there are many figures that do not have any line of symmetry. Examples would be any non-regular polygon, the letter "R", and the number "2."

Distance Formula

The distance formula is used to determine the distance between two points, (x_1, y_1) and (x_2, y_2), on the coordinate plane. Its formula is $d = \sqrt{(x_2 - x_1)^2 + (y_2 - y_1)^2}$

EXAMPLE 53

Find the distance between (3, 4) and (−4, 5).

SOLUTION

Let $(x_1, y_1) = (3, 4)$ and $(x_2, y_2) = (-4, 5)$. Then
$$d = \sqrt{(x_2 - x_1)^2 + (y_2 - y_1)^2} = \sqrt{(-4 - 3)^2 + (5 - 4)^2}$$
$$= \sqrt{(-7)^2 + (1)^2} = \sqrt{49 + 1} = \sqrt{50}$$, which can be also written as $5\sqrt{2}$ units.

EXAMPLE 54

A triangle has vertices at the coordinates (2, 4), (−4, 12) and (10, 10). Determine if the triangle is isosceles.

SOLUTION

We need to determine the length of the 3 sides.
Let $(x_1, y_1) = (2, 4)$ and $(x_2, y_2) = (-4, 12)$
$$d = \sqrt{(x_2 - x_1)^2 + (y_2 - y_1)^2} =$$
$$\sqrt{(-4 - 2)^2 + (12 - 4)^2} = \sqrt{(-6)^2 + (8)^2} = \sqrt{100}$$
$$= 10 \text{ units}$$

Let $(x_1, y_1) = (-4, 12)$ and $(x_2, y_2) = (10, 10)$

$d = \sqrt{(10-(-4)^2 + (10-12)^2} = \sqrt{(14)^2 + (-2)^2} =$

$= \sqrt{200} = 10\sqrt{2}$ units

Let $(x_1, y_1) = (2, 4)$ and $(x_2, y_2) = (10, 10)$

$d = \sqrt{(10-2)^2 + (10-4)^2} = \sqrt{(8)^2 + (6)^2} =$

$= \sqrt{100} = 10 = 10$ units.

Since two of the three sides are equal, the triangle is isosceles.

Midpoint Formula

The midpoint formula is used to determine the midpoint of a line segment. Given a line segment with endpoints (x_1, y_1) and (x_2, y_2), the midpoint has the coordinates $(\frac{x_1 + x_2}{2}, \frac{y_1 + y_2}{2})$.

EXAMPLE 55

> What is the midpoint of the line segment whose endpoints are $(-2, 1)$ and $(2, -5)$.

SOLUTION

Let $(x_1, y_1) = (-2, 1)$ and $(x_2, y_2) = (2, -5)$

$(\frac{x_1 + x_2}{2}, \frac{y_1 + y_2}{2}) = (\frac{-2+2}{2}, \frac{1+(-5)}{2})$

$= (\frac{0}{2}, \frac{-4}{2}) = (0, -2)$

EXAMPLE 56

> One endpoint of the diameter of a circle has coordinates $(-6, -5)$. If the center of the circle is located at $(-3, -2)$, what are the coordinates of the other endpoint?

SOLUTION

Let (x, y) represent the coordinates of the other endpoint. The center must represent the midpoint of

the diameter. Then $(\frac{-6+x}{2}, \frac{-5+y}{2}) = (-3, -2)$. This equality leads to two equations, the first of which is $\frac{-6+x}{2} = -3$. Multiply both sides by 2 to get $-6 + x = -6$, which means that $x = 0$. The second equation is $\frac{-5+y}{2} = -2$. Multiply both sides by 2 to get $-5 + y = -4$, which leads to $y = 1$. Thus, the second endpoint has coordinates $(0, 1)$.

Three-Dimensional Space

Three-dimensional figures are plotted using x-axis, y-axis, and z-axis. Three-dimensional coordinates are represented by (x, y, z). Since the three axes must be drawn on two-dimensional paper, the conventional way in which this is accomplished is shown in Figure 5.68.

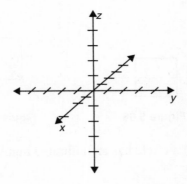

Figure 5.68

The y-axis is horizontal and the z-axis is vertical. You should view the x-axis as if it were protruding from behind the yz-coordinate plane to the front of this plane. So, the positive portion of the x-axis would be aiming directly at you.

Plotting points in isolation would be a virtually impossible mission. The solution devised by mathematicians is to represent each point that has nonzero coordinates by a corner of a rectangular prism. Figures 5.69, 5.70, and 5.71 illustrate the coordinates of points A, B, and C, respectively.

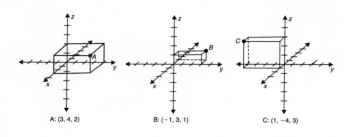

A: (3, 4, 2)

B: (−1, 3, 1)

C: (1, −4, 3)

Figure 5.69   **Figure 5.70**   **Figure 5.71**

If any one of the coordinates of a point is zero, a parallelogram is used to plot the point.

Should two of the coordinates be zero, place a dot on the axis (in the appropriate place) for which the coordinate is nonzero. Of course, the point (0, 0, 0) represents the intersection of all three axes. Figures 5.72, 5.73, 5.74, and 5.75 illustrate these concepts for points D, E, F, and G, respectively.

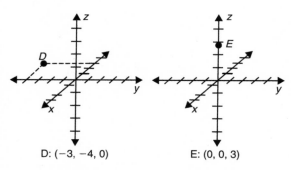

D: (−3, −4, 0)

E: (0, 0, 3)

Figure 5.72   **Figure 5.73**

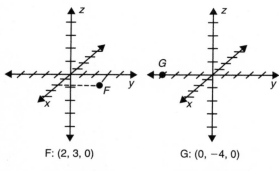

F: (2, 3, 0)

G: (0, −4, 0)

Figure 5.74   **Figure 5.75**

Distance Formula in Three-Dimensional Space

The distance formula for two points (x_1, y_1, z_1) and (x_2, y_2, z_2) is given by

$$d = \sqrt{(x_2 - x_1)^2 + (y_2 - y_1)^2 + (z_2 - z_1)^2}.$$

EXAMPLE 57

What is the distance between $(2, -3, 5)$ and $(6, 0, 4)$?

SOLUTION

$$d = \sqrt{(6-2)^2 + (0+3)^2 + (4-5)^2} = \sqrt{16+9+1} = \sqrt{26}.$$

Spheres

A sphere is a three-dimensional object where all points on the surface are the same distance from the center point. The equation of a sphere with center (r, s, t) is $(x - r)^2 + (y - s)^2 + (z - t)^2 = r^2$. For example, a sphere with a center $(2, 3, 4)$ and a diameter of 24 ($r = 12$) is represented by $(x - 2)^2 + (y - 3)^2 + (z - 4)^2 = 144$.

EXAMPLE 58

What are the coordinates of the center of the sphere whose equation is $x^2 + y^2 + z^2 - 2x + 8y + 10z + 1 = 0$? What is the radius?

SOLUTION

Rewrite the equation as $(x^2 - 2x) + (y^2 + 8y) + (z^2 + 10z) = -1$. Next, complete the square for each of the expressions in parentheses. Then $(x^2 - 2x + 1) + (y^2 + 8y + 16) + (z^2 + 10z + 25) = -1 + 1 + 16 + 25$. This equation simplifies to $(x - 1)^2 + (y + 4)^2 + (z + 5)^2 = 41$. Thus, the center is located at $(1, -4, -5)$ and the radius is $\sqrt{41}$.

Planes

The equation of a plane is usually expressed in the form $a(x - x_0) + b(y - y_0) + c(z - z_0) + d = 0$, where a, b, c, and d are constants. In some cases the equation may appear in an equivalent form as $ax + by + cz = d$. The point (x_0, y_0, z_0) lies in this plane. The stipulation for a, b, c, and d is that they are not all zero. Note that any three noncollinear points determine a plane.

EXAMPLE 59

Given that the equation $3(x - x_0) + 2(y - y_0) - (z - z_0) + d = 0$ contains the points $(0, 4, 0)$ and $(1, 2, 3)$, what is the value of d?

SOLUTION

We'll use the point $(0, 4, 0)$ to represent (x_0, y_0, z_0). Now substitute the values of $(1, 2, 3)$ for x, y, and z. Then $3(1 - 0) + 2(2 - 4) - (3 - 0) + d = 0$. So $3 - 4 - 3 + d = 0$. Thus, $d = 4$.

Chapter 5 Quiz

1. The diagram below shows two concentric circles.

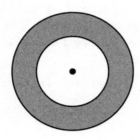

If the radius of the smaller two concentric circles is 6 cm while the radius of the larger circle is 10 cm., what is the area of the shaded region?

(A) 64π cm^2 (C) 4π cm^2

(B) 8π cm^2 (D) 136π cm^2

2. Find the center of the ellipse given by the equation $x^2 + 2x + 3y + 2y^2 = 1$.

(A) $(\frac{3}{4}, -1)$ (C) $(0, 0)$

(B) $(-1, -\frac{3}{4})$ (D) $(1, \frac{3}{4})$

3. The cross-section of a cube cut in half by a plane perpendicular to one of its faces is which of the following?

(A) circle   (C) line

(B) trapezoid   (D) square

4. A triangle has vertices at $(-3, 4)$, $(-3, -4)$, and $(4, -4)$. Which one of the following statements is true about the triangle?

(A) The triangle is isosceles.

(B) Not enough information is given.

(C) The triangle is equilateral.

(D) The triangle is scalene.

5. A spherical water tower holds $10,650\pi$ m^3. What is the approximate diameter of the water tower?

(A) 20 m   (C) 40 m

(B) 104 m   (D) 52 m

6. Given that $\overline{AB} \parallel \overline{CD}$ and $\overline{ST}$ is a transversal which of the following statements is <u>not</u> true?

(A) All angles are right angles.

(B) Corresponding angles are congruent.

(C) Vertical angles are congruent.

(D) Adjacent angles are supplementary.

7. Which of the following has two lines of symmetry?

(A) RADAR   (C) 11

(B) BOB   (D) ▽

8. A contractor needs to determine the dimensions of a roof on a house. What is the most appropriate measure to use?

(A) meter   (C) millimeter

(B) kilometer   (D) gram

9. Write the equation of the graph that has been reflected across the x-axis and moved up 4 units, given $f(x) = x^2$.

(A) $f(x) = 4x^2$ (C) $f(x) = x^2 + 4$

(B) $f(x) = -x^2 + 4$ (D) $f(x) = -x^2 - 4$

10. A gardener wants to plant flowers on the diagonal of a rectangular garden. The garden is 30 feet wide and 40 feet long. What is the length of the diagonal?

(A) 1200 ft   (C) 100 ft

(B) 25 ft   (D) 50 ft

Chapter 5 Quiz Solutions

1. (A)

Subtract the area of the smaller circle from the larger circle using $A = \pi r^2$.

$$A = \pi(10)^2 - \pi(6)^2 = 100\pi - 36\pi = 64\pi$$

2. (B)

Write $x^2 + 2x + 3y + 2y^2 = 1$ in standard notation: $x^2 + 2x + 3y + 2y^2 - 1 = 0$. Find the center by completing the square as follows:

$x^2 + 2x + 3y + 2y^2 - 1 = 0$

$(x^2 + 2x + \_) + (2y^2 + 3y + \_) = 1$

$(x^2 + 2x + 1) + 2(y^2 + \frac{3}{2}y + \frac{9}{16}) = 1 + 1 + 2(\frac{9}{16})$

$(x + 1)^2 + 2(y + \frac{3}{4})^2 = \frac{25}{8}$.

The final step is to divide by $\frac{25}{8}$ to get

$$\frac{(x+1)^2}{25/8} + \frac{(y+\frac{3}{4})^2}{25/16} = 1.$$

Thus, the coordinates of the center are $(-1, -\frac{3}{4})$.

3. (D)

The cross-section is a square. A cube is a prism with all sides equal and all right angles.

4. (D)

The triangle is scalene by the distance formula. The vertices of the triangle are $(-3, 4)$, $(-3, -4)$, and $(4, -4)$. Use the distance formula to determine the length of the sides.

The distance from $(-3, 4)$ to $(-3, -4)$ is given by

$$d = \sqrt{(x_2 - x_1)^2 + (y_2 - y_1)^2}$$
$$= \sqrt{(-3-(-3))^2 + ((-4)-4)^2} = \sqrt{0^2 + (-8)^2}$$
$$= \sqrt{0+64} = \sqrt{64} = 8 \text{ units}$$

The distance from $(-3, 4)$ to $(4, -4)$ is given by

$$d = \sqrt{(x_2 - x_1)^2 + (y_2 - y_1)^2}$$
$$= \sqrt{(4-(-3))^2 + ((-4)-4)^2} = \sqrt{(7)^2 + (-8)^2}$$
$$= \sqrt{49+64} = \sqrt{103} \text{ units.}$$

The distance from $(-3, -4)$ to $(4, -4)$ is given by

$$d = \sqrt{(x_2 - x_1)^2 + (y_2 - y_1)^2}$$
$$= \sqrt{(4-(-3))^2 + ((-4)-(-4))^2} = \sqrt{(-7)^2 + 0^2}$$
$$= \sqrt{49} = 7 \text{ units}$$

The lengths of the three sides are 8 units, $\sqrt{103}$ units, and 7 units. So, the triangle is scalene.

(Note that this triangle has a right angle, but this answer choice is not given.)

5. (C)

Use the volume formula for a sphere: $V = \frac{4}{3}\pi r^3$.

By substitution, $10,650\pi = \frac{4}{3}\pi r^3$. Then $r^3 = \frac{3V}{4\pi}$

$$= \frac{3(10650\pi)}{4\pi} = 7,987.5. \text{ So, } r = \sqrt[3]{7987.5} \approx 20 \text{ m.}$$

Thus, the diameter is $(2)(20) = 40$ m.

6. (A)

Corresponding angles are always congruent for two parallel lines cut by a transversal. Vertical angles are congruent by definition. Adjacent angles are supplementary since when combined they form a straight angle. Finally, not all angles formed when two parallel lines are cut by a transversal are right angles.

7. (C)

The number 11 has both horizontal and vertical lines of symmetry, RADAR has neither horizontal nor vertical lines of symmetry. BOB has horizontal line symmetry only. The inverted isosceles triangle has vertical line symmetry only.

8. (A)

Meters would be most appropriate in measurement of the dimensions of the roof. Kilometers are used to measure long distances (equals 1000 meters). Millimeters are used to measure very small objects (equals $\dfrac{1}{1000}$ of a meter). Grams are used to measure weight, not length.

9. (B)

To reflect across the x-axis, use $y = -f(x)$. To move a function upwards use $y = f(x) + a$. So, the combined process is $y = -f(x) + a$. Thus, the answer is $y = -x^2 + 4$.

10. (D)

A property of a rectangle is that all angles are right angles, so use the Pythagorean theorem to find the length of the diagonal.

$$a^2 + b^2 = c^2$$
$$c^2 = (30)^2 + (40)^2$$
$$c = \sqrt{(30)^2 + (40)^2} = \sqrt{2500} = 50$$

The length of the diagonal is 50 feet.

Data Analysis and Probability

Statistics is a mathematical field that involves the collection, analysis, interpretation or explanation, and presentation of data. The entire group of subjects or items to be studied is called the **population**. A population is represented by N. The part of the population being studied is called the **sample**. A sample is represented by n. The closer a sample size is to the population, the more likely the sample represents the population. Surveys and observations are often used to collect population/sample data to be analyzed. Simulations are sometimes used to replicate data collection typically via computers.

Sampling

Sampling is the process of collecting information about a topic of interest. **Random sampling** is used to ensure sample participants represent the population. Random sampling means population participants have an equally likely chance of being in the sample. Different random sampling techniques are used, depending on the population to survey.

Technique	Method Used	Example
Convenience	Choose those most readily available.	Ask friends.
Stratified	Random selection based on groups	Survey all school districts in a state by randomly choosing several schools within each district.
Systematic	Use a specific rule or formula.	Choose every fifth person on a list to survey, after randomly selecting the first person.

Bias occurs when a sample does not represent the population. Biased samples are not reliable measures of the population.

EXAMPLE 1

For the following illustration, determine the sampling method used and note whether or not the sample could be biased:

Asking individuals who are walking along a particular street about increases in city property taxes.

SOLUTION

This is a convenience sample since participants are readily available. The sample can be biased since the sample does not represent all those that will be impacted by the property tax increase.

Measures of Central Tendency

Measures of central tendency calculate the expected or "middle" values of the data. These are known as the **mean**, **median**, and **mode**.

The **mean** (commonly referred to as average) is the typical data set value. A population mean is denoted as μ. A sample mean is denoted as $\bar{x}$. Whether dealing with a sample or population, the mean is the sum of the data entries divided by the total number of data entries. Mathematically, the mean of a sample is calculated by

$$\bar{x} = \frac{\sum_{i=1}^{n} x_i}{n} = \frac{1}{n}(x_1 + x_2 + \ldots + x_n),$$ where n is the number of data entries and x_i is each data entry. For a population, the formula for the mean would be $\mu = \sum_{i=1}^{N} \frac{x_i}{N}$ $= \frac{1}{N}(x_1 + x_2 + x_3 + \ldots + x_N)$. Note that the numerical values of $\bar{x}$ and μ are equivalent.

EXAMPLE 2

What is the mean for the sample consisting of 24, 18, 50, 22, and 18?

SOLUTION

The sum of the five numbers is 132, so $\bar{x} = \frac{132}{5} = 26.4$.

The **median** is the positional midpoint of the data set. The first step in finding the median is to order the data set, typically from least to greatest. If the data set has an odd number of entries, then the median is the middle value. If the data set has an even number of entries, then the median is the average of the two "middle" data points. If n represents the number of data, the position of the median is <u>always</u> given by $\frac{n+1}{2}$.

EXAMPLE 3

What is the median for the numbers 26, 22, 16, 11, 27, 26, 20, 20, and 15?

SOLUTION

The nine numbers, arranged in order, become 11, 15, 16, 20, 20, 22, 26, 26, and 27. The fifth number is in the middle position, so the median is 20.

EXAMPLE 4

What is the median for the numbers 44, 38, 19, 6, 31, and 37?

SOLUTION

Arranged in order, the six numbers are 6, 19, 31, 37, 38, and 44. The third and fourth numbers occupy the two middle positions. Thus, the median is $\frac{31+37}{2} = 34$.

The **mode** represents the number that occurs most often. If two or more numbers occur the most often, then each number is a mode. If all values occur the same number of times in a data set, then each number is a mode. **Bimodal** describes a data set with two modes. **Trimodal** describes a data set with three modes. In Example 2, 18 is the mode; in Example 3, 20 and 26 are modes; in Example 4, there is no mode because each number occurs only once.

EXAMPLE 5

Find the mean, median, and mode for the data set 2, 5, 3, 7, 8, 5, 5, 1, 6, 7.

SOLUTION

The mean is $\dfrac{(2+5+3+7+8+5+5+1+6+7)}{10}$ $= \dfrac{49}{10} = 4.9$. The ten numbers, arranged in order, are 1, 2, 3, 5, 5, 5, 6, 7, 7, 8. Then the median can be found by locating the two middle numbers, which are the fifth and sixth numbers. Since both these positions are held by the number 5, this means that 5 is the median. We notice that 5 occurs three times, which is more frequently than any other number. Thus, the mode is 5.

A variation of the word *mean* is a weighted mean. A **weighted mean** occurs when some data values contribute more to the average than other data values, due to their frequency. Mathematically, a weighted mean

$$\bar{x}_w = \frac{\sum\limits_{i=1}^{n} w_i x_i}{\sum\limits_{i=1}^{n} w_i} = \frac{w_1 x_1 + w_2 \cdot x_2 + \ldots + w_n x_n}{w_1 + w_2 + \ldots + w_n},$$ where n is

the number of data, x_i is the value of each different data value, and w_i is the associated frequency or "weight." In some cases, the weights are assigned "percents."

EXAMPLE 6

A college professor's syllabus states that exams are worth 70% of a student's final grade, while the final exam is worth 30%. Suppose that a student's exam scores are 95, 91, 85, and 91. If his final exam score is 80, what is the student's final grade?

SOLUTION

This is a weighted average problem. The average of the exams is $\dfrac{95+91+85+91}{4} = \dfrac{362}{4} = 90.5$. Then

the final grade is calculated as $\dfrac{(0.7)(90.5)+(0.3)(80)}{(0.3)+(0.7)}$ $= \dfrac{63.35+24}{1} = 87.35$. The student's final grade is 87.

Skewness

If the mean, median and mode are identical, then the data is known as **symmetrically distributed**. Figure 6.1 illustrates this type of distribution.

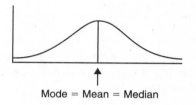

Mode = Mean = Median

Figure 6.1

A distribution is **negatively skewed** (also called "skewed to the left") if the mean is less than the median, which is less than the mode. An example would be the results of an easy exam, in which many students scored high and just a few students scored extremely low. Figure 6.2 illustrates this type of distribution.

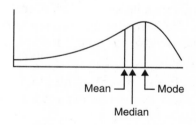

Mean — Mode
Median

Figure 6.2

A distribution is **positively skewed** (also called "skewed to the right") if the mean is greater than the median, which is greater than the mode. An example would be the incomes of the residents of a town in which many of them earn either average or just below average wages; however, a select few earn well above the average income. Figure 6.3 illustrates this type of distribution.

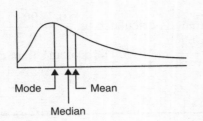

Figure 6.3

Measures of Variability

Measures of variability describe the dispersion (spread) of a data set. The most common measures are **range**, **percentile**, **interquartile range, variance**, and **standard deviation**.

The **range** is the difference between the highest and lowest data values.

The **percentile** of a specific data value x is the percent of all data that lie at or below x. For example, if the number 40 represents the 35th percentile of a data set, it would mean that 35% of data fall at or below the value of 40. Furthermore, we could state that 65% of the data lie above 40.

Percentiles are often used with normal-referenced tests. Frequently referenced percentiles are the 25th, 50th, and 75th percentiles, which are the first (lower) quartile, second quartile (median), and the third (upper) quartile, respectively. The 25th percentile is referred to as Q_1, the median is referred to as Q_2, and the 75th percentile is referred to as Q_3.

We have already shown the rules for identifying the median for a data set. We now explore the rules for finding the values of Q_1 and Q_3.

Let n represent an odd number of data arranged in ascending order. The position of Q_1 is given by $\frac{n+1}{4}$, and the position of Q_3 is given by $\frac{3n+3}{4} = (3)(\frac{n+1}{4})$.

Notice that the position of Q_3 is three times the position of Q_1. Thus, if a distribution has 37 data, the position of Q_1 would be $\frac{37+1}{4} = 9.5$. This implies that the value of Q_1 would be the mean of the 9th and 10th data. Likewise, the position of Q_3 would be $(3)(\frac{37+1}{4}) = 28.5$.

This implies that the value of Q_3 would be the mean of the 28th and 29th data. As expected, the median would be the $\frac{37+1}{2} = 19$th number.

Now let n represent an even number of data. The position of Q_1 is given by $\frac{n+2}{4}$, and the position of Q_3 is given by $\frac{3n+2}{4}$. Thus, if a distribution of has 72 numbers, the position of Q_1 would be $\frac{72+2}{4} = 18.5$. This implies that Q_1 would be the mean of the 18th and 19th data. Similarly, the position of Q_3 would be $\frac{(3)(72)+2}{4} = 54.5$. This implies that the value of Q_3 would be the mean of the 54th and 55th data.

The **interquartile range** (**IQR**) represents the middle 50% of the data. Mathematically, it is the difference between the upper and lower quartiles, that is $Q_3 - Q_1$. The **semi-interquartile range,** although not used very often, is equivalent to half the interquartile range. Thus, it is calculated as $\frac{Q_3 - Q_1}{2}$.

EXAMPLE 7

The electric bills for the month of January for six residents of Somewhere, USA, were $112.50, $76.80, $207.45, $96.30, $145.20, and $134.10. Find the values of the range, Q_1, Q_2, Q_3, and the interquartile range

SOLUTION

Let's first arrange the data in order, from lowest to highest. They will appear as $76.80, $96.30, $112.50, $134.10, $145.20, and $207.45. The range is $207.45 − $76.80 = $130.65.

There are six data, so the position of Q_1 is $\frac{6+2}{4} = 2$, the position of Q_2 is $\frac{6+1}{2} = 3.5$, and the position of Q_3 is $\frac{(3)(6)+2}{4} = 5$. Thus, $Q_1 = $96.30, $Q_2 = \frac{$112.50+$134.10}{2} = 123.30, and $Q_3 = $145.20.

Finally, the interquartile range (IQR) = \$145.20 − \$96.30 = \$48.90.

Variance is a representation of the dispersion (spread) of the data values from the middle (mean) of the distribution. Population and sample variances are calculated slightly differently. The population variance is $\sigma^2 = \dfrac{\sum\limits_{i=1}^{N}(x_i - \bar{x})^2}{N}$, where N is the number of data, x_i is a data value, and $\bar{x}$ is the mean. The sample variance is $s^2 = \dfrac{\sum\limits_{i=1}^{n}(x_i - \bar{x})^2}{n-1}$, where n is the number of data, x_i is a data value, and $\bar{x}$ is the mean.

The **standard deviation** is an approximation of the average distance between the data values and the middle (mean) of the distribution. Mathematically, the standard deviation is the square root of the variance. So, the population standard deviation is $\sigma = \sqrt{\sigma^2}$ and the sample standard deviation is $s = \sqrt{s^2}$. The standard deviation is a powerful statistic, especially when discussing normally distributed data sets.

If we are interested in approximating the variance of a population for which we do not know all the data, the sample variance would be applied. Similarly, the sample standard deviation would be used to approximate the population standard deviation.

EXAMPLE 8

A baseball pitcher threw five pitches to a batter at these speeds (in miles per hour): 80, 93, 88, 96 and 78. Find the standard deviation of the pitch speeds. Consider this data set as a population.

SOLUTION

$$\bar{x} = \frac{80+93+88+96+78}{5} = \frac{435}{5} = 87$$

$$\sigma^2 = \frac{\sum\limits_{i=1}^{n}(x_i - \bar{x})^2}{N} = \frac{\begin{array}{c}(80-87)^2 + (93-87)^2 + (88-87)^2 \\ +(96-87)^2 + (78-87)^2\end{array}}{5}$$

$$= \frac{49+36+1+81+81}{5} = \frac{248}{5} = 49.6. \text{ Then } \sigma = \sqrt{\sigma^2}$$

$$= \sqrt{49.6} \approx 7.04.$$

EXAMPLE 9

A universal typing test was given to 1000 applicants. For a sample of six applicants, the number of errors made was 12, 3, 8, 6, 16, and 15. What is the best estimate of the population variance of the number of errors made on this test?

SOLUTION

The sum of these six data is 60, so $\bar{x} = \dfrac{60}{6} = 10$. Since we want to approximate the population variance based on this sample, we will use the statistic s, which is calculated as the square root of s^2.

$$s^2 = \frac{\begin{array}{c}(12-10)^2 + (3-10)^2 + (8-10)^2 + (6-10)^2 \\ +(16-10)^2 + (15-10)^2\end{array}}{5}$$

$$= \frac{4+49+4+16+36+25}{5} = \frac{134}{5} = 26.8. \text{ There-}$$

fore, $s = \sqrt{26.8} \approx 5.18$.

Representing Data Graphically

Data can be represented many ways. The type of data given often limits the graphical representation possibilities. The graphical representations typically studied in secondary schools are frequency distributions, stem-and-leaf plots, histograms, bar graphs, circle graphs, box-and-whisker plots, line plots, line graphs, and scatters plots. Each representation is discussed below.

Frequency Distributions

Frequency distributions or tables are used to show the number of times a value or class (group) of values occurs in a data set. A **class** of values is a range of values for which the data are included. For example, 90 − 100 is a data class in which the lowest value is 90 and the highest value is 100.

Each of the mean, median, and standard deviation can be calculated from a frequency distribution.

$$\text{Mean} = \bar{x} = \frac{\sum_{i=1}^{n} f_i x_i}{\sum_{i=1}^{n} f_i} = \frac{f_1 x_1 + f_2 x_2 + \ldots + f_n x_n}{f_1 + f_2 + \ldots + f_n},$$

where f_i is the frequency of a data value and x_i is the midpoint of each interval. For non-grouped data, x_i is the actual data value in the frequency table.

The median is found by creating a cumulative distribution table. A cumulative distribution table is the sum of the values for a specific data plus all previous data value frequencies. The table is created by listing classes from greatest to least and totaling data from least to greatest. The class where the median occurs is called the **median class**. The median is calculated using the formula

$$\text{Median} = L + (I)\left(\frac{\frac{N}{2} - c}{f}\right), \text{ where } L \text{ is the lower}$$

boundary in the median class, I is the width of the class interval, N is the total number of data, c is the cumulative frequency of all data that below the median class, and f is the frequency of median class.

The frequency table standard deviation formula also involves frequency counts. Remember that variance is the square of the standard deviation. The standard deviation is found using the formula

$$\sigma = \sqrt{\frac{\sum_{i=1}^{n}(x_i - \bar{x})^2 f_i}{\sum_{i=1}^{n} f_i}} =$$

$$\sqrt{\frac{(x_1 - \bar{x})^2 f_1 + (x_2 - \bar{x})^2 f_2 + \ldots + (x_n - \bar{x})^2 f_n}{f_1 + f_2 + \ldots + f_n}},$$

where x_i is the midpoint of each interval and f_i is the frequency of its associated data value x_i.

EXAMPLE 10

Make a frequency table of the data and then find the mean of the data set 1, 2, 2, 1, 4, 3, 5, 3, 2, 2.

SOLUTION

We will use five "classes" containing each of 1, 2, 3, 4, and 5. For each of these data, the associated frequency will be listed.

Children	Frequency
1	2
2	4
3	2
4	1
5	1

$$\text{Mean} = \bar{x} = \frac{f_1 x_1 + f_2 x_2 + \ldots + f_n x_n}{f_1 + f_2 + \ldots + f_n}$$

$$= \frac{(2)(1) + (4)(2) + (2)(3) + (1)(4) + (1)(5)}{2 + 4 + 2 + 1 + 1} = \frac{25}{10} = 2.5$$

EXAMPLE 11

Twenty test scores on a mathematics tests are: 55, 95, 92, 48, 67, 80, 81, 84, 86, 99, 64, 77, 52, 80, 66, 91, 72, 83, 100, and 50. Make a frequency table of the data and find the median and standard deviation of the data set.

Assume that this is a population.

SOLUTION

Classes are needed due to the large number and spread of data. The classes need to be of the same size (width) and include all of the data values. Due to the wide range of values ($100 - 48 = 52$), we will choose a class sizes of 11 (5 rows of data) to create the frequency distribution table, as shown below.

Test Scores	Frequency
90 − 100	5
79 − 89	6
68 − 78	2
57 − 67	3
46 − 56	4

Now we create a cumulative distribution table, as shown below.

Test Scores	Frequency
90 − 100	20
79 − 89	15
68 − 78	9
57 − 67	7
46 − 56	4

There are a total of 20 data. There are 10 entries below the median. We observe that nine of the data lie below the class 79 − 89. Thus the class 79 − 89 contains the tenth data value and thus represents the median class. Note that with a frequency distribution table, the location of the median is simply $\frac{N}{2}$, where N is the total number of data. Thus, the median is the 10th number. To find the (common) interval width, labeled as I, we calculate the difference between class boundaries. Using the class with the highest data, $I = 100.5 - 89.5 = 11$.

$$\text{Median} = L + (I)\left(\frac{\frac{N}{2} - c}{f}\right), \text{ where } L = 78.5,$$

$I = 11$, $N = 20$, $\frac{N}{2} = 10$, $c = 9$, and $f = 6$. Thus, the median $= 78.5 + (11)(\frac{10-9}{6}) \approx 78.5 + 1.83 = 80.33$.

To find the standard deviation, we first calculate the mean. The value of each x_i is the mean of the lower and upper limit of its respective class. For example, $x_1 = \frac{90+100}{2} = 95$. Similarly, the values of x_2, x_3, x_4, and x_5 are 84, 73, 62, and 51 respectively.

$$\text{Mean} = \bar{x} = \frac{f_1 x_1 + f_2 x_2 + \ldots + f_n x_n}{f_1 + f_2 + \ldots + f_n}$$

$$= \frac{(5)(95) + (6)(84) + (2)(73) + (3)(62) + (4)(51)}{5 + 6 + 2 + 3 + 4}$$

$$= \frac{1515}{20} = 75.75$$

Standard deviation

$$= \sigma = \sqrt{\frac{(x_i - \bar{x})^2 f_1 + (x_i - \bar{x})^2 f_2 + \ldots + (x_i - \bar{x})^2 f_n}{f_1 + f_2 + \ldots + f_n}}$$

$$= \sqrt{\frac{\begin{array}{c}(95 - 75.75)^2 5 + (84 - 75.75)^2 6 + (73 - 75.75)^2 2 + \\ (62 - 75.75)^2 3 + (51 - 75.75)^2 4\end{array}}{5 + 6 + 2 + 3 + 4}}$$

$$= \sqrt{\frac{1852.81 + 408.38 + 15.13 + 567.19 + 2450.25}{20}}$$

$$\approx \sqrt{\frac{5294}{20}} = \sqrt{264.7} \approx 16.27.$$

Stem-and-Leaf Plots

Stem-and-leaf plots are typically used when all the data have a common number of digits. The stem consists of all digits, except the units digit. The leaf contains the units digit of each number that is associated with that stem. The process for creating a stem-and leaf-plot are as follows:

Step One: Order data points from least to greatest

Step Two: Determine the stems

Step Three: Place the leaf for each data point that corresponds to the respective stem

EXAMPLE 12

Create a stem-and-leaf diagram using these data.
61, 48, 61, 81, 63, 59, 70, 54, 77, 60, 47, 83

SOLUTION

Arrange the data in order: 47, 48, 54, 59, 60, 61, 61, 63, 70, 77, 81, and 83. The stems are the left (tens) digits, which are 4, 5, 6, 7, 8.

Create the stem-and-leaf table as shown below.

Stems	Leaves
4	7 8
5	4 9
6	0 1 1 3
7	0 7
8	1 3

Histograms

A histogram is used to display continuous grouped data. The vertical axis represents the frequency of the grouped data. The horizontal axis represents the grouped data. Each grouped data class is represented by a rectangle where the horizontal endpoints are the minimum and maximum class boundaries. The height of the rectangle represents the frequency in the data class. Each rectangle is connected to its adjacent rectangle(s).

EXAMPLE 13

The minutes a class of students typically spend completing homework in one of their classes are listed in the following frequency distribution.

Minutes	Frequency
1 − 15	4
16 − 30	8
31 − 45	4
46 − 60	2

Create a histogram of this data.

SOLUTION

Using the class boundaries for the four classes, we have $0.5 - 15.5$, $15.5 - 30.5$, $30.5 - 45.5$, and $45.5 - 60.5$. We'll use a vertical scale of 2 units.

Figure 6.4 illustrates the histogram.

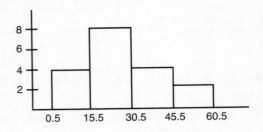

Figure 6.4

Bar Graphs

A bar graph is used to display categorical data. The vertical axis represents the frequency of each category, while the horizontal axis represents the category. Each category is represented by a rectangle, all of which have the same width.

The height represents the associated frequency. The rectangles do not touch and are equally spaced along the horizontal axis.

EXAMPLE 14

The favorite ice cream flavors of students in a mathematics class are listed in the following frequency distribution.

Ice Cream Flavor	Frequency
Chocolate	7
Strawberry	4
Vanilla	10
Other	3

Create a bar graph using the data set.

SOLUTION

The four rectangles will be placed on the horizontal axis. We'll use a scale of 2 units on the vertical axis. Figure 6.5 illustrates the bar graph.

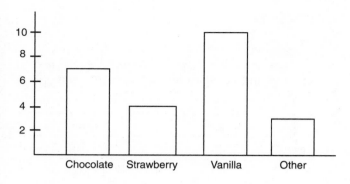

Figure 6.5

Circle Graphs

A circle graph is used to show the part each category represents of all the given categories. Circle graphs are created by determining the percent contribution of a particular category. Each category is illustrated by using a sector of the circle. The central angle of the sector equals the product of the category's percent contribution and 360°.

EXAMPLE 15

Draw a circle graph that represents the following data set.

Budget Item	Amount Spent
Education	$4,000,000
Government Operations	$5,000,000
Public Safety	$8,000,000
Debt	$3,000,000

SOLUTION

We first determine the percent each category represents of all the categories.

Total Expenditures = $4,000,000 + $5,000,000 + $8,000,000 + $3,000,000 = $20,000,000.

Education $= \dfrac{4,000,000}{20,000,000} = 20\%$. Then $(0.20)(360°) = 72°$.

Government Operations $= \dfrac{5,000,000}{20,000,000} = 25\%$. Then $(0.25)(360°) = 90°$.

Public Safety $= \dfrac{8,000,000}{20,000,000} = 40\%$. Then $(0.40)(360°) = 144°$.

Debt $= \dfrac{3,000,000}{20,000,000} = 15\%$. Then $(0.15)(360°) = 54°$.

Figure 6.6 shows the circle graph.

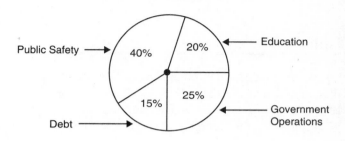

Figure 6.6

Box-and-Whisker Plots

A box-and-whisker plot is a method of displaying the minimum value, first quartile, second quartile, third quartile and maximum value. A rectangular box is drawn using the first and third quartiles as the endpoints of the rectangle. The second quartile (median) is a segment drawn inside the box. The segments that connect to the rectangle are called whiskers. Whisker endpoints are the minimum and maximum data set values. Note that the mean value is <u>not</u> depicted in a box-and-whisker plot.

EXAMPLE 16

Create a box-and-whiskers plot that represents this data: minimum value = 45, maximum value = 98, first quartile = 65, third quartile = 87, and median = 83.

SOLUTION

The choice of numbers on the horizontal scale is arbitrary, provided that they form an arithmetic sequence and are evenly spaced. We'll use a scale from 45 to 100, in intervals of 5. Figure 6.7 shows the complete box-and-whisker plot.

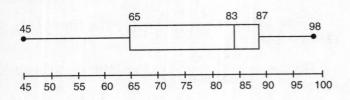

Figure 6.7

Line Plots

A line plot uses a number line to show frequency of data points. The number of marks above a point represents the number of times a data point occurs. This type of graph is usually limited to a small set of data.

EXAMPLE 17

Make a line plot that represents the following data. 1, 2, 2, 1, 4, 3, 5, 3, 2, and 2.

SOLUTION

For easy reading, we arrange the data in order: 1, 1, 2, 2, 2, 2, 3, 3, 4, and 5. We'll use x's to mark the frequencies. Figure 6.8 shows the line plot.

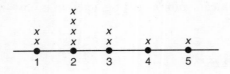

Figure 6.8

Line Graphs

A line graph is used to demonstrate the way in which a quantity varies over a period of time. The horizontal axis represents units of time (evenly spaced) and the vertical axis represents numerical values. Solid lines are used to connect sequential data.

EXAMPLE 18

Consider the following data that shows a person's annual salary for the years 2006 through 2009.

Year	Salary
2006	$85,000
2007	$88,000
2008	$94,000
2009	$92,000

Create a line graph showing this person's salaries over the given time span.

SOLUTION

First place the years along the horizontal axis in an evenly spaced manner. Our vertical axis will contain the numbers from $84,000 to $96,000, with a scale of $2000 for each marking. Note that there is a squiggle line at the base of the vertical axis. This is required since we are not showing values of $2000, $4000, $6000, etc. Finally, plot the data and connect the data using solid lines. Figure 6.9 shows the line graph.

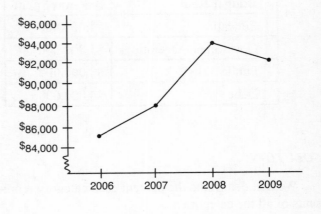

Figure 6.9

Scatter Plots

A scatter plot is used to show the relationship between two variables. Scatter plots are created by plotting points using (x, y) coordinates where x represents the data of the independent variable and y represents the data of the dependent variable.

In using a scatter plot, we may be interested in determining the best linear relationship between two given quantities. The corresponding mathematical relationship is called a **correlation**. The term **correlation coefficient,** denoted as r, is used to describe mathematically the strength of the relationship between the variables. The value of r lies between -1 and 1, inclusive. When two variables both increase or both decrease at the same time, the value of r will be positive. When one variable increases as the other variable decreases, the value of r will be negative. The closer to -1 or to 1 the value of r lies, the stronger the relationship between the variables. Perfect correlation exists when $r = 1$ or $r = -1$. If $r = 0$, then there is no relationship between the changes in the variables. As an example in which $r = 0$, let the number of people in a house represent one variable and the number of pets represent the second variable.

Figures 6.10, 6.11, and 6.12 illustrate the three categories of r values.

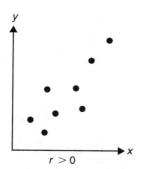

Figure 6.10

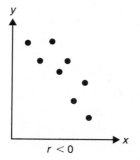

Figure 6.11

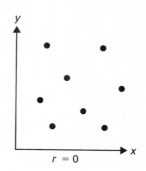

Figure 6.12

The actual value of r is given by the following formula:

$$r = \frac{n\left(\sum xy\right) - \left(\sum x\right)\left(\sum y\right)}{\sqrt{\left[n\left(\sum x^2\right) - \left(\sum x\right)^2\right]\left[n\left(\sum y^2\right) - \left(\sum y\right)^2\right]}},$$

where n represents the number of ordered pairs of values.

Incidentally, the quantity r^2 is called the **coefficient of determination**. This value has important applications in advanced statistical testing, but this topic is beyond the scope of this book.

The kind people who designed your TI-83 calculator did not want you to struggle with the formula for r, so they developed a program to do this intense computation. This procedure will be shown in the following example.

EXAMPLE 19

Ms. Jones was interested in trying to determine whether a correlation existed between students' final exam grade and the number of hours they claimed they studied for this exam. Her class consisted of eight students, for which the results are as follows: The independent variable x represents the number of hours of study, and the dependent variable y represents the exam grade. For ease of reading, Ms. Jones arranged the number of hours of study in ascending order

x	1	1.5	2	2.5	3.5	4	5	6.5
y	70	78	75	82	80	85	83	90

What is the value of r?

SOLUTION

Using the TI-83, press "STAT," then highlight "EDIT" and press "1." You will see three columns, labeled L_1, L_2, and L_3. Next, fill in the column L_1 with x values and the column L_2 with the corresponding y values. After all data has been entered, press "STAT," scroll to "CALC," then press "4" (Linear Regression). Your screen will show "LinReg(ax+b)." Press "Enter" and one of the entries on the screen will show that r is approximately 0.895. This number indicates a strong positive correlation, since this value is close to +1.

Regression Analysis

Regression is the process of determining a mathematical equation that models the relationship between two variables. The higher the correlation between the two variables the better the regression equation will model values in the data set. Regression lines are often used to predict future values. This process is called **extrapolation**. For example, perfect correlations mean the data set variables will fit the equation perfectly. Linear and non-linear relationships can be modeled via regression equations. All linear regression models can be written in the form $y = ax + b$, where a is the slope and b is the y-intercept. This equation can be determined by using the **median-median** or **line-of-best fit** techniques.

A median-median line is best when the data has values that are not close together.

The median of the x scores is found. Then the points on the scatter plot are divided into two categories of points - those with x values lower than the median (called the "left half") and those with x values greater than the median (called the "right half"). Let

$\bar{x}_L$ = the mean of x values that are lower than the median x value,

$\bar{x}_R$ = the mean of x values that are higher than the median x value,

$\bar{y}_L$ = the mean of y values for all points whose x value belongs to the group of x_L's,

$\bar{y}_R$ = the mean of y values for all points whose x value belongs to the group of x_R's.

Then the equation of the median-median line is $y = ax + b$, where $a = \dfrac{\bar{y}_R - \bar{y}_L}{\bar{x}_R - \bar{x}_L}$ and $b = \bar{y} - a\bar{x}$. Note that $\bar{x}$ and $\bar{y}$ represent the means of the x and y values, respectively of <u>all</u> the data.

The equation $y = ax + b$ also applies to the line-of-best fit, which is known as the least squares line. This line is determined by minimizing the sum of the squares of the vertical distances (y values) from each point to the line. The values of a and b are found as follows:

$$a = \frac{n(\sum xy) - (\sum x)(\sum y)}{n(\sum x^2) - (\sum x)^2} \text{ and } b = \frac{\sum y - a(\sum x)}{n}.$$

Fortunately, your TI-83 calculator provides both the median-median line and the least squares line. Return to Example 6.19. After you pressed "STAT" and scrolled to "CALC," you pressed "4", then "Enter." In addition to revealing the value of r (and of r^2), the screen will show that for the least squares line, $a \approx 2.95$ and $b \approx 70.8$.

Thus, the equation for the least squares line is $y = 2.95x + 70.79$.

Figure 6.13 shows both the scatter plot and the least squares line for Example 6.19.

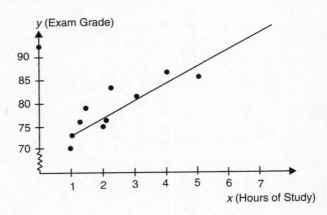

Figure 6.13

To determine the equation of the median-median line for the data of Example 6.19, you would press "STAT," scroll to "CALC," press "3," then "Enter." The screen will show that $a \approx 2.86$ and $b \approx 71.29$. Thus, the associated equation is $y = 2.86x + 71.29$.

EXAMPLE 20

Find the median-median line and the least squares line for the following data. Also, determine the value for 200 roundtrip miles using each equation.

Roundtrip Distance Flown	Price Paid ($)
200	100
640	178
1000	310
150	88
420	150

SOLUTION

After pressing "STAT" and scrolling to "EDIT," remove all current entries for lists L_1 and L_2. Enter the distances flown in L_1 and the prices paid in L_2. The results are as follows: The equation of the median-median line is $y = 0.23x + 52.98$ and the equation of the least squares line is $y = 0.25x + 44.43$.

We already know that when $x = 200$, $y = 100$. Let's use these two equations to "predict" the y value for $x = 200$. For the median-median line equation, $y = (0.23)(200) + 52.98 = \$98.98$. For the least squares line, $y = (0.25)(200) + 44.43 = 94.43$. For this x value, the median-median line equation yields a closer approximation to the actual value of 100.

Had we chosen to "predict" the y value for $x = 1000$, the median-median line equation yields a value of 282.98. The least squares line equation produces a value of 294.43, which would be a better approximation to the actual value of 310.

Probability

Probability is the study of the likelihood for specific actions to occur. A **probability** experiment consists of a well-defined series of related actions that are called **outcomes**.

The component parts of an outcome are called **trials**. The set of all outcomes is called the **sample space** (normally denoted as S). A specific outcome or set of outcomes is called an event.

EXAMPLE 21

A probability experiment consists of tossing a penny twice. List the sample space, state the total number of outcomes, and the event of getting one head and one tail.

SOLUTION

We'll use H to represent heads and T to represent tails. Then there are four outcomes, as shown by the sample space $S = \{HH, HT, TH, TT\}$. The event (E) of getting one head and one tail becomes $E = \{HT, TH\}$.

EXAMPLE 22

Referring to the probability experiment of Example 21, how many outcomes are there for the event in which two tails are shown? How many trials are there for each outcome of S?

SOLUTION

Let F represent the desired event. Then $F = \{TT\}$, so F consists of one outcome. Each of the four outcomes in S consists of two trials.

Theoretical Probability

Theoretical probability is the study of experiments where events are equally likely to happen. The probability of an event E is defined as follows:

$P(E) =$ Number of outcomes in the event divided by the number of outcomes in the sample space.

The probability of any event A [$P(A)$] ranges from 0 to 1, inclusive. This statement can be written as $0 \leq P(A) \leq 1$. If $P(A) = 0$, then A has no chance of occurring. If $P(A) = 1$, then A must occur. The probability of an event A not occurring is called the **complement** of A, and is calculated as $P(\text{not } A) = 1 - P(A)$. The event "not A" can be written as $\overline{A}$.

number of observations in E divided by the total number of observations.

EXAMPLE 23

A probability experiment consists of rolling an ordinary die twice. What is the probability that the sum of the dice is not 7?

SOLUTION

Since the result of each die is any number from 1 to 6, there are $(6)(6) = 36$ outcomes in the sample space. Suppose the outcome $(1, 2)$ represents the result of getting a "1" on the first roll and a "2" on the second roll. Let B represent the event of getting a sum of 7. Then $B = \{(1, 6), (2, 5), (3, 4), (4, 3), (5, 2), (6, 1)\}$.

Since E contains six outcomes, $P(E) = \dfrac{6}{36} = \dfrac{1}{6}$. Thus, $P(\overline{E}) = 1 - \dfrac{1}{6} = \dfrac{5}{6}$.

EXAMPLE 24

A probability experiment consists of drawing one card from an ordinary deck of 52 cards. What is the probability of not drawing a red 4?

SOLUTION

The sample space consists of 52 outcomes, each one corresponding to a different card. Let C represent the event of drawing a red 4. There are two red 4's, namely the four of diamonds and the four of hearts. So $P(C) = \dfrac{2}{52} = \dfrac{1}{26}$. Thus, $P(\overline{C}) = 1 - \dfrac{1}{26} = \dfrac{25}{26}$.

Experimental Probability

Experimental probability is the study of experiments in which observations are recorded or generated by such devices as a computer or a random number table. The probability of an event E is defined as the

EXAMPLE 25

An ordinary die was rolled 1800 times and the results of each outcome is recorded as follows:

Outcome	Frequency
1	120
2	140
3	250
4	450
5	300
6	540

Based on this chart, what is the probability that in rolling this die, it will land on a 3 or a 4?

SOLUTION

The number of times in which this die has landed on 3 or 4 is $250 + 450 = 700$. Since this die was rolled 1800 times, the required probability is $\dfrac{700}{1800} = \dfrac{7}{18}$.

EXAMPLE 26

An ordinary (six-sided) die was rolled 100 times with these outcomes.

Outcome	Rolls
1	10
2	18
3	22
4	14
5	20
6	16

Determine the values of P(1) and P(not 5).

SOLUTION

$$P(1) = \frac{10}{100} = 0.1$$
$$P(\text{not } 5) = 1 - P(5) = 1 - \frac{20}{100} = \frac{80}{100} = 0.8.$$

Compound events

Compound events are those that consists of two or more "actions." An example would be tossing a coin once and drawing one card from a deck of cards.

Mutually exclusive or **disjoint events** are events that cannot happen simultaneously. An example would be rolling a die once and getting both a 2 and 6.

Inclusive events are those that can occur simultaneously. As an example, suppose the probability experiment consists of tossing a coin three times. Let X represent the event of getting exactly one tail and let Y represent the event of getting exactly two heads.

Independent events are two or more events for which the occurrence of one event has no effect on the probability that the other event (s) will occur. For example, A represents the event of getting an even number when rolling a die once. B represents the event of drawing a picture card when drawing one card from a deck.

Dependent events are two or more events for which the occurrence of one event affects the probability of the occurrence of the other event(s). For example, suppose the probability experiment consists of two cards from a deck, one at a time, with no replacement of the first card when drawing the second card. Event C is drawing a black card and event D is drawing a red 5.

Conditional probability is the probability of an event occurring based on the occurrence of a previous event. The symbol $P(A \mid B)$ means the probability that event A occurs, given that event B has already occurred. In the example given in the previous paragraph, $P(D \mid C)$ means the probability that a red 5 is drawn for the second card, given that a black card has been drawn for the first card. Below is a chart that summarizes the most common formulas that are used with compound events. Notice that the abbreviation for $P(A$ and $B)$ is $P(A \cap B)$. Also, the abbreviation for $P(A$ or $B)$ is $P(A \cup B)$.

Event	Probability Formulas
Independent Events	$P(A \text{ and } B) = P(A \cap B) = P(A) \times P(B)$
Conditional	$P(A \mid B) = \dfrac{P(A \cap B)}{P(B)}, P(B) \neq 0$
Dependent Events	$P(A \cap B) = P(A) \times P(B \mid A)$
Mutually exclusive	$P(A \text{ or } B) = P(A \cup B) = P(A) + P(B)$
Inclusive	$P(A \cup B) = P(A) + P(B) - P(A \cap B)$

Some compound events contain outcomes in which the phrase "with replacement" is used; others contain outcomes in which the phrase "without replacement" is used. Probability experiments that may involve either "with replacement" or "without replacement" include examples such as (a) drawing two or more cards from a deck, (b) selecting people from a group, and (c) selecting a particular color marble from a bag of marbles.

EXAMPLE 27

In drawing one card from a deck, what is the probability that it is a king, given that the card is a face card?

SOLUTION

Let A represent the event of getting a king and let B represent the event of getting a face card. Recall that the 12 face cards of a deck are the jack, queen, and king of each of the four suits. There are four kings in the deck, and by definition, each is a face card. Then

$$P(A \mid B) = \frac{P(A \cap B)}{P(B)} = \frac{4/52}{12/52} = \frac{4}{12} = \frac{1}{3}.$$

Alternative Solution: Since the given card is known to be a face card, we may restrict our sample space to simply the 12 face cards. Of these, there are four kings. Thus, the required probability is $\frac{4}{12} = \frac{1}{3}.$

EXAMPLE 28

In rolling an ordinary die twice, what is the probability of getting a 6, followed by a 2?

SOLUTION

Since these are independent events, we can use the formula $P(A \cap B) = P(A) \times P(B)$. The probability of getting any single number is $\frac{1}{6}$, Therefore, $P(A \cap B) = \frac{1}{6} \times \frac{1}{6} = \frac{1}{36}$.

EXAMPLE 29

What is the probability of rolling a 3 or any even number on a 20-sided die?

SOLUTION

These are mutually exclusive events, so we use the formula $P(A \cup B) = P(A) + P(B)$. Let event A represent the event of rolling a 3 and let B represent the event of rolling an even number. Then $P(A) = \frac{1}{20}$ and $P(B) = \frac{10}{20}$. Therefore, $P(A \cup B) = \frac{1}{20} + \frac{10}{20} = \frac{11}{20}$.

EXAMPLE 30

A box contains 8 red balls, 6 green balls, and 6 black balls. What is the probability that a red ball is drawn on the first draw and a black ball is drawn on the second draw, if the first ball is not replaced prior to the drawing of the second ball?

SOLUTION

Since the first ball is not replaced prior to drawing the second ball, these events are dependent. Let A represent the event of drawing a red ball and let B represent

the event of drawing a black ball. We'll use the formula $P(A \cap B) = P(A) \times P(B \mid A)$.

We know that $P(A) = \frac{8}{20} = \frac{2}{5}$. In order to determine the value of $P(B \mid A)$, we must recognize that at the time that one of the six black balls is drawn, there are 19 (not 20) balls remaining in the box. This means that $P(B \mid A) = \frac{6}{19}$. Thus, $P(A \cap B) = \frac{2}{5} \times \frac{6}{19} = \frac{12}{95}$.

EXAMPLE 31

A box contains 8 red balls, 10 green balls, and 7 black balls. What is the probability that a red ball is drawn on the first draw and a green ball is drawn on the second draw, if the first ball is replaced prior to the drawing of the second ball?

SOLUTION

Since the first ball is replaced before the second ball is drawn, these events are independent. Let A represent the event of drawing the red ball and let B represent the event of drawing the green ball. There is a total of 25 balls, so $P(A) = \frac{8}{25}$ and $P(B) = \frac{10}{25} = \frac{2}{5}$. Finally, $P(A \cap B) = \frac{8}{25} \times \frac{2}{5} = \frac{16}{125}$.

EXAMPLE 32

In drawing one card from a deck, what is the probability that the card is either a queen or a diamond?

SOLUTION

These are inclusive events, since a card may be both a queen and a diamond. Let A represent the event of drawing a queen and let B represent the event of drawing a diamond. Then $P(A \cup B) = P(A) + P(B) - P(A$ and $B) = \frac{4}{52} + \frac{13}{52} - \frac{1}{52} = \frac{16}{52} = \frac{4}{13}$.

EXAMPLE 33

Look at the following Venn diagram that involves 90 people in a room. (Figure 6.14)

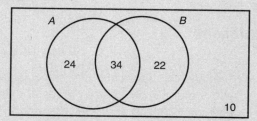

Figure 6.14

Circle A represents the category of males and circle B represents the category of people over the age of 50. One person will be randomly selected.

(a) What is the probability of selecting a female who is over the age of 50?

(b) What is the probability of selecting a person who is not over the age of 50?

(c) Given that the person selected is a female, what is the probability that she is over the age of 50?

(d) What is the probability of selecting a person who is male or who is over the age of 50?

SOLUTION

(a) Of the $34 + 22 = 56$ people over the age of 50, the number of females is 22. Therefore, the required probability is $\dfrac{22}{90} = \dfrac{11}{45}$.

(b) There are $24 + 10 = 34$ people who are not over the age of 50. Therefore, the required probability is $\dfrac{34}{90} = \dfrac{17}{45}$.

(c) From part (a), we know that there are 22 females over the age of 50. The number of females whose age is at most 50 must be 10, since this category is not found within any circle. So, there are a total of $22 + 10 = 32$ females, of which 22 are over the age of 50. Thus, the required probability is $\dfrac{22}{32} = \dfrac{11}{16}$.

(d) The quickest way to get this answer is to first add 24, 34, and 22 to get 80.

Thus, the required probability is $\dfrac{80}{90} = \dfrac{8}{9}$.

Alternate solution for part (d):

$$P(A \cup B) = P(A) + P(B) - P(A \cap B) = \frac{58}{90} + \frac{56}{90} - \frac{34}{90}$$

$$= \frac{80}{90} = \frac{8}{9}$$

Odds

Odds are calculated using the ratio of the probability of successful events to the probability of unsuccessful events. Odds in favor of an event A are written in the form $a{:}b$, (read as "a to b"), where $a = P(A)$ and $b = P(\overline{A})$. Odds against an event A are written in the form $b{:}a$. Also, the probability that event A will occur as $\dfrac{a}{a+b}$.

EXAMPLE 34

The probability of winning a contest is $\dfrac{1}{1250}$. What are the odds of winning?

SOLUTION

Since $a = 1$ and $a + b = 1250$, we determine that $b = 1249$. Therefore the odds are $1 : 1249$

EXAMPLE 35

What are the odds in favor of getting two 1's or two 2's in a single roll of a pair of six-sided dice?

SOLUTION

Whether rolling one die twice or two dice once, the number of outcomes is 36. There is only one way to get two 1's and one way to get two 2's. This means that there are $36 - 2 = 34$ ways (outcomes) that result in neither two 1's nor two 2's. Thus, the odds are 2 : 34, which reduces to 1 : 17.

Counting Techniques

The **Addition Counting Principle** states, "If one group contains m objects and a second group contains n objects and the groups have no objects in common, then there are a total of $m + n$ objects." The **Fundamental Counting Principle** states, "If there are m ways in which one event can occur and n ways in which a second event can occur, then there are $m \times n$ ways in which both events can occur."

EXAMPLE 36

A security firm creates a 5- digit code, for which each digit equally likely to occur. Find the total number of codes.

SOLUTION

This is a problem in which replacement of digits is allowed. There are a total of ten digits. (Remember to include zero.) Thus, the answer is $10 \times 10 \times 10 \times 10 \times 10 = 100{,}000$ codes.

EXAMPLE 37

Another security firm creates a 4- digit code, for which there is no repetition of digits. Assuming that each digit is equally likely to occur, find the total number of codes.

SOLUTION

For the first digit chosen, there are ten possibilities. But, for the second digit chosen, there are only nine possibilities. (The previous digit chosen is not eligible to be chosen again.) Similarly, there are eight possibilities for the third digit and seven possibilities for the fourth digit. Thus, the answer is $10 \times 9 \times 8 \times 7 = 5040$ codes.

Tree Diagrams

Tree diagrams are used to display a sequence of outcomes and to compute probabilities. They are especially effective when the number of outcomes for each event is small.

EXAMPLE 38

A sandwich shop is running a special where a customer has the choice of 3 breads (white, wheat, and raisin) and 3 meats (turkey, ham, and bologna).

(a) Draw a tree diagram to determine the number of possible outcomes.

(b) Use the Fundamental Counting Principle to determine the number of outcomes.

(c) Using the tree diagram, find the probability that a customer will choose a sandwich that consists of either turkey or ham on wheat bread.

SOLUTION

(a) Figure 6.15 illustrates the tree diagram that lists all possibilities. (T = Turkey, H = Ham, B = Bologna)

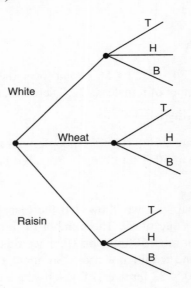

Figure 6.15

(b) Since there are three choices of breads and three choices of meats, the number of outcomes is $(3)(3) = 9$.

(c) Follow the center branch in the first group that is named "wheat." Then, there are two branches that lead to either turkey or ham. Of the nine items listed on the far right of the tree diagram, two of them result from wheat bread and either turkey or ham. Therefore, the required probability is $\frac{2}{9}$.

Tree diagrams also can be used to represent selections that contain probabilities.

EXAMPLE 39

The tree diagram in Figure 6.16 represents the probability that a basketball player can make two free throws. We will assume that his making or missing the first free throw <u>does</u> have an effect on the probability that he will make (or miss) the second free throw.

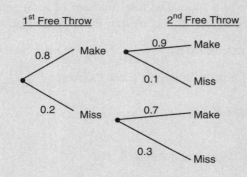

Figure 6.16

Based on this tree diagram, what is the probability that he misses his first free throw and makes his second free throw?

SOLUTION

The probability that he misses his first free throw is 0.2. The probability that he makes his second free throw, given that he has missed his first free throw, is 0.7.

By using the formula $P(A \cap B) = P(A) \times P(B \mid A)$ that applies to dependent events, the required probability is $(0.2)(0.7) = 0.14$.

Expected Value

The **expected value** of any quantity is the theoretical average value after performing the probability experiment an infinite number of times. Mathematically, it is calculated as follows. Let X represent the given quantity and let $E(X)$ represent its expected value. Then $E(X) = \sum_{1}^{n} (X_i) \times P(X_i)]$, where n represents the number of different values of X.

EXAMPLE 40

Based on previous experience, a public speaker has developed a probability distribution for the number of speeches that she makes in one week. Each week, she made at least one speech, but never more than five speeches.

x	1	2	3	4	5
$P(X)$	0.3	0.1	0.2	0.2	0.2

What is the value of $E(X)$?

SOLUTION

$E(X) = (1)(0.3) + (2)(0.1) + (3)(0.2) + (4)(0.2) + (5)(0.2) = 2.9$. This means that 2.9 is the expected (or average) number of speeches that she will make per week.

EXAMPLE 41

A game consists of spinning a 4-color spinner (red, blue, green, and yellow). The probability that the spinner will stop at any one color is 0.25. The game costs $5 to play. A player wins $8 if the spinner stops on red or blue. A player wins $1 if the spinner stops on green or yellow. What is the expected value of the game?

SOLUTION

Expected value of the game = Expected winnings − Cost of the game.

Let X represent the expected winnings. X can assume the values of 1 and 8. Then $E(X) = 8(\frac{1}{4}) + 8(\frac{1}{4}) + 1(\frac{1}{4}) + 1(\frac{1}{4}) = \$4.50$. Thus, the expected value of the game is $\$4.50 − \$5.00 = −\$0.50$. This means that the player should expect to lose an average of 50 cents per game when playing this game over time.

NOTE:

An easy way to check this answer is to assume that the player plays this game four times. Suppose that the spinner stops at each of the four colors in the following order: red, blue, green, yellow. Then the player would collect $\$8 + \$8 + \$1 + \$1 = \$18$.

However, the cost for playing the four games is $(4)(\$5) = \$20$. So, the player actually lost $2. If we divide the loss of $2 by the four games, we arrive at an average loss of $0.50 per game.

NOTE:

Games of chance are designed so that the customer can win money over a short period of time, but the probability is high that he or she will lose money over a long period of time.

Factorials

The symbol $n!$ is read as "n factorial", where $n! = n \times (n−1) \times (n−2) \times (\cdots) \times 1$. This definition only applies to nonnegative integers. Thus, $(\frac{1}{3})!$ and $(−2)!$ have no meaning.

By definition, $0! = 1$.

The TI-83 calculator has a factorial button, which is especially useful for large numbers.

In order to calculate 19!, do the following steps: press 19, press "MATH," scroll to "PRB, press 4, press "Enter." The result will be 1.216...E 17. This is interpreted as the number 1.216×10^{17}.

EXAMPLE 42

What is the value of 6!?

SOLUTION

$6! = 6 \times 5 \times 4 \times 3 \times 2 \times 1 = 720$

Permutations

A **permutation** is an arrangement of n distinct objects in a **specific order**. An arrangement of r distinct objects taken with regard to order from a set of n distinct objects, where $r \leq n$, is called a permutation of n objects taken r at a time. The total number of arrangements is denoted by nPr and is written in the form P(n, r) or $_nP_r$ and is calculated as $\frac{n!}{(n−r)!}$. Since we have used the capital P for probability, we'll use the form $_nP_r$.

EXAMPLE 43

What is the value of $_5P_3$?

SOLUTION

$_5P_3 = \frac{5!}{2!} = \frac{5 \times 4 \times 3 \times 2 \times 1}{2 \times 1} = 5 \times 4 \times 3 = 60$. (Be sure your denominator is $(n − r)!$, not $r!$)

EXAMPLE 44

A class consists of ten students. Each of four students will be selected sequentially to answer four different questions. In how many ways can this happen?

SOLUTION

We have $n = 10$ and $r = 4$. Thus, $\dfrac{10!}{6!} = 10 \times 9 \times 8 \times 7 = 5040$.

NOTE:

> Your TI-83 calculator does have a feature for permutations. In order to calculate $_{10}P_4$, do the following in sequence: press 10, press "MATH," scroll to "PRB," press 2, then press 4. At this point your calculator screen should display the following: 10 nPr 4. Now press "Enter" and the number 5040 should appear.

There also exist permutation problems in which there are identical (also called indistinguishable) elements. In such instances, an adjustment must be made in order to determine the number of different arrangements.

EXAMPLE 45

> In how many different ways can all the letters of the word "BROOM" be arranged to form a sequence of 5 letters?

SOLUTION

The five letters in the word "BROOM" are not all different. Thus, the answer will not be $5! = 120$. The reason is that the two Os cannot be distinguished from each other. If we labeled these Os as O_1 and O_2, the sequence BR $O_1 O_2$ M would appear the same as the sequence BR $O_2 O_1$M.

Likewise, the sequence B O_1R O_2M would appear the same as the sequence B O_2R O_1M. The way to handle this situation is to pretend that the word "BROOM" has 5 different letters and then divide by 2!. Thus, the answer is $\dfrac{5!}{2!} = \dfrac{120}{2} = 60$.

EXAMPLE 46

> In how many different ways can the word "ATTENTION" be arranged to form a sequence of nine letters?

SOLUTION

Although there are a total of nine letters, the answer is not simply 9!, which is 362,880. We have three Ts and two N's. We proceed by pretending that the original word has nine different letters, then divide by the product of 3! and 2!. Thus, the answer is $\dfrac{9!}{(3!)(2!)} = \dfrac{362,880}{(6)(2)} = 30,240$.

Combinations

A **combination** is an arrangement of n distinct objects where order does not matter. An arrangement of r distinct objects without regard to order taken from a set of n distinct objects, $r \leq n$, is called a combination of n objects taken r at a time. The total number of combinations is denoted by nCr and is written in the form $C(n, r)$ or $_nC_r$, and is calculated as $\dfrac{n!}{(r!)(n-r)!}$. We'll use the form $_nC_r$ in our examples.

EXAMPLE 47

> What is the value of $_5C_3$?

SOLUTION

$$_5C_3 = \frac{5!}{(3!)(2!)} = \frac{5 \times 4 \times 3 \times 2 \times 1}{(3 \times 2 \times 1)(2 \times 1)} = \frac{5 \times 4}{2} = 10.$$

EXAMPLE 48

> A class of 20 students is selecting a committee of four students to plan a class party. How many committees are possible?

SOLUTION

The word "committee" implies that the order in which the students are selected does not matter. Then

$$_{20}C_4 = \frac{20!}{(4!)(16!)} = \frac{20 \times 19 \times 18 \times \cdots \times 1}{(4 \times 3 \times 2 \times 1)(16 \times 15 \times 14 \times \cdots \times 1)}$$

$$= \frac{20 \times 19 \times 18 \times 17}{4 \times 3 \times 2 \times 1} = 4845.$$

NOTE:

Your TI-83 calculator does have a feature for combinations. Follow the same procedure as for permutations, with one exception. After scrolling to "PRB", select 3 instead of 2. After you press "Enter", your calculator screen will contain the value of "$_nC_r$" instead of the value of "$_nP_r$".

EXAMPLE 49

Mr. Fields coaches a high school baseball team. He wishes to select a team of 9 players. There are a total of 25 available players. Assuming that any of these players can play any position, how many different teams are possible?

SOLUTION

The order in which the 9 players are selected is not important. Thus, the answer is $_{25}C_9 = \dfrac{25!}{16! \times 9!} = 2,042,975$. Note that the answer can be found by simply using the TI-83 feature for calculating combinations.

The Binomial Probability Formula

The binomial probability formula can be applied to probability calculations with the following restrictions:

(a) Each trial results in one of two choices, which can be labeled as "success" or "failure."

(b) All trials are independent.

(c) The probability of success must be the same for each trial.

The probability for X successes in n trials is given by the formula $P(X) = (_nC_X)(p^x)(1-p)^{n-x}$, where p is the probability for success on any one trial.

EXAMPLE 50

A test consists of 10 true-false items. What is the probability that by randomly guessing, a person gets exactly four correct answers?

SOLUTION

We have $n = 10$ and $X = 4$. The probability of getting a correct answer on any single question is $\dfrac{1}{2}$, which becomes the value of p. Thus, the answer is

$$(_{10}C_4)(\tfrac{1}{2})^4(\tfrac{1}{2})^6 \approx 0.205 .$$

EXAMPLE 51

Three cards are drawn from a deck, one at a time, with replacement. What is the probability that none of the cards are clubs?

SOLUTION

We have $n = 3$ and $X = 0$. On any one draw, the probability of getting a club is $\dfrac{1}{4}$, which becomes the value of p. Thus, the answer is

$$(_3C_0)(\tfrac{1}{4})^0(\tfrac{3}{4})^3 = (\tfrac{3}{4})^3 \approx 0.4219 .$$

NOTE:

Your TI-83 calculator has a feature that will automatically display probabilities for the binomial probability formula (also known as the binomial distribution). We'll show this feature for Example 51, in which $n = 3$, $X = 0$, and $p = \dfrac{1}{4}$.

On your calculator press in sequence "2nd", "DISTR", and the number 0. Your screen will appear as "binompdf(". Fill in the values 3, $\dfrac{1}{4}$, 0, and a right parenthesis. Be sure you have a comma between each number. Press "Enter" and your screen should show .421875, which we have rounded off to 0.4219.

Normal Distributions

The **Law of Large Numbers Theorem** states that as the number of trials of a probability experiment increases, the observed number of "successful" outcomes will get increasingly closer to the theoretical number "successful" outcomes. Another way to state this concept is that the empirical probability will approach the theoretical probability. For example, if a fair coin is flipped, let's identify the number of tails as the number of "successful" outcomes. On any one flip, the theoretical probability of getting tails is 0.5. If this coin is flipped 10,000 times, the expected number of tails is $(0.5)(10,000) = 5000$. The Law of Large Numbers theorem states that we should observe that the actual number of tails is very close to 5000. If we decide to flip this coin 100,000 times, we should observe that the number of tails is extremely close to 50,000.

The most widely used distribution of data is the **normal distribution**. Some examples of this type of distribution are (a) heights of all adult women, (b) weights of all adult men, (c) highest daily temperatures in a given city over a period of time, and (d) the diameters of cylinders manufactured in a factory in which the machines produce them. When graphed, a group of data that is normally distributed will resemble a histogram that is symmetric.

The normal curve has these properties.

a) The mean, median, and mode are equal.

b) The curve is symmetric about the mean.

c) The y-coordinate of the mean is the maximum point on the curve.

d) Approximately 68.3% of the data are within one standard deviation of the mean ($\mu \pm \sigma$)

e) Approximately 95.5% of the data are within two standard deviations of the mean ($\mu \pm 2\sigma$)

f) Approximately 99.7% of the data are within three standard deviations of the mean ($\mu \pm 3\sigma$)

g) The curve never touches the x-axis and all y-values are positive.

h) The curve is continuous and assumes all values of x.

Figure 6.17 illustrates these properties.

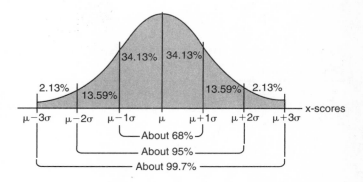

Figure 6.17

Standard Normal Distribution

A **standard normal distribution** is a special case of the normal distribution, in which the mean is zero, the standard deviation is 1, and the area under the curve above the x-axis is 1. Figure 6.18 illustrates the standard normal distribution.

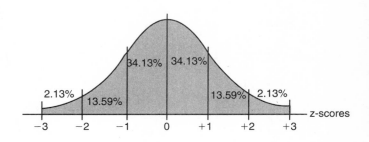

Figure 6.18

The values of x of a normal distribution are called **raw scores**. For a standard normal distribution, the independent values become **z scores**, which are also called **standard scores**. Z-scores are used to determine how many standard deviations from the mean a data value lies. Just as x scores can assume any value, z scores can also assume any value. But, we will discover that a negligible amount of the area of the curve lies greater than 3 or less than -3. For this reason, our z values will be confined to the closed interval $[-3, 3]$. The actual formula for converting x scores to z scores is $z = \dfrac{x - \mu}{\sigma}$, where x is the raw score, μ is the mean, and σ is the standard deviation. Incidentally, this formula applies to <u>any</u> distribution of data, not just those that belong to a normal distribution.

Applications of the Standard Normal Distribution

EXAMPLE 52

A mathematics test was given to both a class that met in the morning and a class that met in the afternoon. For the morning class, the mean was 84 and the standard deviation was 3.4. For the afternoon class, the mean was 82 and the standard deviation was 3.6. For which class would a raw score of 90 correspond to a higher z-score?

SOLUTION

We calculate the z-scores separately.

Morning class: $z = \dfrac{x - \mu}{\sigma} = \dfrac{90 - 84}{3.4} = \dfrac{6}{3.4} \approx 1.76.$

Afternoon class: $z = \dfrac{x - \mu}{\sigma} = \dfrac{90 - 82}{3.6} \approx 2.22.$

Thus, the grade of 90 corresponded to a higher z score in the afternoon class.

NOTE:

A negative z score corresponds to a raw (x) score that lies below the mean. In Example 52, if a person received a raw score of 80 in the morning class, the corresponding z score would be $\dfrac{80 - 84}{3.4} \approx -1.18$. Also, note that a z-score of zero corresponds to a raw score that equals the mean.

Statistics textbooks list a table of values for a standard normal curve, such as the one shown below in Figure 6.19.

z	.00	.01	.02	.03	.04	.05	.06	.07	.08	.09
0.0	.0000	.0040	.0080	.0120	.0160	.0199	.0239	.0278	.0319	.0359
0.1	.0398	.0438	.0478	0.517	.0557	.0596	.0636	.0675	.0714	.0753
0.2	.0793	.0832	.0871	.0910	.0948	.0987	.1026	.1064	.1103	.1141
0.3	.1179	.1217	.1255	.1293	.1331	.1368	.1406	.1443	.1480	.1517
0.4	.1554	.1591	.1628	.1664	.1700	.1736	.1772	.1808	.1844	.1879
0.5	.1915	.1950	.1985	.2019	.2054	.0288	.2123	.2157	2190	.2224
0.6	.2257	.2291	.2324	.2357	.2389	.2422	.2454	.2486	.2517	.2549
0.7	.2580	.2611	.2642	.2673	.2704	.2734	.2764	.2794	.2823	.2852
0.8	.2881	.2910	.2939	.2967	.2995	.3023	.3051	.3078	.3106	.3133
0.9	.3159	.3186	.3212	.3238	.3264	.3289	.3315	.3340	.3365	.3389
1.0	.3413	.3438	.3461	.3485	.3508	.3531	.3554	.3577	.3599	.3621
1.1	.3643	.3665	.3686	.3708	.3729	.3749	.3770	.3790	.3810	.3830
1.2	.3849	.3869	.3888	.3907	.3925	.3944	.3962	.3980	.3997	.4015
1.3	.4032	.4049	.4066	.4082	.4099	.4115	.4131	.4147	.4162	.4177
1.4	.4192	.4207	.4222	.4236	.4251	.4265	.4279	.4292	.4306	.4319
1.5	.4332	.4345	.4357	.4370	.4382	.4394	.4406	.4418	.4429	.4441
1.6	.4452	.4463	.4474	.4484	.4495	.4505	.4515	.4525	.4535	.4545
1.7	.4554	.4564	.4573	.4582	.4591	.4599	.4608	.4616	.4625	.4633
1.8	4641	.4649	.4656	.4664	.4671	.4678	.4686	.4693	.4699	.4706
1.9	.4713	.4719	.4726	.4732	.4738	.4744	.4750	.4756	.4761	.4767
2.0	.4772	.4778	.4783	.4788	.4793	.4798	.4803	.4808	.4812	.4817
2.1	.4821	.4826	.4830	.4834	.4838	.4842	.4846	.4850	.4854	.4857
2.2	.4861	.4864	.4868	.4871	.4875	.4878	.4881	.4884	.4887	.4890
2.3	.4893	.4896	.4898	.4901	.4904	.4906	.4909	.4911	.4913	.4916
2.4	.4918	.4920	.4922	.4925	.4927	.4929	.4931	.4932	.4934	.4936
2.5	.4938	.4940	.4941	.4943	.4945	.4946	.4948	.4949	.4951	.4952
2.6	.4953	.4955	.4956	.4957	.4959	.4960	.4961	.4962	.4963	.4964
2.7	.4965	.4966	.4967	.4968	.4969	.4970	.4971	.4972	.4973	.4974
2.8	.4974	.4975	.4976	.4977	.4977	.4978	4979	.4979	.4980	.4981
2.9	.4981	.4982	.4982	.4983	.4984	.4984	.4985	.4985	.4986	.4986
3.0	.4987	.4987	.4987	.4988	.4988	.4989	.4989	.4989	.4990	.4990

Figure 6.19

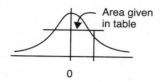

Figure 6.20

The table entries indicate the area of the curve between $z = 0$ and any other z score. We can also determine the area between two given z-scores, as well as the area that lies completely to the right (or to the left) of any z score. The z scores are found by using the left column for the first two digits of the number and using the top row for the hundredths place digit. Due to the symmetry of the standard normal distribution, the area between $z = 0$ a given positive z value is equivalent to the area between $z = 0$ and the opposite of this positive z value.

EXAMPLE 53

What is the area between z = 0 and z = 1?

SOLUTION

We find the number 1.00 by first locating the row with 1.0. Now go to the column indicated by .00. The corresponding table entry is 0.3413, which is the answer.

(We'll insert leading zeros, for decimal numbers less than 1.)

EXAMPLE 54

What is the area between $z = 0$ and $z = -2.25$?

SOLUTION

This question is equivalent to finding the area between $z = 0$ and $z = 2.25$.

Locate the row marked 2.2. Now find the column marked .05 and you should see the table entry of 0.4878, which becomes the answer.

Before we do additional examples, it is imperative that we point out that this table will <u>not</u> be distributed when you take your GACE math certification exam. The good news is that your TI-83 calculator can perform any necessary calculations involving the area between any two z-scores. If we want the area to the left of a specific z value, we can use -1×10^{99} as the lower bound. Likewise, if we want any area to the right of a specific z value, we can use 1×10^{99} as the upper bound. The calculator interprets -1×10^{99} as $-\infty$ and interprets 1×10^{99} as $+\infty$. For the next few examples, a diagram will be shown. Each of these examples refers to a standard normal distribution.

EXAMPLE 55

What is the area between z = −1 and z = 1?

SOLUTION

Figure 6.20 illustrates the desired area of the curve.

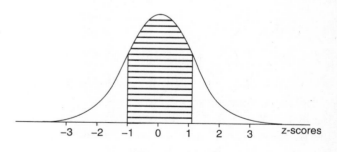

Figure 6.20

First, press in sequence: "2nd," "DISTR," and the number 2. At this point, your TI-83 reads as "normalcdf(". Now press in sequence the numbers −1, 1, 0, 1, followed by a right parenthesis. (Be sure that you have placed commas between these numbers.) Finally, press "Enter," so that your answer should be approximately 0.6827.

NOTE:

The sequence of numbers −1, 1, 0, and 1, refers to the lower bound of z, the upper bound of z, the mean of a standard normal distribution, and the standard deviation of a standard normal distribution, respectively.

EXAMPLE 56

What percent of the area lies to the right of $z = 0.8$?

SOLUTION

The diagram appears below as Figure 6.21.

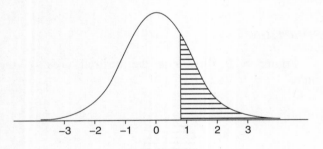

Figure 6.21

As in Example 55, first, press in sequence: "2ⁿᵈ," "DISTR," and the number 2. Now press in sequence the numbers 0.8, 1×10^{99}, 0, 1, followed by a right parenthesis. Press "Enter" and your result is approximately 0.2119, which is slightly more that 21%.

EXAMPLE 57

What is the area between $z = -1.5$ and $z = -0.5$?

SOLUTION

The diagram appears below as Figure 6.22.

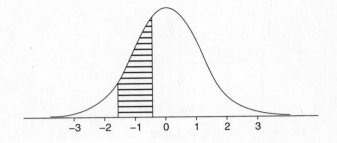

Figure 6.22

Follow the steps up to the point where your calculator reads as "normalcdft." Now press in sequence −1.5, −0.5, 0, 1, then a right parenthesis. Finally, press "Enter" to get the answer of approximately 0.2417.

Applications of the Normal Distribution

The steps we followed to solve Examples 55, 56, and 57 can be applied to any normal distributions, provided that we know the mean and standard deviation. In some cases, the word "probability" will be used in place of "area" or "percent." The procedure for finding a probability is identical to that of finding a percent or area. We assume a normal distribution for each of Examples 58, 59, and 60.

EXAMPLE 58

The mean age of the chief operating officers (COOs) in the United States is 54 years old, with a standard deviation of 5 years. What percent of these COOs are younger than 47 years old?

SOLUTION

The phrase "younger than 47" must be changed to "between -1×10^{99} and 47." After pressing "2ⁿᵈ," "DISTR," the numbers 2, -1×10^{99}, 47, 54, 5, and a right parenthesis, your calculator screen should show the following: "normalcdf(-1×10^{99}, 47, 54, 5)." Press "Enter" to reveal the approximate answer of 0.0808, which is 8.08%.

NOTE:

The mean and standard deviation appear as the third and fourth numbers respectively following the left parenthesis after "normalcdf."

EXAMPLE 59

The Time is Tight company makes watches. The mean lifetime of these watches is 38 months, with a standard deviation of 4 months. What percent of this company's watches will last longer than 35 months?

SOLUTION

In order to use our TI-83 calculator, the phrase "longer than 35" must be changed to "between 35 and 1×10^{99}." After pressing "2nd," "DISTR," the numbers 2, 35, 1×10^{99}, 38," and 4, a right parenthesis, and "Enter," your answer should be approximately 0.7734, which is 77.34%.

EXAMPLE 60

The amount of coffee dispensed in the paper cups of an automatic machine has a mean of 5.5 ounces and a standard deviation of 0.3 ounces. A paper cup is randomly selected. What is the probability that it will contain between 5.2 and 5.6 ounces of coffee?

SOLUTION

By this time, you probably know the sequence of steps by heart! When the calculator screen shows "normalcdf (5.2, 5.6, 5.5, 0.3)," press "Enter" to display approximately 0.4719, which expresses the required probability.

Central Limit Theorem

In some instances, we are interested in drawing conclusions concerning a sample taken from a population

of normally distributed data. Let's return to Example 59, which involves the Time is Tight company. Suppose this company made 100,000 watches in a year. If you were to consider all samples of 20 watches each, there would be a total of $_{100,000}C_{20} \approx 4.10 \times 10^{81}$ different samples. Each one of these 4.10×10^{81} samples would have a sample mean. This group of 4.10×10^{81} means is called the **distribution of sample means**. If you could then determine the mean of this distribution of sample means, you would find that it equals 38 months. This number matches exactly the mean of all watches made by this company. (Please do not try to perform this experiment, for it would take more years than a lifetime!).

In addition, this huge sample of 4.10×10^{81} numbers would also have a standard deviation. Statisticians have proven that this value would equal $\frac{4}{\sqrt{20}} \approx 0.89$ months. You recall that 4 months is the standard deviation of the population of all the watches this company makes.

Without any formal proof, let's generalize the information in the previous two paragraphs. Given a population that is normally distributed, with a mean of μ and a standard deviation of σ, consider the set of sample means of all samples of size n. This distribution of sample means is itself a normal distribution, whose mean equals the mean of the population. In addition, the standard deviation of this distribution is equal to the standard deviation of the population divided by the square root of the size of each sample.

Note that each of the samples <u>must</u> be the same size. The notation for the mean and standard deviation of this distribution of sample means is denoted as $\mu_{\overline{X}}$ and $\sigma_{\overline{X}}$, respectively. Thus, we can write $u_{\overline{X}} = \mu$ and $\sigma_{\overline{X}} = \frac{\sigma}{\sqrt{n}}$. Also, the standard deviation of the distribution of sample means is commonly called the **standard error of the mean**.

The Central Limit Theorem states that as the sample size n increases, the distribution of sample means taken from <u>any</u> population with mean μ and standard deviation σ will approach a normal distribution. Furthermore, this distribution will have a mean of μ and a standard deviation of $\frac{\sigma}{\sqrt{n}}$.

Note that the original population need not be normally distributed. Statisticians have agreed that to apply the Central Limit Theorem, the minimum size of n should be 30. Also, we generally assume that the population size is considerably larger than 30.

EXAMPLE 61

A random sample of 300 students was found to have a mean height of 64 inches and standard deviation of 2.3 inches. What is the standard error of the mean?

(Assume that the population from which the 300 students are drawn is much larger than 300.)

SOLUTION

$$\sigma_{\bar{x}} = \frac{\sigma}{\sqrt{n}} = \frac{2.3}{\sqrt{300}} \approx 0.13.$$

EXAMPLE 62

A popular magazine surveyed its readers to indicate the number of hours of sleep needed per night. The results showed a mean of six hours, with a standard deviation of 1.5 hours. A random group of 100 entries are selected. What is the probability that the sample mean will be less than 5.8 hours? (Assume that a very large number of readers responded.)

SOLUTION

Since the value of n is greater than 30, the distribution of sample means must be normally distributed. For this distribution of sample means, $\mu_{\bar{X}} = \mu = 6$ and $\sigma_{\bar{X}} = \frac{\sigma}{\sqrt{n}} = \frac{1.5}{\sqrt{100}} = 0.15$. We want to find the probability that a value of this distribution is less than 5.8. Following the procedure shown in Examples 55 to 60, your calculator should display the following: "normalcdf (-1×10^{99}, 5.8, 6, 0.15)." Press "Enter" to get the answer of approximately 0.0912.

EXAMPLE 63

The town of Whisper Pines has been keeping statistics on its highest temperature each day for more than 200 years. For that period of time, its mean high temperature has been 47.3 degrees with a standard deviation of 3.6 degrees. A random sample of 64 days is chosen. What is the probability that the sample mean will exceed 48 degrees?

SOLUTION

We are not told whether the population of temperatures is normally distributed. Similar to Example 62, our value of n is greater than 30. Thus, the distribution of sample means can be treated as a normal distribution. We first determine that $\mu = \mu_{\bar{X}} = 47.3$ and $\sigma_{\bar{X}} = \frac{\sigma}{\sqrt{n}} = \frac{3.6}{\sqrt{64}} = 0.45$. Thus, we find that normalcdf $(48, 1 \times 10^{99}, 47.3, 0.45) \approx 0.0599$.

Confidence Intervals

In Examples 58 through 63, we assumed knowledge of the population, and then determined the value of statistics related to samples. More often, we have better information about the sample data and wish to extend this information to draw conclusions about the population data.

For example, we can usually determine the value of a sample mean, $\bar{x}$. Based on this value, we would like to project a good estimate of the mean of the population, μ, from which this sample was extracted. For the following discussion, we will assume that at least one of the following two conditions holds:

(a) the sample size n is at least 30.

(b) the population standard deviation, σ, is known and the population is normally distributed.

If we do not know that value of σ but condition (a) is met, then we may substitute the sample standard deviation, s.

A **confidence interval** for the mean of a population is a two-sided open interval that corresponds to the percent of samples whose mean satisfies that inequality. This confidence interval is given by the expression $\bar{x} \pm (z_c)(\frac{\sigma}{\sqrt{n}})$, when σ is known. This expression changes to $\bar{x} \pm (z_c)(\frac{s}{\sqrt{n}})$, when σ is not known and the sample size is at least 30. The term z_c refers to a **critical z value** of the standard normal distribution. It will be easier to understand these terms, once we show some examples.

EXAMPLE 64

A survey of 60 homeowners in Maryland was conducted, during which time it was discovered that the average age of their homes was 25 years, with a sample standard deviation of 4 years. What is the 95% confidence interval for the age of all homes in Maryland?

SOLUTION

Our aim is to create an open interval for which the probability is 95% that this range of values includes the true mean of the population (μ). Since $n = 60$, we know that the distribution of all samples of size 60, from the population of Maryland homes, is normally distributed. Here are the known quantities thus far: $\bar{x} = 25$, $s = 4$, and $n = 60$. The critical z value, known as z_c, is computed as the z value for which $(\frac{100-95}{2})\% =$ 2.5% of all z values are larger than z_c, and 2.5% of all z values are smaller than $-z_c$. Essentially, we want include the middle 95% of a normal distribution. Using a table of standard normal values, to the nearest hundredth, $z_c = 1.96$. If we don't have this table, the TI-83 calculator does have this feature. Press "2nd", "DISTR," then press 3. The screen will display "invNorm(." At this point, you want to enter the decimal equivalent of the percent of the area under the normal curve that lies to the left of z_c. This decimal value is $1 - 0.025 = 0.975$. Now insert a right parenthesis and press "Enter." The screen will show a value which is approximately 1.96. This implies that 2.5% of the area lies to the right of $z_c = 1.96$ and 2.5% of the area lies to the left of $-z_c$,

which is -1.96. Figure 6.23 illustrates this 95% confidence interval.

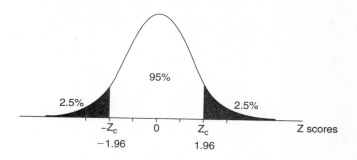

Figure 6.23

The required interval for the population mean becomes $25 \pm (1.96)\frac{4}{\sqrt{60}} \approx 25 \pm 1.01$. The more common way to write this interval is $23.99 < \mu < 26.01$.

NOTE:

For Example 64, the number 1.01 is also known as the **maximum error of estimate**. In general, the expression $(z_c)(\frac{s}{\sqrt{n}})$ or $(z_c)(\frac{\sigma}{\sqrt{n}})$ is the maximum error of estimate when determining a confidence interval for the population mean, given a particular sample mean.

EXAMPLE 65

The heights of a particular type of plant are normally distributed. The heights of 400 plants were measured with a mean of 26 inches and a standard deviation of 4.8 inches. To the nearest hundredth, what is the 90% confidence interval for the mean height of all these plants?

SOLUTION

In order to determine the critical z values, we first compute $(\frac{100-90}{2})\% = 5\%$. This means that 5% of the values lie above z_c and 5% of the values lie below $-z_c$. Since we want a z_c value for which 95% of the area lies to its left, our calculator should display "invNorm(0.95)," whose value is approximately 1.645. Figure 6.24 illustrates this 90% confidence interval.

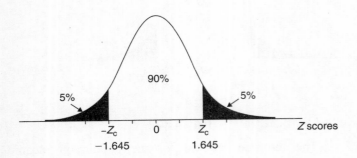

Figure 6.24

Using the values $\bar{x} = 26$, s = 4.8, and $n = 400$, the required interval for the population mean is $26 \pm (1.645)(\frac{4.8}{\sqrt{400}}) \approx 26 \pm 0.39$. The interval may also be written as $25.61 < \mu < 26.39$.

Your TI-83 calculator is programmed to provide confidence intervals for the population mean, even without the calculation of the critical z values. All that is needed is the sample mean, standard deviation, number of data in the sample, and the desired percent confidence interval. We'll show this process for Example 65.

Press "STAT," scroll to "TESTS," and press 7. At this point, your screen will display "ZInterval" at the top. On the second line, highlight "Stats." Now follow these steps:

For σ, fill in the value of s, which is 4.8. For $\bar{x}$, fill in 26. For n, fill in 400. For "C-Level," fill in 0.90. Scroll to "Calculate" and press "Enter." On the second line, your screen will show (25.605, 26.395), which is equivalent to $25.605 < \mu < 26.395$

Suppose the we are given a sample size less than 30 from a normally distributed population, but we do not know the value of σ. In this scenario, we cannot use the formulas in Examples 64 and 65 to create a confidence interval for μ. However, we can use a t scores in place of z scores. A t-distribution is a family of curves that approaches the curve of the standard normal distribution, as n approaches 30. Critical t values will replace

critical z values, so that the confidence interval becomes $\bar{x} \pm (t_c)(\frac{s}{\sqrt{n}})$. Statistics textbooks do contain tables of critical t values, but our friendly TI-83 is already programmed to do the necessary calculations, even without these critical t values. We'll show the steps in the next two examples.

EXAMPLE 66

In a small city in Michigan, a survey of 16 schools was conducted to determine the number of teachers in each school. The results showed a mean of 35 with a sample standard deviation of 5. Assuming that the population of the number of teachers in each Michigan school is normally distributed, what is the 90% confidence interval for the mean number of teachers in all Michigan schools?

SOLUTION

The formula to use would be $\bar{x} \pm (t_c)(\frac{s}{\sqrt{n}})$; however, we would need the value of t_c. Using the TI-83, follow these steps: Press "STAT," scroll to "TESTS," and press 8. At this point, your screen will display "Tinterval" at the top. On the second line highlight "Stats." For $\bar{x}$, fill in 35. For s_x, fill in 5. For n, fill in 16. For "C-Level," fill in 0.90. Now scroll to "Calculate" and press "Enter." On the second line, your screen will show (32.809, 37.191), which is equivalent to $32.809 < \mu < 37.191$.

EXAMPLE 67

The Texas State Police recorded the speed for each of twenty-four randomly selected automobiles on a busy road. Their mean speed was 43 miles per hour, with a standard deviation of 5.5 miles per hour. Assuming that the speeds of all automobiles on this road are normally distributed, what is the 98% confidence interval for the mean speed of all automobiles on this road?

SOLUTION

As in Example 66, press "STATS," scroll to "TESTS," then press "8." Now enter 43, 5.5, 24, and .98 for $\bar{x}$, s_x, n, and C-Level, respectively. By scrolling to "Calculate" and pressing "Enter," your answer should be (40.193, 45.807). This is equivalent to $40.193 < \mu < 45.807$.

NOTE:

The "Tinterval" feature was necessary in Examples 66 and 67 because even though the population was normal, the sample size was less than 30 and the value of σ was not known. Figure 6.25 provides a helpful Flow Chart to assist you in deciding which of Tinterval or Zinterval to use when calculating a confidence interval.

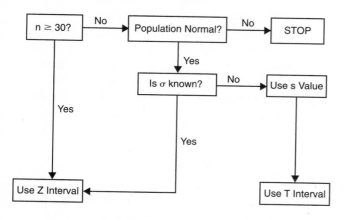

If $n \geq 30$ and σ is not known, use the value of s.

Figure 6.25

Statistical Hypothesis Testing

Statistical hypothesis testing is a process by which decisions are made concerning claims about population values. Although there are several population statistics of interest, our discussion will be confined to testing claims about a population mean, based on the results of a sample mean and sample standard deviation. This discussion is very closely aligned with our study of confidence intervals.

A **null hypothesis**, symbolized as H_0, is one that states that there is no statistical difference between the sample mean and the population mean.

An **alternative hypothesis**, symbolized as H_1, is one that states that there is a statistical difference between the sample mean and the population mean.

A **critical region** (also called a **rejection region**) is the range of values for which there is a significant statistical difference between the sample mean and the population mean. As a consequence, the null hypothesis (H_0) should be rejected.

A **noncritical region** is the range of values for which the difference between the sample mean and the population mean is attributed to chance. As a consequence, the null hypothesis should not be rejected.

Let μ_0 represent a specific value for the population mean. There are three different types of hypothesis testing to consider:

Type 1: H_0: $\mu \leq \mu_0$ and H_1: $\mu > \mu_0$

Type 2: H_0: $\mu \geq \mu_0$ and H_1: $\mu < \mu_0$

Type 3: H_0: $\mu = \mu_0$ and H_1: $\mu \neq \mu_0$:

Types 1 and 2 are called a **one-tailed test**, whereas Type 3 is called a **two-tailed test**.

A one-tailed test is one in which there is a critical region either on the left side or the right side of the mean. A two-tailed test is one in which there is a critical region on each side of the mean. Note that for any of these types of hypothesis testing, H_0 <u>must</u> contain an equals sign.

For any of these three types of hypothesis testing, a **Type I error** occurs if H_0 is rejected when it is actually true. This is equivalent to accepting the alternative hypothesis (H_1) when H_1 is actually false. The maximum probability of committing a Type I error is called the **level of significance**, and is designated as α.

A **Type II error** occurs if H_0 is not rejected when it is actually false. The maximum probability of committing a Type II error is designated as β. However, the study of Type II errors is beyond the scope of this book.

In each of our examples, a claim will be made about the value of the population mean. A sample will be considered, in which the sample mean and standard deviation are given. Based on this information, we will either reject the claim or fail to reject the claim concerning the value of the population mean. When a claim cannot be rejected, statisticians hesitate to use the phrase "accept the claim" because only a single sample is being used.

EXAMPLE 68

Among all the homeowners of Dallas County, a noted researcher has claimed that the average age of their homes is 19 years. A current study of 50 homes reveals an average age of 21 years, with a sample standard deviation of 2 years. At the 5% level of significance, what decision should be made concerning the researcher's claim?

SOLUTION

In this example, our null hypothesis is $H_0: \mu = 19$ and our alternative hypothesis is $H_1: \mu \neq 19$. So, this is a two-tailed test. Since $n \geq 30$, we will use the Z-test on our TI-83 calculator. The procedure is as follows: Press "STAT," scroll to "TESTS," and press "1." At this point, your screen should read "Z-Test." On the first line below "Z-Test," highlight "Stats." For the values of μ_0, σ, $\bar{x}$, and n, input the values 19, 2, 21, and 50, respectively. For the line beginning "μ:", be sure to highlight "$\neq \mu_0$". Now press "Calculate." Note that the p value is about 1.54×10^{-12}, which means that the probability of obtaining a sample mean value of 21 if the actual population mean were really 19 is only about 1.54×10^{-12}. Thus, since $1.54 \times 10^{-12} < 0.05$, the researcher's claim is rejected. (Note that since σ is unknown, the value of s is used).

EXAMPLE 69

A machine is set to produce widgets with a mean length of 6 cm. Widgets that are too long or short cannot be sold. Forty bolts have been sampled. The sample mean is 6.03 cm and the sample standard deviation is 0.12 cm. At the 10% level of significance, is the machine producing widgets that have a mean length of 6 cm.?

SOLUTION

Our null hypothesis is H_0; $\mu = 6$ cm. and our alternative hypothesis is $H_1: \mu \neq 6$ cm. As with Example 68, we have a two-tailed test. Following the instructions of the previous example, after we have pressed "STATS," scrolled to "TESTS," and pressed "1," we again highlight "Stats," then input 6, .12, 6.03, and 40 for μ_0, σ, $\bar{x}$, and n, respectively. We highlight "$\neq \mu_0$", then press "Calculate." Note that the p value is about 0.114, which represents the probability of getting a sample mean of 6.03 if the population mean were actually 6. Since 0.114 > 0.10, we cannot reject the null hypothesis. Another way to state this conclusion is that there is not significant evidence to reject H_0.

EXAMPLE 70

Among all hospitals in Oklahoma, a state health official has claimed that the average noise level is at least equal to 60 decibels. A recent study of 40 hospitals shows a mean noise level of 59 decibels, with a standard deviation of 4 decibels. At the 5% level of significance, what decision should be made concerning the health official's claim?

SOLUTION

Based on the wording of the state health official, our null hypothesis is $H_0: \mu \geq 60$ and our alternative hypothesis is $H_1: \mu < 60$. In essence, we are seeking to determine if the sample noise level of 59 decibels is _significantly_ less than 60 decibels. On your calculator, follow the procedure for Examples 68 and 69 in using the Z-Test. The key numbers to input are as follows: 60, 4, 59, and 40 for the values of μ_0, σ, $\bar{x}$, and n, respectively. Now on the line beginning "μ:", you must highlight "$< \mu_0$". After you press "Calculate," the p value is approximately 0.057. Since 0.057 is greater than our level of significance (5%), we cannot reject the state health official's claim.

NOTE:

We need to emphasize an important concept regarding the solution to Example 70. While it is true that the value of 59 is not greater than or equal to 60, at the 5% level of significance, 59 is <u>not</u> <u>significantly</u> lower than 60. In each of Examples 68, 69, and 70, you will notice that the sample size is at least 30. When the sample size is less than 30, we need to use the t-test feature of the TI 83 calculator. In addition, we <u>must</u> have a population that is normally distributed. (In hypothesis testing, this condition is not required whenever the sample size is at least 30.)

EXAMPLE 71

It has been already established that the time required for math professors to grade a student's final exam is normally distributed. A well-known educator claims that the mean time for this distribution is 10.5 minutes. A current study involving 15 mathematics professors at a local college showed that the mean time was 10.1 minutes, with a standard deviation of 0.7 minutes. At the 2% level of significance, what decision should be made concerning the educator's claim?

SOLUTION

Since this is a two-tailed test, our null hypothesis is $H_0: \mu = 10.5$ and our alternative hypothesis is $H_1: \mu \neq 10.5$. Since $n < 30$, we will need to apply the t-test on the TI 83 calculator. Press "STAT," scroll to "TESTS," and press 2. At this point, your screen should show "T-Test." On the second line, be sure to highlight "Stats." The val-

ues of $\mu_0, \bar{x}, s_x$, and n become 10.5, 10.1, 0.7, and 15, respectively. Then highlight "$\mu: \neq \mu_0$", and press "Calculate." The p value is about 0.044, which is larger than our given significance level of 0.02. Therefore, the educator's claim (which is H_0), cannot be rejected.

EXAMPLE 72

Along Interstate 81, many motorists seem to obey the posted speed limit. A Department of Transportation official has claimed that the average speed is no greater than 62 miles per hour. A recent study of a random sample of 25 vehicles that use this interstate revealed that their average speed was actually 65 miles per hour, with a standard deviation of 2.5 miles per hour. At the 1% level of significance, what decision should be made concerning the Department of Transportation official's claim? Assume that the average speed is normally distributed.

SOLUTION

Based on the wording of the statement that the average speed is "no greater than 62" miles per hour, our null hypothesis is $H_0: \mu \leq 62$. Then the alternative hypothesis is $H_1: \mu > 62$. Since $n < 30$, σ is unknown, and the distribution is normal, we will use T-Test. Following the procedure in Example 71, the numbers to enter when you reach the screen with T-Test on the top line are 62, 65, 2.5, and 25. These numbers correspond to $\mu_0, \bar{x}, x, s_x$, and n, respectively. Then be sure to highlight $\mu > \mu_0$ before pressing "Calculate". The result yields a p value of about 1.70×10^{-6}. Since this number is less than 0.01, we must reject the official's claim. We conclude that the speed of 65 miles per hour is significantly greater than 62 miles per hour.

Chapter 6 Quiz

1. Which of the following is true of the data set 10, 7, 5, 4, 8, 7, 8?

   (A) The mean equals the median.

   (B) The mean is less than the median.

   (C) The mode does not exist.

   (D) There is one mode.

2. A fair spinner has two colors: blue and yellow. $P(\text{Blue}) = \frac{3}{4}$ and $P(\text{Yellow}) = \frac{1}{4}$. A person wins $20 if the spinner lands on yellow and $2 if the spinner lands on blue. It costs $10 to play. How much should a person expect to win/lose per game?

   (A) Win $6.50   (C) Lose $3.50

   (B) Win $16.50   (D) Lose $11.50

3. Which of the following best represents a positive correlation between the variables?

   (A) Hours watching television and money saved on groceries

   (B) The number of kilowatt-hours used in a month and the cost of electric bill

   (C) Height and weight of people

   (D) The age of an appliance and its value

4. A machine is designed to produce bolts with a mean length of 3 cm. We wish to test the null hypothesis $H_0: \mu = 3$ vs. the alternative hypothesis $H_1: \mu \neq 3$. Fifty bolts will be sampled. At the 0.10 level of significance, for which mean and standard deviation is the machine working properly?

   (A) $\bar{x} = 3.01$, $\sigma = 0.01$

   (B) $\bar{x} = 3.001$, $\sigma = 0.01$

   (C) $\bar{x} = 2.996$, $\sigma = 0.01$

   (D) $\bar{x} = 2.97$, $\sigma = 0.1$

5. In how many different ways can the letters w, x, y, and z be arranged if the first letter must be w?

   (A) 1   (C) 24

   (B) 6   (D) 256

6. A bag contains 6 blue marbles, 4 red marbles, and 8 green marbles. With one random draw, what is the probability of selecting a blue or red marble?

   (A) $\frac{2}{9}$ (C) $\frac{4}{9}$

   (B) $\frac{1}{3}$ (D) $\frac{5}{9}$

7. Approximately 95% of the data in a normal curve occurs between which two values?

   (A) $\mu - \sigma$ and $\mu + \sigma$

   (B) $\mu - 2\sigma$ and $\mu + 2\sigma$

   (C) $\mu - 3\sigma$ and $\mu + 3\sigma$

   (D) $\mu - 4\sigma$ and $\mu + 4\sigma$

8. The following stem-and-leaf plot represents the test scores for a class.

Stems	Leaves
5	5 7
6	8 8 8
7	4 7 8 8 9
9	1 3 4 8

   What is the class mean?

   (A) 78   (C) 77.5

   (B) 68   (D) 77

9. A person is interested in determining whether or not to open a restaurant in a particular neighborhood. Which of the following is the best method of collecting data to answer the question?

(A) Randomly select neighborhood residents on different days at different times.

(B) Randomly select individuals who are in the neighborhood on a Monday afternoon.

(C) Select each of the neighborhood business owners.

(D) Select each of the individuals who teach at the neighborhood high school.

10. A bag contains 10 pennies, 15 nickels, 5 dimes, and 20 quarters. Three coins will be drawn, one at a time, without any replacement of coins. What is the probability of drawing three nickels?

(A) $\dfrac{3375}{117600}$

(C) $\dfrac{2730}{117600}$

(B) $\dfrac{3375}{125000}$

(D) $\dfrac{2730}{125000}$

Chapter 6 Quiz Solutions

1. (A)

The mean $= \dfrac{10+7+5+4+8+7+8}{7} = \dfrac{49}{7}$ $= 7$. In order, from least to greatest, the data appear as 4, 5, 7, 7, 8, 8, 10. Thus, the median is the fourth number, which is 7. Therefore, the mean and median are equal. Note that both 7 and 8 are modes.

2. (C)

$P(\text{Blue}) = \dfrac{3}{4}$ and $P(\text{Yellow}) = \dfrac{1}{4}$. Thus, the expected value of the game is $\dfrac{3}{4}$ ($2) + $\dfrac{1}{4}$ ($20) = $6.50. Since the cost of the game is $10, a person can expect to lose $10 - $6.50 = $3.50 per game.

3. (B)

The cost of an electric bill is based on the number of kilowatt hours. As kilowatt-hours increases the higher the bill. Answer choices (A) and (C) have no correlation, while answer choice (D) has a negative correlation.

4. (B)

The quickest way to solve this question is to use the TI-83 calculator feature on hypothesis testing with Z-tests for each answer choice. If the displayed value of p is greater than 0.10, then we accept H_0. The procedure is to press "STAT," scroll to "TESTS," and press option 1. Then highlight "Stats" and fill in the values for μ, σ, $\bar{x}$, and n. Be sure that "$\mu: \neq \mu_0$" is highlighted, then press "Calculate." For each answer choice, the value of μ_0 is 3 and the value of n is 50. For answer choice (B), the p value is 0.479, which is greater than 0.10. Thus, the null hypothesis cannot be rejected. This means that the machine is working properly. For answer choices (A), (C), and (D), the p values are 1.55×10^{-12}, 0.0047, and 0.039, respectively.

5. (B)

Since the first letter is w, the number of arrangements apply only to the letters x, y, and z. The number of ways to arrange 3 items is $3! = 6$.

6. (D)

There is a total of 10 marbles that are either blue or red. Thus, the required probability is $\frac{10}{18} = \frac{5}{9}$.

7. (B)

Use the "InvNorm" feature of the TI-83 calculator. The z values that include the central 95% is equivalent to the positive z value for which 97.5% of the data lies to its left. The value of InvNorm(0.975) is approximately 1.96, which is nearest to 2. Since $\sigma = 1$ in a Standard Normal Distribution, 1.96 represents about two standard deviations.

8. (D)

The mean is calculated as follows:

$$\frac{55 + 57 + 68 + 68 + 68 + 74 + 77 + 78 + 78 + 79 + 91 + 93 + 94 + 98}{14}$$

$$= \frac{1078}{14} = 77.$$

9. (A)

Randomly selecting neighborhood residents on different days and at different times.

10. (C)

On the first draw, the probability of selecting a nickel is $\frac{15}{50}$. For the second draw, there are 14 nickels left out of a total of 49 coins. The probability of drawing this second nickel is $\frac{14}{49}$. After both nickels have been drawn, there are 13 nickels left out of a total of 48 coins. The probability of drawing this third nickel is $\frac{13}{48}$. Thus, the probability of drawing three nickels is $\frac{15}{50} \cdot \frac{14}{49} \cdot \frac{13}{48}$

$$= \frac{2730}{117600}.$$

CHAPTER 7

Mathematical Processes and Perspectives

Proofs

Proofs are used to determine whether or not mathematical arguments are true. Proofs are constructed from a set of logical statements that can be made based on given information or information learned from given information. There are several methods used to prove mathematical arguments.

Indirect Proof

Indirect proof is based on the principle of eliminating alternatives to the given statement, and once all alternatives have been dismissed, given statement must be true. The process to use for an indirect proof is:

1. Assume that the negation of the statement to be proved;

2. Demonstrate that the negation leads to a contradiction;

3. Conclude that the negation is incorrect; and

4. Conclude that the original given statement is therefore true.

The negation of a simple statement is usually accomplished by negating the verb. For example, the negation of "It is snowing" would be "It is not snowing." If the statement contains the conjunction "and," we can create the negation by prefacing the statement with "it is false that." For example, the negation of "Jim is going bowling and Jane is going shopping" would be " It is false that Jim is going bowling and Jane is going shopping."

The negation of a conditional statement is accomplished by just negating the conclusion. Consider the statement, "If its batteries are working, then a flashlight will turn on." The negation would be, "If its batteries are working, then a flashlight will not turn on."

EXAMPLE 1

Given the statement "A right triangle has a least one acute angle," write the negation.

SOLUTION

A right triangle has no acute angles.

EXAMPLE 2

Given the statement "If the weather is chilly, then we will not have a picnic," write the negation.

SOLUTION

If the weather is chilly, then we will have a picnic.

EXAMPLE 3

Use an indirect proof to prove that a right triangle has a least one acute angle.

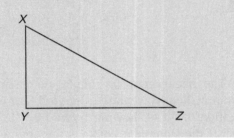

SOLUTION

Given: $\triangle XYZ$ and $m\angle Y = 90$

Prove: $m\angle X < 90$ or $m\angle Z < 90$

1. Suppose $\triangle XYZ$ has no acute angles.

2. Then, $m\angle X \geq 90$ and $m\angle Z \geq 90$. So, $m\angle X + m\angle Y + m\angle Z \geq 270$. We know the sum of the measures of a triangle equal 180 degrees. Therefore, it is not possible (contradiction) for $m\angle X + m\angle Y + m\angle Z \geq 270$.

3. Therefore, the original statement (#1) that $\triangle XYZ$ has no acute angles is false.

4. Thus, $\triangle XYZ$ has a least one acute angle.

Direct Proof

Direct proof is a method of showing the truth or falsehood of a given statement by using established facts.

EXAMPLE 4

Use direct proof to demonstrate that the sum of two even integers is an even integer.

SOLUTION

Two even integers, x and y, can be represented respectively as $x = 2a$ and $y = 2b$, where a and b are any integers. Then $x + y = 2a + 2b = 2(a + b)$. Since $(a + b)$ is an integer, two times an integer is always an even integer.

Counterexamples

Counterexamples are used when attempting to prove that a given statement is false. Only a single counterexample is sufficient for such a proof.

EXAMPLE 5

Use a counterexample to disprove the statement "The quotient of any two integers is a rational number."

SOLUTION

A rational number is defined as the quotient of two integers for which the divisor is not zero. Thus, a quotient such as $\frac{5}{0}$ is not defined, and therefore is not a rational number.

Reasoning

Two types of reasoning are used to draw conclusions that are based on factual information; namely, inductive and deductive **Inductive reasoning** involves drawing general conclusions from a set of given facts. **Deductive reasoning** is moving from ideas you know to conclusions that must follow from these ideas.

Deductive Reasoning

This type of reasoning involves the application of a generally accepted or proven theory to a specific example. For example, the Pythagorean theorem states that for any right triangle, the sum of the squares of the two legs equals the square of the hypotenuse. Using deductive reasoning, if we know that the two legs of a right triangle are 5 and 12, then we can determine that the length of the hypotenuse c, can be found using the equation $5^2 + 12^2 = 13^2$.

As a second example, consider the statement that in any triangle, the medians must meet intersect at a common interior point. (A median of a triangle is a segment whose endpoints are a vertex and the midpoint of the opposite side.) By deductive reasoning, if we draw any triangle ABC, then the three medians will intersect at one point in the interior of this triangle.

Inductive Reasoning

This process is the reverse of inductive reasoning. We use specific examples, then generalize our conclusion(s). For example, we note that $1 + 5 + 9 = 15$, which is an odd number. Also, $3 + 13 + 27 = 43$, another odd number. Using induction, our generalization would be that in adding three odd numbers, the sum is an odd number.

As a second example, note that $1 = 1^2$, $1 + 3 = 4 = 2^2$, and $1 + 3 + 5 = 9 = 3^2$. Using induction, our generalization would be the sum of any number of consecutive odd numbers, beginning with 1, results in a perfect square.

EXAMPLE 6

State whether the following is an example of inductive or deductive reasoning: Every time you draw a triangle the sum of the measures of the interior angles equals 180 degrees regardless of the size of the triangle. Therefore you conclude that the sum of the measures of the interior angles of any triangle equals 180 degrees.

SOLUTION

This is an example of inductive reasoning, since you are making a general conclusion, based upon specific circumstances.

Problem Solving Strategies

There are several strategies that can be used to help you solve a problem. These are: finding a pattern, making a table, guessing and checking, making a list, estimating, working backwards, and drawing a diagram.

EXAMPLE 7

Choose an appropriate problem-solving strategy to solve the following problem.

Gregory asks Steve, Beth, and Mark to form a line in front of the class. How many different ways could the students form a line?

SOLUTION

In the absence of knowledge about the concept of combinations, making a list works best, since the number of possible ways is rather small. (The actual answer is six.)

EXAMPLE 8

Choose an appropriate problem-solving strategy to solve the following problem.

There are 4 white chips, 5 blue chips, and 3 brown chips in a bag. What is the probability of drawing a brown chip?

SOLUTION

If a person does not know the basics of probability, drawing a diagram works best because the contents inside the bag can be easily counted (The answer is $\frac{3}{12}$, which reduces to $\frac{1}{4}$.)

EXAMPLE 9

Choose an appropriate problem-solving strategy to solve the following problem.

Bill and Gene sold 21 raffle tickets together. Bill sold twice as many tickets as Gene. How many tickets did Bill and Gene each sell?

SOLUTION

This problem can be solved with knowledge of elementary algebra. Without such knowledge, a guess-and-check method works best. One could begin by assuming that Gene sold 5 tickets. Then Bill would have sold $(2)(5) = 10$ tickets. Since this total of 15 would be too small, the next step would be to choose a number slightly higher than 5. (The actual answer is that Gene sold 7 tickets and Bill sold 14 tickets.)

EXAMPLE 10

Choose an appropriate problem-solving strategy to solve the following problem.

Sally took a train from Selma to Savannah. The train arrived in Savannah at 11:10 P.M. It took 2 hours and 25 minutes to travel from Charleston to Savannah. It took 1 hour to travel from Florence to Charleston. It took 3 hours and 15 minutes to travel from Selma to Charleston. At what time did Sally leave Selma?

SOLUTION

The quickest method would be to work backwards, since the final time was given. (The answer is 4:30 PM.)

EXAMPLE 11

Choose an appropriate problem-solving strategy to solve the following problem.

You save $3 on Monday. Each Monday after that you place in your savings account double the amount you saved the week before. If this pattern continues, how much would you place in your savings account on the sixth Monday?

SOLUTION

This problem could be solved by using a formula for geometric sequences, but since we only need to find the sixth entry, making a table of values would be very appropriate. In this table, you can create two columns, one for the numbered day (1 through 6) and the other for the amount of money deposited each Monday. (The answer is $96.)

EXAMPLE 12

Choose an appropriate problem-solving strategy to solve the following problem.

A large machine contains jellybeans that come in four different colors: red, green, yellow, and brown. The machine dispenses the jellybeans in this order. What is the color of the 95th jellybean?

SOLUTION

Finding a pattern works best, since the sequence in which the jellybeans are dispensed is repeated continuously. The key to finding the correct color is to assign each color a number, then determine which of the numbers (1 through 4) corresponds to the 95th jellybean. (The answer is yellow.)

Connecting Areas of Mathematics

Often, mathematical properties can be used that span different subject areas of mathematics such as geometry and algebra.

EXAMPLE 13

The coordinates of a triangle are $(0, 0)$, $(3, 0)$ and $(0, 3)$. The following mapping is used to create a new triangle $(x, y) \rightarrow$
$(x + 2, y - 2)$. What are the coordinates of the new triangle?

SOLUTION

The mapping is a translation of the original triangle. The resulting triangle is 2 units to the right and 2 units down from the original triangle. The new coordinates are $(2, -2)$, $(5, -2)$ and $(2, 1)$.

Set Theory

A **set** represents a collection of objects, commonly referred to as **elements**. Sets are denoted by a capital letter and they are written by using braces. Their elements are listed within these braces, separated by commas. For example, if set T consists of the elements 1, 3, 5, and 7, we can write T = {1, 3, 5, 7}. In fact, the order is irrelevant, so that we could have written T = {7, 3, 1, 5}. The symbol U is used to represent a **Universal Set**, which contains of all elements under consideration for a given discussion. Following is a table that lists the common symbols used for sets, along with the associated definition and example. For this table, let U = {1, 2, 3, 4, 5, 6, 7, 8, 9}, A = {1, 2, 3, 4, 5}, B = {2, 6, 8}, and C = {9}.

Notation	Definition	Example
$\cup$	Union (All of the elements in two sets combined with no element repeated)	$A \cup B =$ {1, 2, 3, 4, 5, 6, 8}
$\cap$	Intersection (Elements two sets have in common)	$A \cap B = \{2\}$
$\in$	Is an element of a given set	$3 \in A$
$\notin$	Is not an element of a given set	$3 \notin B$
ϕ	Empty set (Two sets that have no elements in common)	$A \cap C = \phi$
A'	Complement (All elements that are not in A that are in the given universe)	$A' = \{6, 7, 8, 9\}$

$\subset$	Proper Subset (All elements of a set are part of a given set)	$\{3, 5\} \subset A$
$\not\subset$	Not a proper subset (Not all elements of a set are part of a given set)	$\{3, 5\} \not\subset B$ $\{2, 6\} \not\subset A$

For the following five examples, let S = {2, 4, 6, 8, 10}; X = {1, 3, 5, 7, 9}; Y = {4, 7, 9}; and U = {1, 2, 3, 4, ..., 10}

EXAMPLE 14

Express $X \cup Y$ as a set of elements.

SOLUTION

We use all elements that are found in at least one of X or Y. Thus the answer is {1, 3, 4, 5, 7, 9}. (Note that no number is repeated when writing sets.)

EXAMPLE 15

Express $S \cap X$ as a set of elements.

SOLUTION

Since these two sets have no common elements, the answer is ϕ.

EXAMPLE 16

Express $(S \cup X) \cap Y$ as a set of elements.

SOLUTION

$S \cup X = \{1, 2, 3, ..., 10\}$. Then $\{1, 2, 3, ..., 10\} \cap Y = \{4, 7, 9\}$.

EXAMPLE 17

> Express S ∪ (X ∩ Y) as a set of elements.

SOLUTION

(X ∩ Y) = {7, 9}. Then S ∪ {7, 9} = {2, 4, 6, 7, 8, 9, 10}.

Notice how the answer in Example 17 differs from the answer in Example 16. Just as with algebraic operations, the placement of parentheses affects the answer.

EXAMPLE 18

> Express X′ ∪ Y′ as a set of elements.

SOLUTION

Remember that X′ means all elements that do not belong to X but do belong to U. So, X′ = {2, 4, 6, 8, 10}. In similar fashion, Y′ = {1, 2, 3, 5, 6, 8, 10}. Thus, X′ ∪ Y′ = {1, 2, 3, 4, 5, 6, 8, 10}.

Venn Diagrams

Venn diagrams are graphical illustrations that show that relationships among sets. We use a rectangle to represent the Universal Set (U) and then use circles within this rectangle to represent proper subsets of U. Following are some Venn diagrams with explanations.

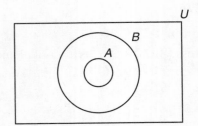

Figure 7.1

In Figure 7.1, set A is a subset of set B.

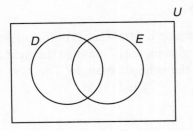

Figure 7.2

In Figure 7.2, sets D and E contain some common element(s).

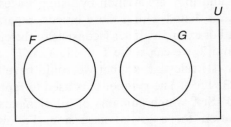

Figure 7.3

In Figure 7.3, sets F and G contain no common elements.

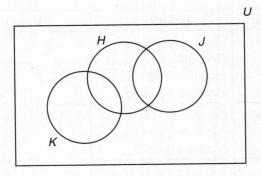

Figure 7.4

In Figure 7.4, sets H and J contain common elements. Also, set K contains elements common to H but not to J.

When a Venn diagram is used to illustrate the intersection or union of sets, the required region is shaded.

For the following examples, use the information concerning sets from Examples 14 through 18.

EXAMPLE 19

Using a Venn diagram, express the region X ∪ Y.

SOLUTION

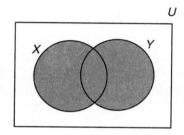

EXAMPLE 20

Using a Venn diagram, express the region X′.

SOLUTION

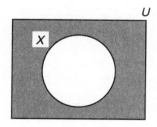

EXAMPLE 21

Using a Venn diagram, express the region S′ ∩ Y.

SOLUTION

First note that S and Y do contain common elements, so their circles must overlap. The shaded region contains elements that are not in S but are in Y.

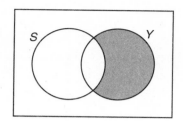

Translating Mathematical Language

Mathematics can be written in both English and symbolic language. With respect to mathematical expressions, equations, and inequalities, here is a list of the most commonly used symbols:

=	Equals	+	Add
<	Less than	−	Subtract
>	Greater than	×	Multiply
≤	Less than or equal to	÷	Divide
≥	Greater than or equal to		

EXAMPLE 22

Write in mathematical symbols: Two times a number plus four is eleven.

SOLUTION

Letting x represent the number, the answer is $2x + 4 = 11$.

EXAMPLE 23

Write in mathematical symbols: Six less than the quotient of ten and a number is greater than four.

SOLUTION

Letting y represent the number, the answer is $\frac{10}{y} - 6 > 4$.

EXAMPLE 24

Write as a sentence using words: $3(x + 2) = 5x$.

SOLUTION

The answer is "Three times the quantity of a number added to two equals five times that number."

The Number Line and Mathematical Phrases

The word *inclusive* means including a specific number. When used in interval notation, the symbols are $\leq$ and $\geq$. As denoted on a number line, we use a circle that is shaded (also called a black dot). The word "exclusive" means not including a specific number. When used in interval notation, the symbols are $<$ and $>$. On a number line, we use a circle that is not shaded. On occasion, an interval may contain both a closed circle and an open circle.

EXAMPLE 25

Write in interval notation: A number lies between 4 and –4, inclusive. (Use x for the number.)

SOLUTION

The answer is $-4 \leq x \leq 4$.

EXAMPLE 26

Graph the inequality from Example 25 on a number line.

SOLUTION

We use a closed circle at –4 and 4, and then shade the section of the number line between these two numbers.

EXAMPLE 27

Write in interval notation: A number lies between 1 and 5, not inclusive. (Use x for the number.)

SOLUTION

The answer is $1 < x < 5$.

EXAMPLE 28

Graph the inequality from Example 27 on a number line.

SOLUTION

We use an open circle at 1 and 5, and then shade the section of the number line between these two numbers.

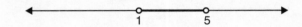

EXAMPLE 29

Write in interval notation: A number lies between 3 and 7, including 7. (Use x for the number.)

SOLUTION

The answer is $3 < x \leq 7$.

EXAMPLE 30

Graph the inequality from Example 29 on a number line.

SOLUTION

We use an open circle at 3, a closed circle at 7, and then shade the section of the number line between these two numbers.

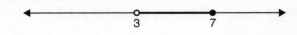

Choosing an Appropriate Model

The ability to determine the correct mathematical model to use in solving a problem is extremely important. There are many ways to represent and also analyze data. These ways include entering data in matrices, creating a circle graph, making a scatterplot, or creating a box-and-whiskers plot.

EXAMPLE 31

A cell phone customer wants to compare the prices of two companies' cell phone packages. The customer wants to know which package is least costly, given the number of minutes used each month. What type of mathematical model can be used to best answer this question?

SOLUTION

A system of equations is the best model. A system of equations is used to compare continuous data. The intersection of the two equations is known as the break-even point. Values above the break-even point mean that one package is more expensive than the other. Likewise, values below the break-even point indicate that one package is less expensive than the other.

EXAMPLE 32

A person wants to look at the relationship between height and shoe size. What type of mathematical model can be used to best answer this question?

SOLUTION

A scatter plot is the best model. A scatter plot will allow the individual to visually see if there appears to be a correlation between the two variables (height and shoe size).

Analyzing Faulty Mathematical Reasoning

Many mathematical arguments appear to be true but may not be true, after a careful analysis of the logic and/or steps.

EXAMPLE 33

Determine the faulty reasoning in the following mathematical series of steps. Assume that $a \neq 0$ and $b \neq 0$.

$a = b$
$a^2 = b^2$
$a^2 - b^2 = 0$
$(a - b)(a + b) = 0$
$$\frac{(a-b)(a+b)}{(a-b)} = \frac{0}{(a-b)}$$
$(a + b) = 0$

SOLUTION

Since $a = b$, the expression $a - b$ has a value of zero. The erroneous step is division by zero on the fifth line.

EXAMPLE 34

Determine the faulty reasoning in the following series of statements.

If it is raining, then I carry an umbrella.
I am carrying an umbrella.
Therefore, it is raining.

SOLUTION

The implication is that if it is raining, then an umbrella is being carried. However the converse is not necessarily true. If I am carrying an umbrella, then the weather might be snow or perhaps I am bringing the umbrella home from the office.

43. Consider a unit circle, with the angle θ in standard position, and point P on this circle with the coordinates (m, n). Which one of the following represents $\cot \theta$?

A. $\dfrac{m}{n}$

B. $\dfrac{n}{m}$

C. $\dfrac{1}{m}$

D. $\dfrac{1}{n}$

44. What is the product of $9 - 2i$ and $9 + 2i$?

A. $77i$

B. $-11 + 77i$

C. $11 + 77i$

D. $36 + 77i$

45. The graph of which one of the following trigonometric functions has a period of $\dfrac{2\pi}{3}$ radians and has a phase shift of $\dfrac{\pi}{3}$ radians to the right of the graph of $y = \sin x$? (x is measured in radians)

A. $y = 3\sin(2x - \pi)$

B. $y = 2\sin(3x - \pi)$

C. $y = \sin(2x - 3\pi)$

D. $y = \sin(3x - 2\pi)$

46. Suppose the function $g(x)$ has a local maximum value at $x = -1$. Which one of the following statements is <u>completely</u> correct?

A. $g'(-1) < 0$ and $g''(-1) = 0$

B. $g'(-1) > 0$ and $g''(-1) = 0$

C. $g'(-1) = 0$ and $g''(-1) < 0$

D. $g'(-1) = 0$ and $g''(-1) > 0$

47. A system of two linear equations in x and y has an infinite number of solutions. Which one of the following is a valid conclusion concerning the graphs of these two equations?

A. They represent parallel lines.

B. They are perpendicular to each other.

C. They intersect at $(0, 0)$.

D. They represent the same line.

48. The line segment whose endpoints are $(3, 4)$ and $(7, 6)$ is reflected over the x-axis. Which one of the following represents <u>both</u> endpoints of the resulting segment?

A. $(-3, 4)$ and $(-7, 6)$

B. $(3, -4)$ and $(7, -6)$

C. $(3, -4)$ and $(7, -2)$

D. $(-3, 4)$ and $(-7, 2)$

49. What is the complete solution set to $(x - 5)(x - 3)(x + 1) < 0$?

A. $\{x : -1 < x < 3\} \cup \{x : x > 5\}$

B. $\{x : -5 < x < -3\} \cup \{x : x > 1\}$

C. $\{x : 3 < x < 5\} \cup \{x : x < -1\}$

D. $\{x : 1 < x < 5\} \cup \{x : x < -3\}$

50. If $\sec \theta = -\dfrac{25}{7}$ and θ lies in the third quadrant, what is the value of $\tan \theta$?

A. $-\dfrac{24}{7}$

B. $-\dfrac{7}{24}$

C. $\dfrac{7}{24}$

D. $\dfrac{24}{7}$

51. A moving object has a velocity $v(t)$ given by the equation $v(t) = t^1 - 9t + 20/$ sec., where t is measured in seconds. What is the distance traveled from $t = 2$ to $t = 5$?

A. $4\dfrac{1}{2}$

B. $4\dfrac{5}{6}$

C. $5\dfrac{1}{2}$

D. $5\dfrac{5}{6}$

52. Which one of the following is a fourth root of $8 + 8\sqrt{3}i$?

A. $\sqrt{2}(\cos 15° + i \sin 15°)$

B. $2(\cos 15° + i \sin 15°)$

C. $\sqrt{2}(\cos 45° + i \sin 45°)$

D. $2(\cos 45° + i \sin 45°)$

53. To the nearest hundredth, what is the area bounded by the curves whose equations are $y = 10x$ and $y = 2x^2$?

A. 41.67   C. 28.33

B. 34.33   D. 21.67

54. Which one of the following is <u>completely</u> correct regarding the number whose exact value is 2.605×10^{20}?

A. It has 20 digits, including 17 zeros.

B. It has 20 digits, including 18 zeros.

C. It has 21 digits, including 17 zeros.

D. It has 21 digits, including 18 zeros.

55. Consider the following connected graph.

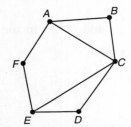

How many odd vertices are there?

A. 4   C. 2

B. 3   D. 1

56. If $(3^b)^c$ represents a positive integer greater than 3, then which one of the following is possible?

A. One of b and c is a negative number and the other is a positive number.

B. Each of b and c is a proper fraction.

C. One of b and c is zero.

D. Each of b and c is a negative number

57. What is the rectangular form of the equation $r = -4\cos\theta$, where r and θ represent polar coordinates?

A. $x^2 + y^2 + 4x = 0$

B. $x^2 + y^2 - 16x = 0$

C. $x^2 + y^2 + 4y = 0$

D. $x^2 + y^2 - 16y = 0$

58. A triangle has sides of 8, 11, and 13. To the nearest degree, what is the measure of the angle between the sides whose lengths are 8 and 11?

A. 70°   C. 80°

B. 75°   D. 85°

59. For which one of the following does its graph have the equation $x = -5$ as its axis of symmetry?

A. $y = 5x^2 + 30x + 50$

B. $y = 5x^2 - 30x + 40$

C. $y = 3x^2 - 30x + 60$

D. $y = 3x^2 + 30x + 70$

60. If $\sqrt{24} + \sqrt{n}$ can be written using a single radical number, which one of the following could represent the value of n?

A. 12   C. 54

B. 20   D. 72

Constructed-Response Questions

61. The cost of 3 apples and 4 pears is $3.77. The cost of 5 apples and 6 pears is $5.87. What is the cost of 7 apples and 9 pears?

- Write a system of equations that models this situation and identify the meaning of each variable.
- Solve the system of equations.
- Verify that the solution satisfies the given conditions.

62. Consider the following table of values for a quadratic function:

x	−1	1	2
$f(x)$	−3	5	15

- If $f(x) = ax^2 + bx + c$, determine the value of each of a, b, and c.
- Determine the y-intercept of the graph of this function.

ANSWER KEY – MATHEMATICS PRACTICE TEST 1

Question	Answer	Objective	Description
1	D	0002	Real and Complex Numbers
2	A	0005	Quadratic Functions
3	D	0003	Functions and Relations
4	C	0002	Real and Complex Numbers
5	D	0003	Functions and Relations
6	B	0001	Number Theory
7	C	0007	Trigonometric Functions, Identities
8	A	0001	Number Theory
9	C	0002	Real and Complex Numbers
10	A	0002	Real and Complex Numbers
11	B	0006	Nonlinear Functions
12	A	0004	Linear Equations and Systems
13	D	0006	Nonlinear Functions
14	B	0001	Number Theory
15	C	0005	Quadratic Functions
16	D	0004	Linear Equations and Systems
17	C	0005	Quadratic Functions
18	C	0004	Linear Equations and Systems
19	A	0007	Trigonometric Functions, Identities
20	B	0005	Quadratic Functions
21	D	0003	Functions and Relations
22	A	0001	Number Theory
23	B	0004	Linear Equations and Systems
24	A	0005	Quadratic Functions
25	B	0003	Functions and Relations
26	D	0008	Calculus
27	C	0001	Number Theory

Question	Answer	Objective	Description
28	C	0007	Trigonometric Functions, Identities
29	B	0002	Real and Complex Numbers
30	B	0005	Quadratic Functions
31	A	0006	Nonlinear Functions
32	A	0006	Nonlinear Functions
33	A	0006	Nonlinear Functions
34	D	0003	Functions and Relations
35	B	0001	Number Theory
36	C	0003	Functions and Relations
37	C	0008	Calculus
38	A	0003	Functions and Relations
39	B	0008	Calculus
40	B	0006	Nonlinear Functions
41	C	0001	Number Theory
42	C	0008	Calculus
43	A	0007	Trigonometric Functions, Identities
44	D	0002	Real and Complex Numbers
45	B	0007	Trigonometric Functions, Identities
46	C	0008	Calculus
47	D	0004	Linear Equations and Systems
48	B	0003	Functions and Relations
49	C	0006	Nonlinear Functions
50	D	0007	Trigonometric Functions, Identities
51	B	0008	Calculus
52	B	0002	Real and Complex Numbers
53	A	0008	Calculus
54	D	0001	Number Theory
55	C	0004	Linear Equations and Systems

Question	Answer	Objective	Description
56	D	0002	Real and Complex Numbers
57	A	0002	Real and Complex Numbers
58	D	0007	Trigonometric Functions, Identities
59	D	0005	Quadratic Functions
60	C	0002	Real and Complex Numbers
61	C-R	0004	Linear Equations and Systems
62	C-R	0005	Quadratic Functions

Objectives Checklist – Practice Test 1 – Code 022
Multiple-Choice Questions

Objective   0001   _____/8

6	8	14	22	27	35	41	54

Objective   0002   _____/10

1	4	9	10	29	44	52	56	57	60

Objective   0003   _____/8

3	5	21	25	34	36	38	48

Objective   0004   _____/6

12	16	18	23	47	55

Objective   0005   _____/7

2	15	17	20	24	30	59

Objective   0006   _____/7

11	13	31	32	33	40	49

Objective   0007   _____/7

7	19	28	43	45	50	58

Objective   0008   _____/7

26	37	39	42	46	51	53

Objectives Checklist – Practice Test 1 – Code 022
Constructed-Response Questions

Objective   0004   _____ First Bullet, _____ Second Bullet

61

Objective   0005   _____ First Bullet, _____ Second Bullet _____ Third Bullet

62

DETAILED SOLUTIONS: PRACTICE TEST 1 (022)

1. D.

Recall that $i^2 = -1$. Then $(a + bi)(a - bi) = a^2 - b^2i^2 = a^2 + b^2$, which is a real number.

2. A.

If there is exactly one real root, the discriminant of $f(x)$ must be zero. Then $m^2 - (4)(2)(50) = 0$. Thus, $m = \pm\sqrt{400} = \pm 20$.

3. D.

The expression $4x^4 - 36y$ is equivalent to $4(x^4 - 9y)$, which illustrates Common Term factoring.

4. C.

If x, y, and z are any real numbers, the Associative Law of Multiplication states that $(x \cdot y) \cdot z = x \cdot (y \cdot z)$. In this example, $x = 7$, $y = 8$, and $z = 3$.

5. D.

When the graph of $y = 5x^2 - 7$ is shifted 2 units to the right and 4 units down, x is replaced by $x - 2$ and -7 is replaced by -11. The new equation becomes $y = 5(x - 2)^2 - 11$, which simplifies to $y = 5x^2 - 20x + 9$.

6. B.

Given $x > y$, subtract x from each side of the inequality to get $0 > y - x$. This means that $y - x$ is a negative number.

7. C.

The measure of $\angle B$ is $180° - 65° - 35° = 80°$. Using the Law of Sines, $\dfrac{AC}{\sin 80°} = \dfrac{15}{\sin 35°}$.

Then $AC = \dfrac{(15)(\sin 80°)}{\sin 35°} \approx 25.75$.

8. A.

$-|-14| + (-6) = -14 - 6 = -20$, which is the lowest value of the four answer choices. The values of answer choices B, C, and D are -8, 20, and 8, respectively.

9. C.

The dot product of the vectors $\vec{v}_1 = -\mathbf{i} + 4\mathbf{j}$ and $\vec{v}_2 = 3\mathbf{i} + y\mathbf{j}$, written as $\vec{v}_1 \bullet \vec{v}_2$, can be calculated as $(-3)(3) + (4)(y)$. Since the dot product is known to be 21, we have $-3 + 4y = 21$. Thus, $y = 6$.

10. A.

Given any vector $\mathbf{v}$, its unit vector is represented by $\dfrac{v}{|v|}$. In this example, $v = 5\mathbf{i} + 3\mathbf{j}$ and $|\mathbf{v}| = \sqrt{5^2 + 3^2} = \sqrt{34}$.

11. B.

Using the rules of logarithms, rewrite the equation as $\log_b(\dfrac{M}{N}) = \log_b(3^M)$. Then $\dfrac{M}{N} = 3^M$, which leads to $N = \dfrac{M}{3^M}$.

12. A.

Matrix A has 2 rows and 3 columns, whereas matrix B has 3 rows and 1 column. The matrix AB must have 2 rows and 1 column, and would appear as $\begin{bmatrix} x \\ y \end{bmatrix}$. The value of x is found by multiplying each element of the first row of A by each element of B, then adding these products. So $x = (2)(4) + (0)(3) + (-2)(1) = 6$. The value of y is found by multiplying each element of the second row of A by each element of B, then adding these products. So $y = (-1)(4) + (1)(3) + (1)(1) = 0$.

13. D.

If $x = t + 3$ and $y = t^2 + 5t$, then $t = x - 3$. By substitution, $y = (x - 3)^2 + 5(x - 3) = x^2 - 6x + 9 + 5x - 15 = x^2 - x - 6$. So, the y-intercept must be -6.

14. B.

$24 = 2^3 \times 3$, $36 = 2^2 \times 3^2$, and $54 = 2 \times 3^3$. The greatest common factor is found by using the lowest exponent shown for each common base. For the base of 2, the lowest exponent is 1. For the base of 3, the lowest exponent is also 1. Thus, the greatest common factor is given by $2 \times 3 = 6$.

15. C.

For the parabola written in the form $y = a(x - h)^2 + k$, its highest point is given by (h, k), with the additional requirement that a is negative. If the highest point is $(1, -7)$, then $h = 1$ and $k = -7$. Answer choice (C) meets these requirements and $a = -1$.

16. D.

The equation $x = -1$ is a vertical line, and thus has an undefined slope.

17. C.

Factor the left side of the inequality to get $(x - 4)(x + 1) < 0$. For the situation in which $x - 4 < 0$ and $x + 1 > 0$, the solution is $-1 < x < 4$. For the situation in which $x - 4 > 0$ and $x + 1 < 0$, there would be no solution. The only possible answer is $-1 < x < 4$.

18. C.

The maximum value of the objective function is located at one of the vertices of the feasible region defined by the constraints. Solving $y = -x + 12$ and $y = -\frac{5}{4}x + 13$ simultaneously, the point of intersection is $(4, 8)$. Solving $y = -\frac{5}{4}x + 13$ and $y = -3x + 27$ simultaneously, the point of intersection is $(8, 3)$. The y-intercept of $y = -x + 12$ is the point $(0, 12)$ and the x-intercept of $y = -3x + 27$ is the point $(9, 0)$. The feasible region is the area bounded by the five vertices $(0, 0)$, $(9, 0)$, $(0, 12)$, $(4, 8)$, and $(8, 3)$. Any other x-intercepts or y-intercepts are outside the feasible region. We already know that $(0, 0)$ cannot possibly be a maximum value for $C = 5x + 3y$, so we just need to test the other four vertices. At $(9, 0)$, $C = (5)(9) + (3)(0) = 45$.

At $(0, 12)$, $C = (5)(0) + (3)(12) = 36$. At $(4, 8)$, $C = (5)(4) + (3)(8) = 44$; At $(8, 3)$, $C = (5)(8) + (3)(3) = 49$. Thus, 49 is the maximum value for C.

19. A.

Rewrite the equation as $(2\cos\theta - 3)(2\cos\theta + 1) = 0$. If $2\cos\theta - 3 = 0$, then $\cos\theta = \frac{3}{2}$, which is impossible. If $2\cos\theta + 1 = 0$, then $\cos\theta = -\frac{1}{2}$. This means that $\theta = \cos^{-1}(-\frac{1}{2}) = 120°$ or $240°$.

20. B.

Rewrite $y = 5x^2 + 2x + 9$ as $y = 5(x^2 + \frac{2}{5}x + \_) + 9$. Now put $\frac{1}{25}$ in the blank space inside the parentheses and add $5(\frac{1}{25}) = \frac{1}{5}$ to the left side so that the equation reads as $y + \frac{1}{5} = 5(x^2 + \frac{2}{5}x + \frac{1}{25}) + 9$. By factoring the right side and isolating y, we get $y = 5(x + \frac{1}{5})^2 + \frac{44}{5}$. Thus, the vertex of this parabola is given by $(-\frac{1}{5}, \frac{44}{5})$.

21. D.

$a_2 = (2)(a_1) + 6 = (2)(-1) + 6 = 4$.
$a_3 = (2)(a_2) + 6 = (2)(4) + 6 = 14$.
$a_4 = (2)(a_3) + 6 = (2)(14) + 6 = 34$.
Finally, $a_3 + a_4 = 48$.

22. A.

Given any two numbers in prime factorization form, the least common multiple is found by selecting the highest exponent that is used for each different prime factor of the two numbers. Then multiply these prime factors containing the correct associated exponents. For the prime factors of 2, 3, 5, and 7, the corresponding exponents are 6, 3, 5, and 3, respectively. Thus, the least common multiple is $2^6 \times 3^3 \times 5^5 \times 7^3$.

23. B.

Multiplying the top equation by 5 and the bottom equation by 4, the resulting equations become $15x + 20y = 80$
$$8x - 20y = 104$$
Then add these equations to get $23x = 184$, so $x = 8$. By substituting this value of x into $3x + 4y = 16$, we get $24 + 4y = 16$. Then $4y = -8$, so $y = -2$. Thus, the sum of x and y is 6.

24. A.

If $x = -1$, then $y = (-1)^2 + (-1) - 4 = -4$, which is the value of a. If $y = 2$, then $2 = x^2 + x - 4$. This equation simplifies to $x^2 + x - 6 = 0$. By factoring the left side, we get $(x + 3)(x - 2) = 0$. So, $x = -3$ or $x = 2$. Thus, $b = -3$ or $b = 2$. If $b = -3$, then $a + 2b = -4 + (2)(-3) = -10$. The second possible answer would be found by letting $b = 2$. In that case, $a + 2b = -4 + (2)(2) = 0$.

25. B.

For the equation $x - y = 2$, the x-intercept is determined by solving $x - 0 = 2$, which leads to $x = 2$. The y-intercept is determined by solving $0 - y = 2$, which leads to $y = -2$.

26. D.

A vertical cross-sectional area can be represented by $\pi(\frac{1}{2}x^{3/2})^2 = \frac{1}{4}\pi x^3$. When rotated about the x-axis, the volume generated is given by
$$\int_0^4 (\frac{1}{4}\pi x^3) dx = \frac{1}{16}\pi x^4 \Big]_0^4 = 16\pi$$

27. C.

$$(\frac{1}{3})(\frac{2}{3} + \frac{3}{2}) = (\frac{1}{3})(\frac{13}{6}) = \frac{13}{18}.$$

28. C.

If the secant of an angle θ is 2, we can assign the number 2 to the hypotenuse and the number 1 to the adjacent side of a right triangle. Then the opposite side is $\sqrt{2^2 - 1^2} = \sqrt{3}$. So the sine of this angle θ must be $\frac{\sqrt{3}}{2}$. Thus,
$$\sin(\sec^{-1}(2)) = \sin(\sin^{-1}(\frac{\sqrt{3}}{2})) = \frac{\sqrt{3}}{2}.$$

29. B.

The associated right triangle would be found in the fourth quadrant. The length of the hypotenuse is $\sqrt{6^2 + 8^2} = \sqrt{100} = 1$. The reference angle can be found by $\tan^{-1}(\frac{6}{8}) \approx 37°$. This means that the fourth quadrant angle is $360° - 37° = 323°$. The polar representation is in the form $r(\cos\theta + i\sin\theta)$, in which r is the hypotenuse.

30. B.

The vertex of the graph of a quadratic function must be either the highest or the lowest point. Since the function is not defined for $y = 0$, the graph does not cross the x-axis. Thus, the vertex $(4, 3)$ must represent the lowest point.

31. A.

The amount that is <u>present</u> after 3 hours is given by $A = 500(\frac{1}{2})^{3/10} \approx 406.13$ grams. Thus, the amount of grams that has decayed is $500 - 406.13 = 93.87$.

32. A.

$h(-5) = 2 - (-5) = 7$, $h(-0.5) = 3(-0.5)^2 + 1 = 1.75$, and $h(2) = 2^3 = 8$. The sum of the three numbers 7, 1.75, and 8 is 16.75.

33. A.

If the degree of the denominator of a rational function is higher than the degree of the numerator, then the horizontal asymptote is $y = 0$.

34. D.

Write the given function as $y = \frac{8 - 3x}{5}$. Now switch the variables so that it reads as $x = \frac{8 - 3y}{5}$. Solving this equation for y, multiply both sides by 5 to get $5x = 8 - 3y$. Then $3y = 8 - 5x$, which leads to $y = \frac{8 - 5x}{3}$.

35. B.

For the number $5^9 \times 7^4$, the total number of integral factors is given by the product $(9 + 1)(4 + 1) = 50$. The rule for finding this number is to add 1 to each exponent of a base used in prime factor form, then multiply these "adjusted" exponents.

36. C.

We can write $m = \dfrac{k}{n^2}$, where k is a constant. Substituting $m = 4$ and $n = 3$, $4 = \dfrac{k}{3^2} = \dfrac{k}{9}$. So $k = 36$. Using this value of k and substituting $n = 6$, we get $m = \dfrac{36}{6^2} = \dfrac{36}{36} = 1$.

37. C.

$f'(x) = 3x^2 - 2x = x(3x - 2)$ and $f''(x) = 6x - 2$. If $x(3x - 2) > 0$, then either both factors are positive or both factors are negative. If both are positive, then $x > \dfrac{2}{3}$. If both are negative, then $x < 0$. Thus far, the allowable values of x are $x > \dfrac{2}{3}$ or $x < 0$. Now if $6x - 2 > 0$, then $x > \dfrac{1}{3}$. Finally, the intersection of $\{x \mid x > \dfrac{2}{3} \text{ or } x < 0\}$ and $\{x \mid x > \dfrac{1}{3}\}$ is $\{x \mid x > \dfrac{2}{3}\}$.

38. A.

$z = kxy$, where k is a constant. By substitution, $135 = (k)(9)(20) = 180k$. So, $k = 0.75$, which means that $z = 0.75xy$. Now using the values $z = 84$ and $y = 7$, we can write $84 = (0.75)(x)(7) = 5.25x$. Finally, $x = 84 \div 5.25 = 16$.

39. B.

If each term of an infinite sequence increases and there exists an upper bound for each term, then the sequence must converge. This is not the only set of requirements for a sequence to converge, but it is sufficient.

40. B.

By the definition of logarithms, rewrite the original equation as $c^{y+1} = x$. Then using the rules of exponents, replace c^{y+1} with $c^y \times c$.

41. C.

$(3 + 2) = 5$ should be done first, followed by $20 \div 5 = 4$, followed by $4 \times 10 = 40$, followed by $25 + 40 = 65$. The operation 5×10 is <u>not</u> a correct step.

42. C.

The expression $\lim_{x \to k} [f(x) - f(k)] / (x - k)$ is the definition of the derivative of $f(x)$ as x approaches k. The information that $f(x) < L$ has no effect on this definition. Also, note that the limit value may not be L.

43. A.

The cotangent of an angle is the ratio of the adjacent side to the opposite side. The adjacent side is the x-coordinate of P and the opposite side is the y-coordinate of P. Thus, $\cot \theta = \dfrac{m}{n}$.

44. D.

$(9 - 2i)(2 + 9i) = 18 + 81i - 4i - 18i^2 = 36 + 77i$. Note that $i^2 = -1$.

45. B.

For a trigonometric function written in the form $y = A \sin(Bx - C)$, its period is $\dfrac{2\pi}{B}$ and its phase shift is $\dfrac{C}{B}$ in the positive x direction. Thus, for $y = 2\sin(3x - \pi)$, the period is $\dfrac{2\pi}{3}$ and its phase shift to the right is $\dfrac{\pi}{3}$.

46. C.

At the place where a function has a local maximum at a point, its first derivative is zero and its second derivative is negative.

47. D.

If the graphs of two equations are the same line, then there are an infinite number of solutions. An example would be the equations $x + 2y = 5$ and $2x + 4y = 10$.

48. B.

In reflecting a point over the x-axis, the x-coordinate remains the same and the y-coordinate changes sign. Thus, $(3, 4)$ becomes $(3, -4)$ and $(7, 6)$ becomes $(7, -6)$.

49. C.

There are four possible cases:
Case 1: $x - 5 > 0$, $x - 3 > 0$, and $x + 1 < 0$. This has no answer.
Case 2: $x - 5 > 0$, $x - 3 < 0$, and $x + 1 > 0$. This has no answer.
Case 3: $x - 5 < 0$, $x - 3 > 0$, and $x + 1 > 0$. These imply that $3 < x < 5$.
Case 4: $x - 5 < 0$, $x - 3 < 0$, and $x + 1 < 0$. These imply that $x < -1$.
The final answer is the union of cases 3 and 4.

50. D.

The secant of an angle is the ratio of the hypotenuse to the adjacent side of a right triangle. If this ratio is $-\dfrac{25}{7}$ in the third quadrant, then the opposite side is given by the negative y value in the equation $7^2 + y^2 = 25^2$. Then $y^2 = 25^2 - 7^2 = 576$, so $y = -\sqrt{576} = -24$. Finally, the tangent of an angle is the ratio of the opposite side to the adjacent side, which becomes $\dfrac{-24}{-7} = \dfrac{24}{7}$.

51. B.

First solve $t^2 - 9t + 20 = 0$ to determine the time subintervals when the velocity is positive and when it is negative. $t^2 - 9t + 20 = (t - 5)(t - 4)$, so $t = 5$ or $t = 4$. In the interval from $t = 2$ to $t = 4$, the velocity is positive. The corresponding distance is $\int_2^4 (t^2 - 9t + 20)dt = |\dfrac{t^3}{3} - \dfrac{9t^2}{2} + 20t \Big|_2^4 =$

$(\dfrac{64}{3} - 72 + 80) - (\dfrac{8}{3} - 18 + 40) = \dfrac{88}{3} - \dfrac{74}{3} = 4\dfrac{2}{3}$.

In the interval from $t = 4$ to $t = 5$, the velocity is negative. The corresponding distance is

$|\int_4^5 (t^2 - 9t + 20)dt| = |(\dfrac{t^3}{3} - \dfrac{9t^2}{2} + 20t)\Big|_4^5 = |(\dfrac{125}{3}$

$- \dfrac{225}{2} + 100) - (\dfrac{64}{3} - 72 + 80)| = |\dfrac{175}{6} - \dfrac{88}{3}| = \dfrac{1}{6}$.

The total distance becomes $4\dfrac{2}{3} + \dfrac{1}{6} = 4\dfrac{5}{6}$.

52. B.

The hypotenuse of a right triangle whose legs are 8 and $8\sqrt{3}$ is calculated as $\sqrt{8^2 + (8\sqrt{3})^2}$ $= \sqrt{64 + 192} = 16$. The reference angle of the first quadrant right triangle can be calculated as $\cos^{-1}(\dfrac{8}{16}) = 60°$. So the polar form of $8 + 8\sqrt{3}i$ is $16(\cos 60° + i \sin 60°)$. Then one of this number's fourth roots is $(16)^{\frac{1}{4}}(\cos \dfrac{60°}{4} + i \sin \dfrac{60°}{4}) = 2(\cos 15° + i \sin 15°)$.

Incidentally, the other three roots are $2(\cos 105° + i \sin 105°)$, $2(\cos 195° + i \sin 195°)$, and $2(\cos 285° + i \sin 285°)$.

53. A.

The points of intersection are $(0, 0)$ and $(5, 50)$. The area is given by $\int_0^5 (10x - 2x^2)dx$ $= 5x^2 - \dfrac{2}{3}x^3 \Big|_0^5 = (125 - \dfrac{250}{3}) - (0 - 0) \approx 41.67$.

54. D.

When the decimal point of 2.605 is moved 20 digits to the right, there will be a total of 21 digits. This will include an additional 17 zeros to the right of the digit 5, so that the entire number will have 18 zeros.

55. C.

Points A and E are odd vertices, since they are connected to an odd number of edges. Each of these points is connected to 3 edges.

GACE MATHEMATICS ASSESSMENT

Constructed-Response Solutions

56. D.

$(3^b)^c = 3^{bc} > 3$. Then, since $3^1 = 3$, this means that $bc > 1$. If each of b and c is a negative number, their product is a positive number. None of the other three answer choices will yield a value greater than 1 for bc.

57. A.

Multiply both sides of the equation by r to get $r^2 = -4r\cos\theta$. We can replace r^2 by $x^2 + y^2$. Also, $\cos\theta = \dfrac{x}{r}$. Then $x^2 + y^2 = (-4r)(\dfrac{x}{r}) = -4x$. Then rewrite the last equation as $x^2 + y^2 + 4x = 0$.

58. D.

Let θ represent the angle between the sides of 8 and 11. By the Law of Cosines, $13^2 = 8^2 + 11^2 - (2)(8)(11)(\cos\theta)$. Simplify this equation to $169 = 64 + 121 - 176\cos\theta$. Then $-16 = -176\cos\theta$, so that $\theta = \cos^{-1}(\dfrac{16}{176}) \approx 85°$.

59. D.

Rewrite $y = 3x^2 + 30x + 70$ as $y = 3(x^2 + 10x + \_\_) + 70$. To create a perfect trinomial square, replace the blank by 25. This means that $(3)(25) = 75$ must be added to the left side of the equation, which now appears as $y + 75 = 3(x^2 + 10x + 25) + 70$. Factoring the expression in parentheses and isolating y, we get $y = 3(x + 5)^2 - 5$. The axis of symmetry is given by the equation $x = -5$.

60. C.

$\sqrt{24} + \sqrt{54} = \sqrt{4 \times 6} + \sqrt{9 \times 6} = 2\sqrt{6} + 3\sqrt{6} = 5\sqrt{6}$ or $\sqrt{150}$, which represents a single radical number.

61.

- Let x represent the cost of one apple and let y represent the cost of one pear. Then the appropriate equations are $3x + 4y = \$3.77$ and $5x + 6y = \$5.87$.
- Multiply the first equation by 3 and multiply the second equation by 2. The new equations are $9x + 12y = \$11.31$ and $10x + 12y = \$11.74$. Subtracting the first of these new equations from the second yields $x = \$0.43$. Substitute this value of x into the equation $3x + 4y = \$3.77$ so that it reads $(3)(\$0.43) + 4y = \$3.77$. The next steps are $\$1.29 + 4y = \$3.77$, $4y = \$2.48$, then $y = \$0.62$. Finally, the cost of 7 apples and 9 pears becomes $(7)(\$0.43) + (9)(\$0.62) = \$8.59$.
- To check the solution, we note that three apples and four pears cost $(3)(\$0.43) + (4)(\$0.62) = \$3.77$ and that five apples and six pears cost $(5)(\$0.43) + (6)(\$0.62) = \$5.87$.

62.

- $f(-1) = -3 = (a)(-1)^2 + (b)(-1) + c$, which simplifies to $-3 = a - b + c$. $f(1) = 5 = (a)(1)^2 + (b)(1) + c$, which simplifies to $5 = a + b + c$. Also, $f(2) = 15 = (a)(2)^2 + (b)(2) + c$, which simplifies to $15 = 4a + 2b + c$. By subtracting $-3 = a - b + c$ from $5 = a + b + c$, we find that $8 = 2b$, so $b = 4$. Now the equation $-3 = a - b + c$ becomes $-3 = a - 4 + c$, which simplifies to $1 = a + c$. Likewise, $15 = 4a + 2b + c$ becomes $15 = 4a + 8 + c$, which simplifies to $7 = 4a + c$. By subtracting $1 = a + c$ from $7 = 4a + c$, we find that $6 = 3a$, so $a = 2$. Finally, using the values of $a = 2$ and $b = 4$, we can rewrite the equation $5 = a + b + c$ as $5 = 2 + 4 + c$. Thus, $c = -1$.
- The quadratic function is $f(x) = 2x^2 + 4x - 1$. The y-intercept is found by substituting $x = 0$. Thus, the y-intercept is $2(0)^2 + 4(0) - 1 = -1$.

Practice Test 1
Exam Questions for
Mathematics (Code 023)

GACE Mathematics Assessment

ANSWER SHEET FOR PRACTICE TEST 1 (CODE 023)

1 _____   16 _____   31 _____   46 _____

2 _____   17 _____   32 _____   47 _____

3 _____   18 _____   33 _____   48 _____

4 _____   19 _____   34 _____   49 _____

5 _____   20 _____   35 _____   50 _____

6 _____   21 _____   36 _____   51 _____

7 _____   22 _____   37 _____   52 _____

8 _____   23 _____   38 _____   53 _____

9 _____   24 _____   39 _____   54 _____

10 _____   25 _____   40 _____   55 _____

11 _____   26 _____   41 _____   56 _____

12 _____   27 _____   42 _____   57 _____

13 _____   28 _____   43 _____   58 _____

14 _____   29 _____   44 _____   59 _____

15 _____   30 _____   45 _____   60 _____

ANSWER SHEET FOR CONSTRUCTED-RESPONSE QUESTIONS
PRACTICE TEST 1 (023)

1. In $\triangle ABC$, each of the sides is an integer. If $AB = 8$ and $BC = 12$, which one of the following could <u>not</u> be the length of $\overline{AC}$?

   A. 18   C. 6

   B. 14   D. 4

2. Which one of the following represents the equation of a sphere with its center at $(5, -3, 2)$ and a radius of 9 ?

   A. $(x+5)^2 + (y-3)^2 + (z+2)^2 = 81$

   B. $(x-5)^2 + (y+3)^2 + (z-2)^2 = 81$

   C. $(x+5)^2 + (y-3)^2 + (z+2)^2 = 18$

   D. $(x-5)^2 + (y+3)^2 + (z-2)^2 = 18$

3. A book publishing company's expenses are sub-divided into six major categories. If the company financial advisor is interested in summarizing how the expense of each category compares to the to-tal expenses, which of the following would be the best representation?

   A. Bar graph   C. Histogram

   B. Time series graph   D. Pie graph

4. If the point $(-5, -2)$ is rotated 90 degrees clock-wise around $(0, 0)$, what will be the coordinates of its new location?

   A. $(5, 2)$ C. $(-2, -5)$

   B. $(-5, 2)$ D. $(-2, 5)$

5. A principal at Center High School is interested in conducting a study to find out the level of service given by the cafeteria staff. He would like to make the study as impartial as possible. Which one of the following groups of students should be polled in or-der to be assured of getting a random sample?

   A. A group of students chosen from the first period in which lunch is served

   B. A group of students who take the bus to school

   C. A group of students chosen from each period in which lunch is served

   D. A group of students who only buy snacks for lunch

6. The mean height of high school girls is 65 inches, with a standard deviation of 2.5 inches. Assume a normal distribution. What is the probability, to the nearest thousandth, that a randomly selected high school girl is less than 66.0 inches tall?

   A. 0.655   C. 0.523

   B. 0.589   D. 0.345

7. An inductive mathematical proof is to be provided for a specific proposition. After showing that this statement is true for $n = 1$, what is the next step in the proof?

   A. Assume that the statement is true for $n = k$, where $k > 1$.

   B. Assume that the statement is only true for a specific $k > 1$.

   C. Find a specific $k > 1$ for which the proposition is false.

   D. Find a specific $k > 1$ for which the proposition may be either true or false.

8. Suppose you are given a multiple-choice question in which there is a lengthy equation of degree 5 in the variables x and y. Each answer choice has an answer for x and an answer for y. Which of the fol-lowing would be the best approach for selecting the correct set of answers?

   A. Estimating the answers based on using just the terms with degree 5

   B. Substituting each of the answer choices into the original equation

   C. Removing any 5th degree terms, then solving the resulting equation

   D. Drawing a table to identify all plausible values of x and y

9. Consider the statement " If it rains on Sunday, then Julie will not play golf." What is the inverse of this statement?

   A. If Julie did play golf, then it did not rain on Sunday.

   B. If Julie did play golf, then it rained on Sunday.

   C. If it does not rain on Sunday, then Julie will not play golf.

   D. If it does not rain on Sunday, then Julie will play golf.

10. Maureen is driving a distance of 150 miles at 50 miles per hour. At what speed does she need to drive for the next 7 hours in order for her average speed for the entire trip to be 60.5 miles per hour?

    A. 63 miles per hour

    B. 65 miles per hour

    C. 68 miles per hour

    D. 70 miles per hour

11. Ruth can run at a speed of 8 miles per hour. To the nearest tenth of a yard, how many yards can she travel in 20 seconds?

    A. 78.2   C. 57.3

    B. 67.8   D. 46.9

12. In the diagram below, $\overline{FH}$ is a secant and $\overline{FG}$ is a tangent to the circle whose center is point P. Point J lies on both the circle and on $\overline{FH}$.

    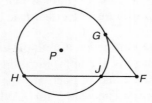

    If $FJ = 4$ and $HJ = 8$, what is the length of $\overline{FG}$, to the nearest hundredth?

    A. 6.93   C. 5.66

    B. 6.30   D. 5.23

13. Which one of the following represents a net for a cube?

    A.

    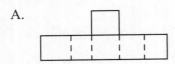

    B.

    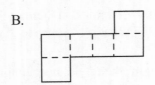

    C.

    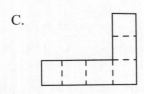

D.

14. Which one of the following has the answer of $_6C_3$?

    A. The number of groups of 3 children from a total of 6 children.

    B. The number of ways of arranging 3 books on a shelf with 6 slots.

    C. The number of ways of getting any number on a six-sided die when it is rolled three times.

    D. The number of ways of arranging nine marbles, 3 of which are identical white marbles and 6 of which are identical black marbles.

15. A researcher is interested in determining the relationship between the age (in years) of a particular type of copy machine and its annual maintenance cost. She collects the following data from five companies that use this type of machine.

Age (X)	2	3	4	7	8
Cost (Y)	$60	$80	$130	$200	$250

    Let $Y = aX + b$ represent the line of best fit. Which pair of equations would be used to solve for the values of a and b?

    A. $700 = 20a + b$ and $4220 = 142a + 20b$

    B. $700 = 24a + b$ and $4240 = 142a + 24b$

    C. $720 = 20a + b$ and $4260 = 142a + 20b$

    D. $720 = 24a + b$ and $4280 = 142a + 24b$

16. When drawn in the xy-coordinate plane, lines l_1 and l_2 are parallel to each other. If l_1 contains the points $(0,5)$ and $(3, -4)$, which one of the following conditions concerning l_2 is not possible?

    A. It contains the point $(1, 2)$.

    B. It contains the point $(5, 0)$.

    C. It has a slope of -3.

    D. It has a y-intercept of 3.

17. From a normal distribution of data, a sample of 64 data is extracted. The mean of this sample is 27 and its standard deviation is 4. Which one of the following represents a 99% confidence interval for the mean of the entire population?

    A. $26.02 < \mu < 27.98$

    B. $25.83 < \mu < 28.17$

    C. $25.71 < \mu < 28.29$

    D. $25.45 < \mu < 28.55$

18. Line l_1 lies in plane m and line l_2 lies in plane n. If plane m is parallel to plane n, which one of the following conclusions is valid concerning lines l_1 and l_2?

    A. They are either skew to each other or parallel to each other.

    B. They must be parallel to each other.

    C. They must be skew to each other.

    D. They are neither parallel to each other nor are they skew to each other.

19. Mario took a sample of 400 homeowners in a large city, and discovered that the average price of their homes was $150,000 with a standard deviation of $15,000. If he constructs a 95% confidence interval for the true average price of all homes in this city, what is the maximum error of estimate?

    A. $712   C. $1234

    B. $950   D. $1470

20. The perimeter of a rectangle is twice the perimeter of a triangle. Each side of both figures is an integer. If the length and width of the rectangle are 10 and 9, respectively, what is the largest possible side of the triangle?

    A. 11   C. 9

    B. 10   D. 8

21. The word *range* in everyday language can refer to "all possibilities." However, if y is a function of x, what is the meaning of "range"?

    A. The permissible values of x

    B. The permissible values of y

    C. The smallest value of x

    D. The largest value of y

22. A soil conservationist wishes to summarize his collection of samples by weight. The lowest (first) class has a lower boundary of 3.5 grams and an upper boundary of 6.5 grams. Each class will have the same width. What is the upper <u>limit</u> of the second class?

    A. 9   C. 11

    B. 10   D. 12

23. Which one of the following describes a set of data with the highest interquartile range?

    A. $Q_1=9$, $Q_2=13$, and $Q_3=22$.

    B. $Q_1=12$, $Q_2=15$, and $Q_3=24$.

    C. $Q_1=15$, $Q_2=20$, and $Q_3=25$.

    D. $Q_1=18$, $Q_2=28$, and $Q_3=29$.

24. A right circular cone and a sphere have equal radii. The volume of the cone is 75π and its height is 9. What is the volume of the sphere?

    A. $\dfrac{500\pi}{3}$ C. $\dfrac{500\pi}{9}$

    B. $\dfrac{400\pi}{3}$ D. $\dfrac{400\pi}{9}$

25. Which one of the following equations represents an ellipse whose center is at $(-2, 1)$ and whose major axis is parallel to the y-axis?

    A. $\dfrac{(x-2)^2}{16}+\dfrac{(y+1)^2}{25}=1$

    B. $\dfrac{(x-2)^2}{25}+\dfrac{(y+1)^2}{16}=1$

    C. $\dfrac{(x+2)^2}{16}+\dfrac{(y-1)^2}{25}=1$

    D. $\dfrac{(x+2)^2}{25}+\dfrac{(y-1)^2}{16}=1$

26. Which one of the following is a valid meaning of $\theta=\cot^{-1} 0.6$?

    A. θ represents the value of the cotangent of 0.6 degrees.

    B. θ represents the value of the cotangent of $\dfrac{1}{0.6}$ degrees.

C. θ represents an angle whose cotangent value is $\dfrac{1}{0.6}$.

D. θ represents an angle whose cotangent ratio is 0.6 .

27. Which one of the following would be a main purpose for using the technique of linear programming in a two-variable problem?

    A. To minimize one variable while maximizing the other variable

    B. To minimize each variable by using a line of least squares

    C. To maximize a specific function in which there are limitations on the size of each variable

    D. To maximize a specific function by introducing new limitations on one of the variables

28. Alice is an excellent bowler, although she has never bowled 300. She has kept a record of her last 25 games in a stem-and-leaf plot format, as shown below.

    18 | 6 8 9
    19 | 2 3
    20 | 1 3
    21 | 8
    22 | 1 4 5 7 7
    23 | 2 3 6 8
    24 | 7 8
    25 | 4 5 9
    26 | 3 6 8

    How much higher is her third quartile score than her median score?

    A. 15   C. 21

    B. 18   D. 24

29. Two triangles are similar. The sides of one triangle are 9, 16, and 21. If the largest side of the second triangle is 70, what is the smallest side of this second triangle?

    A. 30   C. 48

    B. 39   D. 57

30. A gallon of Quick-Dry paint can cover a rectangular wall that measures 12 feet wide by 10 feet high. Which one of the following rectangular sections of this wall could a quart of this paint cover without any paint left over?

    A. 6 feet wide by 5 feet high

    B. 4 feet wide by 2.5 feet high

    C. 10 feet wide by 2.4 feet high

    D. 3 feet wide by 2.5 feet high

31. The following Venn Diagram illustrates the favorite ice cream flavor(s) of a sample of 40 people. (V = vanilla, C = chocolate, and S = strawberry)

    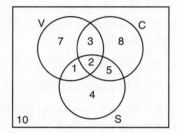

    What is the combined number of people who like exactly two of these three flavors or who like only strawberry?

    A. 15   C. 11

    B. 13   D. 9

32. What type of figure is formed by the intersection of a plane and a cone such that the plane is perpendicular to the base of the cone, but does not pass through its vertex?

    A. Parabola   C. Circle

    B. Hyperbola   D. Ellipse

33. A "weighted" penny was tossed three times. This triple tossing was repeated 80 times and the results are shown below. (H = Heads, T = Tails)

Outcome:	HHH	HHT	HTH	THH	HTT	THT	TTH	TTT
Frequency:	8	11	6	9	5	10	13	18

    Based on this chart, if Fred now tosses this penny three times, what is the probability that the penny lands on tails exactly twice?

A. 0.28   C. 0.475

B. 0.35   D. 0.575

34. Which one of the following represents a half-open interval?

   A. The set of all integers between -100 and $+100$, inclusive

   B. The set of all fractions greater than $\frac{1}{2}$ but less than $\frac{3}{4}$

   C. The set of all numbers greater than $8\frac{1}{2}$

   D. The set of all numbers less than or equal to 3

35. Mr. Chen gave his statistics class a quiz, on which the mean grade was 80 and the standard deviation was 2. Instead of giving each student a grade based on a total of 100, he gave each student a z-score grade. One of his students received a z-score grade of 2.5. What conclusion can you draw concerning this student's grade?

   A. The student's grade was below the mode grade.

   B. The student's grade was better than the median grade.

   C. The student's grade was better than the mean grade.

   D. Mr. Chen made an error, since each student's grade must be an integer.

36. The difference of 10 and 4 is to be divided by 3. This quotient is to be added to 4. Which one of the following correctly identifies these instructions?

   A. $10 - 4 \div 3 + 4$

   B. $(10 - 4) \div 3 + 4$

   C. $(10 - 4) \div (3 + 4)$

   D. $10 - 4 \div (3 + 4)$

37. A jar contains ten marbles, of which six are green and the rest are yellow. Debra will draw two marbles, one at a time, with no replacement of the first marble when the second marble is drawn. What is the probability that Debra will draw two green marbles?

   A. $\frac{6}{25}$ C. $\frac{9}{25}$

B. $\frac{1}{3}$ D. $\frac{2}{3}$

38. Peter states: "All isosceles triangles are acute." If Maria wants to present a counterexample, which one of the following should she use?

   A. A triangle with angles of 20°, 20°, and 140°

   B. A triangle with angles of 50°, 50°, and 80°

   C. A triangle with angles of 50°, 60°, and 70°

   D. A triangle with angles of 15°, 30°, and 135°

39. A company that makes transparent-tape dispensers claims that the weights of these dispensers are approximately normally distributed with a mean weight of 20 ounces and a standard deviation of 1.2 ounces. An inspector selects 2000 random samples of 64 dispensers each and calculates the mean weight for each sample. If the company's claim is accurate, what is the expected standard deviation for the means of all the samples?

   A. 0.10   C. 0.15

   B. 0.12   D. 0.20

40. Consider the following circle graph, in which the residents of the town of Peopleville rated the quality of their mayor.

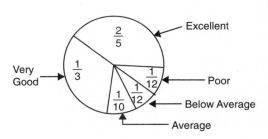

   If 1320 residents rated the mayor as either "very good" or "excellent," how many residents rated the mayor as "average"?

   A. 276   C. 180

   B. 228   D. 132

41. For which one of the following situations would a line graph be best suited?

   A. Showing a comparison of earnings power, identified by gender

   B. Showing the percent of a family's budget that is devoted to buying food

C. Showing a trend of auto purchases over a period of six months

D. Showing a comparison among different types of college degrees offered

42. The mean salt content of the newest brand of soup is 6 grams, with a standard deviation of 1.2 grams. Assume that the amount of salt content is normally distributed for all cans of this brand of soup. If a sample of 50 cans of this soup is selected, what is the probability that its mean salt content will be greater than 6.2 grams?

A. 14.7%   C. 6.4%

B. 11.9%   D. 3.6%

43. Which one of the following is correct about the graph of the parabola $y^2 = 24(x-3)$?

A. The directrix is $x = -6$.

B. The axis of symmetry is $x = 0$.

C. The focus is located at $(-6, 0)$.

D. The vertex is located at $(3, 0)$.

44. A set consists of only distinguishable elements, and may be listed in any order. Which one of the following sets is equivalent to $\{5, 3, 9, 10, 1\}$?

A. $\{1, 1, 5, 3, 9, 9, 9, 10\}$

B. $\{9, 9, 5, 3, 1, 1, 1\}$

C. $\{10, 3, 9, 5, 1, 1, 6\}$

D. $\{5, 1, 3, 3, 10, 10\}$

45. Point A is located at $(-4, 6)$. If the slope of $\overline{AB}$ is $-\dfrac{3}{4}$, which one of the following could represent the location of point B?

A. $(-7, 10)$ C. $(5, 18)$

B. $(4, 12)$ D. $(12, -6)$

46. Let A and B represent events, where $P(A)$ means the probability of A occurring and $P(B)$ means the probability of B occurring. Which one of the following set of conditions implies that events A and B are independent?

A. $P(A) = 0.5$, $P(B) = 0.4$, and $P(A \text{ and } B) = 0.2$

B. $P(A) = 0.5$, $P(B) = 0.8$, and $P(A \text{ and } B) = 0.3$

C. $P(A) = 0.6$, $P(B) = 0.3$, and $P(A \text{ or } B) = 0.9$

D. $P(A) = 0.6$, $P(B) = 0.7$, and $P(A \text{ or } B) = 0.8$

47. Which one of the following is an example of valid deductive reasoning?

A. Every integer is a real number. Every fraction is a real number. Therefore, every integer is a fraction.

B. The product of two negative numbers is positive. The product of X and Y is positive. Therefore, each of X and Y is negative.

C. Every rectangle has a length and a width. Figure $ABCD$ is a rectangle. Therefore, $ABCD$ has a length and a width.

D. Every square has four sides. Figure $EFGH$ has four sides. Therefore, $EFGH$ is a square.

48. Which one of the following would be an appropriate question for using the equation $(10)(x-3) = (8)(x)$?

A. Two people are biking the same distance. The faster person is biking 3 miles per hour faster than the slower person. The faster person is biking for 10 hours and the slower person is biking for 8 hours. What are their speeds?

B. Two people are driving at the same speed. The faster person is driving 3 miles farther than the slower person. The faster person is driving for 8 hours and the slower person is driving for 10 hours. What are their distances?

C. Two people are biking the same distance. The faster person is biking 3 miles per hour faster than the slower person. The faster person is biking for 8 hours and the slower person is biking for 10 hours. What are their speeds?

D. Two people are driving at the same speed. The faster person is driving 3 miles farther than the slower person. The faster person is driving for 10 hours and the slower person is driving for 8 hours. What are their distances?

49. All four sides of a quadrilateral are congruent and the diagonals are perpendicular bisectors of each other. Which one of the following figures does this describe?

A. Rectangle

B. Rhombus

C. Parallelogram

D. Isosceles trapezoid

50. Consider the following circle, with center P and a sector bounded by $\overline{PQ}$, $\overline{PR}$, and $\overset{\frown}{QR}$.

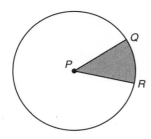

If $PQ = 8$ and the length of $\overset{\frown}{QR}$ is 1.5 π, what is the area of the sector?

A. 4π

C. 9π

B. 6π

D. 12π

51. Rectangle ABCD is situated in the xy-coordinate plane with coordinates $(-2, 5)$, $(12, 5)$, $(12, -1)$, and $(-2, -1)$, respectively. What is the distance from point C to the midpoint of $\overline{AB}$, to the nearest hundredth?

A. 8.06

C. 9.22

B. 8.64

D. 9.80

52. How many numbers, between 100 and 999 have a middle digit of 5?

A. 50

C. 81

B. 72

D. 90

53. For which one of the following set of conditions must events R and S be mutually exclusive?

A. $P(R) = 0.3$, $P(S) = 0.4$, and $P(R \cup S) = 0.7$

B. $P(R) = 0.5$, $P(S) = 0.3$, and $P(R \mid S) = 0.2$

C. $P(R) = 0.6$, $P(S) = 0.4$, and $P(R \cap S) = 0.24$

D. $P(R) = P(S) = 0.5$

54. A spherical balloon has a specific radius, represented as r. The balloon is inflated so that its new surface area is 64 times as large as its original surface area. What is the ratio of its new radius to its original radius?

A. $32 : 1$

C. $8 : 1$

B. $16 : 1$

D. $4 : 1$

55. Two groups consisting of an equal number of data, X and Y, have the same mean. However, the standard deviation of X is larger than the standard deviation of Y. Which conclusion is correct concerning the sum of the squares of differences between each data value and the mean of its associated group?

A. It is larger for the data in group X, provided that the median of X is greater than the median for Y.

B. It must be larger for the data in group X.

C. It must be larger for the data in group Y.

D. It is larger for the data in group Y, provided that the range of Y is larger than the range of X.

56. Which one of the following represents an equation of the plane that contains the points $(0, -5, 1)$, $(4, 3, 2)$, and $(5, -1, 3)$?

A. $3x - y - 4z - 1 = 0$

B. $3x + y + z - 17 = 0$

C. $4x + y - 12z + 17 = 0$

D. $4x - y - 8z + 3 = 0$

57. The solution to which one of the following situations would require knowledge of <u>both</u> algebra and geometry?

A. Writing a proof that a median of a triangle divides it into two triangles of equal area

B. Determining the measure of each angle of a triangle, given that one angle is double a second angle, which is 5 degrees more than a third angle

C. Finding the speed of the faster of two cars, given their times, distances traveled, and relationship between their speeds

D. Calculating the volume of a sphere, given the size of its radius

Practice Test 2
Exam Questions for
Mathematics (Code 022)

GACE Mathematics Assessment

ANSWER SHEET FOR PRACTICE TEST 2 (CODE 022)

1 _____   16 _____   31 _____   46 _____

2 _____   17 _____   32 _____   47 _____

3 _____   18 _____   33 _____   48 _____

4 _____   19 _____   34 _____   49 _____

5 _____   20 _____   35 _____   50 _____

6 _____   21 _____   36 _____   51 _____

7 _____   22 _____   37 _____   52 _____

8 _____   23 _____   38 _____   53 _____

9 _____   24 _____   39 _____   54 _____

10 _____   25 _____   40 _____   55 _____

11 _____   26 _____   41 _____   56 _____

12 _____   27 _____   42 _____   57 _____

13 _____   28 _____   43 _____   58 _____

14 _____   29 _____   44 _____   59 _____

15 _____   30 _____   45 _____   60 _____

ANSWER SHEET FOR CONSTRUCTED-RESPONSE QUESTIONS
PRACTICE TEST 2 (022)

1. Consider a unit circle, with the angle θ in standard position. Point P is on this circle with coordinates (x, z). Which one of the following represents $\csc\theta$?

   A. $\dfrac{x}{z}$

   B. $\dfrac{z}{x}$

   C. $\dfrac{1}{z}$

   D. $\dfrac{1}{x}$

2. What is the value of $\lim_{x \to -2} \dfrac{4x^2 + 3x - 10}{x + 2}$?

   A. 4

   B. 0

   C. −13

   D. −16

3. Which principle provides the steps for the subtraction of integers?

   A. Change the sign of the first number, then follow the rules of addition.

   B. Change the sign of the second number, then follow the rules of addition.

   C. Change the sign of both numbers, then take the absolute value of their sum.

   D. Change the sign of both numbers, then take the absolute value of their difference.

4. In which of the following situations would DeMoivre's Theorem be used?

   A. Finding the zeros of the polynomial $f(x) = x^2 - x - 6$

   B. Determining the fourth roots of 12

   C. Locating the endpoints of the central 95% of the data of a normal curve

   D. Solving for the maximum value of the objective function in a linear programming problem

5. Which of the following is equivalent to $\left(\dfrac{2^a}{2^b}\right)^c$?

   A. 2^{ab-c}

   B. 2^{a-b-c}

   C. 2^{a+c-b}

   D. 2^{ac-bc}

6. Look at the following graph of $g(x) = \begin{cases} \dfrac{1}{x-1}, & 1 < x \le 5 \\ -x - 1, & x \le -1 \end{cases}$

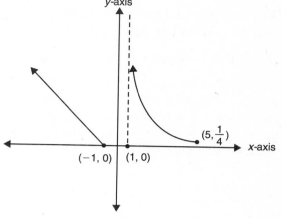

   For which of the following values does $\lim g(x)$ not exist?

   A. −3

   B. −1

   C. 1

   D. 5

7. On the closed interval $[a, b]$, the function $f(x)$ is increasing and is concave downward. Which of the following statements is true about the first and second derivatives of $f(x)$ on $[a, b]$?

   A. $f'(x) > 0$ and $f''(x) < 0$

   B. $f'(x) > 0$ and $f''(x) > 0$.

   C. $f'(x) < 0$ and $f''(x) < 0$.

   D. $f'(x) < 0$ and $f''(x) > 0$.

8. If $h(x) = \sqrt{\dfrac{3x - 2}{5}}$, which one of the following represents $h^{-1}(x)$?

   A. $\dfrac{5x^2 - 3}{2}$

   B. $\dfrac{5x^2 + 2}{3}$

   C. $\dfrac{2x^2 - 5}{3}$

   D. $\dfrac{2x^2 + 3}{5}$

9. The statement $(7)(x + yz) = 7x + 7yz$ is an example of which property?

   A. Distributive property of multiplication over addition

   B. Associative property of multiplication

C.   Associative property of addition

D.   Commutative property of multiplication

10.   The half-life of a substance is the time required in order for half of it to decay. Consider the formula $A = A_0(\frac{1}{2})^{t/h}$, where A is the amount of the substance present at any time t. A_0 is the initial amount (when $t = 0$) and h is its half-life. Suppose that the initial amount is 60 grams and its half-life is 12 hours. To the nearest gram, how many grams have decayed after nine hours?

A.   36

B.   30

C.   24

D.   18

11.   What is the multiplicative inverse of the matrix $\begin{bmatrix} 9 & 3 \\ 2 & 1 \end{bmatrix}$?

A. $\begin{bmatrix} \frac{1}{3} & -\frac{2}{3} \\ -1 & 3 \end{bmatrix}$

C. $\begin{bmatrix} -1 & 3 \\ \frac{1}{3} & -\frac{2}{3} \end{bmatrix}$

B. $\begin{bmatrix} -1 & \frac{1}{3} \\ 3 & -\frac{2}{3} \end{bmatrix}$

D. $\begin{bmatrix} \frac{1}{3} & -1 \\ -\frac{2}{3} & 3 \end{bmatrix}$

12.   The figure below shows the graph of $f(x) = -x^2 + 16$ and triangle ABC.

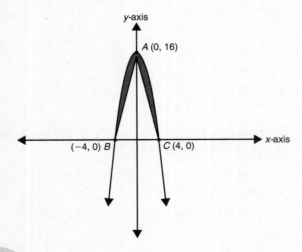

What is the area of the shaded region?

A. $15.\overline{6}$

C. $19.\overline{3}$

B. $17.\overline{6}$

D. $21.\overline{3}$

13.   Which of the following illustrates the Fundamental Theorem of Arithmetic?

A. $2^4 \times 6^2 \times 7$

C. $3^2 \times 7^5 \times 11^4$

B. $5^7 \times 9^3 \times 12^6$

D. $2^{-2} \times 3^4 \times 5$

14.   Consider the following graph.

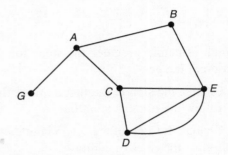

How many even vertices are there?

A.   1

B.   2

C.   3

D.   4

15.   The distance from the earth to the moon is approximately 384,400 kilometers. What is the scientific notation for the distance traveled (in kilometers) on a roundtrip from earth to moon and back to earth?

A. 7.688×10^5

C. 1.922×10^5

B. 768.8×10^3

D. 19.22×10^4

16.   What is the simplified form of $(2 + 3i)(-2 - 3i) + (4 - i)$?

A. $1 - 13i$

C. $-9 - 13i$

B. $9 - 13i$

D. $1 + 13i$

17.   If $f(x) = -x^2 + x$ and $g(x) = x^3$, what is the value of $g[f(-2)]$?

A. -216

C.   8

B. -56

D.   48

18. What is the solution set for $2x^2 + 5x - 12 > 0$?

    A. $\{x : -\dfrac{3}{2} < x < 4\}$

    B. $\{x : -4 < x < \dfrac{3}{2}\}$

    C. $\{x : x < -\dfrac{3}{2} \text{ or } x > 4\}$

    D. $\{x : x < -4 \text{ or } x > \dfrac{3}{2}\}$

19. Additive inverses do <u>not</u> exist in which one of the following?

    A. {rational numbers}

    B. {irrational numbers}

    C. {whole numbers}

    D. {integers}

20. The x-intercept of line l is $(-2, 0)$ and the slope of l is $\dfrac{1}{4}$. Which of the following represents the equation of a line with the same y-intercept as l?

    A. $10x - 2y = -1$

    B. $10x + 2y = -1$

    C. $8x + 3y = -4$

    D. $8x - 3y = -4$

21. What is the equation of the slant asymptote for $h(x) = \dfrac{-6x^3 + 4x^2 - 1}{2x^2 + 1}$?

    A. $y = -3x + 1$

    B. $y = -3x - 1$

    C. $y = -3x - 2$

    D. $y = -3x + 2$

22. In the table shown below, $y = 3x^2 - x - 4$

x	1	a	b
y	-2	0	6

    Which one of the following is a possible value of ab?

    A. 5

    B. $\dfrac{8}{3}$

    C. $-\dfrac{5}{3}$

    D. -6

23. To the nearest tenth, what is the length of the curve $f(x) = 1.5\,x^2 - 2x$ on the closed interval $[2, 5]$?

    A. 40.5   C. 30.8

    B. 35.6   D. 25.7

24. With respect to $f(x) = \sin x$, the graph of $y = \sin(Bx - C)$ represents a phase shift of π units to the right. If the period of $y = \sin(Bx - C)$ is 4π, what is the value of C?

    A. 2π C. $\dfrac{\pi}{2}$

    B. π D. $\dfrac{\pi}{4}$

25. Which one of the following functions has the same domain as the function $f(x) = \dfrac{x + 4}{2x^2 - 2}$?

    A. $g(x) = \dfrac{x - 4}{(x - 1)(x + 1)}$

    B. $g(x) = \dfrac{x + 4}{(2)(x^2 - 2)}$

    C. $g(x) = \dfrac{x - 4}{(x - 2)(x + 1)}$

    D. $g(x) = \dfrac{x + 4}{(2x)(x - 1)}$

26. Two cars are at the finish line of a circular track that is 1.5 miles long. In the time that one car has traveled three laps, the other car has traveled five laps. Assuming that each car travels at a constant speed and that they are traveling in the same direction, how many miles will each car have traveled when they next meet at the finish line?

    A. 7.5   C. 18

    B. 15   D. 22.5

27. Given that $\begin{bmatrix} 0 & 4 \\ 5 & 0 \end{bmatrix} \times \begin{bmatrix} a & b \\ c & d \end{bmatrix} = \begin{bmatrix} 8 & 12 \\ 40 & 20 \end{bmatrix}$, what is the value of $a + b - c - d$?

    A. 5   C. 13

    B. 7   D. 17

$(-\frac{x^3}{3}+16x) = \left[-\frac{x^3}{3}+16x\right]_{-4}^{4} = (-\frac{64}{3}+64) - (\frac{64}{3}-64) = 85.3$. The area of $\triangle ABC$ is $(\frac{1}{2})(8)(16) = 64$. Thus, the shaded area is $85.\overline{3} - 64 = 21.\overline{3}$.

13. C.

The Fundamental Theorem of Arithmetic states that any integer greater than 1 can be written as a unique product of prime numbers (except for order).

14. B.

Vertex B has 2 edges and vertex E has 4 edges.

15. A.

The roundtrip distance is $(384,400)(2) = 768,800$ kilometers. In scientific notation, this number becomes 7.688×10^5.

16. B.

$(2 + 3i)(-2 - 3i) + (4 - i) = -4 - 6i - 6i - 9i^2 + 4 - i$. Then since $i^2 = -1$, the previous expression can be further simplified to $(-4 + 9 + 4) + (-6i - 6i - i) = 9 - 13i$.

17. A.

$f(-2) = -(-2)^2 + (-2) = -6$. Then $g[f(-2)] = g(-6) = (-6)^3 = -216$.

18. D.

Factor the left side so that the inequality reads as $(2x - 3)(x + 4) > 0$. This inequality is true if both factors are positive or both are negative. If both factors are positive, then we have $2x - 3 > 0$ and $x + 4 > 0$. This is equivalent to $x > \frac{3}{2}$ and $x > -4$. The solution to this compound inequality is $x > \frac{3}{2}$.

If both factors are negative, then we have $2x - 3 < 0$ and $x + 4 < 0$. This is equivalent to $x < \frac{3}{2}$ and $x < -4$. The solution to this compound inequality is $x < -4$.

19. C.

The additive inverse property states that for every element a, there must exist an element $-a$ such that $a + (-a) = 0$. The set of whole numbers can be written as $\{0, 1, 2, 3, 4, ...\}$. The additive inverse for a number such as 2 would be -2, but -2 is not an element of the set of whole numbers.

20. A.

The equation for line l is $y - 0 = \frac{1}{4}(x - [-2])$, which can be simplified to $y = \frac{1}{4}x + \frac{1}{2}$. This means that the y-intercept of l is $(0, \frac{1}{2})$. The line that is represented by $10x - 2y = -1$ also has a y-intercept of $(0, \frac{1}{2})$, since $(10)(0) - (2)(\frac{1}{2}) = -1$. The point $(0, \frac{1}{2})$ does not satisfy any of answer choices (B), (C), or (D).

21. D.

By long division, $\frac{-6x^3 + 4x^2 - 1}{2x^2 + 1} = -3x + 2 + \frac{3x - 3}{2x^2 + 1}$. The remainder is not used, so that the equation of the slant asymptote is $y = -3x + 2$.

22. B.

The value(s) of a is (are) found by solving $0 = 3a^2 - a - 4$. Using factoring, $0 = (3a - 4)(a + 1)$. So, $a = \frac{4}{3}$ or $a = -1$. The value(s) of b is (are) found by solving $6 = 3b^2 - b - 4$, which can be written as $0 = 3b^2 - b - 10$. Using factoring, $0 = (3b + 5)(b - 2)$. So, $b = -\frac{5}{3}$ or $b = 2$. Using all four combinations, the possible values of ab are $\dfrac{8}{3}$, $\dfrac{5}{3}$, -2, and $-\dfrac{20}{9}$.

23. D.

$f'(x) = 3x - 2$, so $\sqrt{1 + [f'(x)]^2} = \sqrt{1 + (3x - 2)^2}$ $= \sqrt{9x^2 - 12x + 5}$. The length of $f(x)$ on $[2, 5]$ is given by $\displaystyle\int_2^5 \sqrt{9x^2 - 12x + 5}\,dx$. This integral can be evaluated using the TI-83 calculator as follows: Press "y =" and enter $\sqrt{9x^2 - 12x + 5}$. Press "Graph" and the graph of this function will appear on your screen. Now press "2nd", "CALC", and the number 7. The graph will appear with the words "Lower Limit" at the bottom left. Press the number 2, then press "Enter." At the bottom left will be the words "Upper Limit." Press the number 5 and press "Enter." Your screen will show the shaded area bounded by $x = 2$, $x = 5$, the curve, and the x-axis. The bottom of the screen will show the answer as $\displaystyle\int f(x)\,dx = 25.695283$.

24. C.

The phase shift to the right of π units means that $\dfrac{C}{B} = \pi$. The period of this function is 4π, so $\dfrac{2\pi}{B} = 4\pi$. Solving this equation, we get $B = \dfrac{1}{2}$. Thus, $\dfrac{C}{1/2} = \pi$, so $C = \dfrac{\pi}{2}$.

25. A.

The domain of $f(x)$ is all numbers that satisfy the inequality $2x^2 - 2 \neq 0$. Since $2x^2 - 2 = (2)(x - 1)(x + 1)$, the domain is all reals except 1 and -1. The domain of $g(x) = \dfrac{x - 4}{(x - 1)(x + 1)}$ is also all reals except 1 and -1.

26. D.

The least common multiple of 3 and 5 is 15. This number represents the number of miles that the two cars will need to travel in order to meet

again at the finish line. Then $(15)(1.5) = 22.5$ miles is the distance that each car has traveled.

27. B.

Using the rules for matrix multiplication, $\begin{bmatrix} 0 & 4 \\ 5 & 0 \end{bmatrix} \times \begin{bmatrix} a & b \\ c & d \end{bmatrix} = \begin{bmatrix} 4c & 4d \\ 5a & 5b \end{bmatrix}$. Then $5a = 40$, $5b = 20$, $4c = 8$, and $4d = 12$. Therefore $a + b - c - d = 8 + 4 - 2 - 3 = 7$

28. C.

$120 = 2^3 \times 3 \times 5$ and $128 = 2^7$. So the greatest common factor of these two numbers is $2^3 = 8$. Then the number of groups for the first class is $\dfrac{120}{8} = 15$ and the number of groups for the second class is $\dfrac{128}{8} = 16$. Thus, there are a total of 31 groups.

29. D. $\log_b\left(\dfrac{X^2}{Y^3}\right) = \log_b X^2 - \log_b Y^3 =$

$2\log_b X - 3\log_b Y = 2C - 3D$.

30. D.

Using triangle PRS, $PR = (18)(\sin 44°) \approx 12.5$. Now use the value of PR in triangle PQR. Then $QR = \dfrac{PR}{\tan 20°} = \dfrac{12.5}{\tan 20°} \approx 34.3$.

31. B.

The function $g(x) = \dfrac{3x^2 + 12x + 12}{x^2}$ has a domain of all real numbers except zero. Its zeros are found by solving $3x^2 + 12x + 12 = 0$. The left side of this equation factors as $(3)(x + 2)^2$, so the only zero is -2.

32. D.

The axis of symmetry is the vertical line whose equation is $x = 5$. For any point on a parabola, its image under a reflection over the axis of symmetry must also lie on the parabola. The point $(0, -8)$ lies 5 units to the left of the axis of symmetry. The image of the reflection of

(0, −8) is found by adding 5 units to the x value of the axis of symmetry and leaving the y value unchanged. Thus, the point (10, −8) must lie on the parabola.

33. C.

Each of $\sqrt[a]{4^3}$ and $\sqrt[b]{3^5}$ must be a positive integer. If $\sqrt[a]{4^3}$ is a positive integer, $a = 2$ or 3. In order for $\sqrt[b]{3^5}$ to be a positive integer, $b = 5$. Then $a + b = 7$ or 8, so $\sqrt[a]{4^3} + \sqrt[b]{3^5}$ is less than 10. Also, $a < b$.

34. B.

The coordinates of M are $\left(\dfrac{2+(-6)}{2}, \dfrac{7+1}{2}\right)$ = (−2, 4). A 90-degree clockwise rotation changes a point with coordinates of (x, y) to its image with coordinates $(y, -x)$. Thus, the image of (−2, 4) is (4, 2).

35. C.

$a_3 = 2.5 + (2)(0.5) = 3.5$ and $a_4 = 3.5 + (2)(2.5) = 8.5$. Thus, the sum of the first four terms is $0.5 + 2.5 + 3.5 + 8.5 = 15$.

36. B.

The function $y = ax^2 + bx + c$ will have two complex roots if $b^2 - 4ac < 0$. By substitution, $15^2 - (4)(4)(k) < 0$, which simplifies to $16k > 225$. Therefore, $k > 14.0625$. Since we want k to be an integer, the smallest allowable value of k is 15.

37. A.

If $A > 0$, then the lowest point on the graph of $y = A \sin 3x + B$ is represented by $B - A$. Thus, $B - A = 9$.

38. C.

Consider an item that normally retails for \$100. Using the discount available at the first department store, the final price would be \$100 − (0.60)(\$100) = \$40. Using both discounts available at the second department store, the final price would be (0.50)(\$100) − (0.20)(0.50)(\$100) = \$50 − \$10 = \$40.

39. D.

Square both sides of the equation to get $3x^2 + 1 = (x + 2)^2 = x^2 + 4x + 4$. Then the equation can be simplified to $2x^2 - 4x - 5 = 0$. In any quadratic equation of the form $ax^2 + bx + c = 0$, the product of the roots is $\dfrac{c}{a}$. Thus, the product of the roots of $2x^2 - 4x - 5 = 0$ is $-\dfrac{5}{2}$.

40. A.

The vertex of this parabola is (−1, 6). For any parabola in the form $y = a(x - h)^2 + k$ in which $a < 0$, the vertex represents the highest point. Thus, this graph's range is all numbers less than or equal to 6.

41. B.

The rectangular form of a number in the fourth quadrant must be in the form $a + bi$, where $a > 0$ and $b < 0$. These restrictions eliminate answer choices (A) and (D). The magnitude is given by the value of $\sqrt{a^2 + b^2}$. Note that the magnitude of answer choice (B) is $\sqrt{1^2 + (-\sqrt{3})^2} = \sqrt{1+3} = 2$.

42. A.

We can write $Y = kT^2$, where k is a constant. Substituting 27 and 6 for Y and T respectively, yields $27 = k(6)^2 = 36k$. So, $k = \dfrac{27}{36} = \dfrac{3}{4}$. Using the equation $Y = \dfrac{3}{4}T^2$, substitute 36 for Y. Then $36 = \dfrac{3}{4}T^2$, which is equivalent to $48 = T^2$. Thus, the positive value of T is $\sqrt{48} = \sqrt{16} \times \sqrt{3} = 4\sqrt{3}$.

43. A.

When $-5 \leq x \leq 0$, the values of y are $-25 \leq y \leq 0$. When $x > 0$, the values of y are $y > 2$. Thus, the range of y is all numbers greater than or equal to −25, except numbers between 0 and 2, including 2. (Note that although the number 2 is excluded from the range, zero is included.)

44. D.

First rewrite each inequality as follows: $y \geq -\dfrac{a}{5}x + \dfrac{2}{5}$ and $cy \geq -3x + 4$.

The solution lies above line l_1 and below line l_2. Noting that the slope of l_1 is negative, a must be positive in the first inequality. However, for the second inequality, the $\geq$ must change to $\leq$. In order for this change of inequality to occur, c must be negative. In this way, the second inequality can be written as $y \leq -\dfrac{3}{c}x + \dfrac{4}{c}$. As a check, note that with $c < 0$, the slope of $-\dfrac{3}{c}$ is positive and the y-intercept $\dfrac{4}{c}$ is negative. This confirms the properties of line l_2 in the graph. Each of answer choices (A), (B), or (C) would either yield an incorrect solution region or an incorrect description of the given lines.

45. A.

Using DeMoivre's theorem, the number Z can be expressed as $2^4(\cos[4][30]° + i \sin[4][60]°)$ $= 16(\cos 120° + i \sin 120°)$. Then the cube roots of Z can be expressed as $\sqrt[3]{16}(\cos[\dfrac{120 + (k)(360°)}{3}]$ $+ i \sin[\dfrac{120 + (k)(360°)}{3}])$, for $k = 0, 1,$ and 2. Thus, the three cube roots of Z are $\sqrt[3]{16}(\cos 40° + i \sin 40°)$, $\sqrt[3]{16}(\cos 160° + i \sin 160°)$, and $\sqrt[3]{16}(\cos 280° + i \sin 280°)$.

46. B.

The velocity function $v(t)$ is the derivative of $x(t)$, so $v(t) = t^2 + 14t - 3$. We determine that $v(2) = 2^2 + (14)(2) - 3 = 29$ and that $v(6) = 6^2 + (14)(6) - 3 = 117$. Then the average acceleration between $t = 2$ and $t = 6$ is $\dfrac{117 - 29}{6 - 2} = 22$.

47. C.

$\sqrt[3]{72} = (\sqrt[3]{8})(\sqrt[3]{9}) = (2)(\sqrt[3]{9})$ and $\sqrt[3]{1944} = (\sqrt[3]{216})(\sqrt[3]{9}) = (6)(\sqrt[3]{9})$. Therefore, $\sqrt[3]{x} = (6)(\sqrt[3]{9})$

$-(2)(\sqrt[3]{9}) = (4)(\sqrt[3]{9})$. Since $4 = \sqrt[3]{64}$, $x = (64)(9) = 576$.

48. D.

There are four possible sets of factors.
Case 1: $(3x + 7)(x - 1) = 3x^2 + 4x - 7$, which implies that $k = 4$.
Case 2: $(3x - 7)(x + 1) = 3x^2 - 4x - 7$, which implies that $k = -4$.
Case 3: $(3x - 1)(x + 7) = 3x^2 + 20x - 7$, which implies that $k = 20$.
Case 4: $(3x + 1)(x - 7) = 3x^2 - 20x - 7$, which implies that $k = -20$. Since $k > 0$, the only allowable values of k are 4 and 20.

49. C.

Since θ is not in the first quadrant and $\cos \theta > 0$, θ must be in the fourth quadrant. The reference triangle has a horizontal side of 1, a hypotenuse of 4, and a vertical side whose length is $\sqrt{4^2 - 1^2} = \sqrt{15}$. Thus, $\sin \theta = -\dfrac{\sqrt{15}}{4}$.

50. A.

Using the Law of Sines, $\dfrac{a}{\sin \angle A} = \dfrac{b}{\sin \angle B}$. By substitution, $\dfrac{45}{\sin 65°} = \dfrac{26}{\sin \angle B}$. Cross-multiplying, $(45)(\sin \angle B) = (26)(\sin 65°) \approx 23.564$. Thus, $\angle B = \sin^{-1}(\dfrac{23.564}{45}) \approx \sin^{-1}(0.5236) \approx 32°$.

51. C.

Use the formula $\dfrac{dA}{dt} = (\dfrac{dA}{dr}) \times (\dfrac{dr}{dt})$. Since $A = \pi r^2$, $\dfrac{dA}{dr} = 2\pi r$. So, when $r = 3$, $\dfrac{dA}{dr} = 6\pi$. We are given that $\dfrac{dA}{dt} = 10$. Then $10 = 6\pi \times (\dfrac{dr}{dt})$, which means that $\dfrac{dr}{dt} = \dfrac{10}{6\pi} = \dfrac{5}{3\pi}$.

52. D.

$(\dfrac{3}{4})(\dfrac{1}{6} - \dfrac{1}{8}) = (\dfrac{3}{4})(\dfrac{1}{24}) = \dfrac{3}{96} = \dfrac{1}{32}$.

53. D.

If a rational function has no horizontal asymptote, then the degree of the numerator must be greater than the degree of the denominator. The degree of the denominator of $k(x)$ is 6.

54. B.

Since we have the values for two sides and an included angle, we can use the Law of Cosines. So $(JM)^2 = (JL)^2 + (LM)^2 - (2)(JL)(LM)(\cos\angle L)$. By substitution, $(JM)^2 = (10)^2 + (34)^2 - (2)(10)(34)(\cos 127°)$. Simplifying, we get $(JM)^2 = 100 + 1156 - (680)(-0.6018) \approx 1665.22$. Thus, $JM = \sqrt{1665.22} \approx 40.81$.

55. C.

Let $Q = 10^{\log_{10} x}$. Then $\log_{10} Q = \log_{10}(10^{\log_{10} x}) = (\log_{10} x)(\log_{10} 10)$. But $\log_{10} 10 = 1$, which means that $\log_{10} Q = \log_{10} x$. Thus, $Q = x$.

56. D.

Whole numbers consist of all positive integers and zero, so they are mutually exclusive from the set of negative numbers. Answer choice (A) is wrong because all natural numbers are whole numbers. Answer choice (B) is wrong because all repeating decimals are rational numbers. Answer choice (C) is wrong because negative numbers include both rational and irrational numbers.

57. A.

When written in standard form $Ax + By = C$, the equation of each of two parallel lines must be a multiple of the other. Therefore, $qx - 12y = 21$ must be a multiple of $x - py = 7$. Since $21 = (3)(7)$, each coefficient of the second equation must be three times the corresponding coefficient of the first equation. So, $q = (3)(1) = 3$ and $p = \frac{12}{3} = 4$. Thus, $\frac{q}{p} = \frac{3}{4}$.

58. B.

Given a number in prime factorization form, the total number of factors can be found by adding 1 to each exponent, then finding the product of these increased exponents. Then $36 = (m + 1)$

$(2 + 1)(1 + 1)$, which simplifies to $36 = (m + 1)(6)$. Thus, $m + 1 = 6$, so $m = 5$.

59. B.

Since $t = x - 1$, we can write $y = (x - 1)^2 + 5(x - 1) + 1 = x^2 - 2x + 1 + 5x - 5 + 1 = x^2 + 3x - 3$. In the form $y = Ax^2 + Bx + C$, the product of the zeros is $\frac{C}{A}$. Thus, for $y = x^2 + 3x - 3$, the product of its zeros is $\frac{-3}{1} = -3$. Answer choice (A) is wrong because the y-intercept is $(0, -3)$. Answer choice (C) is wrong because when the function is written as $y = (x + \frac{3}{2})^2 - \frac{21}{4}$, the vertex is $(-\frac{3}{2}, -\frac{21}{4})$. Answer choice (D) is wrong because in the form $y = Ax^2 + Bx + C$, the sum of the zeros is $-\frac{B}{A}$. So, the sum of the zeros for $y = x^2 + 3x - 3$ is $-\frac{3}{1} = -3$.

60. C.

By definition, $\sec\theta = -\frac{30}{OR} = -7.5$, so $OR = 4$. Then $RT = \sqrt{30^2 - 4^2} = \sqrt{884} \approx 29.73$. Thus, the coordinates of T are $(-4, -29.73)$.

Constructed-Response Solutions

61.

- For the graph of $y = A\sin(Bx - C) + D$, the lowest function value is represented by $D - A$. Since $A = 1$, we have $Q - 1 = 6$. Thus, $Q = 7$. The period is represented by $\frac{2\pi}{B}$, which becomes $\frac{2\pi}{\frac{1}{2}} = 4\pi$.

- The period is represented by $\frac{2\pi}{C}$, which means that $\frac{2\pi}{C} = 3\pi$. Thus, $C = \frac{2\pi}{3\pi} = \frac{2}{3}$. The highest function value is represented by $D + A$. Therefore, $D + \frac{1}{5} = 2$. Thus, $D = \frac{9}{5}$.

62.

- Using the x values of -1, 0, 1, 2, 3, the five points become $(-1, -6)$, $(0, -1)$, $(1, 3)$, $(2, 10)$, and $(3, 29)$.

- $F(x)$ is not differentiable at $x = 1$ because its limit as x approaches 1 from the left is 4, whereas its limit as x approaches 1 from the right is $1^3 + 2 = 3$. These two limits are not equal.

- For $x \geq 1$, $F'(x) = 3x^2$. Then $F'(2) = 12$, which represents the slope of the tangent line. So, the equation of the tangent line is of the form $y = 12x + b$. Substituting $(2, 10)$ leads to $10 = (12)(2) + b$, so $b = -14$. Thus, the equation of the tangent line is $y = 12x - 14$.

- $F(1) = 3$ and $F(3) = 29$. The slope of the secant line that joins $(1, F(1))$ and $(3, F(3))$ equals $\dfrac{F(3) - F(1)}{3 - 1} = \dfrac{29 - 3}{2} = 13$. Since $F'(c) = 3c^2$ for $1 < c < 3$, this implies that $3c^2 = 13$. Thus, $c = \sqrt{\dfrac{13}{3}} \approx 2.08$.

Practice Test 2
Exam Questions for Mathematics (Code 023)

GACE Mathematics Assessment

ANSWER SHEET FOR PRACTICE TEST 2 (CODE 023)

1 _____   16 _____   31 _____   46 _____

2 _____   17 _____   32 _____   47 _____

3 _____   18 _____   33 _____   48 _____

4 _____   19 _____   34 _____   49 _____

5 _____   20 _____   35 _____   50 _____

6 _____   21 _____   36 _____   51 _____

7 _____   22 _____   37 _____   52 _____

8 _____   23 _____   38 _____   53 _____

9 _____   24 _____   39 _____   54 _____

10 _____   25 _____   40 _____   55 _____

11 _____   26 _____   41 _____   56 _____

12 _____   27 _____   42 _____   57 _____

13 _____   28 _____   43 _____   58 _____

14 _____   29 _____   44 _____   59 _____

15 _____   30 _____   45 _____   60 _____

ANSWER SHEET FOR CONSTRUCTED-RESPONSE QUESTIONS
PRACTICE TEST 2 (023)

1. When Caroline drove from work to home yesterday, she drove at 30 miles per hour for the first 20 minutes, and then rested for 10 minutes. Finally, she drove at 45 miles per hour for the remaining 20 minutes. Which of the following line graphs could represent her trip? (The y-axis represents distance from home and the x-axis represents time.)

A.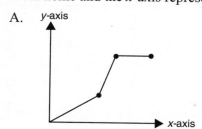

B.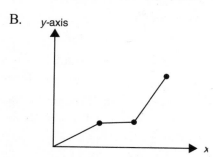

C.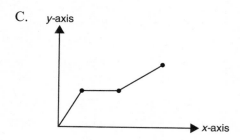

D.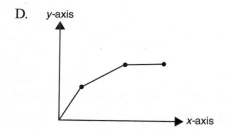

2. In a game of poker, each player is dealt five cards. To the nearest thousandth, what is the probability that a player's hand consists of exactly four diamonds?

A. 0.011

B. 0.009

C. 0.006

D. 0.004

3. If $f(x) = \dfrac{x+3}{2}$, which one of the following statements is true about $f^{-1}(x)$?

A. $f^{-1}(x) = \dfrac{2}{x+3}$

B. $f^{-1}(x) = \dfrac{-x-3}{2}$

C. Its graph is a reflection of the graph of $f(x)$ about the y-axis.

D. Its graph is a reflection of the graph of $f(x)$ about the line $y = x$.

4. In the diagram below, $TUXY$ is a rectangle and $UVWX$ is a square.

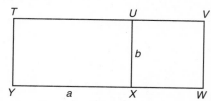

Which expression represents the area of rectangle $TVWY$?

A. $(a + b)^2$

B. $a^2 + b^2$

C. $ab + b^2$

D. $ab + a^2$

5. For inequalities such as $-11x < 44$, the solution is given as $x > -4$. Which rule for reversing the order of inequalities is being used?

A. Division of a smaller coefficient

B. Division of a larger coefficient

C. Division in which the constant term is negative

D. Division in which the coefficient of the variable term is negative

6. In using algebra tiles to demonstrate the factoring of the expression $2x^2 + 13x + 15$, which of the following could represent the composition of one of the six rows of tiles?

A. Three tiles labeled as x^2 and two tiles labeled as x

B. Two tiles labeled as x^2 and three tiles labeled as x

Class	Frequency
9 − 12	3
13 − 16	4
17 − 20	1
21 − 24	12

C. Two tiles labeled as x^2, one tile labeled as x, and two tiles labeled as 1

D. One tile labeled as $2x^2$ and four tiles labeled as 1

7. The diagonals of quadrilateral $ABCD$ bisect each other, but they are not perpendicular to each other. Which of the following could describe $ABCD$?

(A) Square   (C) Rhombus

(B) Pentagon   (D) Rectangle

A. $23.8\overline{3}$ C. $22.8\overline{3}$

B. $23.1\overline{6}$ D. $22.1\overline{6}$

8. Which one of the following equations represents the graph of a parabola whose vertex is its highest point and whose axis of symmetry is $x = 6$?

A. $y = -2(x + 6)^2 + 3$

B. $y = 2(x - 6)^2 + 3$

C. $y = -2(x - 6)^2 - 3$

D. $y = 2(x + 6)^2 - 3$

12. In how many different ways can all the letters of the word "SCHOOLS" be arranged to form a sequence of seven letters?

A. 1260   C. 3780

B. 2520   D. 5040

9. Consider $\triangle DEG$, with angle bisector $\overline{DF}$, as shown below.

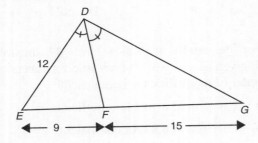

What is the perimeter of $\triangle DEG$?

A. 58.4   C. 54

B. 56   D. 52.6

13. The amount of hot chocolate dispensed in the paper cups of a vending machine is normally distributed, with a mean of 4.5 ounces and a standard deviation of 0.2 ounces. What percent of all the paper cups will have more than 4.8 ounces of hot chocolate? (Nearest tenth of one percent)

A. 6.1%   C. 7.3%

B. 6.7%   D. 7.9%

14. Look at the following diagram.

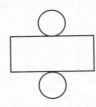

This represents the net of which geometric figure?

A. Cone   C. Cube

B. Cylinder   D. Pyramid

10. The mean weight of 36 apples and oranges is 5.9 ounces. If the mean weight of the 20 apples is 5.5 ounces, what is the mean weight of the oranges?

A. 6.6 ounces   C. 6.4 ounces

B. 6.5 ounces   D. 6.3 ounces

15. Which statement is sufficient to prove that events M and N are dependent?

A. $P(M \mid N) = 1$ C. $P(M) + P(N) < 1$

B. $P(M) + P(N) = 1$ D. $P(M \mid N) = P(M)$

11. What is the value of the third quartile for the following grouped frequency distribution?

16. Consider the following three statements. The greatest common factor of 9 and 10 is 1. The greatest common factor of 16 and 17 is 1. The greatest common factor of 102 and 103 is 1. Which conclusion would be valid by using the process of induction?

    A. The product of any two consecutive numbers is an integer.

    B. The greatest common factor of any two integers is 1.

    C. The difference of any two integers is less than either integer.

    D. The greatest common factor of any two consecutive integers is 1.

17. What type of figure is formed by the intersection of a plane and a cone such that the plane is parallel to the base of the cone, but does not pass through the vertex?

    A. Circle   C. Hyperbola

    B. Ellipse   D. Parabola

18. In a geometry class, a teacher may need to have a set of Pythagorean triples handy in order to present examples and exercises on the Pythagorean theorem. Knowing that 3, 4, and 5 represent the smallest group of Pythagorean triples, how do you generate other related Pythagorean triples?

    A. Multiply these numbers by any positive integer greater than 1.

    B. Square each of these numbers.

    C. Add a fixed number to each of these numbers.

    D. Multiply these numbers by squared numbers only.

19. Point A is reflected across the line $y = -x$ so that the coordinates of its image point are $(-3, 7)$. What are the coordinates of A?

    A. $(7, 3)$ C. $(-7, -3)$

    B. $(7, -3)$ D. $(-7, 3)$

20. A population is normally distributed with a mean of 60 and a standard deviation of 9. A distribution (V) consists of all sample means of size 25. Which of the following is <u>completely</u> correct for the mean and standard deviation of V?

    A. Mean = 12 and standard deviation $= \dfrac{3}{25}$.

    B. Mean = 12 and standard deviation $= \dfrac{9}{5}$.

    C. Mean = 60 and standard deviation $= \dfrac{3}{25}$.

    D. Mean = 60 and standard deviation $= \dfrac{9}{5}$.

21. You are given the information that for a non-zero integer x, $\dfrac{3x+6}{x}$ is a positive integer. Which one of the following approaches would be best in order to find the value of x?

    A. $\dfrac{3x+6}{x} = m$, where m is an integer.

    B. $\dfrac{3x+6}{x} = \dfrac{m}{n}$, where m is divisible by n.

    C. $\dfrac{3x+6}{x} = \dfrac{3x}{x} + \dfrac{6}{x}$

    D. $\dfrac{3x+6}{x} = \dfrac{3(x+2)}{x}$

22. The radius of a circle is 10 inches. If the area of a sector is 35π square inches, what is the measure, in degrees, of the central angle?

    A. $126°$ C. $114°$

    B. $120°$ D. $108°$

23. For which one of the following set of conditions must the T-Test be used in creating a confidence interval for an unknown population mean?

    A. The sample size is greater than 30 and the population standard deviation is unknown.

    B. The sample size is greater than 30, the population is normally distributed and the population standard deviation is known.

C. The sample size is less than 30, the population is normally distributed, and the population standard deviation is unknown.

D. The sample size is less than 30 and the population is not normally distributed.

24. For a normally distributed population, which of the following is the closest approximation to the percent of data within two standard deviations of the mean?

(A) 85%   (C) 95%

(B) 90%   (D) 98%

25. Nick drives from home to work, a distance of 15 miles, in 20 minutes. What is his speed in yards per second?

A. 1320   C. 132

B. 440   D. 22

26. Which shortcut could a student use to multiply 48 by 52 using mental math?

A. the sum of cubes

B. the difference of cubes

C. the sum of squares

D. the difference of squares

27. Each face of a cube is sliced along dotted lines to produce a number of smaller cubes, as shown below.

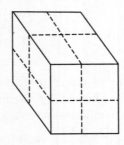

If the total surface area of all the smaller cubes is 300 square inches, what is the volume of one of the smaller cubes, in cubic inches to the nearest tenth?

A. 10.4   C. 29.7

B. 15.6   D. 42.9

28. Look at the following boxplot.

Which statement concerning this distribution must be true?

A. It is positively skewed.

B. It is negatively skewed.

C. Its mean is 32.

D. Its interquartile range is 37.

29. A national toy distributor uses the mathematical model $f(x) = -.064x^2 + x + 12$ to gauge advertising costs versus units sold (in millions) for a new doll. Using this model, what is the maximum sales volume for this doll?

A. 9.2 million   C. 15.9 million

B. 10.2 million   D. 17.2 million

30. What are the equations of the asymptotes for the curve whose equation is $\dfrac{(x-3)^2}{16} - \dfrac{y^2}{25} = 1$?

A. $y - 3 = \pm\dfrac{4}{5}x$ C. $y - 3 = \pm\dfrac{5}{4}x$

B. $y = \pm\dfrac{4}{5}(x-3)$ D. $y = \pm\dfrac{5}{4}(x-3)$

31. The line segment with endpoints $(2, 7)$ and $(-6, 1)$ is rotated 90° clockwise. If M is the midpoint of the original line segment, what are the coordinates of M'?

A. $(-4, -2)$ C. $(2, -4)$

B. $(4, 2)$ D. $(-2, 4)$

32. Suppose X represents a set of ten individual numbers. Each number is then multiplied by four then subtracted by two. This new set of ten individual numbers is represented by Y. The variance of set Y is 9. What is the variance of set X?

A. $\dfrac{1}{16}$ C. $\dfrac{4}{9}$

B. $\dfrac{1}{4}$ D. $\dfrac{9}{16}$

33. In the following diagram, P is the center of the circle.

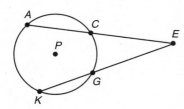

If $EC = 15$, $AC = 12$, and $EG = (2)(GK)$, then to the nearest tenth, what is the value of GK?

A. 7.5   C. 10.7

B. 8.2   D. 11.6

34. In the literal equation $ax + b = 5$, where a and b are constants, what is the most direct approach in solving for x?

A Subtract b from 5, then divide by a.

B. Square both sides of the equation, then isolate x.

C. Assume that $b = 1$, then isolate x.

D. Combine $ax + b$ into the single term axb, then divide 5 by ab.

35. At the XYZ company, each employee is given an identification badge. From left to right, the badge consists of two different letters, followed by three different digits. The only other restriction is that zero must not appear as one of the digits. Consider the following eight potential identification badges: AB987, RR346, 213MN, LK344, J9K25, WR697, MT148, and GH502. How many of these would not be legitimate identification badges?

A. 6   C. 4

B. 5   D. 3

36. Mr. Griffin would like to divide his class into groups of the same size. If he divides the class into groups of six, there will be two students left over. Assuming that the class size is between 15 and 36, how many possibilities are there for the number of students in Mr. Griffin's class?

A. 2   C. 4

B. 3   D. 5

37. Given a normal distribution of data, a sample is extracted. If the inequality $30 - (1.96)(\frac{5}{\sqrt{100}}) < \mu < 30 + (1.96)(\frac{5}{\sqrt{100}})$ represents a 95% confidence interval for the mean of the population, which one of the following is completely true about this sample?

A. There are 100 data and the sample mean is 5.

B. There are 10 data and the sample standard deviation is 5.

C. The sample mean is 5 and the number of data is 30.

D. The sample mean is 30 and the sample standard deviation is 5.

38. Ms. Taylor gave her statistics class a quiz. The results showed that the mean grade was 76 and the standard deviation was 6. Each student was given a z-score grade. If Tommy's z-score grade was 2.5, what was his actual grade?

A. 91   C. 85

B. 88   D. 82

39. A room contains 20 people, for which the mean weight is 150 pounds. When two people leave the room, the mean weight for the remaining 18 people is 145 pounds. Which of the following is the correct way to calculate the mean weight of the two people who left?

A. Calculate $(20 - 18)(150 - 145)$, then multiply this product by 20.

B. Calculate $(20)(150) + (2)(145)$, then divide this sum by 18.

C. Calculate $(20)(150) - (18)(145)$, then divide this difference by 2.

D. Calculate $(\frac{20+18}{2})(\frac{145+150}{2})$, then divide this product by 20.

40. An experiment consists of rolling a seven-sided die twice. The faces of the die are numbered 1, 2, 3, 4, 5, 6, 7. The event of getting an odd number on both rolls contains how many different outcomes?

A. 49   C. 14

B. 16   D. 8

41. An ordinary six-sided die is rolled. To the nearest hundredth, what is the probability that the first time that a "2" appears is on the fifth roll?

A. 0.14   C. 0.10

B. 0.12   D. 0.08

42. Given the equation $2x^3 - x^2 - 14x - 56 = 0$, a teacher wishes to show her class the quickest way to identify possible rational roots. How should this be accomplished?

A. List all factors in the form $\frac{p}{q}$, for which p is a factor of 2 and q is a factor of 56.

B. List all factors in the form $\frac{p}{q}$, for which p is a factor of 56 and q is a factor of 2.

C. List all factors in the form pq, for which p is a factor of 2 and q is a factor of 14.

D. List all factors in the form $p + q$, for which p is a factor of 14 and q is a factor of 56.

43. Which equation represents the graph of an ellipse that has a vertical major axis of length 12?

(A) $\dfrac{x^2}{16} + \dfrac{y^2}{36} = 1$ (C) $\dfrac{x^2}{144} + \dfrac{y^2}{64} = 1$

(B) $\dfrac{x^2}{36} + \dfrac{y^2}{16} = 1$ (D) $\dfrac{x^2}{64} + \dfrac{y^2}{144} = 1$

44. Consider the following three statements: One pax is worth five pexes. One pex is worth two pyxes. One pix is worth four pyxes. Which of the following shows the correct order of the value of each of these, from lowest to highest?

(A) pyx, pex, pax, pix

(B) pyx, pix, pax, pex

(C) pyx, pix, pex, pax

(D) pyx, pex, pix, pax

45. A scale factor of $\frac{3}{5}$ is applied to $\triangle TUV$ in creating $\triangle XYZ$. The area of $\triangle TUV$ is 30. What is the area of $\triangle XYZ$?

A. 10.8   C. 50

B. 18   D. $83.\overline{3}$

46. Consider the following stem-and-leaf plot.

```
1 | 2 3 4
2 | 0 0 1 6
3 | 1 6 9
4 | 5 7
```

What percent of the data lies above the mean?

A. 50%   C. $33\frac{1}{3}$%

B. $41\frac{2}{3}$%   (D) 25%

47. The probability that event M will occur is 0.24 and the probability that event N will occur is 0.42. If the probability that at least one of M and N will occur is 0.57, what is the probability that both M and N will occur?

A. 0.04   C. 0.30

B. 0.09   D. 0.39

48. What is the equation of an ellipse with its center located at $(6, 0)$, a horizontal major axis of length 14, and a minor axis of length 8?

A. $\dfrac{(x-6)^2}{49} + \dfrac{y^2}{16} = 1$

B. $\dfrac{(x+6)^2}{49} + \dfrac{y^2}{16} = 1$

C. $\dfrac{(x-6)^2}{16} + \dfrac{y^2}{49} = 1$

D. $\dfrac{(x+6)^2}{16} + \dfrac{y^2}{49} = 1$

49. Point A is located at $(-2, 1)$ and point B is located at $(-6, 2)$. Line l is perpendicular to $\overleftrightarrow{AB}$ and contains the point $(0, 6)$. What is the x-coordinate of the point of intersection of $\overleftrightarrow{AB}$ and l?

A. $-\dfrac{26}{15}$ C. $-\dfrac{22}{15}$

B. $-\dfrac{26}{17}$ D. $-\dfrac{22}{17}$

A. $\dfrac{12}{35}$ C. $\dfrac{1}{7}$

B. $\dfrac{1}{5}$ D. $\dfrac{4}{35}$

50. Among all auto shops in Nebraska, a claim has been made that the mean time needed to rotate the tires on a car is 16 minutes. Recently, a study of 20 auto shops revealed a mean time of 17 minutes, with a sample standard deviation of 1.5 minutes. At the 1% level of confidence, which one of the following conclusions is correct?

A. The p value is 0.003 and the claim of $\mu_0 = 16$ is rejected.

B. The p value is 0.003 and the claim of $\mu_0 = 16$ cannot be rejected.

C. The p value is 0.008 and the claim of $\mu_0 = 16$ is rejected.

D. The p value is 0.008 and the claim of $\mu_0 = 16$ cannot be rejected.

51. The area of a rhombus is 240 square inches. The length of one diagonal is three times the length of the other diagonal. To the nearest tenth, what is the sum of the lengths of the diagonals?

A. 36.8   C. 50.6

B. 43.7   D. 57.5

52. Look at the following Venn diagram.

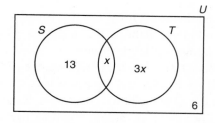

The Universal Set (U) represents the students in a ninth grade class consisting of of 35 students. S represents the students who enjoy mathematics and T represents the students who enjoy history. A student is randomly selected. What is the probability that this student enjoys history but does not enjoy mathermatics?

53. Two cones are similar and the volume of the smaller cone is 54 cubic meters. If the ratio of their areas is $\dfrac{9}{25}$, what is the volume of the larger cone?

A. 100 cubic meters

B. 150 cubic meters

C   200 cubic meters

D. 250 cubic meters

54. How many four-digit numbers are possible in which the following three conditions hold?

(a) The leftmost digit cannot be zero.

(b) No digit may be 5.

(c) There is no repetition of any digit.

A. 5832   C. 2688

B. 3024   D. 1680

55. If a grouped frequency distribution is negatively skewed, which one of the following inequalities is correct?

A. mean < mode < median

B. mean < median < mode

C. median < mode < mean

D. median < mean < mode

56. The function $f(x) = 3x^2 - x$ is translated two units to the left and one unit up to become $g(x)$. Which of the following represents $g(x)$?

(A) $3x^2 - 13x + 15$ (C) $3x^2 - 11x - 15$

(B) $3x^2 + 11x + 11$ (D) $3x^2 + 13x + 11$

57. Triangle TUV is acute and isosceles. If the measure of $\angle T$ is 42°, what conclusion can be reached about the measure of $\angle U$?

A. It must be 42°

B. It may be either 42° or 69°

C.   It must be 69°

D.   It must be more than 90°

58. Which of the following could represent the correct situation for the equation $(0.50)(6) + (0.65)(x) = (0.55)(6 + x)$?

A.   A bike is traveling for 0.50 hours. What is the required speed, in miles per hour for the next 0.65 miles in order for the trip to take 0.55 hours?

B.   A bike is traveling for 6 hours and goes 0.50 miles. What is the time required if the distance is increased to $0.65 + 0.55$ miles?

C.   How many pounds of cashews at $0.65 per pound must be removed from a 6-pound mixture of peanuts and cashews worth $0.50 per pound to produce a mixture worth $0.55 per pound?

D.   How many pounds of cashews at $0.65 per pound must be added to 6 pounds of peanuts at $0.50 per pound in order to produce a mixture worth $0.55 per pound?

59. A rectangular prism has a height of 24 cm., a width of 20cm., and a volume of 7200 cubic cm. What is the surface area, in square centimeters?

A.   880   C.   2280

B.   1140   D.   4560

60. At High Tech High School, 32% of the students are in the freshman class, 25% are in the sopho-more class, 16% are in the junior class, and the remaining students are in the senior class. Using a pie graph, to the nearest degree, how many de-grees are in the central angle that represents the students in the senior class?

A.   93°   C.   97°

B.   95°   D.   99°

Constructed-Response Questions

61. In the diagram below, isosceles trapezoid *DFHJ* is similar to isosceles trapezoid *MPRT*. They both represent two floors on which carpets will be placed. The dimensions given are in units of feet.

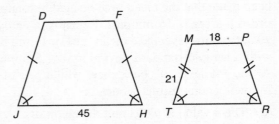

*   If the ratio of the area of *DFHJ* to that of *MPRT* is $\dfrac{25}{9}$, determine the perimeter of trapezoid *MPRT*.
*   Carpets cost $5 per <u>square</u> <u>yard</u>. If the cost to carpet *DFHJ* is $750, find the measure of the height of *DFHJ*.

62. An elementary school teacher brings a set of blocks to her class. The chart below shows the number of blocks of each color and shape. The total number of blocks is 35, of which 20 are blue. One block will be randomly drawn.

	Square	Round	Triangular
Blue	10	6	x
Yellow	5	y	2

*   Find the probability that it is round and yellow.
*   Find the probability that it is blue, given that it is known to be triangular.
*   The teacher decides to remove one of the round yellow blocks and replace it with a round blue block. One block will be drawn. Find the prob-ability that it is square or yellow, but not both.

ANSWER KEY – MATHEMATICS PRACTICE TEST 2 (023)

Question	Answer	Objective	Description
1	B	0015	Representations of Math Concepts
2	A	0013	Applications of Probability
3	D	0015	Representations of Math Concepts
4	C	0009	Measurement
5	D	0015	Representations of Math Concepts
6	B	0016	Mathematical Reasoning
7	D	0010	Euclidean Geometry
8	C	0011	Coordinate, Transform. Geometry
9	B	0010	Euclidean Geometry
10	C	0012	Collection and Description of Data
11	C	0012	Collection and Description of Data
12	A	0013	Applications of Probability
13	B	0014	Statistical Inference
14	B	0009	Measurement
15	A	0013	Applications of Probability
16	D	0016	Mathematical Reasoning
17	A	0009	Measurement
18	A	0016	Euclidean Geometry
19	D	0011	Coordinate, Transform. Geometry
20	D	0014	Statistical Inference
21	C	0016	Mathematical Reasoning
22	A	0009	Measurement
23	C	0014	Statistical Inference
24	C	0014	Statistical Inference
25	D	0009	Measurement
26	D	0016	Mathematical Reasoning
27	B	0009	Measurement

Question	Answer	Objective	Description
28	B	0012	Collection and Description of Data
29	C	0015	Representations of Math Concepts
30	D	0011	Coordinate, Transform. Geometry
31	B	0011	Coordinate, Transform. Geometry
32	D	0012	Collection and Description of Data
33	B	0010	Euclidean Geometry
34	A	0016	Mathematical Reasoning
35	B	0015	Representations of Math Concepts
36	B	0015	Representations of Math Concepts
37	D	0014	Statistical Inference
38	A	0014	Statistical Inference
39	C	0015	Statistical Inference
40	B	0013	Applications of Probability
41	D	0013	Applications of Probability
42	B	0016	Statistical Inference
43	A	0011	Coordinate, Transform. Geometry
44	D	0016	Mathematical Reasoning
45	A	0009	Measurement
46	B	0012	Collection and Description of Data
47	B	0013	Applications of Probability
48	A	0011	Coordinate, Transform. Geometry
49	D	0011	Coordinate, Transform. Geometry
50	C	0014	Statistical Inference
51	C	0010	Euclidean Geometry
52	A	0013	Applications of Probability
53	D	0009	Measurement
54	C	0013	Applications of Probability
55	B	0012	Collection and Description of Data

Question	Answer	Objective	Description
56	B	0011	Coordinate, Transform. Geometry
57	C	0010	Euclidean Geometry
58	D	0015	Representations of Math Concepts
59	C	0009	Measurement
60	C	0012	Collection and Description of Data
61	C-R	0009	Measurement
62	C-R	0013	Applications of Probability

Objectives Checklist – Practice Test 2 – Code 023
Multiple-Choice Questions

Objective 0009   _____/9

4	14	17	22	25	27	45	53	59

Objective 0010   _____/5

7	9	33	51	57

Objective 0011   _____/8

8	19	30	31	43	48	49	56

Objective 0012   _____/7

10	11	28	32	46	55	60

Objective 0013   _____/8

2	12	15	40	41	47	52	54

Objective   0014   ____/7

13	20	23	24	37	38	50

Objective   0015   ____/8

1	3	5	29	35	36	39	58

Objective   0016   ____/8

6	16	18	21	26	34	42	44

Objectives Checklist − Practice Test 2 − Code 022
Constructed-Response Questions

Objective   0009   _____ First Bullet, _____ Second Bullet.

61

Objective   0013   _____ First Bullet, _____ Second Bullet _____ Third Bullet

62

DETAILED SOLUTIONS: PRACTICE TEST 2 (023)

1. (B)

The slope of the first line segment shows Caroline traveling for a distance at 30 miles per hour. Since she rested for some time, the second line segment must be horizontal. Finally, her speed increased to 45 miles per hour for the last part of the trip. Since 45 is greater than 30, the slope of the third line segment must be steeper than that of the first line segment.

2. (A)

There are 13 diamonds in a deck of cards, so the required probability is found by using the Hypergeometric distribution $\frac{(_{13}C_4)(_{39}C_1)}{_{52}C_5} \approx 0.011$.

3. (D)

For any point (x, y) that belongs to the graph of $f(x)$, the point (y, x) must belong to the graph of $f^{-1}(x)$. Thus, the graph of $f^{-1}(x)$ must be a reflection of the graph of $f(x)$ over the line $y = x$. (The expression for $f^{-1}(x)$ is $2x - 3$.)

4. (C)

Since $UX = b$, the area of $TUXY$ is ab and the area of $UVWX$ is b^2. Thus, the area of $TVWY$ is the sum of these two pieces, which is $ab + b^2$.

5. (D)

Whenever an inequality contains a variable term that has a negative coefficient, operations of multiplication or division require that the order of inequality be reversed.

6. (B)

Here is how the tiles should appear:

	X	X	I	I	I
X	X^2	X^2	X	X	X
I	X	X	I	I	I
I	X	X	I	I	I
I	X	X	I	I	I
I	X	X	I	I	I
I	X	X	I	I	I

In this formation, the tiles in a row appear as either two labeled x^2 and three labeled x, or as two labeled x and three labeled as 1. If the rows and columns are switched, then the rows are labeled as follows: one labeled as x^2 and five labeled as x, or one labeled as x and five labeled as 1.

7. (D)

$ABCD$ could be either a general parallelogram or a rectangle. In a square and a rhombus, the diagonals are perpendicular to each other. A pentagon is not a quadrilateral.

8. (C)

In the form $y = a(x - h)^2 + k$, the axis of symmetry is $x = h$. If $a < 0$, the parabola has a highest point.

9. (B)

Since $\overline{DF}$ is an angle bisector, $\frac{12}{9} = \frac{DG}{15}$. Then $DG = \frac{180}{9} = 20$. Thus, the perimeter of ΔDEG is $12 + 9 + 15 + 20 = 56$.

10. (C)

The total weight of the oranges is $(36)(5.9) - (20)(5.5) = 102.4$ ounces. Thus, the mean weight of the oranges is $\frac{102.4}{16} = 6.4$ ounces.

11. (C)

The third quartile is the 15th number, so its value is $20.5 + (\frac{15-8}{12})(4) = 22.8\overline{3}$.

12. (A)

There are seven letters, including two s's and two o's. The total number of arrangements is $\frac{7!}{(2!)(2!)} = 1260$.

13. (B)

Your TI − 83 calculator screen should read as follows. "normalcdf (4.8, 1 × 10⁹⁹, 4.5, 0.2)." By pressing "Enter," the result is approximately 6.7%.

14. (B)

The net of a cylinder consists of a rectangle and two circles.

15. (A)

If $P(M \mid N) = 1$, then the probability of M occurring is a certainty, given that N has occurred. This implies that the two events are dependent.

16. (D)

The three given statements demonstrate that the greatest common factor of any two consecutive integers is 1.

17. (A)

As a plane parallel to the base of a cone passes through the cone, but not at the vertex, the intersection is a circle.

18. (A)

Let m be an arbitrary positive integer. Then multiplying the numbers 3, 4, and 5 by m results in $3m$, $4m$, and $5m$. Applying the Pythagorean theorem to these numbers gives $(5m)^2 = (3m)^2 + (4m)^2$, which leads to $25m^2 = 9m^2 + 16m^2$, or more simply, $25 = 9 + 16$. The result indicates that the generated numbers satisfy the Pythagorean theorem.

19. (D)

When a point (x, y) is reflected across the line $y = -x$, the coordinates of its image become $(-y, -x)$. Thus, the pre-image of $(-3, 7)$ is $(-7, 3)$.

20. (D)

The mean of V is identical to the mean of the population and the standard deviation of V equals the standard deviation of the population divided by the square root of the common size of each sample size. Thus, the mean of V is 60 and the standard deviation of V is $\frac{9}{\sqrt{25}} = \frac{9}{5}$.

21. (C)

Using the decomposition method, we get $\frac{3x + 6}{x} = \frac{3x}{x} + \frac{6}{x}$. This yields $3 + \frac{6}{x}$. Then, x must be 1, 2, 3, or 6 in order for $3 + \frac{6}{x}$ to be a positive integer.

22. (A)

The area of the circle is $(\pi)(10^2) = 100\pi$. Let x represent the measure of the central angle. Then $\frac{35\pi}{100\pi} = \frac{x}{360°}$. Thus, $x = \frac{(35\pi)(360°)}{100\pi} = 126°$.

23. (C)

The conditions for using the T-Test are the following: a) sample size under 30, b) normal distribution for the population, and c) the value of σ unknown. Note that answer choice (D) would not allow the use of either the T-Test or the Z-Test.

24. (C)

Using the TI-83 calculator, press "2nd," "Distr," and the number 2. Then enter the numbers −2, 2, 0, 1. End with a right parenthesis and press "Enter." The entry on the screen will be approximately 0.95.

25. (D)

Fifteen miles in 20 minutes is equivalent to $\frac{15}{20} = 0.75$ miles per minute. Then 0.75 miles per minute is equivalent to $\frac{0.75}{60} = 0.0125$ miles per second. Finally, 0.0125 miles is equivalent to $(0.0125)(1760) = 22$ yards.

26. (D)

The difference of squares, $a^2 - b^2$, can be used to calculate $(48)(52)$. $(50 - 2)(50 + 2) = 2500 - 4 = 2496$.

27. (B)

When the large cube is sliced, there will be a total of 8 smaller cubes. Let s represent the length of one side of a smaller cube. Since the total surface area is 300, $(8)(6s^2) = 300$. Then $s^2 = 6.25$, so $s = 2.5$. Thus, the volume is $2.5^3 \approx 15.6$.

28. (B)

When the x value of the left tail of a boxplot is longer than its right tail, the distribution is negatively skewed.

29. (C)

Find the x value of the vertex by using the expression $\frac{-b}{2a}$. $\frac{-b}{2a} = \frac{-1}{2(-.064)} \approx 7.8$ million.

Place 7.8 (million) into the formula to find the units sold. $f(x) = -.064(7.8)^2 + 7.8 + 12 = 15.9$. The toy company will spend \$7.8 million in advertising to reach a peak sales volume of 15.9 million dolls.

30. (D)

For the general hyperbola $\frac{(x-h)^2}{a^2} - \frac{(y-k)^2}{b^2} = 1$, the equations of the asymptotes are $y - k = \pm\frac{b}{a}(x - h)$. In this example, $k = 0$, $h =$

3, $a = 4$, and $b = 5$. Thus, the equations of the asymptotes are $y = \pm\frac{5}{4}(x - 3)$.

31. (B)

The coordinates of M are $(-2, 4)$. A 90°-clockwise rotation changes a point with coordinates of (x, y) to its image with coordinates of $(y, -x)$. Thus, the image of $(-2, 4)$ is $(4, 2)$.

32. (D)

$Y = 4X - 2$. Then the variance of Y is $4^2 = 16$ times the variance of X. Thus, the variance of X is $(\frac{1}{16})$(the variance of Y) $= \frac{9}{16}$.

33. (B)

$EA = 27$ and letting $x = GK$ and $2x = EG$, we can represent EK by $3x$. Then $(27)(15) = (3x)(2x) = 6x^2$. Then $x^2 = 67.5$, so $x \approx 8.2$.

34. (A)

The most direct approach is to subtract b from 5, which results in $ax = 5 - b$. The final step is to divide by a, which yields the solution $x = \frac{5-b}{a}$.

35. (B)

The five that would not qualify for identification badges are RR346, 213MN, LK344, J9K25, and GH502.

36. (B)

The only three possibilities for the size of Mr. Griffin's class are 20, 26, and 32. When each of these numbers is divided by 6, the remainder is 2.

37. (D)

A 95% confidence interval for the mean of the population is given in the form $\overline{x} - (1.96)(\frac{s}{\sqrt{n}}) < \mu < \overline{x} + (1.96)(\frac{s}{\sqrt{n}})$, where $\overline{x}$

is the sample mean, s is the sample standard deviation, and n is the size of the sample.

38. (A)

Let x represent Tommy's actual grade. Then $x = 76 + (2.5)(6) = 91$.

39. (C)

Find the total weight of all 20 people, then subtract the total weight of the remaining 18 people. This difference represents the combined weight of the two people who left. Finally, divide this combined weight by 2 in order to find the mean weight of these two people, which is 195 pounds.

40. (B)

Any one of the four odd numbers may appear on each roll, so the number of outcomes is $(4)(4) = 16$.

41. (D)

This is a geometric distribution in which $p = \frac{1}{6}$. Thus, the required probability is $(\frac{1}{6})(\frac{5}{6})^4 \approx 0.08$.

42. (B)

The only possible rational roots can be written in the form $\frac{p}{q}$, where p is a factor of 56 and q is a factor of 2.

43. (A)

If $a > b$, then $\frac{x^2}{b^2} + \frac{y^2}{a^2} = 1$ represents the equation of an ellipse with a vertical major axis with a length of $2a$. Given that $2a = 12$, it follows that $a^2 = 36$. Only answer choice (A) has both 36 as the value of a^2 and has a value lower than 36 for b^2.

44. (D)

Suppose a pyx were worth one cent. Then one pex would be worth two cents and one pix would be worth four cents. In addition, one pax would be worth ten cents. Thus, the correct order

of their values from lowest to highest are: pyx, pex, pix, pax.

45. (A)

The ratio of the areas from $\triangle XYZ$ to $\triangle TUV$ is $(\frac{3}{5})^2 = \frac{9}{25}$. Let x represent the area of $\triangle XYZ$. Then $\frac{x}{30} = \frac{9}{25}$, so $x = 10.8$.

46. (B)

The mean is $\dfrac{12+13+14+20+20+21 \\ +26+31+36+39+45+47}{12} = 27$.

There are five values greater than 27, so the required percent is $\frac{5}{12} = 41\frac{2}{3}\%$.

47. (B)

The probability that at least one of M and N will occur, written as $P(M \cup N)$, is given by the formula $P(M \cup N) = P(M) + P(N) - P(M \cap N)$, where $P(M \cap N)$ represents the probability that both M and N occur. By substitution, $0.57 = 0.24 + 0.42 - P(M \cap N)$. Thus, $P(M \cap N) = 0.24 + 0.42 - 0.57 = 0.09$.

48. (A)

The equation of an ellipse whose center is located at (h, k) and that has a horizontal major axis is $\frac{(x-h)^2}{a^2} + \frac{(y-k)^2}{b^2} = 1$. The length of the major axis is $2a$ and the length of the minor axis is $2b$. For this question, $a = 7$, $b = 4$, $h = 6$, and $k = 0$.

49. (D)

The slope of $\overrightarrow{AB}$ is $\frac{2-1}{-6+2} = -\frac{1}{4}$. Using point A, $1 = (-\frac{1}{4})(-2) + b$, so $b = \frac{1}{2}$. The equation of $\overrightarrow{AB}$ is $y = -\frac{1}{4}x + \frac{1}{2}$. The slope of l must be the negative reciprocal of $-\frac{1}{4}$, which is 4. Since the y-intercept of l is 6, the equation of l is $y = 4x + 6$. To find the point of intersection, we solve $-\dfrac{1}{4}x + \dfrac{1}{2} = 4x + 6$. Then $\dfrac{17}{4}x = -\dfrac{11}{2}$, so $x = (-\dfrac{11}{2})(\dfrac{4}{17}) = -\dfrac{22}{17}$.

50. (C)

Press "Stat," scroll to "Tests," press 2, then enter 16 for μ_0, enter 17 for $\bar{x}$, enter 1.5 for $s_{\bar{x}}$, enter 20 for n, highlight $\mu_0 \neq \mu_0$, then press "Calculate." The p value will be approximately 0.008, and since $0.008 < 0.01$, the claim is rejected.

51. (C)

Let x and $3x$ represent the lengths of the diagonals. Then, $(\dfrac{1}{2})(x)(3x) = 240$. This equation simplifies to $x^2 = 160$, so $x \approx 12.65$ and $3x \approx 37.95$. Thus, their sum is approximately 50.6.

52. (A)

The required number of students who enjoy history but not mathematics is the value of $3x$. The total number of students, which is 35, is represented by the sum of 13, x, $3x$, and 6. Thus, $13 + x + 3x + 6 = 35$. This equation simplifies to $4x = 35 - 6 - 13 = 16$. Then $x = 4$, so $3x = 12$. Therefore, the required probability is $\dfrac{12}{35}$.

53. (D)

The ratio of their corresponding linear dimensions is $\sqrt{\dfrac{9}{25}} = \dfrac{3}{5}$, so the ratio of their volumes must be $(\dfrac{3}{5})^3 = \dfrac{27}{125}$. Let v represent the volume of the larger cone. Then $\dfrac{27}{125} = \dfrac{54}{v}$, so $v = 250$.

54. (C)

Since neither zero nor 5 may appear in the leftmost position, there are eight choices for the leftmost digit. The next selection also has eight choices, since it will exclude both 5 and the digit used for the leftmost digit. Each succeeding selection will have one less choice. So, the third selection has seven choices and the final selection has six choices. The answer becomes $(8)(8)(7)(6) = 2688$.

55. (B)

In a negatively skewed distribution, the frequencies of the higher numbers tend to be larger than those of the lower numbers. This implies that the mean is less than the median, which is less than the mode.

56. (B)

By translating $f(x)$ two units to the left and one unit up, the function becomes $3(x + 2)^2 - (x + 2) + 1 = 3x^2 + 12x + 12 - x - 2 + 1 = 3x^2 + 11x + 11$.

57. (C)

If the measure of $\angle U$ is 69°, then the measure of $\angle V$ is $180° - 69° - 42° = 69°$. So triangle TUV would be isosceles and scalene. Note that $\angle U$ cannot be 42°, since this would mean that $\angle V$ would be $180° - 42° - 42° = 96°$, an obtuse angle.

58. (D)

Let x represents the number of pounds of cashews needed. The value of the peanuts is $(\$0.50)(6)$ and the value of the cashews is $(\$0.65)(x)$. The mixture will contain $6 + x$ pounds, so its value will be $(\$0.55)(6 + x)$.

59. (C)

The height is equal to $\dfrac{7200}{(24)(20)} = 15$ cm. Thus, the surface area is $(2)(15)(20) + (2)(15)(24) + (2)(20)(24) = 2280$ cubic cm.

60. (C)

The percent of students in the senior class is $100 - 32 - 25 - 16 = 27\%$. Thus, the measure of the central angle is $(0.27)(360°) \approx 97°$.

Constructed-Response Solutions

61.

- The ratio of the corresponding sides of $DFHJ$ to $MPRT$ is $\sqrt{\dfrac{25}{9}} = \dfrac{5}{3}$. Then $\dfrac{5}{3} = \dfrac{45}{TR}$. By cross-multiplying, we get $(5)(TR) = 135$, so $TR = 27$ feet. Thus, the perimeter of $MPRT$ is $21 + 18 + 21 + 27 = 87$ feet.

- The area of $DFHJ$ is $\dfrac{\$750}{\$5} = 150$ square yards, which is equivalent to 1350 square feet. (1 square yard is equivalent to 9 square feet.) Next, we determine the value of DF by using the proportion $\dfrac{DF}{18} = \dfrac{45}{27}$. By cross-multiplying, $(27)(DF) = 810$, which means that $DF = 30$ feet. Finally, let x represent the height of $DFHJ$. Then $1350 = (\dfrac{1}{2})(x)(45+30)$. This equation simplifies to $1350 = 37.5x$; thus, $x = 36$ feet.

62.

- The value of x is $20 - 10 - 6 = 4$. There are $35 - 20 = 15$ yellow blocks, so the value of y is $15 - 5 - 2 = 8$. Thus, the required probability is $\dfrac{8}{35}$.

- Since $x = 4$, there are 6 triangular blocks. Thus, the required probability is $\dfrac{4}{6}$, which reduces to $\dfrac{2}{3}$.

- After the replacement, there will be 7 round blue and 7 round yellow blocks. The number of blocks that are square or yellow but not both become $10 + 7 + 2 = 19$. Thus, the required probability is $\dfrac{19}{35}$.

Index

Table of Contents

Unit 6 Study Skills

Final Reviews

Lesson

Synonyms and Antonyms

■ A **synonym** is a word that has the same or nearly the same meaning as one or more other words.   EXAMPLES: sick – ill   sad – unhappy

A. Write a synonym for each word below.

1. discover _____
2. ridiculous _____
3. difficult _____

4. weary _____
5. beautiful _____
6. inquire _____

7. capable _____
8. funny _____
9. honest _____

B. Rewrite the following sentences, using synonyms for the underlined words.

1. The vacant lot became the neighborhood playground.

_____

2. His broken leg slowly began to mend.

_____

3. The Barkers returned from their trip weary, but happy.

_____

4. The energetic dog bounded across the lawn.

_____

■ An **antonym** is a word that has the opposite meaning of another word.
EXAMPLES: high – low   giant – tiny

C. Write an antonym for each word below.

1. graceful _____
2. difficult _____
3. generous _____

4. hastily _____
5. deflate _____
6. valuable _____

7. definite _____
8. superior _____
9. abundance _____

D. For each underlined word, underline the correct antonym.

1. Her failure was no surprise to those who knew her well.   (success, defeat)
2. Dr. Fenton always has a mean greeting for her patients.   (sarcastic, friendly)
3. His cowardly actions went unnoticed.   (courageous, fearful)
4. Our car is old and dependable.   (valuable, unreliable)
5. His vague answer cleared up the misunderstanding.   (rambling, specific)

Lesson 2

Homonyms

> ■ A **homonym** is a word that sounds the same as another word but has a different spelling and a different meaning.
> EXAMPLES: their – they're – there   hear – here

A. Underline the correct homonym(s) in each sentence below.

1. What is the (weight, wait) of that rocket?

2. The (sale, sail) on the lake will be rough today.

3. Don't you like to (brows, browse) around in a bookstore?

4. We spent several (days, daze) at an old-fashioned (in, inn).

5. The ship was caught in an ice (flow, floe).

6. A large (boulder, bolder) rolled down the mountainside.

7. Why is that crowd on the (pier, peer)?

8. They asked the bank for a (lone, loan).

9. We drove four miles in a foggy (missed, mist).

10. Don't you like to (sea, see) a field of golden wheat?

11. Jack (threw, through) the ball (threw, through) the garage window.

12. We (buy, by) our fish from the market down on the (beach, beech).

13. The band will march down the middle (aisle, isle) of the auditorium.

14. Who is the (principal, principle) of your school?

15. The United States Congress (meats, meets) in the capitol in Washington, D.C.

16. The farmer caught the horse by the (rain, reign, rein).

17. She stepped on the (break, brake) suddenly.

18. (Their, There) are too many people to get on this boat.

19. The wren (flew, flue) in a (strait, straight) line.

20. We were not (allowed, aloud) to visit the museum yesterday.

B. Write a homonym for each word below.

1. weigh _____

2. steal _____

3. sail _____

4. fare _____

5. maid _____

6. deer _____

7. ate _____

8. vain _____

9. strait _____

10. threw _____

11. soar _____

12. bored _____

13. see _____

14. sent _____

15. pare _____

16. peace _____

17. sun _____

18. blue _____

Homographs

■ A **homograph** is a word that has the same spelling as another word but a different meaning and sometimes a different pronunciation.
    EXAMPLE: base, meaning "the bottom on which a statue stands," and base, meaning "mean and selfish"

A. Write the homograph for each pair of meanings below.

1. **a.** a large animal   **b.** to support or carry   _____

2. **a.** a person that jumps   **b.** a type of dress   _____

3. **a.** a cutting tool   **b.** the past tense of see   _____

4. **a.** to hit   **b.** a sweetened beverage   _____

5. **a.** to be silent   **b.** a type of flower   _____

6. **a.** a glass container   **b.** to rattle or shake   _____

7. **a.** a round object   **b.** a formal dance   _____

8. **a.** part of the eye   **b.** a student   _____

B. Fill in each blank with a homograph from the box.

ball	punch	bear	jar
jumper	mum	saw	pupil

1. Jim and I _____ that movie last week.

2. The pitcher threw the _____ to home plate.

3. Joan's new _____ fit her very well.

4. Sharpen that _____ before you cut the wood.

5. That yellow _____ is the prettiest flower in the vase.

6. Jerry made a delicious _____ for the party.

7. The _____ was filled with strawberry jam.

8. The new _____ made new friends in school.

9. That _____ had two cubs yesterday.

10. My parents attended a formal _____ in Boston, Massachusetts.

Lesson 4

Prefixes

> ■ A **prefix** added to the beginning of a base word changes the meaning of the word.
>
> EXAMPLE: in-, meaning "not," + the base word <u>visible</u> = <u>invisible</u>, meaning "not visible"
>
> EXAMPLES:
>
> | prefix | meaning | prefix | meaning |
> |--------|---------|--------|---------|
> | in- | not | re- | again |
> | dis- | not | fore- | before |
> | un- | not | mis- | wrong |
> | im- | not | co- | together |
> | il- | not, non | pre- | before |

A. On the blank after each sentence, write a new word that means the same as the two underlined words combined. Use prefixes from the examples above. Use a dictionary if needed.

1. Susan was asked to <u>write</u> her report <u>again</u>. _____

2. At first, Susan was <u>not pleased</u> with the idea. _____

3. Then she remembered that the instructor had <u>warned</u> the class <u>before</u> that

   handwriting must be neat. _____

4. Susan looked at her paper and realized that it was <u>not possible</u> to

   read some of the words. _____

5. "I am <u>not certain</u> myself what the last sentence says," she thought. _____

6. "Did I <u>spell</u> that word <u>wrong</u>?" she wondered. _____

7. Susan realized that she tended to be <u>not patient</u> about her work. _____

B. Add a prefix from the examples above to each word to make a new word. Then write the new word on the blank.

1. read _____

2. pure _____

3. wrap _____

4. understand _____

5. mature _____

6. arrange _____

7. equal _____

8. obey _____

9. match _____

10. view _____

11. locate _____

12. fortune _____

13. pay _____

14. fair _____

- A **suffix** added to the end of a base word changes the meaning of the word.
  EXAMPLE: -ward, meaning "toward," + the base word <u>west</u> = <u>westward</u>, meaning "toward the west"
- Sometimes you need to change the spelling of a base word when a suffix is added.
  EXAMPLE: imagine – imagination

EXAMPLES:	suffix	meaning	suffix	meaning
	-less	without	-en	to make
	-ish	of the nature of	-ist	one skilled in
	-ous	full of	-able	able to be
	-er	one who does	-tion	art of
	-hood	state of being	-ful	full of
	-ward	in the direction of	-al	pertaining to
	-ness	quality of	-ible	able to be
	-ment	act or process of	-like	similar to

A. Add a suffix from the examples above to each base word in parentheses. Write the new word in the sentence.

1. Kito wants to be a _____. (paint)

2. He is _____, working after school to earn money for art lessons. (tire)

3. People say that his portraits are very _____. (life)

4. His talent as an _____ was apparent at an early age. (art)

5. In kindergarten his teacher noticed his _____ understanding of shapes and forms. (remark)

6. She gave Kito a great deal of freedom and _____. (encourage)

7. Kito had a _____ for color. (fascinate)

8. Throughout his _____, he entered many contests and competitions. (child)

9. His friends expect that he will become a _____ artist. (fame)

B. Add a suffix from the examples above to each root word. Then write the new word on the blank.

1. rely _____   5. fate _____

2. glory _____   6. comfort _____

3. color _____   7. hope _____

4. occasion _____   8. believe _____

Contractions

> - A **contraction** is a word formed by joining two other words.
> - An **apostrophe** shows where a letter or letters have been left out.
>   EXAMPLE: he would = he'd
> - <u>Won't</u> is an exception.
>   EXAMPLE: will not = won't

A. Write a sentence in which you use a contraction for each pair of words below.

1. I am _____

2. is not _____

3. do not _____

4. where is _____

5. should not _____

6. was not _____

7. were not _____

8. we will _____

9. they are _____

10. I have _____

B. Underline the contractions in the sentences below. Then write the two words that make up each contraction.

1. John and Janet won't be home until dinnertime. _____

2. Let's surprise them by having dinner ready. _____

3. Yes, that's a great idea. _____

4. I don't know what to cook. _____

5. I think we'd better have spaghetti. _____

6. Yes, we can't fail with that. _____

7. It's John's favorite. _____

8. Besides, you're the best spaghetti cook in the family. _____

9. We'll have so much fun! _____

10. John doesn't know how lucky he is. _____

Lesson 7

Compound Words

> ■ A **compound word** is a word that is made up of two or more words. The meaning of compound words is related to the meaning of each individual word.
>
>   EXAMPLE: sail + boat = sailboat, meaning "a boat that uses sails to move through water"
>
> ■ Compound words may be written as one word, as hyphenated words, or as separate words.
>
>   EXAMPLES: airport   air-condition   air force

A. Combine the words in the list to make compound words. You may use words more than once.

sand	fall	paper	color	home	water	room	play
made	field	under	come	out	stand	mate	back

1. _____

2. _____

3. _____

4. _____

5. _____

6. _____

7. _____

8. _____

9. _____

10. _____

11. _____

12. _____

B. Answer the following questions.

1. The word <u>books</u> sometimes refers to "financial accounts."

    What is a <u>bookkeeper</u>? _____

2. A <u>fast</u> is "a period of time when a person eats little or nothing."

    What does <u>breakfast</u> actually mean? _____

3. <u>Ferry</u> means "to transport across a body of water."

    What is a <u>ferryboat</u>? _____

4. A <u>lord</u> is "a person who has great authority over something."

    What is a <u>landlord</u>? _____

5. <u>Jelly</u> is "a soft, transparent substance." What is a <u>jellyfish</u>?

    _____

6. Since <u>out</u> means "outside of," what is an <u>outlaw</u>?

    _____

Connotation/Denotation

- The **denotation** of a word is its exact meaning as stated in a dictionary.
  EXAMPLE: The denotation of casual is "not fancy or formal."
- The **connotation** of a word is an added meaning that suggests something positive or negative.
  EXAMPLES: **Negative:** Sloppy suggests "very messy." Sloppy has a negative connotation.
  Positive: Casual suggests "informal or relaxed." Casual has a positive connotation.
- Some words are neutral. They do not suggest either good or bad feelings.
  EXAMPLES: calendar, toy, pencil

A. Write (–) if the word has a negative connotation. Write (+) if it has a positive connotation. Write (N) if the word is neutral.

1. _____ lazy
   _____ relaxed

2. _____ determined
   _____ stubborn

3. _____ drug
   _____ remedy

4. _____ clever
   _____ sneaky

5. _____ pretty
   _____ gorgeous

6. _____ grand
   _____ large

7. _____ old
   _____ antique

8. _____ curious
   _____ nosy

9. _____ make
   _____ create

10. _____ weird
    _____ unique

11. _____ criticize
    _____ evaluate

12. _____ snooty
    _____ refined

B. Rewrite the paragraph below. Replace the underlined words with words that do not have a negative connotation.

Jason shoved his way through the mob of people. He swaggered through the doorway and slouched against the wall. His clothes were quite gaudy. He glared at everyone with hostile eyes. Then he snickered and said in a loud tone, "I'm finally here."

_____

_____

_____

_____

_____

_____

_____

> ■ An **idiom** is an expression that has a meaning different from the usual meanings of the individual words within it.
>
> EXAMPLE: We're all in the same boat means "We're in a similar situation," not, "We're all in a watercraft together."

A. Read each sentence. Then write the letter of the corresponding idiom for the underlined word or words.

A. shaken up	**D.** beside herself	**G.** comes through	**J.** down in the dumps
B. fly off the handle	**E.** in a bind	**H.** in the doghouse	**K.** stands up for
C. on cloud nine	**F.** put up with	**I.** on the fence	

1. One day Julia will be <u>sad</u>. _____

2. The next day you may find her <u>unbelievably happy</u>. _____

3. But be careful when Julia is <u>very scared or confused</u>. _____

4. She's liable to <u>become suddenly angry</u>. _____

5. Julia always <u>defends</u> her views, no matter what. _____

6. She won't <u>allow</u> any argument. _____

7. One time when I insisted that she listen to my viewpoint, she was <u>really upset</u>. _____

8. I was <u>out of favor</u> for weeks. _____

9. On the other hand, when a friend of Julia's is <u>in a difficult situation</u>, she really <u>helps</u>. _____ _____

10. Like a true friend, Julia is there when I am <u>unable to make a decision</u>. _____

B. For the underlined idiom in each sentence below, write the usual meaning of the words that make up the idiom.

1. Kelly can't decide whether she wants to go, so our plans are still <u>up in the air</u>. _____undecided_____

2. If I get the job, I'll be <u>walking on air</u>. _____

3. My friend's business is <u>on the skids</u>. _____

4. George's ideas are <u>off the wall</u>. _____

5. That's enough silliness. Let's <u>talk turkey</u>. _____

6. Victor was <u>in hot water</u> for not cleaning the garage. _____

7. The audience was <u>all ears</u> when you spoke. _____

8. The lost book <u>turned up</u> yesterday. _____

9. Jan and I <u>put our heads together</u> to solve the problem. _____

A. Write S before each pair of synonyms. Write A before each pair of antonyms. Write H before each pair of homonyms.

1. _____ study, consider
2. _____ expand, reduce
3. _____ attempt, endeavor
4. _____ away, aweigh
5. _____ grouchy, pleasant
6. _____ move, budge
7. _____ arc, ark
8. _____ response, reply

9. _____ bolder, boulder
10. _____ stride, walk
11. _____ doubting, trustful
12. _____ boy, buoy
13. _____ frolic, romp
14. _____ panicky, poised
15. _____ chilly, chili
16. _____ hangar, hanger

17. _____ shout, yell
18. _____ site, sight
19. _____ civilized, primitive
20. _____ kind, humane
21. _____ stable, changeable
22. _____ compliment, complement
23. _____ simple, difficult
24. _____ outspoken, shy

B. In each sentence below, circle the correct definition for the underlined homograph.

1. Once a month I get a yen to go out for a nice dinner.

   a. a unit of money in Japan   **b.** strong desire

2. My favorite cereal has nuts, dates, and raisins.

   a. sweet, dark fruits   **b.** days, months, and years

3. The batter swung at the pitch but missed the ball.

   a. a baseball player   **b.** a liquid mixture for baking

4. Our choices of dessert included fresh cobbler with ice cream.

   a. a mender of shoes   **b.** a fruit pie with one crust

C. Underline each word that has a prefix. Write its meaning on the line.

1. movie preview _____

2. nonprofit organization _____

3. unusual design _____

4. mistaken identity _____

D. Underline each word that has a suffix. Write its meaning on the line.

1. thoughtless person _____

2. unreadable writing _____

3. unbeatable price _____

4. dangerous curve _____

E. In each sentence, underline the words that could form contractions. Then write the contractions on the lines.

1. It is time for the summer festival at the lake. _____

2. I wonder what is taking them so long. _____

3. You have had enough time to answer that. _____

4. If you won, it would be the happiest day of your life. _____

5. Jessica should not be so impatient with her friends. _____

6. I would like to go with you. _____

F. Underline the compound word in each sentence. Then write its definition on the line.

1. The gash in her forehead needed sixteen stitches. _____

2. Everything you heard is absolutely true. _____

3. Get a Sunday paper at the nearest newsstand. _____

4. My roommate never remembers to water the plants. _____

5. The underwater world is fascinating. _____

6. I buy groceries at the supermarket on the corner. _____

G. Answer the following questions.

1. Would you rather be considered smart or brilliant? _____

2. Would you prefer a helpful or an interfering neighbor? _____

3. Which is more admirable, being thrifty or cheap? _____

4. Which is less polite, to sip a drink or to gulp it? _____

5. Would you rather be considered clumsy or graceful? _____

H. Underline the idiom in each sentence. On the line after each sentence, explain what the idiom means.

1. Sometimes it's hard to make ends meet. _____

2. Jeff's turning over a new leaf now. _____

3. Trying to fool her is skating on thin ice. _____

4. We ran into our old friend at the shopping mall. _____

5. I was all ears when she told me the news. _____

A. Read each sentence. Then combine the base word below the blank and a prefix or suffix from the box to form another word. Write the new word in the blank. You may have to make changes in spelling.

re-	fore-	-ist	-able	-ous	-al	im-	-ful

1. My new desk is a _____ example of French woodworking artistry.
   marvel

2. When our first plan didn't work, we had to _____ our strategy.
   think

3. Her response was a _____ denial of the charges.
   force

4. The Russian _____ astounded the audience with his skill.
   piano

5. Our car has an _____ steering wheel.
   adjust

6. Cleaning the garage before noon seemed an _____ task.
   possible

7. In the second race, Greg moved to the _____ of the competition.
   front

8. She wrote a _____ note to the author of the book she loved.
   person

B. Underline the word that has a positive connotation in each pair.

1. A (group, gang) of employees planned a meeting.

2. The man (walked, stomped) into the room.

3. José (asked, demanded) to see the manager.

4. The (puny, fragile) vase was very old.

5. Do you smell a pleasant (fragrance, odor)?

6. David made a (tasty, bland) stew for dinner.

7. The biscuits were baked to a (golden, dark) brown.

8. The (confident, arrogant) young man spoke at the convention.

9. Dan (wrote, scribbled) a note to his grandmother.

10. The (soiled, filthy) clothes needed to be washed.

11. The boy (leaned, slouched) against the doorway.

12. The (reckless, brave) firefighter entered the burning building.

C. In each pair of sentences below, put a check before the one that contains an idiom.

1. _____ "Keep your chin up. Things aren't as bad as they seem," Joe said.

   _____ "Please keep your chin up while I button the top button," Jill said.

2. _____ Sue was mad at her friend and gave her the cold shoulder.

   _____ Cynthia took the cold shoulder of beef out of the refrigerator.

3. _____ It seemed that the clock slowly ticked off the minutes until lunchtime.

   _____ Beth was ticked off when her friend didn't return her call.

4. _____ Watching clock hands move is for the birds.

   _____ This bag of seed is for the birds.

5. _____ "I've been on a merry-go-round all week," Nancy exclaimed.

   _____ "Mom, we went on a merry-go-round at the carnival!" Jody exclaimed.

6. _____ Jean's problem was so confusing that she was all at sea.

   _____ The sailors were all at sea when the storm began.

7. _____ We often take a walk through the woods to see the wildflowers.

   _____ Craig tells his little sister to take a walk whenever she bothers him.

8. _____ The action of the movie picked up during the second half.

   _____ Joe picked up his clothes and put them away.

D. Put a check before the definition of each underlined idiom.

1. John has a bad temper and flies off the handle at the smallest thing.

   _____ leaps from a wagon

   _____ is easily angered

   _____ soars over a frying pan

2. "Try to keep out of hot water," José told his little brother.

   _____ stay clear of the stove

   _____ take a cold shower

   _____ avoid trouble

3. "You can bank on Juan to keep his promises," Mary said.

   _____ build on

   _____ depend on

   _____ deposit money

4. Ryan kept his head when the fire started, and he called for help.

   _____ didn't let his head fall off

   _____ didn't talk suddenly

   _____ didn't panic

5. Stand up for your rights, and don't let people walk all over you.

   _____ trample you on the ground

   _____ take advantage of you

   _____ step on your feet

6. "I take what Kelly says with a grain of salt," Sarah said.

   _____ very lightly

   _____ by eating a little salt

   _____ seriously

7. Joe refused to swallow the line that Jason gave him.

   _____ drink something

   _____ eat the fishing line

   _____ believe the words

8. Nina nearly jumped out of her skin at the movie about ghosts.

   _____ removed her skin

   _____ was startled and frightened

   _____ split her skin open

Lesson 10

Recognizing Sentences

> ■ A **sentence** is a group of words that expresses a complete thought.
> EXAMPLE: He has not worked since he injured his leg.

■ **Some of the following groups of words are sentences, and some are not. Write <u>S</u> before each group that is a sentence. Punctuate each sentence with a period.**

_____ 1. In planning our work schedule____

_____ 2. December is the last month of the year____

_____ 3. Last year when it snowed for eight days____

_____ 4. Another way to improve the quality of your voice____

_____ 5. The largest city in Illinois is Chicago____

_____ 6. There is no way to know what will happen____

_____ 7. Enter the house very quietly____

_____ 8. On one of our hikes in the park____

_____ 9. Houston is the largest gulf port____

_____ 10. An outstanding quarterback with the ability to throw long passes____

_____ 11. Paul Revere was a silversmith____

_____ 12. Check all your sentences carefully____

_____ 13. High on a wooded hill, the cabin____

_____ 14. The cats had a wonderful time running among the bushes____

_____ 15. After wading a long distance in the stream____

_____ 16. As the hour approached for the program____

_____ 17. Kathleen has been learning to become a mechanic ____

_____ 18. Don't throw those papers away ____

_____ 19. California is the third largest state in the United States ____

_____ 20. There are many mountain streams in the Ozarks____

_____ 21. Before they reached the edge of the cliff____

_____ 22. Many notable Americans are buried in the National Cathedral____

_____ 23. In the early morning, the wind became cold____

_____ 24. The silvery airplane____

_____ 25. From the spaceship onto the carrier____

_____ 26. Here comes the delivery truck____

_____ 27. W. C. Handy is known as the "Father of the Blues"____

_____ 28. While on vacation in Florida____

_____ 29. Sometime tomorrow morning____

_____ 30. Laurie and I picked apples this morning____

- A **declarative sentence** makes a statement. It is followed by a period (.).   EXAMPLE: Insects have six legs.
- An **interrogative sentence** asks a question. It is followed by a question mark (?).   EXAMPLE: What are you eating?
- An **imperative sentence** expresses a command or request. It is followed by a period (.).   EXAMPLE: Open the window.
- An **exclamatory sentence** expresses strong emotion. It can also express a command or request that is made with great excitement. It is followed by an exclamation point (!).   EXAMPLES: The grass is on fire! Hurry over here!

- **Write D for declarative, IN for interrogative, IM for imperative, or E for exclamatory before each sentence. Put the correct punctuation at the end of each sentence.**

_____ 1. What do you consider a fair price____

_____ 2. How many people signed a contract____

_____ 3. Do not leave objects lying on floors and stairways____

_____ 4. Mary Bethune became the first black woman to head a federal agency____

_____ 5. What a cold day it is____

_____ 6. Ryan, where have you been____

_____ 7. Return those books when you have finished with them____

_____ 8. I bought this scarf in Mexico____

_____ 9. Look at that gorgeous sunset____

_____ 10. Copy each problem accurately____

_____ 11. Books are storehouses of knowledge____

_____ 12. My pet snake is loose____

_____ 13. How do forests help prevent floods____

_____ 14. Where did we get the word September____

_____ 15. Listen attentively____

_____ 16. Rice is the most widely eaten food in the world____

_____ 17. Don't lose the book____

_____ 18. Paul's cousins from South Dakota will arrive Saturday____

_____ 19. Did you buy more cereal____

_____ 20. We saw the new tiger exhibit at the zoo____

_____ 21. Put those books on that shelf____

_____ 22. Do you want to help me make bread____

_____ 23. We're out of flour____

_____ 24. Wait for me____

_____ 25. How old is that oak tree____

Complete Subjects and Predicates

- Every sentence has two main parts, a **complete subject** and a **complete predicate.**
- The complete subject includes all the words that tell who or what the sentence is about.

    EXAMPLE: **The southern section of our state**/has many forests.
- The complete predicate includes all the words that state the action or condition of the subject.

    EXAMPLE: The southern section of our state/**has many forests.**

- **Draw a line between the complete subject and the complete predicate in each sentence below.**

    1. An earthquake formed Reelfoot Lake in 1811.

    2. The deepest places in the oceans are in the Mariana Trench in the Pacific.

    3. The seasons are the four divisions of the year.

    4. Many of the people waited instead of crowding into the bus.

    5. The two mechanics have not yet fixed the car.

    6. The first telegraph line was between Baltimore, Maryland, and Washington, D.C.

    7. The territory of Iowa was formed from a part of the Louisiana Purchase.

    8. The origin of the wheat plant is very obscure.

    9. The television tube was a product of many years of experimentation.

    10. The shortest day of the year is in December.

    11. Workers discussed timely topics at the meeting.

    12. Fossils show that ferns 100 feet high once grew in Kansas.

    13. Great deposits of bauxite, from which aluminum is extracted, exist in Arkansas.

    14. The Shoshone live in Wyoming, Idaho, and Nevada.

    15. The citizens of Georgia built Fort Pulaski over one hundred years ago.

    16. Who originated Father's Day?

    17. Many people watched the airliner take off.

    18. Mexican silver mines were worked before the Spanish conquest.

    19. A steamboat was used on the Mississippi River for the first time in 1811.

    20. Who brought in the mail?

    21. Benjamin Franklin was once an apprentice to his brother.

    22. All of the guests enjoyed the picnic.

    23. Annapolis Academy was founded in 1845.

    24. The three cities that we visited were New York, Montreal, and Calgary.

    25. Banff National Park is one of the most popular parks in California.

    26. Many towns in the United States are built around squares.

Lesson 13 — Simple Subjects and Predicates

- The **simple subject** of a sentence is the main word in the complete subject. The simple subject is a noun or a pronoun. Sometimes the simple subject is also the complete subject.   EXAMPLES: The southern **section** of our state/has many forests. **Forests**/are beautiful.
- The **simple predicate** of a sentence is a verb within the complete predicate. The verb may be made up of one word or more than one word.   EXAMPLES: Dogs/**have** good hearing. Maria/**is going.**

■ **Draw a line between the complete subject and the complete predicate in each sentence below. Then underline the simple subject once and the simple predicate twice.**

1. The different meanings for that word/cover half of a dictionary page.
2. A valuable oil is made from peanuts.
3. A beautiful highway winds through the Catskill Mountains.
4. The woman in the black dress studied the painting for over an hour.
5. The meadowlark builds its nest on the ground.
6. The making of ice cream can be much fun.
7. Many stories have been written about the old Spanish Main, the northern coast of South America.
8. His answer to the question was incorrect.
9. Every sentence should begin with a capital letter.
10. The rotation of the earth on its axis causes day and night.
11. In Norway, a narrow inlet of the sea between cliffs is called a fjord.
12. The Dutch cultivated large fields of tulips and hyacinths.
13. The two treasury mints in the United States are located in Philadelphia and Denver.
14. Benjamin Franklin's *Poor Richard's Almanac* is filled with wise sayings.
15. The warm climate of Jamaica attracts many winter tourists.
16. That movie has been shown on television many times.
17. Acres of wheat rippled in the breeze.
18. That mechanic completed the job in record time.
19. The people in that picture were boarding a plane for London.
20. One can find rocks of fantastic shapes in the Garden of the Gods, near Colorado Springs, Colorado.
21. The city of Albuquerque is five thousand feet above sea level.
22. The apple trees have fragrant blossoms.
23. Sequoias, the world's tallest trees, are found in California.
24. John Banister was an early botanist.
25. The tall pine trees hide our tiny cabin.
26. The woman filled the vase with colorful flowers.

Lesson 14

Position of Subjects

- When the subject of a sentence comes before the verb, the sentence is in **natural order.**   EXAMPLE: Henry went to the park.
- When the verb or part of the verb comes before the subject, the sentence is in **inverted order.**   EXAMPLES: Here are the calculators. Down came the rain.
- Many questions are in inverted order.   EXAMPLE: Where is the restaurant?
- Sometimes the subject of a sentence is not expressed, as in a command or request. The understood subject is you.   EXAMPLES: Call about the job now. (You) call about the job now.

■ **Rewrite each inverted sentence in natural order. Underline the simple subject once and the simple predicate twice. Add you as the subject to commands or requests.**

1. When is the movie playing?

   _____

2. Never will I forget my first train trip.

   _____

3. Here is the picture I want to buy.

   _____

4. Seldom has he been ill.

   _____

5. Out went the lights.

   _____

6. There were bookcases on all sides of the room.

   _____

7. Take the roast from the oven.

   _____

8. Around the sharp curve swerved the speeding car.

   _____

9. Get out of the swimming pool.

   _____

10. Study for the spelling test.

    _____

11. There are two children in the pool.

    _____

Compound Subjects and Predicates

> ■ A **compound subject** is made up of two or more simple subjects.
>   EXAMPLE: **Matt** and **Jan**/are great swimmers.
> ■ A **compound predicate** is made up of two or more simple predicates.
>   EXAMPLE: The dog/**ran** and **barked** with joy.

A. Draw a line between the complete subject and the complete predicate in each sentence. Underline the compound subject once or the compound predicate twice in each sentence.

1. Lewis and Clark blazed a trail across the North American continent.

2. The rose and the jasmine are important flowers for perfume manufacturing.

3. Kelly and Amy went with us.

4. Chris swept the floor, dusted the furniture, and washed the windows.

5. Empires flourish and decay.

6. The level of the lake rises and falls several times each year.

7. Juanita and her brother are excellent skaters.

8. Dwight D. Eisenhower and Douglas MacArthur were famous American generals.

9. He turned slowly and then answered my question.

10. Museums, libraries, and art galleries are found in many cities.

11. The typewriters, the desks, and the chairs are all new.

12. The plants grew tall and flowered.

13. Stephanie and Teresa worked hard.

14. He ran and slid into third base.

15. The sales clerk added up the numbers and wrote down the total.

16. Reading and baking are her favorite pastimes.

17. Mary drank iced tea and ate a sandwich.

18. Cars and trucks sped past.

19. Red and blue are his favorite colors.

B. Write two sentences containing compound subjects.

1. _____

2. _____

C. Write two sentences containing compound predicates.

1. _____

2. _____

Combining Sentences

> - Two sentences in which the subjects are different and the predicates are the same can be combined into one sentence. The two subjects are joined by <u>and</u>.   EXAMPLE: **The sun** is part of our solar system. **The nine planets** are part of our solar system. **The sun and nine planets** are part of our solar system.
> - Two sentences in which the subjects are the same and the predicates are different can be combined into one sentence. The two predicates may be joined by <u>or</u>, <u>and</u>, or <u>but</u>.   EXAMPLE: The planets **are the largest bodies moving around the sun.** The planets **have a total of 34 moons.** The planets **are the largest bodies moving around the sun and have a total of 34 moons.**

- **Combine each pair of sentences below. Underline the compound subject or the compound predicate in each sentence that you write.**

  1. The nine planets in our solar system vary in size. The nine planets in our solar system are at different distances from the sun.

  _____

  _____

  2. Mercury does not have any moons. Venus does not have any moons.

  _____

  3. Venus is similar in some ways to the earth. Venus is much hotter than the earth.

  _____

  4. Pluto is the farthest planet from the sun. Pluto takes 248 years to revolve around the sun.

  _____

  5. Planets revolve around the sun in regular paths. Planets also rotate and spin like tops.

  _____

  _____

  6. Mercury revolves around the sun in less than a year. Venus revolves around the sun in less than a year.

  _____

  7. The solar system may have been formed in a collision between the sun and another star. The solar system may have come from a cloud of gas.

  _____

  _____

Lesson 17

Direct Objects

> ■ The **direct object** tells who or what receives the action of the verb. The direct object is a noun or pronoun that follows an action verb.
>
> EXAMPLE: Those countries export **coffee**.
> <small>DO</small>

■ **Underline the verb in each sentence. Then write DO above each direct object.**

1. Juanita's good driving prevented an accident.

2. Every person should have an appreciation of music.

3. Gene, pass the potatoes, please.

4. Do not waste your time on this project.

5. James, did you keep those coupons?

6. Geraldo collects foreign stamps.

7. Eli Whitney invented the cotton gin.

8. Answer my question.

9. We are picking trophies for our bowling league.

10. Who invented the steamboat?

11. I am reading Hemingway's *The Old Man and the Sea*.

12. The North Star guides sailors.

13. The Phoenicians gave the alphabet to civilization.

14. Every person should study world history.

15. Who made this cake?

16. Can you find a direct object in this sentence?

17. Who wrote the story of Johnny Tremain?

18. We bought several curios for our friends.

19. Tamara read the minutes of our last club meeting.

20. Did you ever make a time budget of your own?

21. Mountains have often affected the history of a nation.

22. Emma and Joe baked a pie.

- The **indirect object** is the noun or pronoun that tells to whom or for whom an action is done. In order to have an indirect object, a sentence must have a direct object.
- The indirect object is usually placed between the action verb and the direct object.

                          IO   DO

    EXAMPLE: Who gave **me** this **box** of grapefruit?

- **Underline the verb in each sentence. Then write <u>DO</u> above the direct object and <u>IO</u> above the indirect object.**

1. The pitcher threw David a fast ball.

2. We gave the usher our tickets.

3. The doctor handed Chris the prescription.

4. Mr. Lewis sold us a set of encyclopedias.

5. Have you written Andrea the time of our arrival?

6. The supervisor paid the employee a high salary.

7. Experience should teach us wisdom.

8. Who sent Amy that long letter?

9. Maria, show us that magic trick.

10. I gave the cashier the money for our tickets.

11. Many years ago, a clever writer gave us the story of Robinson Crusoe.

12. A guide always shows visitors the interesting things in this museum.

13. Working crossword puzzles gives many people hours of enjoyment.

14. Carlos, give the group a lecture on saving money.

15. The study of space travel has brought us many new inventions.

16. Dale, please take Sandra these books.

17. Mrs. Yonge gave Joanne several plants.

18. Please give me a drink of water.

19. Who gave the United States flag the name of Old Glory?

20. Will you give me those instructions again?

Independent and Subordinate Clauses

- A **clause** is a group of words that contains a subject and a predicate. There are two kinds of clauses: **independent clauses** and **subordinate clauses.**
- An **independent clause** can stand alone as a sentence because it expresses a complete thought.
    - EXAMPLE: **He recovered the watch** that he had lost.

A. Underline the independent clause in each sentence below.

1. We arrived late because we couldn't find the theater.

2. The play started before we found our seats.

3. We got one of the special programs that were being sold.

4. When the play was over, the audience applauded.

5. After we saw the show, we went for a walk.

6. Although the night was cool, the walk was enjoyable.

7. While we were walking, I noticed the moon.

8. Since it was a full moon, it was shining brightly.

9. We walked along the lake until it became very late.

10. By the time I got home, it was almost midnight.

- A **subordinate clause** has a subject and predicate but cannot stand alone as a sentence because it does not express a complete thought.
- A subordinate clause must be combined with an independent clause to make a sentence.
    - EXAMPLE: We started **when the sun rose.**

B. Underline the subordinate clause in each sentence below.

1. Japan is a country where some trains travel at very fast speeds.

2. The airplane that we saw can land in only a few airports in this country.

3. Henry Hudson discovered the river that bears his name.

4. When you respect others, you win respect for yourself.

5. Diego found the new job that was perfect for him.

6. Colleen is the one who was elected without a run-off.

7. The coin that I purchased is an old French crown.

8. When I awoke, it was broad daylight.

9. Those who would control others must first control themselves.

10. The camel is the only pack animal that can stand the test of the Sahara.

Adjective and Adverb Clauses

> ■ An **adjective clause** is a subordinate clause that modifies a noun or a pronoun. It answers the adjective question <u>Which one?</u> or <u>What kind?</u> It usually modifies the word directly preceding it. Most adjective clauses begin with a **relative pronoun.** A relative pronoun relates an adjective clause to the noun or pronoun that the clause modifies. <u>Who</u>, <u>whom</u>, <u>whose</u>, <u>which</u>, and <u>that</u> are relative pronouns.
>
> EXAMPLE: Always do the work **that is assigned to you.**
> adjective clause
>
> ■ An **adverb clause** is a subordinate clause that modifies a verb, an adjective, or another adverb. It answers the adverb question <u>How?</u> <u>Under what condition?</u> or <u>Why?</u> Words that introduce adverb clauses are called **subordinating conjunctions.** The many subordinating conjunctions include such words as <u>when</u>, <u>after</u>, <u>before</u>, <u>since</u>, <u>although</u>, and <u>because</u>.
>
> EXAMPLE: We left **when the storm clouds gathered.**
> adverb clause

A. Underline the subordinate clause. Then write <u>adjective</u> or <u>adverb</u> on the line.

_____ **1.** John Paul Jones was a hero whose bravery won many victories.

_____ **2.** The person who reads the most books will get a prize.

_____ **3.** He overslept because he hadn't set the alarm.

_____ **4.** Give a rousing cheer when our team comes off the field.

_____ **5.** The parrot repeats many things that he hears.

_____ **6.** The picnic that we planned was canceled.

B. Add a subordinate clause beginning with the word in parentheses to each independent clause below.

1. The package was gone   (when) _____

_____

2. A depot is a place   (where) _____

_____

3. Brad and I cannot go now   (because) _____

_____

4. Tell me the name of the person   (who) _____

_____

Lesson 21

Compound and Complex Sentences

■ A **compound sentence** consists of two or more independent clauses. Each independent clause in a compound sentence can stand alone as a separate sentence. The independent clauses are usually joined by <u>and</u>, <u>but</u>, <u>so</u>, <u>or</u>, <u>for</u>, or <u>yet</u> and a comma.
   EXAMPLE: I like to dance, but Jim likes to sing.

■ Sometimes a **semicolon (;)** is used to join the independent clauses in a compound sentence.
   EXAMPLE: I like to dance; Jim likes to sing.

■ A **complex sentence** consists of one independent clause and one or more subordinate clauses.
   EXAMPLE: **When the fire alarm went off,** everyone left the building.
                        subordinate clause

A. Write CP before each compound sentence. Write CX before each complex sentence.

_____ 1. Our team didn't always win, but we always tried to be good sports.

_____ 2. You may stay, but I am going home.

_____ 3. The rangers who serve in Yellowstone Park know every inch of the ground.

_____ 4. That statement may be correct, but it isn't very polite.

_____ 5. We will meet whenever we can.

_____ 6. The pass was thrown perfectly, but Carlos was too well guarded to catch it.

_____ 7. The toga was worn by ancient Roman youths when they reached the age of twelve.

_____ 8. That song, which is often heard on the radio, was written years ago.

_____ 9. They cannot come for dinner, but they will be here later.

_____ 10. My brother likes dogs, but I prefer cats.

_____ 11. The engine is the heart of the submarine, and the periscope is the eye.

_____ 12. I will call you when it arrives.

_____ 13. Those people who camped here were messy.

_____ 14. Edison was only thirty years old when he invented the talking machine.

_____ 15. She crept silently, for she was afraid.

_____ 16. Move the table, but be careful with it.

_____ 17. Bolivia is the only South American country that does not have a port.

_____ 18. How many stars were in the flag that Key saw "by the dawn's early light"?

_____ 19. The octopus gets its name from two Greek words that mean <u>eight</u> and <u>feet</u>.

_____ 20. You may place the order, but we cannot guarantee shipment.

_____ 21. After the sun set, we built a campfire.

_____ 22. We made hamburgers for dinner, and then we toasted marshmallows.

_____ 23. Some people sang songs; others played games.

_____ 24. When it started to rain, everyone took shelter in their tents.

B. Put brackets [ ] around the independent clauses in each compound sentence below. Then underline the simple subject once and the simple predicate twice in each clause.

1. [The streets are filled with cars], but [the sidewalks are empty].
2. Those apples are too sour to eat, but those pears are perfect.
3. She studies hard, but she saves some time to enjoy herself.
4. They lost track of time, so they were late.
5. Eric had not studied, so he failed the test.
6. Yesterday it rained all day, but today the sun is shining.
7. I set the alarm to get up early, but I couldn't get up.
8. They may sing and dance until dawn, but they will be exhausted.
9. My friend moved to Texas, and I will miss her.
10. They arrived at the theater early, but there was still a long line.
11. Lisa took her dog to the veterinarian, but his office was closed.
12. The black cat leaped, but fortunately it didn't catch the bird.
13. I found a baseball in the bushes, and I gave it to my brother.
14. We loaded the cart with groceries, and we went to the checkout.
15. The stadium was showered with lights, but the stands were empty.
16. The small child whimpered, and her mother hugged her.
17. The dark clouds rolled in, and then it began to rain.

C. In each complex sentence below, underline the subordinate clause.

1. The hummingbird is the only bird that can fly backward.
2. The cat that is sitting in the window is mine.
3. The car that is parked outside is new.
4. Jack, who is a football star, is class president.
5. Bonnie, who is an artist, is also studying computer science.
6. John likes food that is cooked in the microwave.
7. The composer who wrote the music comes from Germany.
8. We missed seeing him because we were late.
9. When Jake arrives, we will tell him what happened.
10. She walked slowly because she had hurt her leg.
11. When she walked to the podium, everyone applauded.
12. If animals could talk, they might have a lot to tell.
13. Many roads that were built in our city are no longer traveled.
14. My address book, which is bright red, is gone.
15. Ann, who is from Geórgia, just started working here today.
16. The crowd cheered when the player came to bat.
17. When he hit the ball, everyone cheered.

Correcting Run-on Sentences

> - Two or more independent clauses that are run together without the correct punctuation are called a **run-on sentence.**
>   EXAMPLE: Your brain is an amazing organ you could not read without it.
> - One way to correct a run-on sentence is to separate it into two sentences.
>   EXAMPLE: Your brain is an amazing organ. You could not read without it.
> - Another way to correct a run-on sentence is to make it into a compound sentence.
>   EXAMPLE: Your brain is an amazing organ, and you could not read without it.
> - Another way to correct a run-on sentence is to use a semicolon.
>   EXAMPLE: Your brain is an amazing organ; you could not read without it.

- **Correct each run-on sentence below by writing it as two sentences or as a compound sentence.**

1. The brain is surrounded by three membranes the skull encloses the brain and these three membranes.

   _____

   _____

2. The brain reaches its full size by the time a person is twenty at that time, it weighs about three pounds.

   _____

   _____

3. The brain helps a person see, hear, touch, smell, and taste it also makes it possible for one to remember and forget, talk and write, and feel emotions.

   _____

   _____

   _____

4. The brain has three main parts these parts are the cerebrum, the cerebellum, and the brain stem.

   _____

   _____

5. A computer is like a human brain however, a computer would have to be the size of a skyscraper to perform all of the functions of the human brain.

   _____

   _____

   _____

- Sentences can be **expanded** by adding details to make them clearer and more interesting.   EXAMPLE: The dog ran. The **big black** dog ran **barking into the street.**
- Details added to sentences may answer these questions: When? Where? How? How often? To what degree? What kind? Which? How many?

A. Expand each sentence below by adding details to answer the questions shown in parentheses. Write the expanded sentence on the line.

1. The crew was ready for liftoff.   (Which? When?)

   _____

2. The shuttle was launched.   (What kind? Where?)

   _____

3. The engines roared.   (How many? To what degree?)

   _____

4. The spacecraft shot up.   (How? Where?)

   _____

5. The astronauts studied the control panels.   (How many? Where?)

   _____

B. Decide how each of the following sentences can be expanded. Write your expanded sentence on the line.

1. The singer ran onto the stage.

   _____

2. The fans leaped up and cheered.

   _____

3. She began to sing.

   _____

4. She strummed the guitar.

   _____

5. The loudspeakers blared.

   _____

6. The fans began dancing.

   _____

A. Label each sentence as follows: Write <u>D</u> for declarative, <u>IN</u> for interrogative, <u>IM</u> for imperative, or <u>E</u> for exclamatory. Punctuate each sentence correctly.

_____ 1. Is that the book I wanted ____

_____ 2. Please, give it to me ____

_____ 3. I read this book ____

_____ 4. That's a fantastic book ____

_____ 5. Who is your favorite author ____

_____ 6. John, put those books in the box ____

_____ 7. We'll sell them at the garage sale ____

_____ 8. Most people would enjoy them ____

_____ 9. I know I did ____

_____ 10. Will we make enough money ____

B. Underline the words in each sentence that are identified in parentheses.

1. (complete subject)   The leaves on the trees in the park turned orange and yellow.

2. (simple subject)   The tourists came to see the changing colors.

3. (direct object)   The children gathered the leaves.

4. (complete predicate)   Some artists painted the colorful scene.

5. (simple predicate)   Camera buffs snapped photographs.

6. (compound predicate)   Dogs jumped and rolled in the piles of crackling leaves.

7. (compound subject)   Adults and children were delighted by the scene.

8. (indirect object)   A toddler handed his mother a bright orange leaf.

9. (direct object)   She happily took the leaf.

10. (indirect object)   Then she gave him a hug.

C. Draw a line between the complete subject and the complete predicate in each sentence. Underline the simple subject once and the simple predicate twice.

1. The crowd of protesting citizens marched down the street.

2. Kara felt the first drops of rain on her face.

3. Under the fence crawled the frightened coyote.

4. All the patrol cars are parked near the police station.

D. Combine each pair of sentences below. Underline the compound subject or the compound predicate in each sentence that you write.

1. The leaves of some trees turn bright colors in the autumn. Some leaves fall off in the autumn.

_____

2. Linda refuses to watch violent movies. Judy refuses to watch violent movies.

_____

3. Tom washed his car. Tom waxed his car.

_____

4. James and Kathryn ride to work together. Kathryn and Kamal ride to work together.

_____

E. Underline the independent clause in each sentence below.

1. After the first act ended, we left the theater.

2. Pat used her computer for the design that won the contest.

3. By the way they were talking, we knew they weren't going.

4. Canada and the United States share a long border that runs east and west.

F. Underline the subordinate clause in each sentence below.

1. I was at the station when the train arrived.

2. The letter that she found had been mailed two years earlier.

3. After he lit the charcoal, he put on the steaks.

4. The heel broke off her shoe while she was walking.

G. Underline the subordinate clause in each sentence. Then identify the clause by writing adjective or adverb on the line.

_____ 1. The person who writes the funniest limerick will appear on television.

_____ 2. She burned the cookies because she wasn't paying attention.

_____ 3. Stand up when the judge enters the courtroom.

_____ 4. He remembered the dress that she wore to the dance.

H. Write CP after each compound sentence and CX after each complex sentence.

1. The bicycle that I wanted is displayed in the window. _____

2. I am going to save my money, and then I'll buy it. _____

3. My boss, who is a generous man, said he would let me work more often. _____

4. I will work more hours whenever I can. _____

5. I want the one that is a slick, silver mountain bike. _____

I. Correct the run-on sentences below.

1. Janet brought the video to my house I popped it into the VCR.

_____

2. Teresa went to the party she took salad and it was good.

_____

3. What was in the salad it contained fresh fruits and walnuts.

_____

4. She gave me the recipe I can copy it for you.

_____

A. Read the sentences in the box. Then answer the questions below.

> **A.** We just rented and moved into an apartment next to the firehouse.
> **B.** The clanging bells and whining sirens go off day and night.
> **C.** The continuous noise is incredible!
> **D.** Shut all the windows.
> **E.** Did you give the landlord the check yet?

1. _____ Which sentence has a compound subject?
2. _____ Which sentence has a compound predicate?
3. _____ Which sentences have direct objects?
4. _____ Which sentence has an indirect object?

5. _____ Which sentence is interrogative?
6. _____ Which sentences are declarative?
7. _____ Which sentence is exclamatory?
8. _____ Which sentence is imperative?

9. What is the complete subject of <u>C</u>? _____

10. What is the simple subject of <u>C</u>? _____

11. What is the complete predicate of <u>B</u>? _____

12. What is the simple predicate of <u>B</u>? _____

B. Underline the independent clause, and circle the subordinate clause in each sentence below.

1. We planned this trip a month ago, after the holidays were over.

2. After we planned the trip, we posted a sign-up sheet.

3. Here is the sign-up sheet that was hanging in the club room.

4. Everyone who is in the ski club plans to take the trip.

5. When everyone packs carefully, the ski gear fits on the bus.

6. When the bus arrives, we will hand out the tickets.

C. Combine each pair of sentences below to form a compound sentence.

1. It is sunny out today. It's still too cold to go to the beach.

_____

2. Maria can't go with us today. She can come tomorrow.

_____

3. Carol said she would meet us. I'll tell her we aren't going.

_____

4. We could go to see that adventure movie. We could go see the new exhibit.

_____

D. Rewrite each inverted sentence below in natural order.

1. Reported on a television bulletin was the news of the storm.

_____

2. Into the hangar taxied the small airplane.

_____

3. Down the ramp came the tired passengers.

_____

E. Create complex sentences by adding a subordinate clause or an independent clause to each group of words.

1. She looked sad _____

2. When she thought about what she said _____

3. This was the time _____

4. After she wrote her apology _____

5. When she wrote it _____

6. Before we left the house _____

F. Rewrite the paragraph below, correcting the run-on sentences.

In space medicine research, new types of miniature equipment for checking how the body functions have been developed on the spacecraft, astronauts' breathing rates, heartbeats, and blood pressure are taken with miniature devices no larger than a pill. These devices detect the information and transmit it to scientists back on Earth they allow the scientists to monitor astronauts' body responses from a long distance and over long periods of time.

_____

_____

_____

_____

_____

G. Read the two sentences below. Then expand each sentence by adding details to make the sentence clearer and more interesting.

1. The acrobats climbed the ladder.

_____

2. They began their act.

_____

Lesson 24 — Common and Proper Nouns

> - There are two main classes of nouns: **common** and **proper nouns.**
> - A **common noun** names any one of a class of objects.
>   EXAMPLES: woman, city, tree
> - A **proper noun** names a particular person, place, or thing. It begins with a capital letter.
>   EXAMPLES: Ms. Patel, Chicago, Empire State Building

A. Underline each noun. Then write C or P above it to show whether it is a common or proper noun.

     P   C

1. Maria is my sister.

2. Honolulu is the chief city and capital of Hawaii.

3. Rainbow Natural Bridge is hidden away in the wild mountainous part of southern Utah.

4. The Declaration of Independence is often called the birth certificate of the United States.

5. Abraham Lincoln, Edgar Allan Poe, and Frederic Chopin were born in the same year.

B. Write a proper noun suggested by each common noun.

1. country _____

2. book _____

3. governor _____

4. state _____

5. athlete _____

6. school _____

7. actor _____

8. day _____

9. car _____

10. lake _____

11. singer _____

12. holiday _____

13. newspaper _____

14. river _____

C. Write a sentence using each proper noun and the common noun for its class.

1. Mexico   Mexico is another country in North America. _____

2. December _____

3. Alaska _____

4. Thanksgiving Day _____

5. Abraham Lincoln _____

6. Tuesday _____

Concrete, Abstract, and Collective Nouns

> ■ A **concrete noun** names things you can see and touch.
> EXAMPLES: apple, dog, fork, book, computer
> ■ An **abstract noun** names an idea, quality, action, or feeling.
> EXAMPLES: bravery, wickedness, goodness
> ■ A **collective noun** names a group of persons or things.
> EXAMPLES: crowd, congress, public, United States

■ **Classify each common noun as concrete, collective, or abstract.**

1. humor _____
2. kindness _____
3. army _____
4. danger _____
5. committee _____
6. towel _____
7. jury _____
8. audience _____
9. bird _____
10. orchestra _____
11. fear _____
12. family _____
13. happiness _____
14. truck _____
15. audience _____
16. honesty _____
17. bracelet _____
18. society _____
19. album _____
20. courage _____
21. faculty _____

22. club _____
23. photograph _____
24. poverty _____
25. class _____
26. swarm _____
27. table _____
28. goodness _____
29. flock _____
30. radio _____
31. mob _____
32. patience _____
33. herd _____
34. banana _____
35. staff _____
36. mercy _____
37. calculator _____
38. coyote _____
39. generosity _____
40. scissors _____
41. sorrow _____
42. independence _____

Singular and Plural Nouns

■ The following chart shows how to change **singular nouns** into **plural nouns**.

Noun	Plural Form	Examples
Most nouns	Add -s	ship, ships nose, noses
Nouns ending in a consonant and -y	Change the -y to -i, and add -es	sky, skies navy, navies
Nouns ending in -o	Add -s or -es	hero, heroes piano, pianos
Most nouns ending in -f or -fe	Change the -f or -fe to -ves	half, halves
Most nouns ending in -ch, -sh, -s, or -x	Add -es	bench, benches bush, bushes tax, taxes
Many two-word or three-word compound nouns	Add -s to the principle word	son-in-law, sons-in-law
Nouns with the same form in the singular and plural	No change	sheep
Nouns with no singular form	No change	scissors
Nouns with irregular plurals	Change the entire word	foot, feet child, children
Figures, symbols, signs, letters, and words considered as words	Add an apostrophe and -s	m, m's 5, 5's and, and's

A. Write the plural for each singular noun.

1. county _____

2. pony _____

3. tomato _____

4. banjo _____

5. match _____

6. window _____

7. century _____

8. trench _____

9. bookcase _____

10. video _____

11. radio _____

12. farm _____

13. fly _____

14. hero _____

15. dress _____

16. boot _____

17. desk _____

18. daisy _____

B. Write the singular form of each word below.

1. mouthfuls _____

2. proofs _____

3. 6's _____

4. calves _____

5. knives _____

6. Joneses _____

7. children _____

8. geese _____

9. wolves _____

10. roofs _____

11. gentlemen _____

12. editors-in-chief _____

13. +'s _____

14. cupfuls _____

15. trout _____

16. mice _____

C. Fill each blank with the plural form of the word in parentheses. You may use a dictionary to check spellings.

1. (box)   Please store these _____ in the garage.

2. (city)   Can you name the four largest _____ in your state?

3. (deer)   The photographers brought back photos of three _____.

4. (flash)   The vivid _____ of lightning frightened everyone.

5. (coach)   That football team employs five _____.

6. (church)   Our small town has several beautiful _____.

7. (potato)   Hot _____ were used as hand warmers in colonial days.

8. (e)   How many _____ are in the word <u>Tennessee</u>?

9. (O'Keefe)   The _____ are having a recital tonight.

10. (fish)   Where did you catch those _____?

11. (scarf)   Dale gave me three _____.

12. (n)   Cynthia, don't make your _____ look like <u>u</u>'s.

13. (radio)   Kirk listens to two _____ so he can hear all the news.

14. (ox)   The _____ wore a yoke around their necks.

15. (pilot)   Those _____ flew four round trips a day.

16. (90)   The teacher gave three _____ on the math test.

17. (woman)   A dozen _____ attended the conference.

18. (i)   Be sure to always dot your _____.

Possessive Nouns

> - A **possessive noun** shows possession of the noun that follows.
>   EXAMPLES: Gerry's football, Donna's gloves
> - Form the possessive of most singular nouns by adding an apostrophe
>   (') and -s.
>   EXAMPLES: José's pillow, Sandy's eyes
> - Form the possessive of most plural nouns ending in -s by adding only
>   an apostrophe.
>   EXAMPLES: birds' nest, lions' den
> - Form the possessive of plural nouns that do not end in -s by adding
>   apostrophe and -s.
>   EXAMPLES: men's wear

■ **Underline the possessive nouns in each sentence.**

1. Steve's glasses are on my desk.

2. Mary is wearing her mother's gold bracelet.

3. My friends' club will meet at our house Monday night.

4. The woman's first statement caused us to change our minds.

5. We have formed a collector's club.

6. Rosa's brother found the child's lost puppy.

7. The Warrens' store was damaged by the recent storm.

8. What are the vice-president's duties?

9. When does the new mayor's term of office begin?

10. Lee, Tony's notebook is on your desk.

11. We went to the women's department.

12. The family's income was reduced.

13. Our day's work is done.

14. The lifeguards' heroism was rewarded.

15. Our team's defeat did not discourage us.

16. Has Joanna opened a children's store?

17. Juan's cooking is improving.

18. We borrowed Jim's hammer.

19. May I see Calvin's picture?

20. I'll meet you at the Lees'.

21. Lucy visited Mark's college.

22. Frank's telephone call was about Jean's accident.

23. Mr. Clark stood at his neighbors' gate.

24. Is that the Masons' parking place?

25. The United States' flag has stars and stripes.

> - An **appositive** is a noun or pronoun that identifies or explains the noun or pronoun it follows.
>   EXAMPLE: My German friend, **Ulrike**, is coming to visit me next month.
> - An **appositive phrase** consists of an appositive and its modifiers.
>   EXAMPLE: Peter's school, **the junior high,** is sponsoring a dance.
> - Use commas to set off an appositive or an appositive phrase that is not essential to the meaning of the sentence.
>   EXAMPLE: Rico's nephew, **a twelve-year-old,** delivers newspapers.
> - Do not use commas if the appositive is essential to the meaning of the sentence.
>   EXAMPLE: The artist **Picasso** is my favorite.

■ **Underline each appositive word or phrase, and circle the noun it identifies.**

1. (Jan Matzeliger,) the inventor of the first shoemaking machine, was born in South America.

2. Niagara Falls, the waterfalls in New York, is not the tallest in the country.

3. Harvard, the oldest university in the United States, is in Massachusetts.

4. My brother Jim lives in Connecticut.

5. Diane Feinstein, a mayor of San Francisco, was San Francisco's first woman mayor.

6. The Sears Tower, one of the tallest buildings in the world, is in Chicago.

7. Scott's cousin Liz sells antique cars.

8. Leontyne Price, the opera singer, was born in Mississippi.

9. The Pilgrim's ship the *Mayflower* had a stormy voyage.

10. Tom's dog Jasmine likes to swim.

11. Dr. Miller, our family physician, is attending a convention with her husband.

12. The swimmer Mark Spitz won seven gold medals in one Olympics.

13. Fort Worth, a city in Texas, is almost midway between the Atlantic and the Pacific.

14. Aunt Lee, my father's sister, is coming to visit.

15. Mr. Diddon, coach of the hockey team, has never had a losing season.

16. Monticello, Jefferson's home, is an example of colonial architecture.

17. The inventor Thomas Edison is responsible for many electrical breakthroughs.

18. Athens, the leading city of ancient Greece, was a center of culture.

19. The Aztec king Montezuma was captured by Cortez.

20. The boll weevil, a small beetle, causes great damage to cotton.

21. The Hoover Dam, a dam in the Colorado River, took five years to build.

22. Antares, a star many times larger than the sun, is the red star in Scorpio.

23. The composer Mozart lived a short but productive life.

24. That is a copperhead, one of the four poisonous snakes found in the United States.

25. Mt. McKinley, a rugged mountain, is the tallest mountain in North America.

- A **verb** is a word that expresses action, being, or state of being.
  EXAMPLES: Leo **traveled** to Europe. Maura **is** an accountant.
- A verb has four principal parts: **present, present participle, past,** and **past participle.**
- For regular verbs, form the present participle by adding -ing to the present. Use a form of the helping verb be with the present participle.
- Form the past and past participle by adding -ed to the present. Use a form of the helping verb have with the past participle.
  EXAMPLES:

Present	Present Participle	Past	Past Participle
listen	(is) listening	listened	(have, had, has) listened
help	(is) helping	helped	(have, had, has) helped
change	(is) changing	changed	(have, had, has) changed

- Irregular verbs form their past and past participle in other ways. A dictionary shows the principal parts of these verbs.

- **Write the present participle, past, and past participle for each verb.**

PRESENT	PRESENT PARTICIPLE	PAST	PAST PARTICIPLE
1. scatter	(is) scattering	scattered	(have, had, has) scattered
2. express			
3. paint			
4. call			
5. cook			
6. observe			
7. look			
8. walk			
9. ramble			
10. shout			
11. notice			
12. order			
13. gaze			
14. borrow			
15. start			
16. work			

Verb Phrases

> ■ A **verb phrase** consists of a main verb and one or more **helping verbs.**
> A helping verb is also called an **auxiliary verb.** In a verb phrase, the
> helping verb or verbs precede the main verb.
>   EXAMPLE: Liz **has been** reading a mystery.
> ■ The helping verbs are
>   am, are, is, was, were, be, being, been
>   has, have, had
>   do, does, did
>   can, could, must, may, might
>   shall, should, will, would

**A. Underline each verb or verb phrase, and circle each helping verb in the
sentences below.**

1. Most people have heard the story of Jonathan Chapman.

2. He was born in 1775 and has become an American legend.

3. You may have heard of him as the barefooted, lovable Johnny Appleseed.

4. As Jonathan Chapman, he had grown up in the woods near Boston, Massachusetts.

5. He had learned about fruit trees in the orchards near his family's farm.

6. He was always interested in the stories he had heard about the Great West.

7. As a young man, he had declared, "I will go west to Pennsylvania and plant my own orchard."

8. Jonathan had done just that, but in a few years, the wilderness had moved farther west.

9. "What should I do now?" Jonathan asked himself.

10. "I will plant other apple orchards!" was his answer.

11. Jonathan could not remain content.

12. Soon he was traveling with the other settlers as the frontier pushed farther and farther west.

13. People called him Johnny Appleseed, that odd man who did not have a home.

14. He would sleep out in the open with his beloved trees.

B. Use each verb phrase in a sentence.

1. should learn _____

2. will occur _____

3. may find _____

4. have tried _____

5. can make _____

6. will go _____

- The **tense** of a verb tells the time of the action or being. There are six main tenses: **present, past, future, present perfect, past perfect,** and **future prefect.**
- Present tense tells about what is happening now.
  EXAMPLES: Emily **sings.** The kittens **are playing.**
- Past tense tells about something that happened in the past.
  EXAMPLES: Emily **sang** in the play. The kittens **were playing** on the porch.
- Future tense tells about something that will happen in the future.
  EXAMPLES: Emily **will sing** in the play. The kittens **will play** on the porch.
- Present perfect tense tells about something that occurred at an indefinite time in the past.
  EXAMPLE: Emily **has sung** the song.
  It is also used to tell about something that began in the past and continues in the present.
  EXAMPLE: The kittens **have been playing** on the porch.
- Past perfect tense tells about something completed at some past time before something else.
  EXAMPLES: Emily **had sung** before you arrived. The kittens **had been playing** on the porch until Tom came home.
- Future perfect tense tells about something that will be completed before some definite future time.
  EXAMPLES: Emily **will have finished** singing by eight o'clock.

- **Underline each verb or verb phrase. Write present, past, future, present perfect, past perfect, or future perfect.**

  1. I brought these vegetables. _____past_____

  2. Yes, I know her. _____

  3. They will close the office tomorrow. _____

  4. The work will continue for several days. _____

  5. His friend has donated the painting to the museum. _____

  6. Alex had told us many stories about his travels. _____

  7. Jesse Owens was a famous track star. _____

  8. She sings well. _____

  9. Mark will have paid for the meal. _____

  10. I will have been in St. Louis for a week. _____

  11. The neighborhood children had been playing baseball. _____

  12. I have anchored the boat. _____

Using Irregular Verbs

A. Write the principal parts of each verb. You may use a dictionary.

PRESENT	PRESENT PARTICIPLE	PAST	PAST PARTICIPLE
1. do	is doing	did	has done
2. come	_____	_____	_____
3. eat	_____	_____	_____
4. go	_____	_____	_____
5. see	_____	_____	_____
6. take	_____	_____	_____

B. Fill in the blank with the correct form of the verb in parentheses.

1. (see) I had never _____ the waterfall before.

2. (see) Have you ever _____ a helicopter?

3. (take) Laura is _____ the hammer with her.

4. (see) We have just _____ a passenger train going over the bridge.

5. (eat) Haven't you _____ your lunch?

6. (go) You should have _____ with us, Jerry.

7. (go) Jaime is _____ to a committee meeting.

8. (eat) Have you ever _____ a spiced olive?

9. (go) Julian has _____ to play a video game.

10. (take) Carey is _____ the photograph now.

11. (do) Who _____ the landscaping around this building?

12. (do) We have _____ a great deal of outside reading on the topic for discussion.

13. (take) Aren't we _____ the wrong road?

14. (come) People have _____ from every state to see the Carlsbad Caverns.

15. (eat) We had _____ different foods in different areas of the country.

16. (see) Thomas, you should have _____ the last game.

17. (come) Most of our people _____ this way on the way to the park.

18. (do) Matt _____ his best to beat his own record in the broad jump.

C. Write the principal parts of each verb. You may use a dictionary.

PRESENT	PRESENT PARTICIPLE	PAST	PAST PARTICIPLE
1. begin	_____	_____	_____
2. drink	_____	_____	_____
3. drive	_____	_____	_____
4. give	_____	_____	_____
5. run	_____	_____	_____

D. Fill in the blank with the correct form of the verb in parentheses.

1. (give) My friend _____ this poem to me.

2. (run) The excited children _____ down the street.

3. (begin) Work on the new building had _____ this week.

4. (begin) I _____ this project yesterday.

5. (drink) Haven't you _____ some of this delicious fruit juice?

6. (drive) Steven, have you ever _____ a car?

7. (give) Gwendolyn Brooks has _____ us many interesting poems.

8. (begin) The supervisor of the crew is _____ to explain the work orders.

9. (run) Rachel, have you _____ into Aunt Sarah?

10. (run) The girl _____ to meet her parents.

11. (begin) That problem _____ last year.

12. (give) James has _____ me a painting for my living room.

13. (begin) Look, it is _____ to rain.

14. (run) They _____ hard to get out of the rain.

15. (give) Mrs. Williams has _____ me a job in her store.

16. (give) Donald, who _____ you this watch?

17. (begin) We haven't _____ eating all the bananas.

18. (drink) Have you _____ from this cup?

19. (begin) We _____ raking the leaves this morning.

20. (run) Michelle is _____ in the 2-mile race.

E. Write the principal parts of each verb. You may use a dictionary.

PRESENT	PRESENT PARTICIPLE	PAST	PAST PARTICIPLE
1. grow	_____	_____	_____
2. know	_____	_____	_____
3. ring	_____	_____	_____
4. sing	_____	_____	_____
5. speak	_____	_____	_____

F. Fill in the blank with the correct form of the verb in parentheses.

1. (sing)   Have you ever _____ a solo?

2. (grow)   In several minutes, my eyes _____ accustomed to the dark.

3. (know)   Bob _____ the answer.

4. (grow)   It has _____ very cold during the last hour.

5. (sing)   Ricardo is _____ although his throat is sore.

6. (ring)   Why hasn't the bell _____?

7. (grow)   Lettuce had first _____ in China.

8. (speak)   Cynthia _____ to Jonathan yesterday.

9. (ring)   The carrier _____ the doorbell.

10. (speak)   Has Rafael _____ to you about his promotion?

11. (speak)   A police officer is _____ to a group of concerned citizens.

12. (sing)   Natalie and her sister _____ on a local TV program last week.

13. (know)   We have _____ the members of that family a long time.

14. (ring)   The mission bells _____ each morning last week.

15. (throw)   Have you _____ away this morning's paper?

16. (grow)   Charles, I believe you have _____ a prize-winning rose.

17. (know)   We have _____ Roberto's brother for three years.

18. (grow)   Because of the rains, the grass is _____ rapidly.

19. (ring)   We _____ the doorbell, but no one answered it.

20. (speak)   Joan has _____ of you quite often, Jeffrey.

G. Write the principal parts of each verb. You may use a dictionary.

PRESENT	PRESENT PARTICIPLE	PAST	PAST PARTICIPLE
1. blow	_____	_____	_____
2. break	_____	_____	_____
3. choose	_____	_____	_____
4. draw	_____	_____	_____
5. fly	_____	_____	_____

H. Fill in the blank with the correct form of the verb in parentheses.

1. (draw) Kim has _____ many cartoons for the daily paper.

2. (blow) The storm _____ tumbleweeds across the prairie.

3. (fly) The tiny mockingbird is _____ from its nest.

4. (choose) We _____ only willing persons for the committee.

5. (choose) Our club has _____ a motto.

6. (blow) Has the five o'clock whistle _____?

7. (break) I accidentally _____ my sister's antique vase.

8. (break) Her promise had not been _____.

9. (choose) The coach is _____ the line-up for today's game.

10. (draw) A famous artist _____ these sketches.

11. (break) One of the windows in the house had _____ during the storm.

12. (break) The handle of my hammer _____ while I was using it.

13. (choose) Has anyone _____ the salad for lunch?

14. (break) Suzanne _____ this chair yesterday.

15. (freeze) Those pipes _____ last February.

16. (choose) Do you think I have _____ wisely?

17. (break) They _____ our winning streak last week.

18. (draw) Have you _____ your map, Lee?

19. (break) Who is _____ these windows?

20. (draw) Their plans for the new house have been _____.

I. Write the principal parts of each verb. You may use a dictionary.

PRESENT	PRESENT PARTICIPLE	PAST	PAST PARTICIPLE
1. become	_____	_____	_____
2. fall	_____	_____	_____
3. ride	_____	_____	_____
4. rise	_____	_____	_____
5. steal	_____	_____	_____
6. show	_____	_____	_____
7. sink	_____	_____	_____
8. swim	_____	_____	_____
9. tear	_____	_____	_____
10. wear	_____	_____	_____

J. Fill in the blank with the correct form of the verb in parentheses.

1. (ride) Have you ever _____ on a tractor?

2. (rise) The temperature has _____ ten degrees this afternoon.

3. (wear) We _____ our sweaters because the night air was very cool.

4. (steal) Look! Carolyn has _____ third base!

5. (ride) How far are we _____ today?

6. (swim) Jeanne is _____ around the pool.

7. (tear) The child _____ his jeans when he fell down.

8. (sink) When his boat _____, Crusoe was tossed about in the sea.

9. (steal) Our new car has been _____.

10. (ride) Have you ever _____ in an airplane?

11. (wear) This wire has almost been _____ in two.

12. (wear) I have _____ this coat for several winters.

13. (rise) The river recently _____ beyond the flood stage.

14. (rise) Diane has _____ from editor to president of the company.

15. (fall) All the pears have _____ from the tree.

- **Mood** is a form of the verb that shows the manner of doing or being. There are three types of moods: **indicative, subjunctive,** and **imperative.**
- **Indicative mood** states a fact or asks a question.
    EXAMPLES: Ben **came** Friday. How many **went** to the meeting?
- **Subjunctive mood** can indicate a wish or a contrary-to-fact condition. Use <u>were</u> to express the subjunctive.
    EXAMPLE: I would help you, if I **were** able. (I am not able.)
- **Imperative mood** expresses a command or a request.
    EXAMPLES: **Ask** no more questions. Let's **start** immediately.

■ **Give the mood of each underlined word.**

1. <u>Come</u> here at once. _____

2. I <u>did</u> not <u>see</u> Carolyn. _____

3. If I <u>were</u> not so tired, I would go to a movie. _____

4. <u>Call</u> for him at once. _____

5. Where <u>has</u> Brittany <u>moved</u>? _____

6. Who <u>invented</u> the sewing machine? _____

7. Juanita <u>came</u> Saturday. _____

8. Paul wishes it <u>were</u> true. _____

9. <u>Come</u> here, Jennifer. _____

10. I wish it <u>were</u> summer. _____

11. <u>Be</u> home early. _____

12. <u>Ring</u> the bell immediately. _____

13. The members of the band <u>sold</u> birthday calendars. _____

14. If I <u>were</u> you, I'd stop that. _____

15. Zachary <u>likes</u> my new sweater. _____

16. My friends <u>painted</u> the entire house. _____

17. If this <u>were</u> a sunny day, I would go with you. _____

18. <u>Tell</u> us where you went. _____

19. He greeted me as though I <u>were</u> a stranger. _____

Transitive and Intransitive Verbs

> - There are two kinds of action verbs: **transitive** and **intransitive.**
> - A transitive verb has a direct object.
>   EXAMPLE: Columbus **discovered** America.
> - An intransitive verb does not need an object to complete its meaning. Linking verbs are always intransitive.
>   EXAMPLES: The wind **howled.** He **is** afraid.

A. Underline each verb, and classify it as transitive or intransitive.

1. We <u>walked</u> into the new school. _____intransitive_____

2. Ornithology is the study of birds. _____

3. Move those blocks now! _____

4. Everyone listened carefully. _____

5. The workers wore special uniforms. _____

6. We built a barbecue pit in our backyard. _____

7. What is the name of this picture? _____

8. He lives in Germany. _____

9. Who elected the principal of Stuart High? _____

10. Leroy paid the bill. _____

11. We send many good customers to them. _____

12. London is the capital city of Great Britain. _____

13. Frank drew many excellent cartoons. _____

14. We study hard for tests. _____

15. The frightened children cried loudly. _____

16. Lora made this poster. _____

17. Thousands of people ran in the race. _____

18. We learned three new songs. _____

19. The stray dogs barked. _____

20. Please bring me a book about famous Canadian scientists. _____

21. Joseph baked a lemon meringue pie. _____

B. Underline each verb or verb phrase, and classify it as transitive or intransitive.

1. The President of the United States signed the new law. _____

2. The workers repaired the telephone lines. _____

3. The factory shipped the shoes. _____

4. Wasteful cutting of timber may cause a shortage of lumber. _____

5. Wolf was Rip Van Winkle's sole friend. _____

6. The city of Mobile, Alabama, has a wonderful harbor. _____

7. Explain your meaning, please. _____

8. The wind whistled down the chimney. _____

9. The heavy floods blocked traffic for miles. _____

10. Many leaves have dropped in our yard. _____

11. Inventions change our way of living. _____

12. Birmingham, England, attracts many tourists. _____

13. Dorothea Lange was a famous photographer. _____

14. Julio has a fine collection of coins. _____

15. Who invented the lightning rod? _____

16. We cooked our steaks over an open fire. _____

17. Madame Curie discovered radium. _____

18. Gene traveled through North America and South America. _____

19. Cole Porter composed "Night and Day." _____

20. Amelia Earhart was a famous pilot. _____

21. The tornado destroyed several stores. _____

22. Paul exercises every day. _____

23. We talked for hours. _____

24. Have you ever seen Plymouth Rock? _____

25. Abandoned campfires often cause great forest fires. _____

26. He is studying hard for the exam. _____

27. The United States bought Alaska in 1867. _____

Active and Passive Voice

> - **Voice** refers to the relation of a subject to the action expressed by the verb.
> - In the **active voice,** the subject does the action.
>   - EXAMPLE: The club **made** these decorations.
> - In the **passive voice,** the subject is acted upon.
>   - EXAMPLE: These decorations **were made** by the club.
> - Only transitive verbs can be used in the passive voice.

■ **Underline each verb. Then write active or passive.**

___passive___ **1.** The phonograph <u>was invented</u> by Edison.

_____ **2.** Tim hit a home run.

_____ **3.** The bell was rung by the caretaker.

_____ **4.** The football was thrown out of bounds.

_____ **5.** Ricardo has bought some new fishing tackle.

_____ **6.** The decision of the committee was announced yesterday.

_____ **7.** Steve blamed Paul for making him late.

_____ **8.** The first three people were selected for the job openings.

_____ **9.** Carl typed the letter.

_____ **10.** Angela quickly stated the reason for not attending.

_____ **11.** Andrew flopped into the chair.

_____ **12.** Many songs were written by Foster.

_____ **13.** The police officer gave me a ticket.

_____ **14.** Dr. Koneru held a press conference.

_____ **15.** Rosa has bought a new car.

_____ **16.** His heart was broken by the cruelty of his friends.

_____ **17.** Senator Dale shook their hands.

_____ **18.** The boat was carried to the landing.

_____ **19.** The party was given for her birthday.

_____ **20.** Pam wrote the winning essay.

> - A **gerund** is the present participle of a verb form ending in -ing that is used as a noun.
> - A gerund may be the subject, direct object, or object of a preposition.
>   EXAMPLES: **Exercising** is vital to good health. (subject)
>   Tanya enjoys **exercising**. (direct object)
>   I have thought of **exercising**. (object of preposition)

- **Underline each gerund.**

1. We enjoy living on the farm.

2. Airplanes are used in fighting forest fires.

3. Landing an airplane requires skill.

4. Climbing Pikes Peak is quite an experience.

5. The moaning of the wind through the pines lulled me to sleep.

6. The dog's barking awakened everyone in the house.

7. Keeping his temper is difficult for John.

8. Sue objected to our hanging the picture in this room.

9. Laughing aloud is encouraged by the comedian.

10. Being treasurer of this club is a responsibility.

11. Making a speech makes me nervous.

12. Winning this game will place our soccer team first in the league.

13. It was my first attempt at pitching horseshoes.

14. Rapid eating will make digestion difficult.

15. Playing golf is a favorite pastime in many countries.

16. Planning a party requires much thought.

17. We have completed our packing for the trip to the mountains.

18. The howling of the dogs disturbed our sleep.

19. I am tired of doing this work.

20. We are fond of living here.

21. Native Americans once spent much time planting, hunting, and fishing.

22. Neat writing is important in school.

23. I enjoy skating on this pond.

24. Jason taught us the rules of boating.

25. Pressing the wrong button can be very dangerous.

26. Airplanes are used in the mapping of large areas.

27. Swimming in this lake is my favorite sport.

28. I enjoy driving a car.

Infinitives

> - An **infinitive** is the base form of the verb, commonly preceded by <u>to</u>.
> - An infinitive may be used as a noun, adverb, or adjective.
>   EXAMPLES: **To know** him is **to like** him. (noun) She came here **to study.** (adverb) That is the movie **to see.** (adjective)

- **Underline each infinitive.**

1. I want <u>to go</u> home before it gets any colder.

2. We went to see the play while Emilio was here.

3. I prepared the salad to serve for lunch.

4. To shoot firecrackers in the city limits is against the law in some places.

5. I like to walk in the country.

6. They were taught to stand, to sit, to walk, and to dance gracefully.

7. Gradually people learned to use fire and to make tools.

8. I need to get a new coat.

9. We plan to make the trip in four hours.

10. Carol, are you too tired to clean the kitchen?

11. Jack, try to be on time in the morning.

12. Anthony plans to travel in Canada during August.

13. Who taught you to play golf?

14. We were taught to rise early.

15. We were hoping to see you at the reunion.

16. Pay one fee to enter the amusement park.

17. Jennifer, I forgot to mail your package.

18. To cook this turkey will require several hours.

19. The children ran to meet their friend.

20. We are learning to speak Spanish.

21. We are planning to exhibit our artwork next week.

22. To succeed as an artist was Rick's dream.

23. We went to see the parade.

24. We are ready to eat.

25. It was easy to see the reason for that actor's popularity.

26. The only way to have a friend is to be one.

27. Madame Curie was the only woman to receive the Nobel Prize a second time.

28. To score the most points is the object of the game.

29. We need to go grocery shopping.

30. Do you want to paint the fence on Saturday?

Participles

> ■ A **present** or **past participle** is a verb form that may be used as an adjective.
>
> EXAMPLES: A **dripping** faucet can be a nuisance. **Wilted** flowers were removed from the vase.

■ **Underline each participle.**

1. We saw a running deer in the forest.

2. The chart showing sales figures is very helpful.

3. The scampering cat ran to the nearest tree.

4. A team of deep-sea divers discovered the hidden treasure.

5. We saw the thunderstorm advancing across the plains.

6. Biting insects hovered over our campsite at night.

7. His foot, struck by the falling timbers, was injured.

8. The whispering pines filled the air with their fresh scent.

9. People preparing for a career in aviation should master mathematics.

10. We drove slowly, enjoying every minute of the drive.

11. Onions are among the largest vegetable crops produced in the United States.

12. The truck, burdened with its load, traveled slowly over the rough road.

13. Jan, thinking about her new job, was very happy.

14. Several passengers injured in the wreck were brought to the local hospital.

15. That expanding city will soon be the largest one in the state.

16. The fire, fanned by the high winds, threatened the entire area.

17. The rude person, shoving others aside, went to see the manager.

18. The lake, frozen solidly, looked like a huge mirror.

19. The man playing the trombone is my brother.

20. The cleaned apartment was ready for new tenants.

21. Teasing children ran at Rip Van Winkle's heels.

22. Balloons lifting weather instruments are released daily by many weather stations.

23. The chirping bird flew from tree to tree.

24. The surviving pilot described the accident.

25. The dedicated artist worked patiently.

26. Homing pigeons were used in the experiment.

27. The whistling youngster skipped happily down the road.

28. Ironed shirts were stacked neatly at the cleaners.

29. Those standing near the fence should form a second line.

30. The child ran to his loving father, who comforted him.

> - The verb <u>lie</u> means "to recline" or "to occupy a certain place." It does not take an object.
>   > EXAMPLE: The baby is **lying** in her crib.
> - The verb <u>lay</u> means "to place." It takes an object.
>   > EXAMPLE: **Lay** the plates on the shelf.
> - The following are forms of <u>lie</u> and <u>lay</u>:
>
> | Present | Present Participle | Past | Past Participle |
> |---------|-------------------|------|-----------------|
> | lie | lying | lay | (have) lain |
> | lay | laying | laid | (have) laid |

A. Circle the correct word in parentheses to complete each sentence.

1. Canada (lays, lies) to the north of the United States.

2. (Lay, Lie) these books on the table.

3. My cat was (laying, lying) on the floor.

4. Stuart likes to (lay, lie) in the shade.

5. James (lay, laid) the morning paper by his plate.

6. She (lay, laid) the letter on the table.

7. I have (lain, laid) awake for hours the last two nights.

8. He is not able to (lay, lie) on his left side.

9. Carol (lay, laid) her book aside and went to the door.

10. Where (lies, lays) the land to which these ships are going?

11. The dogs had (laid, lain) under the porch all night.

12. I (lay, laid) a long time beside the swimming pool.

13. California (lays, lies) to the east of the Pacific Ocean.

B. Write four sentences, each with a different form of <u>lie</u>, and write four sentences, each with a different form of <u>lay</u>.

1. a. _____

   b. _____

   c. _____

   d. _____

2. a. _____

   b. _____

   c. _____

   d. _____

- The verb <u>sit</u> means "to take a resting position."
    EXAMPLE: Please **sit** in that chair.
- The verb <u>set</u> means "to place."
    EXAMPLE: **Set** the cups on the saucers.
- The verb <u>learn</u> means "to acquire knowledge."
    EXAMPLE: I want to **learn** how to tap dance.
- The verb <u>teach</u> means "to give knowledge to" or "to instruct."
    EXAMPLE: Please **teach** me to tap dance.

Present	Present Participle	Past	Past Participle
sit	sitting	sat	(have) sat
set	setting	set	(have) set
learn	learning	learned	(have) learned
teach	teaching	taught	(have) taught

- **Circle the correct word in parentheses.**

1. Please (sit, set) this table on the patio.

2. My friend is (learning, teaching) us to swim this summer.

3. You should (learn, teach) to eat more slowly.

4. Where do you prefer to (sit, set)?

5. The little dog is always found (sitting, setting) by its owner.

6. Such an experience should (learn, teach) you a lesson.

7. In a theater I always like to (sit, set) near the aisle.

8. I (sat, set) in a reserved seat at the last game.

9. Let me (learn, teach) you a shorter way to do this.

10. Alberto, please (sit, set) down on the step.

11. If you (learn, teach) me how to play tennis, I'll try to (learn, teach) well.

12. With tired sighs, we (sat, set) down on the couch.

13. Andrew, have you (sit, set) out the plants?

14. Jerry, did you (learn, teach) your dog all these tricks?

15. We watched the workers as they (sat, set) stone upon stone.

16. Marcy has (learned, taught) me to water-ski.

17. You can (learn, teach) some animals more easily than others.

18. Mona, do you like to (sit, set) by the window?

19. The first-aid course has (learned, taught) me important procedures.

20. Who (learned, taught) you how to ride a bike?

21. Please (sit, set) these chairs on the rug.

22. Manuel has (sat, set) his work aside.

23. Claire is (learning, teaching) children how to sail in August.

24. All the students are (sitting, setting) quietly.

Pronouns

- A **pronoun** is a word used in place of a noun.
- A **personal pronoun** is chosen based on the way it is used in the sentence.
  A **subject pronoun** is used in the subject of a sentence and after a linking verb.
  EXAMPLES: **He** is a chemist. The chemist is **he**.
  An **object pronoun** is used after an action verb or a preposition.
  EXAMPLES: Jan gave **me** the gift. Jan gave the gift to **me**.
  A **possessive pronoun** is used to show ownership of something.
  EXAMPLES: The new car is **ours.** That is **our** car.

- **Underline each pronoun.**

1. Brian, do you have my ticket to the play?

2. Just between you and me, I want to go with them.

3. Carol, will you help me carry our trunk?

4. May I go with you?

5. We saw him standing in line to go to a movie.

6. Just be sure to find Carol and me.

7. We will be ready when they come for us.

8. She sent this box of frozen steaks to Andrea and me.

9. She asked you and me to be on her bowling team.

10. We saw them go into the building on the corner.

11. Last week we sent flowers to our sick friend.

12. He must choose their dinner.

13. She is my English instructor.

14. They have never invited us to go with them.

15. The first-place winner is she.

16. Can he compete against you?

17. She made the dinner for us.

18. Liz and I are going on vacation in June.

19. Where is your umbrella?

20. Sharon gave me a book to read.

21. Do you know where our cottage is?

22. If I lend you my car, will you take care of it?

23. I gave him my word that we would visit her.

24. When they saw us fishing, Bob and Diane changed their clothes.

25. Your toes are peeking through your socks.

26. Marie showed us how to fasten her bike to our car.

Using *Its* and *It's*

> ■ It's is a contraction for "it is."   EXAMPLE: **It's** a beautiful day.
> ■ Its is a personal pronoun.   EXAMPLE: The dog hurt **its** leg.

A. Underline the correct word in each sentence.

1. Our town is proud of (its, it's) elected officials.

2. (Its, It's) time for the curtain to rise.

3. Tell me when (its, it's) time for that television program.

4. (Its, It's) a mile from our house to the grocery store.

5. I think (its, it's) too cold to walk.

6. (Its, It's) almost time for the show to start.

7. (Its, It's) noon already.

8. (Its, It's) time to give the puppy (its, it's) bath.

9. The cat is playing with (its, it's) toy.

10. (Its, It's) time for us to start home.

11. It looks like (its, it's) going to rain.

12. This dog has lost (its, it's) collar.

13. I think that bird has hurt (its, it's) wing.

14. I do believe (its, it's) getting colder.

15. The dog is looking for (its, it's) owner.

16. (Its, It's) a long and very interesting story.

17. Do you know (its, it's) color was green?

18. The pony shook (its, it's) head and ran to the stable.

19. Do you think (its, it's) too late to call?

20. The bear cub imitated (its, it's) mother.

B. Write three sentences of your own in which you use its.

1. _____

2. _____

3. _____

C. Write three sentences of your own in which you use it's.

1. _____

2. _____

3. _____

> - A **demonstrative pronoun** is used to point out a specific person or thing.
> - This and that are used in place of singular nouns. This refers to a person or thing nearby, and that refers to a person or thing farther away.
>   EXAMPLES: **This** is mine. **That** is the right one.
> - These and those are used in place of plural nouns. These points to persons or things nearby, and those points to persons or things farther away.
>   EXAMPLES: **These** are the best ones. **Those** don't look ripe.

A. Underline each demonstrative pronoun.

1. Those are the books I lost.

2. That is where Anne lives.

3. I'm not sure these are my scissors.

4. This is my pen; that is Pam's book.

5. I think those are interesting books.

6. Is that your first mistake?

7. This is Gretchen's timecard.

8. Give these to your friend.

9. These are Stephanie's shoes.

10. Please don't mention this.

11. I think those are just rumors.

12. Will this be our last chance?

13. Dave, those are your messages.

14. These are large peaches.

15. Sorry, that was my last piece.

16. Who told you that?

> - An **indefinite pronoun** does not refer to a specific person or thing.
>   EXAMPLE: **Many** are called, but **few** are chosen.
> - The indefinite pronouns anybody, anyone, anything, each, everyone, everybody, everything, nobody, no one, nothing, one, somebody, someone, and something are singular. They take singular verbs.
>   EXAMPLE: **Everyone is** ready.
> - The indefinite pronouns both, few, many, several, and some are plural. They take plural verbs.
>   EXAMPLE: **Several are** ready.

B. Underline each indefinite pronoun.

1. Both worked hard.

2. Let each help decorate.

3. Several have called about the job.

4. Unfortunately, some never learn.

5. Everyone was delighted at our party.

6. I think someone forgot this sweater.

7. Some asked for pens.

8. He thinks that each is right.

9. Has anyone seen my wallet?

10. Will someone wash the dishes?

11. Both of the singers are here.

12. One is absent.

13. Each must carry a bag.

14. Some always succeed.

15. Did someone leave this lunch?

16. Everybody is to be here early.

Antecedents

- An **antecedent** is the word to which a pronoun refers.
    EXAMPLE: **Stars** are lovely when **they** shine.
- A pronoun must agree with its antecedent in **gender (masculine, feminine,** or **neuter)** and **number (singular** or **plural).**
    EXAMPLES: **Susan** helped **her** friend. The **people** went in **their** cars.
- If the antecedent is an indefinite pronoun, it is correct to use a masculine pronoun. However, it is now common to use both a masculine and feminine pronoun.
    EXAMPLES: **Someone** lost **his** dog. **Someone** lost **his or her** dog.

■ **Underline the correct pronoun, and circle its antecedent.**

1. (Everyone) should work hard at (their, <u>his or her</u>) job.

2. Each of the children willingly did (his or her, their) share of the camp duties.

3. Sophia gave me (her, their) coat to wear.

4. I took (my, our) friend to the ceremony.

5. All members were asked to bring (his or her, their) contributions today.

6. The women have had (her, their) vacation.

7. Someone has left (her or his, their) automobile across the driveway.

8. If each does (his or her, their) best, our chorus will win.

9. Would you tell Joanne that (her, his) soup is ready?

10. Every woman did (her, their) best to make the program a success.

11. Never judge anyone entirely by (his or her, their) looks.

12. Each student should do (his or her, their) own work.

13. I lost (my, our) favorite earring at the dance.

14. Each woman takes (her, their) own equipment on the camping trip.

15. Each one has a right to (his or her, their) own opinion in this matter.

16. (His, Her) sense of humor is what I like best about Joseph.

17. Some man has left (his, their) raincoat.

18. The two waiters dropped (his, their) trays when they bumped into each other.

19. Has each student received (his or her, their) report card?

20. Every person is expected to do (her or his, their) best.

21. We knew that every man at the meeting expressed (his, their) opinion.

22. Every woman furnishes (her, their) own transportation.

23. Jeff and Tom found (his, their) cabin in the dark.

24. Cliff brings his dog every time (he, she) visits.

25. The bird was in (their, its) nest.

26. Mark read (his, her) final essay for me.

Relative Pronouns

> ■ A **relative pronoun** is a pronoun that can introduce a subordinate clause. The relative pronouns are <u>who</u>, <u>whom</u>, <u>whose</u> (referring to persons); <u>which</u> (referring to things); and <u>that</u> (referring to persons or things).
> ■ A **subordinate clause**, when introduced by a relative pronoun, serves as an adjective. It modifies a word, or antecedent, in the main clause.
> EXAMPLES: Tom knows the author **whose** articles we read in class. The family for **whom** I work is from Canada. The movie **that** won the prize is playing.

■ **Underline each relative pronoun, and circle its antecedent.**

1. The (letter) that was published in our daily paper was very long.

2. It was Karen who sang the most difficult song.

3. Robert Burns, who wrote "My Heart's in the Highlands," was Scottish.

4. It was Sylvia who wanted Zach's address.

5. The shop that was filled with video games is going out of business.

6. My parents live in a New England farmhouse that was built many years ago.

7. This is the pearl that is so valuable.

8. The bridge, which is made of wood, was built two hundred years ago.

9. Did you see the animal that ran across the road?

10. Good roads have opened up many regions that were formerly impassable.

11. For our Thanksgiving dinner, we had a turkey that weighed twenty pounds.

12. This story, which was written by Eudora Welty, is most interesting.

13. Anna is a person whom you can trust.

14. We ate the delicious hamburgers that Andrew had prepared.

15. Food that is eaten in pleasant surroundings is usually digested easily.

16. This is the first painting that I did.

17. The sweater that you want is too expensive.

18. She is the one whom we watched at the track meet.

19. The only money that they spent was for food.

20. Your friend is one person who is inconsiderate.

21. A rare animal that lives in our city zoo was featured on the evening news.

22. Heather is one of the guests whom I invited.

23. Is this the file for which you've been searching?

24. Leonardo da Vinci is the artist whose work they most admire.

25. The science museum is an attraction that is visited by many tourists.

26. Charles Dickens is a writer whom I've read extensively.

> ■ Use <u>who</u> as a subject pronoun.   EXAMPLE: **Who** is your favorite rock star?
> ■ Use <u>whom</u> as an object pronoun.   EXAMPLE: **Whom** did Karen call?
> By rearranging the sentence (Karen did call **whom**?), you can see that
> <u>whom</u> follows the verb and functions as the object. It can also function
> as the object of a preposition.   EXAMPLE: For **whom** are you looking?

■ **Complete each sentence with <u>who</u> or <u>whom</u>.**

1. _____ told you about our plans?

2. _____ is our greatest living scientist?

3. _____ did Armando send for?

4. _____ are those women?

5. _____ is your instructor?

6. _____ is your friend?

7. To _____ is that package addressed?

8. For _____ shall I ask?

9. _____ do you think can take my place?

10. From _____ did you borrow that costume?

11. _____ have the people elected?

12. _____ does she look like?

13. With _____ do you plan to study?

14. _____ is the new employee?

15. _____ do I resemble, my mother or my father?

16. The person _____ I called is my sister.

17. For _____ is this letter?

18. _____ will we select?

19. _____ told us about Frank?

20. _____ did he call?

21. _____ sat next to me?

■ **Underline the correct pronoun.**

1. It was (I, me) who brought the telegram.

2. (He, Him) and (I, me) are friends.

3. She used a sentence (who, that) contained a clause.

4. Neither (he, him) nor (she, her) was to blame.

5. Megan, will you sit between Dana and (I, me)?

6. The person (who, which) taught us how to swim has moved.

7. (Who, Whom) do you want?

8. Between you and (I, me), I do not believe that rumor.

9. I was not the only person (who, whom) she helped.

10. Lupe, please let Carla and (I, me) go with you.

11. For (who, whom) did Joanne knit this sweater?

12. A misunderstanding arose between (she, her) and (I, me).

13. Did you and (she, her) speak to (he, him) about the meeting?

14. The doctor (who, which) examined the sick child was very gentle.

15. That is a fox, and (them, those) are coyotes.

16. Is that (she, her) in your car?

17. Calvin invited Zachary and (I, me) to go swimming.

18. Everyone will write (his or her, their) name.

19. Between you and (I, me), I am disappointed.

20. (Those, That) are my books.

21. Patricia chose you and (I, me).

22. Have you ever played tennis with Brenda and (he, him)?

23. (These, This) are very expensive.

24. It is (he, him) who always plans our refreshments.

25. Were Charles and (he, him) ill yesterday?

26. (Those, That) are the singers we want to hear.

27. Our boss will tell Andy and (I, me).

28. Was it (he, him) who won the prize?

29. The person (who, whom) we met comes from Brazil.

30. Both want (his or her, their) papers.

31. (Who, Whom) walked three miles this morning?

32. Was it (she, her) who called this morning?

33. No one should comb (his or her, their) hair in public.

34. I thanked the woman (who, whom) helped me.

Lesson 48

Adjectives

> ■ An **adjective** is a word that modifies a noun or a pronoun.
>   EXAMPLE: He has **red** hair.
> ■ A **descriptive adjective** usually tells **what kind, which one,** or **how many.**
>   EXAMPLES: **dreary** weather, **this** camera, **two** tickets
> ■ A **proper adjective** is an adjective that is formed from a proper noun. It always begins with a capital letter.
>   EXAMPLES: **Swedish** history, **Mexican** food
> ■ The articles a, an, and the are called **limiting adjectives.**

A. Underline each adjective.

1. The old delicatessen sells fabulous Greek pastries.

2. The little dog is a very affectionate pet.

3. The weary traveler lay down upon the soft, green turf.

4. The storm was accompanied with a magnificent display of vivid lightning.

5. Every motorist should have good eyes, good ears, and good judgment.

6. Every child in the United States knows about the famous ride of Paul Revere.

7. Fleecy, white clouds were floating overhead.

8. On every side were lofty peaks.

9. We have many clear, bright days in December.

10. Washington was a person of courage and honor.

11. The beautiful memorial fountain was placed near the main entrance of the city park.

12. Cautious movements are required in dangerous areas.

13. Alaska, with its fertile soil, extensive forests, and valuable mines, is a great state.

14. He has a massive head, a broad, deep brow, and large, black eyes.

15. The rain dashed against the windows with a dreary sound.

16. Exercise should be a part of your daily routine.

17. The main street is bordered by stately elms.

18. Show a friendly attitude toward your classmates.

19. The second seat in the fourth row is broken.

20. The bright, colorful leaves of the maple make a wonderful sight in autumn.

21. The old, dusty books were donated to the library.

22. Yellow and green parrots talked to the curious children.

23. The steaming blueberry pie was set on the table.

24. An elegant woman stepped out of the black limousine.

25. Can you hear the chirping baby robins?

26. The salesperson waited on the first customer in line.

B. Form a proper adjective from each proper noun, and use it in a sentence.

1. Puerto Rico _____

2. Ireland _____

3. South America _____

4. Britain _____

5. France _____

6. Rome _____

7. Canada _____

8. England _____

9. Russia _____

C. Write three adjectives to describe each noun.

1. a friend _____ _____ _____

2. a TV program _____ _____ _____

3. a book _____ _____ _____

4. a sunset _____ _____ _____

5. a conversation _____ _____ _____

6. a soldier _____ _____ _____

7. a party _____ _____ _____

8. a pet _____ _____ _____

9. a child _____ _____ _____

10. a tree _____ _____ _____

D. Write two adjectives that could be substituted for the following common adjectives.

1. pretty _____ _____

2. little _____ _____

3. smart _____ _____

4. big _____ _____

5. nice _____ _____

6. good _____ _____

Demonstrative Adjectives

> - A **demonstrative adjective** is one that points out a specific person or thing.
> - <u>This</u> and <u>that</u> modify singular nouns. <u>This</u> points to a person or thing nearby, and <u>that</u> points to a person or thing farther away.
>   EXAMPLES: **This** pasta is delicious! **That** road will lead us to town.
> - <u>These</u> and <u>those</u> describe plural nouns. <u>These</u> points to people or things nearby, and <u>those</u> points to people or things farther away.
>   EXAMPLES: **These** sunglasses are very stylish. **Those** plants grow well in shady areas.
> - The word <u>them</u> is a pronoun. Never use it to describe a noun.

■ **Underline the correct word.**

1. Please hand me one of (those, them) pencils.

2. Who are (those, them) people?

3. Was your report made from (these, them) articles?

4. Have you heard (those, them) harmonica players?

5. (These, Them) ten problems are very difficult.

6. I do not like (that, those) loud music.

7. I like (this, these) kind of soft lead pencil.

8. (Those, Them) shoes are too small for you.

9. Where did you buy (those, them) cantaloupes?

10. Most people like (that, those) kind of mystery story.

11. Please look carefully for (those, them) receipts.

12. Sylvia, please take your brother (these, them) books.

13. (Those, Them) advertisements are very confusing.

14. (Those, Them) buildings are not open to the public.

15. Where did you find (that, those) uniform?

16. Please seat (these, them) guests.

17. Rich lives in (this, these) building.

18. (Those, Them) actors were exceptionally convincing in their roles.

19. Kelly, I sent you (that, these) brochure you requested.

20. Did you see (this, those) new outfits in the store?

21. Mark and Melissa painted (this, these) scenery.

22. (Those, Them) computer programs have been quite helpful.

23. Anna, would you like to read (these, them) memos?

24. (This, These) pair of sandals feels comfortable.

25. Is (that, those) the correct phone number?

Lesson 50
Comparing with Adjectives

- An adjective has three degrees of comparison: **positive, comparative,** and **superlative.**
- The simple form of an adjective is called the **positive** degree.
    - EXAMPLE: Cornell is **happy.**
- When two people or things are being compared, the **comparative** degree is used.
    - EXAMPLE: Cornell is **happier** than Katya.
- When three or more people or things are being compared, the **superlative** degree is used.
    - EXAMPLE: Cornell is the **happiest** person I know.
- For all adjectives of one syllable and a few adjectives of two syllables, add -er to form the comparative degree and -est to form the superlative degree.
    - EXAMPLE: tall—taller—tallest
- For some adjectives of two syllables, and all adjectives of three or more syllables, use more or less to form the comparative and most or least to form the superlative.
    - EXAMPLES: He is **more** educated than I remember. That is the **most** beautiful horse on the farm. Yoko is **less** active than Mason. Brooke is the **least** active of all.
- Some adjectives have irregular comparisons.
    - EXAMPLES: good, better, best   bad, worse, worst

A. Write the comparative and superlative forms of each adjective.

POSITIVE	COMPARATIVE	SUPERLATIVE
1. gentle		
2. helpful		
3. difficult		
4. troublesome		
5. high		
6. delicious		
7. intelligent		
8. soft		

B. Complete each sentence, using the correct degree of comparison for each adjective in parentheses.

1. (difficult)   This is the _____ problem I have ever faced.

2. (lovely)   A rose is _____ than its thorns.

3. (agreeable)   Ann is _____ in the morning than in the evening.

> - An **adverb** is a word that modifies a verb, an adjective, or another adverb.
>   EXAMPLES: Kevin spoke **casually**. Carmen's attitude is **very** positive.
>   We did the job **too** carelessly.
> - An adverb usually tells **how, when, where, to what extent,** or **how often.**
> - Many adverbs end in <u>-ly</u>.

- **Underline each adverb in the sentences below.**

1. Preventive medicine has advanced rapidly.
2. The surface of the lake is very quiet.
3. Slowly and surely the tortoise won the race.
4. Afterward the child slept soundly.
5. Tom Sawyer's fence was carefully and thoroughly whitewashed.
6. The horse ran gracefully through the woods.
7. Slowly but steadily the river rose.
8. Jane, you read too rapidly.
9. Liz always dresses stylishly and neatly.
10. The driver turned quickly and abruptly.
11. Was the firefighter seriously injured?
12. Cynthia was extremely cautious as she moved slowly away from the danger.
13. Always try to speak correctly and clearly.
14. The assistant typed rapidly.
15. She came in very quietly.
16. Julio worked patiently and carefully.
17. We searched everywhere.
18. Our holidays passed too quickly.
19. The giant airplane landed gently.
20. We looked here, there, and everywhere for Sue's lost ring.
21. Come here immediately!
22. The flags were waving gaily everywhere.
23. Slowly the long freight train climbed the steep grade.
24. Overhead the stars twinkled brightly.
25. Wash your hands thoroughly before eating.
26. Scott caught the ball and speedily passed it to his teammate.
27. Carefully check every belt and hose in the car.
28. They were quite late.
29. He sees too many movies.

Comparing with Adverbs

- An **adverb** has three degrees of comparison: **positive, comparative,** and **superlative.**
- The simple form of the adverb is called the **positive** degree.
   EXAMPLE: Alex worked **hard** on his project.
- When two actions are being compared, the **comparative** degree is used.
   EXAMPLE: Alex worked **harder** than Justin.
- When three or more actions are being compared, the **superlative** degree is used.
   EXAMPLE: Alex worked the **hardest** of all.
- Use -er to form the comparative degree, and use -est to form the superlative degree of one-syllable adverbs.
- Use more and most with longer adverbs and with adverbs that end in ly.
   EXAMPLE: Karen finished **more quickly** than Sally. Sally works the **most carefully** of the two.
- Some adverbs have irregular comparative and superlative degrees.
   EXAMPLES: well, better, best   badly, worse, worst

A. Write the comparative and superlative form of each adverb.

POSITIVE	COMPARATIVE	SUPERLATIVE
1. fast		
2. carefully		
3. quietly		
4. slow		
5. frequently		
6. proudly		
7. evenly		
8. long		

B. Complete each sentence using the correct degree of comparison for each adverb in parentheses. Some of the forms are irregular.

1. (seriously) Does Angela take her job _____ than Beth?

2. (high) Which of the kites flew _____ ?

3. (thoroughly) Who cleaned his plate _____ , Juan or Bruce?

4. (badly) This is the _____ I've ever done on a test.

5. (diligently) Carl works _____ than Mario!

6. (well) Lisa skis the _____ of everyone in her family.

Lesson 53

Using Adjectives and Adverbs

■ **Underline the correct word.**

1. Always drive very (careful, carefully).

2. The lake seems (calm, calmly) today.

3. The storm raged (furious, furiously).

4. The dog waited (patient, patiently) for its owner.

5. Nicole's letters are always (cheerful, cheerfully) written.

6. Although our team played (good, well), we lost the game.

7. Always answer your mail (prompt, promptly).

8. James speaks (respectful, respectfully) to everyone.

9. Tara is (happy, happily) with her new work.

10. Write this address (legible, legibly).

11. The time passed (slow, slowly).

12. The robin chirped (happy, happily) from its nest.

13. We were (sure, surely) glad to hear from him.

14. Rebecca tries to do her work (good, well).

15. I think Brenda will (easy, easily) win that contest.

16. We had to talk (loud, loudly) to be heard.

17. Yesterday the sun shone (bright, brightly) all day.

18. He says he sleeps (good, well) every night.

19. The elevator went up (quick, quickly) to the top floor.

20. The storm began very (sudden, suddenly).

21. You did react very (cautious, cautiously).

22. Every student should do this work (accurate, accurately).

23. Eric rode his bike (furious, furiously) to get home on time.

24. The paint on the house is (new, newly).

25. The mist fell (steady, steadily) all evening.

26. The river looked (beautiful, beautifully) in the moonlight.

27. The salesperson always answers questions (courteous, courteously).

28. He always does (good, well) when selling that product.

29. Ryan can swim (good, well).

30. I was (real, really) excited about going to San Francisco.

31. I think he talks (foolish, foolishly).

32. It seems (foolish, foolishly) to me.

33. That bell rang too (loud, loudly) for this small room.

34. Our grass seems to grow very (rapid, rapidly).

Prepositions and Prepositional Phrases

> - A **preposition** is a word that shows the relationship of a noun or a pronoun to another word in the sentence.
>   EXAMPLES: I saw her coming **around** the **corner.**
>   She placed the present **on** the **chair.**
> - These are some commonly used prepositions:
>
> | about | against | at | between | from | of | through | until |
> |-------|---------|----|---------|------|-----|---------|-------|
> | above | along | before | by | in | off | to | up |
> | across | among | behind | down | into | on | toward | upon |
> | after | around | beneath | for | near | over | under | with |
>
> - A **prepositional phrase** is a group of words that begins with a preposition and ends with a noun or pronoun.
>   EXAMPLE: We borrowed the lawn mower **from Ken.**
> - The noun or pronoun in the prepositional phrase is called the **object of the preposition.**
>   EXAMPLE: Megan hurried **down** the **stairs.**

- **Underline each prepositional phrase. Then circle each preposition.**

1. Salt Lake City, Utah's capital and largest city, was founded (in) 1847.

2. Sir Authur Conan Doyle is famous for creating the beloved detective Sherlock Holmes.

3. Standard time was adopted in the United States in 1884.

4. The geographic center of the United States is in Kansas.

5. The first safety lamp for miners was invented by Sir Humphrey Davy in 1816.

6. Many people of North Borneo live in houses that have been built on stilts in the Brunei River.

7. The children were charmed by the magician's tricks.

8. We visited the Royal Ontario Museum in Canada.

9. The first automobile show was held in New York City in 1900.

10. Self-government in the United States began in Jamestown in 1619.

11. The first street railway in the world was built in New York in 1832.

12. The inventor of the telephone was born in Scotland.

13. Who is the inventor of the printing press?

14. The shadowy outline of the giant skyscrapers loomed before us.

15. Our small boat bobbed in the waves.

16. The swivel chair was invented by Thomas Jefferson.

17. A raging storm fell upon the quiet valley.

18. I was lulled to sleep by the patter of the rain.

19. We found acorns beneath the tree.

20. That cow is standing in the middle of the road.

21. The child ran across the yard and around the tree.

22. A pine tree fell across the brook.

23. The first census of our country was taken in 1790.

24. Tons of violets are made into perfume each year.

25. The heart of a person pumps more than four quarts of blood in one minute.

26. The United States Patent Office was established in 1836.

27. One of the secrets of success is the wise use of leisure time.

28. The school board held its annual banquet at this hotel.

29. Duke Ellington was born in Washington, D.C.

30. Deposits of iron ore exist near the western end of the Great Lakes.

31. The bridge across this stream was destroyed by the recent storm.

32. Many herds of cattle once grazed on these plains.

33. The huddle in football was first used by a team from Georgia University in 1896.

34. The first skyscraper was built in Chicago.

35. Travelers of a century ago journeyed by stagecoach.

36. The tower of Delhi in India is a monument to the skill of its builders.

37. The quiet of the evening was broken by the rumbling of thunder.

38. The parachutist was injured when her parachute caught in a tree.

39. Aviation was born on a sand dune in North Carolina in 1903.

40. The first trolley car was installed in Richmond in 1885.

41. A box of rusty nails was in the corner of the garage.

42. Don't stand near the edge of that steep cliff.

43. The ground was covered with a deep snow.

44. Twenty cars were involved in the accident on the expressway.

45. The study of geography teaches us about the layout of other lands.

46. A thin column of smoke rose from the chimney of the cabin.

47. In the distance, we saw the top of the snow-capped peak.

48. Place the book upon the shelf.

49. At one time, Philadelphia was the capital of the United States.

50. The football sailed between the goal posts.

51. The report of the secretary was given at the beginning of the meeting.

52. A group of cheering fans waited at the entrance.

53. The hot air balloon drifted toward the ground.

54. Let's have our picnic beneath this huge tree.

55. In the glow of the fading light, we drove along the road.

56. Emily lives near the new mall.

57. Look in the card catalog to see if this book is in the library.

58. The tour guide led us through the halls of the mansion.

59. The theater group is meeting to discuss its productions for next year.

Conjunctions

- A **conjunction** is a word used to join words or groups of words.
  EXAMPLE: Jenna **and** her sister are in Arizona.
- These are some commonly used conjunctions:

although	because	however	or	that	when	while
and	but	if	since	though	whereas	yet
as	for	nor	than	unless	whether	

- Some conjunctions are used in pairs. These include either . . .or, neither . . . nor, and not only . . . but also.

- **Underline each conjunction.**

1. He and I are friends.

2. David likes tennis, whereas Jim prefers running.

3. We had to wait since it was raining.

4. We left early, but we missed the train.

5. The show was not only long but also boring.

6. Neither the chairs nor the tables had been dusted.

7. Hail and sleet fell during the storm.

8. Neither Carmen nor Kara was able to attend the meeting.

9. I have neither time nor energy to waste.

10. Bowling and tennis are my favorite sports.

11. Either Dan or Don will bring a portable radio.

12. The people in the car and the people in the van exchanged greetings.

13. Neither cookies nor cake is on your diet.

14. Although I like to take photographs, I am not a good photographer.

15. Did you see Charles when he visited here?

16. We are packing our bags since our vacation trip begins tomorrow.

17. She cannot concentrate while you are making so much noise.

18. Unless you hurry, the party will be over before you arrive.

19. We enjoyed the visit although we were very tired.

20. Both mammals and birds are warm-blooded.

21. She is one performer who can both sing and dance.

22. Unless you have some objections, I will submit this report.

23. Neither dogs nor cats are allowed in this park.

24. April watered the plants while Luis mowed the lawn.

25. I will see you when you are feeling better.

26. Either Ms. Andretti or Ms. Garcia will teach that course.

27. We got here late because we lost our directions.

Double Negatives

> ■ The **adverbs** <u>not</u>, <u>never</u>, <u>hardly</u>, <u>scarcely</u>, <u>seldom</u>, <u>none</u>, and <u>nothing</u> should not be used with a negative verb. One clause cannot properly contain two negatives.
>
> EXAMPLES: There wasn't anything left in the refrigerator. (Correct)
> There wasn't nothing left in the refrigerator. (Incorrect)

■ **Underline the correct word.**

1. We couldn't see (anything, nothing) through the fog.

2. The suspect wouldn't admit (anything, nothing).

3. I don't know (any, none) of the people on this bus.

4. Rosa couldn't do (anything, nothing) about changing the time of our program.

5. We didn't have (any, no) printed programs.

6. I don't want (any, no) cereal for breakfast this morning.

7. You must not speak to (anyone, no one) about our surprise party plans.

8. There isn't (any, no) ink in this pen.

9. Didn't you make (any, no) copies for the other people?

10. I haven't had (any, no) time to repair the lawn mower.

11. She hasn't said (anything, nothing) about her accident.

12. Hardly (anything, nothing) pleases him.

13. There aren't (any, no) pears in this supermarket.

14. There isn't (any, no) newspaper in that little town.

15. There wasn't (anybody, nobody) in the house.

16. Please don't ask him (any, no) questions.

17. I haven't solved (any, none) of my problems.

18. I haven't done (anything, nothing) to offend Greg.

19. We don't have (any, no) water pressure.

20. Our team wasn't (any, no) match for the opposing team.

21. I couldn't hear (anything, nothing) because of the airplane's noise.

22. The salesperson didn't have (any, no) samples on display.

23. I haven't (any, no) money with me.

24. Hasn't he cooked (any, none) of the pasta?

25. We haven't (any, no) more packages to wrap.

26. Wasn't there (anyone, no one) at home?

27. My dog has never harmed (anybody, nobody).

28. They seldom have (anyone, no one) absent from their meetings.

29. There weren't (any, no) clouds in the sky.

A. Write C or P above each underlined noun to show whether it is a common or proper noun. Then identify each common noun as concrete, collective, or abstract.

_____ **1.** Mayor Murayama has a great deal of integrity.

_____ **2.** The public recognizes Julia's singing talent.

_____ **3.** Her computer is exactly like Craig's.

_____ **4.** Jim's sensitivity to others makes him well-liked.

B. Complete each sentence with the plural form of the word in parentheses.

1. (woman)   The _____ in the choir are rehearsing tonight.

2. (calf)   We stopped at the side of the road to watch the

_____ grazing.

3. (porch)   I like old Victorian homes with enclosed _____.

4. (potato)   Will you please put the _____ in the oven?

5. (sister-in-law)   Gina has three _____.

C. Fill in each blank with the possessive form of the word in parentheses.

1. (children)   Hoan's favorite author is appearing at the _____

bookstore.

2. (lawyers)   Rachel is attending a _____ conference.

3. (candidate)   Did you hear that _____ most recent speech?

4. (men)   The basketball team is practicing in the _____ gym.

D. Underline each verb phrase.

1. I should have been more thoughtful.

2. Tom is designing a newsletter for our company.

3. Did you mop the floor?

4. Your package might arrive this week.

5. We will leave tomorrow morning.

6. Dave has washed the car.

7. Chris is paying the bills.

8. Lucy and I have opened the package.

E. Underline each verb. Then identify each as transitive or intransitive.

1. I enjoyed my visit to the art museum.   _____

2. The strong winds howled.   _____

3. We studied the videotape of the incident.   _____

F. Fill in the blank with the correct form of the verb in parentheses.

1. (eat) She has already _____ breakfast.

2. (do) Some people have _____ strange things.

3. (come) Kamal _____ to the meeting late.

4. (draw) Andrew's performance _____ a standing ovation.

5. (speak) James has _____ to me about the problem.

G. Identify the mood of each underlined verb as <u>indicative</u>, <u>subjunctive</u>, or <u>imperative</u>.

1. <u>Show</u> us your new house. _____

2. Who <u>forgot</u> to turn on the porch light? _____

3. I'd be glad about it if I <u>were</u> you. _____

4. Juan <u>bought</u> a new car. _____

H. Identify each underlined word or words as a <u>gerund</u>, an <u>infinitive</u>, or a <u>participle</u>.

1. <u>Crumpled</u> newspapers covered the floor. _____

2. <u>Inviting</u> them to the same party was a mistake. _____

3. I would like <u>to learn</u> a foreign language. _____

4. <u>Shopping</u> for gifts takes a great deal of time. _____

5. We are ready <u>to go</u>. _____

I. Identify each underlined pronoun as a <u>subject</u>, an <u>object</u>, or a <u>possessive</u> pronoun.

1. <u>Our</u> families live hundreds of miles apart. _____

2. James sent <u>me</u> his new address. _____

3. <u>They</u> have moved three times in two years. _____

4. I received a package from <u>them</u> yesterday. _____

5. Laura and <u>I</u> are working on the problem. _____

J. Underline each adjective. Circle each adverb.

1. These trails can be extremely hazardous.

2. After the long hike, we felt weary.

3. The large jar was soon filled with fresh strawberries.

4. Although it was small, the suitcase was quite heavy.

5. With a graceful movement, the horse suddenly jumped across the stream.

6. We will need two volunteers immediately.

A. Read the following paragraphs.

Tibet, which is a remote land in south-central Asia, is often called the Roof of the World or Land of the Snows. Its mountains and plateaus are the highest in the world. The capital of Tibet, Lhasa, is 12,000 feet high.

Tibetans, who are sometimes called the hermit people, follow a simple way of life. They are a short and sturdy people and do heavy physical work. Some are nomads, herders who roam about in the northern uplands of the country. Once a year, the nomads come to the low regions to sell their products and to buy things that they need. They live in tents made of yak hair. A yak is about the size of a small ox and has long hair. Yaks are good companions to the nomads because they can live and work in the high altitudes.

B. Write two appositives from the paragraph above.

_____   _____

C. Write four relative pronouns and their antecedents.

1. _____ _____   3. _____ _____

2. _____ _____   4. _____ _____

D. Write three prepositional phrases.

1. _____

2. _____

3. _____

E. Write one superlative adjective.

_____

F. Write one indefinite pronoun.

_____

G. Write two intransitive verbs.

_____   _____

H. Write two infinitives.

_____   _____

I. Write two conjunctions.

_____   _____

J. Read the following paragraphs.

If you were to guess which people were the first to learn to write, would you guess the Egyptians? Experts believe thousands of years ago, around 3100 B.C., Egyptians first began writing. Much of their writing was done to record historical events. Later, writings were used on pyramids to ensure peace for the kings buried in them. The writings were in hieroglyphics, a system of writing based on pictures.

Egyptian pyramids are notable for a number of reasons. The oldest pyramid is called Saqqarah. It was built with hundreds of steps running up to the top and was the first building in the country made entirely of stone. It clearly shows how advanced the ancient Egyptian culture was, both artistically and mechanically.

Another incredible monument is the Great Sphinx—a half-lion, half-man stone structure built for King Khafre. Historians have been able to learn much about the ancient Egyptian people by studying these buildings and the materials in them. Fortunately, the climate in Egypt was dry, so the writings and artifacts were well-preserved.

K. Write a subjunctive verb from the paragraph above.

_____

L. Write two adverbs.

_____   _____

M. Write two passive verbs.

_____   _____

N. Write an appositive.

_____

O. Write two abstract nouns.

_____   _____

P. Write two concrete nouns.

_____   _____

Q. Write two conjunctions.

_____   _____

R. Write two prepositional phrases.

_____   _____

_____   _____

> - **Capitalize** the first word of a sentence and of each line of poetry.
>   EXAMPLES: Maria wrote a poem. It began as follows:
>   One cold, starry night
>   I saw the stars taking flight.
> - Capitalize all proper nouns.
>   EXAMPLES: Ellen Kennan, Uncle John, First Street, Spain, Virginia, White
>   Mountains, New Year's Day, March, Niles High School, *Sea Voyager*
> - Capitalize the first word of a quotation.
>   EXAMPLE: Tonya said, "Everyone should learn a poem."
> - Capitalize the first, last, and all important words in the titles of books, poems,
>   stories, and songs.
>   EXAMPLES: "Somewhere Over the Rainbow"; *The Call of the Wild*
> - Capitalize all proper adjectives. A proper adjective is an adjective that is
>   made from a proper noun.
>   EXAMPLES: the French language, German food, American tourists

A. Circle each letter that should be capitalized. Write the capital letter above it.

1. henry wadsworth longfellow wove the history of america into his poems

   "evangeline" and "the courtship of miles standish."

2. "the midnight ride of paul revere" is another of longfellow's poems.

3. The british ship *titanic* sank on its first trip from england to the united states.

4. the first law course offered by an american college was taught by george wythe.

5. he taught many famous people, including thomas jefferson and james monroe.

6. The mississippi river flows through vicksburg, mississippi, and new orleans, louisiana.

7. "what time do the church bells ring?" asked amelia.

8. robert answered, "i believe they ring every half hour."

9. Many centuries ago, vikings lived in what is now known as norway, sweden, and denmark.

10. the song "the battle hymn of the republic" was written by julia ward howe.

11. Mr. james nelson lives in chicago, illinois.

12. he asked, "have you ever seen a waterfall?"

13. The president of the united states lives in the white house.

14. Last summer I visited a hopi reservation.

15. The sequoia national park is on the western slope of the sierra nevada mountains in california.

> - Capitalize a person's title when it comes before a name.
>   EXAMPLES: Doctor Lerner, Judge Kennedy, Governor Thompson
> - Capitalize abbreviations of titles.
>   EXAMPLES: Mr. J. D. Little, Dr. Simon, Pres. Clinton

B. Circle each letter that should be capitalized. Write the capital letter above it.

1. mayor jones and senator small attended the awards banquet Friday night.

2. dr. fox is a veterinarian at the local animal hospital.

3. The invitation said to respond to ms. hilary johnson.

4. No one expected judge randall to rule in favor of the defendant.

5. We were disappointed that gov. dickson couldn't speak at graduation.

6. In his place will be senator christopher larson.

7. The speaker will be introduced by supt. adams.

8. Will miss alden be the new history instructor?

9. dr. tabor is a surgeon at Parkside Hospital.

10. His first patient was mr. william benton.

> - Capitalize abbreviations of days and months, parts of addresses, and titles of members of the armed forces. Also capitalize all letters in the abbreviations of states.
>   EXAMPLES: Fri.; Aug.; 267 N. Concord Ave.; Col. Fernando Gonzales; Hartford, CT; Athens, GA

C. Circle each letter that should be capitalized. Write the capital letter above it.

1. When is maj. hanson expected back from his trip overseas?

2. The garage sale is at 101 w. charles st.

3. Have you ever been to orlando, fl?

4. There is a house for sale at the corner of maple ave. and sunset st.

5. Everyone in our company has the first mon. off in september for Labor Day.

6. The highest award for service was given to gen. t. j. quint.

7. The letter from memphis, tn, took only two days to arrive.

8. Did you know that col. kravitz will be stationed in dover, nh?

9. His address will be 1611 falmouth harbor, dover, nh 03805.

- Use a **period** at the end of a declarative sentence.
  EXAMPLE: We are going to Mexico on our vacation.
- Use a **question mark** at the end of an interrogative sentence.
  EXAMPLE: Do you know whose picture is on the one-dollar bill?

A. Use a period or question mark to end each sentence below.

1. Does this road wind uphill all the way to Carol's house____

2. Los Angeles, Mexico City, and Rome have all been sites of the Olympic Games____

3. Were there really one hundred people standing in line at the theater____

4. Wisconsin raises hay, corn, and oats____

5. Pablo, Tom, Carlos, and Ling were nominated as candidates____

6. Whom did you see, Elizabeth____

7. Haydn, Mozart, Mendelssohn, and Beethoven composed symphonies____

8. Hummingbirds and barn swallows migrate____

9. Do you think that Napoleon was an able leader____

10. Does Louise live in Los Angeles, California____

11. Who wrote the Declaration of Independence____

12. We flew from Seattle, Washington, to Miami, Florida____

13. Roy Avery is a guest of Mr. and Mrs. Benson____

14. Anna, have you read "The Gift of the Magi" by O. Henry____

B. Add the correct end punctuation where needed in the paragraphs below.

Have you ever heard of Harriet Tubman and the Underground Railroad____ During the Civil War in the United States, Harriet Tubman, a former slave, helped more than three hundred slaves escape to freedom____ Tubman led slaves on the dangerous route of the Underground Railroad____ It was not actually a railroad but a series of secret homes and shelters that led through the South to the free North and Canada____ How dangerous was her work____ There were large rewards offered by slaveholders for her capture____ But Tubman was never caught____ She said proudly, "I never lost a passenger____" She was called the Moses of her people____

During the war, she worked as a spy for the Union army____ An excellent guide, she would lead soldiers into enemy camps____ She also served as a nurse and cook for the soldiers____ She was well respected among leading abolitionists of the time____ She was also a strong supporter of women's rights____

Do you know what she did after the war____ She settled in Auburn, New York, and took care of her parents and any other needy black person____ She was always low on money but never refused anyone____ Later, she set up a home for poor African Americans____

> ■ Use a **period** at the end of an imperative sentence.
>   EXAMPLE: Please answer the telephone.
> ■ Use an **exclamation point** at the end of an exclamatory sentence and after an interjection that shows strong feeling. If a command expresses great excitement, use an exclamation point at the end of the sentence.
>   EXAMPLES: Ouch! Follow that car! The ringing is so loud! My ears hurt!

C. Add periods or exclamation points where needed in each sentence below.

1. I love to hike in the mountains____

2. Just look at the view in the distance____

3. Be sure to wear the right kind of shoes____

4. Ouch____ My blister is killing me____

5. Talk quietly and walk softly____

6. Don't scare away the wildlife____

7. Look____ It's a bald eagle____

8. I can't believe how big it is____

9. Take a picture before it flies away____

10. Its wings are bigger than I had ever imagined____

11. It's one of the most breathtaking sights I've ever seen____

12. Oh, look this way____ Here comes another one____

13. This is the luckiest day of my life____

14. Sit down on that tree stump____

15. Pick another place to sit____

D. Add the correct end punctuation where needed in the paragraphs below.

Which animal do you think has been on Earth longer, the dog or the cat____ If you answered the cat, you're right____ About 5,000 years ago in Egypt, cats became accepted household pets____ That was a long time ago____ Cats were actually worshipped in ancient Egypt____

The different members of the cat family have certain things in common____ House cats and wild cats all walk on the tips of their toes____ Isn't that incredible____ Even though all cats don't like water, they can all swim____ Another thing that all cats have in common is a keen hunting ability____ Part of this is due to their eyesight____ They see well at night and in dim light____ Did you know that the cat is the only animal that purrs____ A cat uses its whiskers to feel____ Its sense of touch is located in its whiskers____ The coat of a cat can be long-haired or short-haired, solid-colored or striped____ Some cats even have spots____ Can you name any types of cats____

■ Use a **comma** between words or groups of words that are in a series.
  EXAMPLE: Colorado, Canadian, Ohio, Mississippi, and Missouri are names of well-known American rivers.
■ Use a comma before a conjunction in a compound sentence.
  EXAMPLE: Once the rivers were used mainly for transportation, but today they are used for recreation and industry.
■ Use a comma after a subordinate clause when it begins a sentence.
  EXAMPLE: When I got to the theater, the movie had already begun.

A. Add commas where needed in the sentences below.

1. Anita Travis and José went to the tennis tournament.

2. Before they found their seats the first match had already begun.

3. It was a close game and they weren't disappointed by the final score.

4. They had come to cheer for Antonio Fergas and he was the winner.

5. Although his opponent was very good Fergas never missed returning a serve.

6. While they watched the match Anita clapped cheered and kept score.

7. Travis and José watched a number of different matches but Anita followed Fergas.

8. He was signing autographs and Anita was first in line.

9. Antonio asked her name signed a tennis ball and shook her hand.

10. Because they enjoyed the match so much Travis José and Anita made plans to come back for the final match the next day.

11. They planned to see the men's women's and doubles' finals.

12. Fergas won the entire tournament and he became the youngest champion in the history of the tournament.

■ Use a comma to set off a quotation from the rest of the sentence.
  EXAMPLES: "We'd better leave early," said Travis.
  Travis said, "We'd better leave early."
■ Use two commas to set off a divided quotation. Do not capitalize the first word of the second part of the quotation.
  EXAMPLE: "We'd better leave," Travis said, "or we'll be stuck in traffic."

B. Add commas to the quotations below.

1. "The first match starts at 9:00 A.M." said Travis.

2. Anita asked "Do you want to get seats in the same section as yesterday?"

3. "That's fine with me" said José.

4. José said "Fergas's first match is in Court B."

5. "I'll bring the binoculars" said Anita "and you can bring the cooler."

> - Use a comma to set off the name of a person who is being addressed.
>   EXAMPLE: Philip, would you like to leave now?
> - Use a comma to set off words like yes, no, well, oh, first, next, and finally at the beginning of a sentence.
>   EXAMPLE: Well, we better get going.
> - Use a comma to set off an appositive.
>   EXAMPLE: Alan, Philip's brother, is a doctor in Saint Louis.

C. Add commas where needed in the sentences below.

1. Dr. Perillo a nutritionist is an expert on proper eating.

2. "Students it's important to eat a well-balanced diet," she said.

3. "Yes but how do we know what the right foods are?" asked one student.

4. "First you need to look carefully at your eating habits," said Dr. Perillo.

5. "Yes you will keep a journal of the foods you eat," she said.

6. "Dr. Perillo what do you mean by the right servings?" asked Emilio.

7. "Okay good question," she said.

8. "A serving Emilio is a certain amount of a food," said Dr. Perillo.

9. "Dave a cross-country runner will need more calories than a less active student," explained Dr. Perillo.

10. "Class remember to eat foods from the five basic food groups," she said.

D. Add commas where needed in the paragraphs below.

Our neighbor Patrick has fruit trees on his property. "Patrick what kinds of fruit do you grow?" I asked. "Well I grow peaches apricots pears and plums" he replied. "Wow! That's quite a variety" I said. Patrick's son Jonathan helps his dad care for the trees. "Oh it's constant work and care" Jonathan said "but the delicious results are worth the effort." After harvesting the fruit Jonathan's mother Allison cans the fruit for use throughout the year. She makes preserves and she gives them as gifts for special occasions. Allison sells some of her preserves to Chris Simon the owner of a local shop. People come from all over the county to buy Allison's preserves.

Jonathan's aunt Christina grows corn tomatoes beans and squash in her garden. Each year she selects her best vegetables and enters them in the fair. She has won blue ribbons medals and certificates for her vegetables. "Oh I just like being outside. That's why I enjoy gardening" Christina said. Christina's specialty squash-and-tomato bread is one of the most delicious breads I have ever tasted.

Using Quotation Marks and Apostrophes

> - Use **quotation marks** to show the exact words of a speaker. Use a comma or another punctuation mark to separate the quotation from the rest of the sentence. A quotation may be placed at the beginning or at the end of a sentence. Begin the quote with a capital letter. Be sure to include all the speaker's words within the quotation marks.
>   EXAMPLES: "Let's go to the movie," said Sharon.
>   "What time," asked Mark, "does the movie begin?"

A. Add quotation marks and other punctuation where needed in the sentences below.

1. Mary, do you think this is Christine's pen asked Heather.

2. Heather said I don't know. It looks like the kind she uses.

3. Well, I think it's out of ink, Mary replied.

4. Have you seen Barbara's car? asked Sandy.

5. No said Beth. I haven't gotten over to her apartment this week.

6. Sandy said It sure is pretty. I can't wait to ride in it.

7. I can't believe how late it is exclaimed Alan.

8. Paul asked Where are you going on vacation this summer?

9. My brother and I are visiting our parents in Maine said Peter.

10. Tell me, Alison said how many cats do you have?

11. Alison said The last time we counted, there were four.

12. Will you be taking the bus home asked James or do you need a ride?

> - Use an **apostrophe** in a contraction to show where a letter or letters have been taken out.
>   EXAMPLE: **Let's** go to the store. I **can't** go until tomorrow.
> - Use an apostrophe to form a possessive noun. Add -'s to most singular nouns. Add -' to most plural nouns. Add -'s to a few nouns that have irregular plurals.
>   EXAMPLES: **Maria's** sons are musicians. The **sons'** voices are magnificent. They sing in a **children's** choir.

B. Write the words in which an apostrophe has been left out. Insert apostrophes where they are needed.

1. Im sorry I cant make it to the concert. _____ _____

2. I cant go until Beths project is completed. _____ _____

3. Ill need two nights notice. _____ _____

4. Ive heard that the bandleaders favorite piece will be played last. _____ _____

5. Isnt it one of Cole Porters songs? _____ _____

Using Colons and Semicolons

- Use a **colon** after the greeting in a business letter.
  EXAMPLES: Dear Mrs. Miller: Dear Sirs:
- Use a colon between the hour and the minutes when writing the time.
  EXAMPLES: 11:45   3:30   9:10
- Use a colon to introduce a list.
  EXAMPLE: The shopping cart contained the following items: milk, eggs, crackers, apples, soap, and paper towels.

A. Add colons where needed in the sentences below.

1. At 9 1 0 this morning, we'll be leaving for the natural history museum.

2. Please bring the following materials with you pencils, paper, erasers, and a notebook.

3. The bus will be back at 4 0 0 to pick us up.

4. The special exhibit on birds contains the following types prehistoric birds, sea birds, and domestic birds.

5. The letter we wrote to the museum began "Dear Sir Please let us know when the special exhibition on penguins will be shown at your museum."

6. He told us that we could find out more about the following kinds of penguins the Emperor, the Adélie, and the Magellan.

7. We were afraid there would be so much to see that we wouldn't be ready to leave at 3 3 0 when the museum closed.

- Use a **semicolon** between the clauses of a compound sentence that are closely related but not connected by a conjunction. Do not capitalize the word after a semicolon.
  EXAMPLE: Hummingbirds and barn swallows migrate; most sparrows live in one place all year.

B. Rewrite each sentence below, adding semicolons where needed.

1. Colleen is a clever teacher she is also an inspiring one.

   _____

2. Her lectures are interesting they are full of information.

   _____

3. She has a college degree in history world history is her specialty.

   _____

4. She begins her classes by answering questions she ends them by asking questions.

   _____

Lesson 62

Using Other Punctuation

■ Use a **hyphen** between the parts of some compound words.
   EXAMPLE: poverty-stricken   sixty-three   two-thirds
               part-time   able-bodied   brother-in-law
               hard-boiled   short-term   red-hot
■ Use a hyphen to separate the syllables of a word that is carried over
   from one line to the next.
   EXAMPLE: So many things were going on at once that no one could pos-
   sibly guess how the play would end.

A. Add hyphens where needed in the sentences below.

1. The director told us that there would be room for only two busloads, or
   eighty four people.

2. The play was going to be in an old fashioned theater.

3. Between acts the theater was completely dark, but the orchestra con
   tinued to play anyway.

4. The theater was so small that there were seats for only ninety two people.

5. The vice president was played by Alan Lowe.

■ Use a **dash** to set off words that interrupt the main thought of a
   sentence or to show a sudden change of thought.
   EXAMPLES: We were surprised—even shocked—by the news.
   It was Wednesday—no it was Friday—that I was sick.

B. Add dashes where needed in the sentences below.

1. There was a loud boom what a fright from the back of the theater.

2. We all turned around I even jumped up to see what it was.

3. It was part of the play imagine that meant to add suspense.

4. I'd love to see the play again maybe next week and bring Andrea.

■ **Underline** the titles of books, plays, magazines, films, and television series.
   EXAMPLE: We read Romeo and Juliet last term.
■ Underline foreign words and phrases.
   EXAMPLE: "Adieu," said the French actor to his co-star.

C. In the sentences below, underline where needed.

1. We saw the movie Of Mice and Men after we had read the novel.

2. In Spanish, "Hasta la vista" means "See you later."

3. My favorite book is Little Women.

4. I took a copy of Life magazine out of the library.

A. Circle each letter that should be capitalized. Then add the correct end punctuation.

1. last thanksgiving we spent the holiday at my aunt's house in florida____

2. it was wonderful to be warm in november____

3. we visited the riverdale gardens, sea world, and the ringling museum____

4. one day, we went to see the ship *ocean dream*____

5. the boat's captain, mr. harvey land, took us on a tour____

6. he asked if any of us had been to crystal island____

7. when we answered no, he said he'd take us there on friday____

8. after that journey, I read *seafaring around the world*____

B. Add punctuation where needed in the sentences below.

1. We saw twenty four kinds of fish off the coast of Florida said Paul.

2. Did you snorkel asked Marie or did you stay on the ship?

3. Paul answered We began to snorkel in the shallow water at 2 0 0.

4. The captains first mate Jake is an experienced diver.

5. He offered to give us lessons said Paul.

6. What would he teach you asked Andrew.

7. Hed teach us said Paul how to approach the fish without scaring them away.

8. That must be great exclaimed Marie.

9. Yes I cant wait to learn said Paul.

10. Paul said I think hed be a fine teacher I know hes a great swimmer.

C. Punctuate the letter below. Then circle each letter that should be capitalized.

1200 s. clarke st

chicago, il 60202

june 10, 2004

Dear mr anderson,

    i cant tell you how much we appreciated the time you spent with us in florida____ it was the greatest trip ever____ because of our trip my sister and I plan to take introduction to oceanography at the seaworld institute here in chicago____ the course is offered to people of all ages at the alcott aquarium____ dont you think its funny that chicago has the seaworld institute and we arent even near the ocean____ the closest thing we have is lake michigan____ thanks again for all your help and time____

Sincerely,

paul mendoza

D. Rewrite the letter below. Capitalize necessary letters, and add needed punctuation.

1907 e adams blvd

phoenix az 94733

aug 18 2004

dear kmol radio

i listened with interest to peter katz and filipa guerra on your 1000 show talk about town last friday night____ though i tried to call in the lines were always busy____ i thought id try writing it will at least make me feel better____

i really couldnt believe my own ears____ what in the world do those two have in common with the public in general____ mr katz said hed never had to work a day in his life____ ms guerra said shed never been out of the state of new mexico____ well most of the people in arizona have to work____ many have come from another state____ neither of them has the right to tell working class people how to live____ my suggestions are these take a survey show it to your guests and demand an on air apology from them____

by the way i have long wondered what kmol your call letters stand for if anything____ would you please answer that sometime on the air____ thanks for your time____

yours truly

erica mallet

_____

_____

_____

_____

_____

_____

_____

_____

_____

_____

_____

_____

_____

A. Add punctuation where needed in the paragraphs below. Circle each letter that should be capitalized. Be sure to underline book titles.

have you ever heard the story called "the dog and his bone"____ there once was a dog that had a new bone____ this is a great bone said the dog to himself____ the dog decided to take a walk and carried the bone proudly in its mouth____ he went down a dirt road and over a bridge____ as he was crossing the bridge he looked down into the river____ wow said the dog look at that big bone in the water____ the dog thought to himself id rather have that bone than the one i have right now____ can you guess what happened next____ well the dog opened his mouth and dropped the bone a foolish thing to do into the river____ when the splash of the bone hitting the water stopped the dog looked for the bigger bone____ however he didnt see it anymore____ what he did see was his old bone sinking to the bottom of the river____

_____

there is an incredible man scott targot who lives in my town____ his nickname is the ironman____ people call him ironman targot because he has won several triathlons____ do you know what a triathlon is____ some people consider it the ultimate sports contest____ athletes have to swim for 2.4 miles ride a bike for 112 miles and run for 26.2 miles____ just one of those alone is a lot of work____ scott will train from february to august in preparation for a triathlon in hawaii____ scott says i wouldnt want to be doing anything else with my time____ each day during training he gets up at 7 0 0 loosens up for a half hour then runs from 7 3 0 to 8 3 0____ after he cools down a little he takes a 20 mile bike ride____ at the end of the ride he swims for an hour and a half____ yes i get tired he says but i usually feel refreshed after swimming____ last he lifts light weights and takes a break to do some reading____ his favorite book is you can do it____

a triathlon is supposed to be completed in less than seventeen hours____ the record is less than half that time____ thats my goal says scott____ hes still trying to break 14 hours and ten minutes____ scotts usually one of the top finishers____

B. Write a sentence to illustrate each use of punctuation.

1. Comma   (three uses)

_____

_____

_____

2. Quotation mark   (two uses)

_____

_____

_____

3. Apostrophe   (two uses)

_____

_____

4. Colon   (two uses)

_____

_____

5. Semicolon   (one use)

_____

6. Hyphen   (two uses)

_____

_____

7. Dash   (one use)

_____

8. Underlining   (two uses)

_____

_____

C. Write a short paragraph about someone you admire. Follow all capitalization and punctuation rules.

_____

_____

_____

_____

Lesson 63 — Writing Sentences

> ■ Every sentence has a base consisting of a simple subject and a simple predicate.
>   EXAMPLE: <u>People</u> <u>applied</u>.
>
> ■ Expand the meaning of a sentence by adding adjectives, adverbs, and prepositional phrases to the sentence base.
>   EXAMPLE: **Several** people applied **at the technical institute last week.**

A. Expand the meaning of each sentence base below by adding adjectives, adverbs, and prepositional phrases. Write your expanded sentence.

1. (Visitors toured.) _____

2. (Machines roared.) _____

3. (People lifted.) _____

4. (Work stopped.) _____

5. (Buzzer sounded.) _____

B. Imagine two different scenes for each sentence base below. Write an expanded sentence to describe each scene you imagine.

1. (Day began.) **a.** _____

    b. _____

2. (Workers operated.) **a.** _____

    b. _____

3. (Supervisor explained.) **a.** _____

    b. _____

4. (Shipment arrived.) **a.** _____

    b. _____

5. (People unpacked.) **a.** _____

    b. _____

6. (Automobiles appeared.) **a.** _____

    b. _____

7. (Friend cooked.) **a.** _____

    b. _____

> - A **paragraph** is a group of sentences about one **main idea.** All the sentences in a paragraph relate to the main idea.
> - The first sentence in a paragraph is always indented.
>   EXAMPLE:
>   People work for a variety of reasons. One of the most important reasons people work is to earn money to buy goods and services they need. Work can also provide enjoyment or lead to achieving personal goals.

A. In each paragraph below, cross out the sentence that is not related to the main idea of the paragraph. Then write a new sentence that is related.

1.   Bob and Todd have been friends since the day Bob's family first moved into the neighborhood. The boys were in the same class in both kindergarten and first grade. A few years later, they joined Scouts and worked together to earn merit badges. Bob's dad is an experienced carpenter. In junior high school, Bob was a star pitcher, while Todd led their team in batting.

_____

2.   Rita's first job was at the swimming pool. Because she was a good swimmer and had passed a lifesaving course, she was asked to demonstrate swimming strokes during swimming instruction. She was not old enough to be an instructor. Sometimes she got jobs baby-sitting for families with children in the swimming program.

_____

B. Choose one of the topics below, and write a paragraph of three or four sentences that are related to it.

a. Your first job   c. The job you'd most like to have
b. The job everyone wants   d. Jobs in your community

_____

_____

_____

_____

_____

_____

_____

_____

_____

Writing Topic Sentences

> ■ The **topic sentence** states the main idea of a paragraph. It is often placed at the beginning of a paragraph.
> EXAMPLE:
> Young people can learn various skills by working in a fast-food restaurant. They can learn how to use machines to cook food in a uniform way, how to handle money, and how to work with customers and with other employees.

A. Underline the topic sentence in each paragraph below.

1. Working in a fast-food restaurant is a good first job for young people. The hours are flexible. No previous experience is needed. The work is not hard.

2. A popular ice cream parlor in our town hires young people. Some work serving customers. Some work making special desserts. Others do cleanup and light maintenance.

3. Computers are used in fast-food restaurants. The cash register has a computer that totals purchase prices and computes change. Ovens and deep fryers have computers that regulate cooking temperatures.

B. Write a topic sentence for each group of related sentences.

1. Working may conflict with other activities. There may not be enough time for you to complete housework. You may miss out on having fun with friends.

   Topic Sentence: _____

2. Kate manages the kitchen, plans the menus, and orders all the food. Jesse supervises the dining room. Jesse's sister does the bookkeeping for the restaurant. On weekends, my brother and I help clear the tables.

   Topic Sentence: _____

3. The dining room was decorated with advertisements from the Fifties. The band played only music from the Fifties, and the waiters and waitresses all wore black slacks and bright pink bow ties.

   Topic Sentence: _____

C. Write a topic sentence for one of the topics below.

      a. The best restaurant I've ever gone to   **c.** The job of waiter
      b. Restaurants in our town   **d.** The worst meal I've ever eaten

_____

_____

Writing Supporting Details

> ■ The idea expressed in a topic sentence can be developed with sentences containing **supporting details.** Details can include facts, examples, and reasons.

A. Circle the topic sentence, and underline four supporting details in the paragraph below.

In almost every professional sport, there are far more applicants than available jobs. Consider professional football. Every season, several hundred players are selected by twenty-eight professional football teams. Of those chosen, only about ten percent are actually signed by a professional team. Furthermore, this number shrinks each year because team owners want smaller and smaller teams.

B. Answer the following questions about the supporting details you underlined.

1. What is one supporting detail that is a fact?

_____

_____

_____

_____

2. What is a supporting detail that is a reason?

_____

_____

C. Read each topic sentence below, and write three supporting details for each.

1. People who want a career in sports could teach physical education.

_____

_____

_____

2. Professional sports teams employ people other than players.

_____

_____

_____

_____

Topic and Audience

- The **topic** of a piece of writing is the subject written about.
- The **audience** is the person or persons who will read what is written.
  EXAMPLES: parents, teen-agers, school officials, engineers

A. Choose the most likely audience for each topic listed below.

        a. parents   **c.** job counselors
        b. high-school students   **d.** computer hobbyists

_____ **1.** future of personal computers   _____ **3.** jobs of the future

_____ **2.** benefits of a college education   _____ **4.** paying for college

B. Read the paragraph below, and answer the questions that follow.

      The evening was full of surprises. First, Brenda forgot to tell me she had five children. I had seen only two of them at the store with her. She also forgot to mention the cats—to which I am violently allergic. Also, I wasn't prepared to fix the children dinner. I wrongly assumed that Brenda would have fed them before I came. After getting everyone settled, I wondered if I should do the dishes. I figured that anyone with five children would appreciate having that job done.

1. What is the topic? _____

2. Name two possible audiences for the paragraph.

_____

_____

3. Explain why each audience might be interested.

_____

_____

_____

_____

C. Choose two topics that interest you. Write a topic sentence for a paragraph about each topic. Then name an audience for each paragraph.

1. Topic Sentence: _____

    Audience: _____

2. Topic Sentence: _____

    Audience: _____

> ■ **Brainstorming** is a way to bring as many ideas to mind as you can. You
> can brainstorm by yourself or with others. As you brainstorm, write down
> your ideas. It is not necessary to write your ideas in sentence form.

A. Brainstorm about the things you would do if you were president of a major corporation. Write your ideas below.

1. _____
2. _____
3. _____
4. _____

B. Read the topics below. Choose one topic, and circle it. Then brainstorm about its advantages and disadvantages. Write down as many ideas as you can.

    a. volunteering   **d.** bicycle helmet laws

    b. eating healthy   **e.** automatic seat belts

    c. mediating disagreements   **f.** self-defense training

1. _____
2. _____
3. _____
4. _____
5. _____
6. _____

C. Now write a brief paragraph about the topic you chose in Exercise B that explains either the advantages or disadvantages of the topic.

_____
_____
_____
_____
_____

- Before you write, organize your thoughts by making an **outline.** An outline consists of the title of the topic, headings for the main ideas, and subheadings for the supporting details.
- Main headings are listed after Roman numerals. Subheadings are listed after capital letters. Details are listed after Arabic numerals.

EXAMPLE:

Topic	Should Young People Be Paid for Doing Chores?
Main heading	I. Benefits to parents
Subheadings	A. Chores get done
	B. More leisure time
Main heading	II. Benefits to young people
Subheading	A. Learn useful skills
Details	1. Clean and do laundry
	2. Budget time
Subheading	B. Become responsible

- **Choose a topic that interests you. Then write an outline for that topic, using the example outline as a guide.**

_____

_____

_____

_____

_____

_____

_____

_____

_____

_____

_____

_____

_____

_____

Persuasive Composition

> ■ The writer of a **persuasive composition** tries to convince others to accept a personal opinion.

A. Read the following persuasive composition.

Everyone Should Learn to Use a Computer

Knowing how to use a computer is an essential skill for everyone who wants to succeed in today's world. One basic computer program that everyone should learn to use is the word processing program. Most types of writing are easily and professionally produced with a word processing program. For example, everyone must occasionally write a business letter. Using a computer allows you to arrange and rearrange information easily, making your writing more clear and accurate. Word processing programs can help you check your spelling and grammar. A computer makes it easy to correct mistakes.

Computers can be used for much more than word processing, however. Other areas of interest and opportunity in the field of computers are graphic design, programming, and creating new games. Jobs in the computer field are growing, and strong computer skills can serve you well now and into the future.

B. Answer the questions below.

1. List three facts the writer includes to persuade the reader.

_____

_____

_____

_____

_____

2. List two reasons the writer includes in the composition.

_____

_____

_____

3. List one example the writer uses to support the topic.

_____

_____

_____

C. Choose one of the topic sentences below. Write a short paragraph in which you use facts to persuade your audience about the topic.

   1. The driver and front-seat passenger in a car face various consequences if they don't wear seat belts.

   2. More people should car-pool or use public transportation.

_____

_____

_____

_____

_____

_____

D. Choose one of the topic sentences below. Write a short paragraph in which you use reasons to persuade your audience about the topic.

   1. Wearing seat belts ensures all passengers of a safer ride.

   2. The most important subject a person can learn about is _____ .

_____

_____

_____

_____

_____

_____

E. Choose one of the topic sentences below. Write a short paragraph in which you use an example to persuade your audience about the topic.

   1. I know someone who wore a seat belt and survived a serious collision.

   2. _____ make the best pets.

_____

_____

_____

_____

_____

_____

Revising and Proofreading

> ■ **Revising** gives you a chance to rethink and review what you have
> written and to improve your writing. Revise by adding words and
> information, by deleting unneeded words and information, and by moving
> words, sentences, and paragraphs around.
> ■ **Proofreading** has to do with checking spelling, punctuation, grammar,
> and capitalization. Use proofreader's marks to show changes needed.

Proofreader's Marks

	Reverse the order.	Take something out.
Capitalize.	Add a period.	Correct spelling.
Make a small letter.	Add quotation marks.	Indent for new paragraph.
Add a comma.	Add something.	Move something.

A. Rewrite the paragraph below. Correct the errors by following the proofreader's marks.

¶ personal safety is one of the most important social issues today. Adults and children are worried

about staying safe in all these places their homes, their schools, and the places they go to have

fun. one of the best things a person can do is to act with confidence and awarness. Confidents

means "believing" and awareness means seeing." Several studies have shone that people who

act with confidence and awareness do not look like easy targets which is what criminals look for.

_____

_____

_____

_____

_____

_____

_____

_____

B. Read the paragraphs below. Use proofreader's marks to revise and proofread the paragraphs. Then write your revised paragraphs below.

When your outside your home, your body Language is important very. if you straigt stand, walk purposefully and pay attention to what is around you you will discourage Criminals because you appear strong and alert. along with confidence and awareness Another tool you can use all the time is your voice you can yell. Crimnals dont like to draw to attention themselves and they don't like to be seen. Yelling may sometimes be embarrassing, but your safety is more important than worrying about imbarrassment.

at home, its important to always keep your doors and windows locked you should never opent the door to someone you don't know. You don't have to be polite to somebody who may be trying to do you harm. This also applys to the telephone. If sombody you don't know calls and tries to keep you engaged in a conservation, just hang up. you don't have to be polite to somebody who is intruding in your life, especially if you don't know the person. always Keep your safety in mind and act in a way that discourages criminals from bothering you

_____

_____

_____

_____

_____

_____

_____

_____

_____

_____

_____

_____

A. Add adjectives, adverbs, and/or prepositional phrases to expand each sentence. Then write each expanded sentence.

1. (Producer recorded.) _____

2. (Notebook slipped.) _____

3. (Music started.) _____

4. (Crowd cheered.) _____

B. Write a topic sentence for the paragraph below. Name a possible audience for the paragraph.

   The job is not difficult as long as you are not afraid of dogs. Most dog owners have leashes, so the only materials you need are a notebook on which to write down your appointments and a pair of walking—or running, for some dogs—shoes. People who need to be away most of the day really appreciate the service and are willing to pay what you ask.

Topic Sentence: _____

Audience: _____

C. Read the topic sentence. Then underline the sentences that contain supporting details. Label each sentence fact, example, or reason, depending on the kind of supporting details it contains.

Topic Sentence: The widest variety of jobs is found in a hospital.

1. A hospital is a vital part of a community it serves.

   _____

2. A hospital employs technicians, secretaries, doctors, nurses, and business managers.

   _____

3. Many people are needed to carry out a hospital's many functions.

   _____

4. Our local hospital is the largest employer in our county.

   _____

5. A hospital's various facilities, such as its operating rooms, specialized departments, and food service, must work together efficiently.

   _____

6. I had a broken arm set in the emergency room last summer.

   _____

D. Write the items in outline form.

Topic: Pruning trees takes great skill.
Rake tree trash
Climb the tree
Choose and trim bad wood

Cleaning up
Haul trash
Brace your body firmly
Pruning the tree

_____

_____

_____

_____

_____

_____

_____

_____

E. Read the persuasive paragraph. Then answer the questions below.

Everyone Should Vote

Elections are important, no matter what they are for. Voting in an election is democracy in action. Unless you take advantage of this privilege, you are letting a few people make your decisions for you. These decisions may be as small as who becomes class president or as important as who becomes the leader of an entire nation. Exercise your rights and make your beliefs and wishes known—vote in every election you possibly can.

1. What is one reason the writer gives for everyone to vote?

_____

2. What is one example the writer gives for the importance of voting?

_____

F. Read the paragraph below. Use proofreader's marks to revise and proofread the paragraph. Then write your revised paragraph below.

Artists choose from his materials that already are in existents to create their works of art all materials have there own qualities. artists must know the characteristicks of their chosen materyal. They must work with it and not aginst it materials are shaped in many ways cutting melting, hammering, and wearving are some of those waze.

_____

_____

_____

_____

Using What You've Learned

A. Choose one of the topic sentences below. Write a short paragraph in which you use facts to persuade your audience about the topic.

1. Certain rules that apply to children do not apply to adults.
2. Community recycling programs benefit the environment.
3. A regular fitness program has many benefits.

_____

_____

_____

_____

_____

B. Choose one of the topic sentences below. Write a short paragraph in which you use reasons to persuade your audience about the topic.

1. Being a teacher is one of the most important jobs a person can have.
2. It is important to protect endangered animals from extinction.
3. High-school students should be required to take a driver-education course.

_____

_____

_____

_____

_____

C. Choose one of the topic sentences below. Write a short paragraph in which you use an example to persuade your audience about the topic.

1. Dogs can be trained to be more than just pets.
2. A high-school diploma is necessary for obtaining many jobs.
3. You can learn a great deal about life from books.

_____

_____

_____

_____

_____

D. Choose another topic from Exercises A, B, or C. Write a statement for a composition in which you wish to persuade your audience to consider your idea about the topic.

_____

E. Write a short outline of your ideas. Include main headings, subheadings, and details.

_____

_____

_____

_____

_____

_____

_____

_____

_____

_____

F. Write the first and second paragraphs of a short composition that persuades people about your idea. Use the outline you wrote as a guide. Then revise your paragraphs, and proofread them.

_____

_____

_____

_____

_____

_____

_____

_____

_____

_____

_____

_____

Lesson 72 — Dictionary: Syllables

- A **syllable** is a part of a word that is pronounced at one time. Dictionary entry words are divided into syllables to show how they can be divided at the end of a writing line.
- A **hyphen** (-) is placed between syllables to separate them.
   EXAMPLE: neigh-bor-hood
- If a word has a beginning or ending syllable of only one letter, do not divide it so that one letter stands alone.
   EXAMPLES: a-bout   bur-y

A. Find each word in a dictionary. Then write each word with a hyphen between each syllable.

1. rummage _____
2. nevertheless _____
3. abominable _____
4. silhouette _____
5. biological _____
6. stationery _____
7. correspondence _____
8. character _____
9. enthusiasm _____
10. abandon _____

11. treacherous _____
12. effortless _____
13. romantic _____
14. nautical _____
15. accelerate _____
16. financial _____
17. significance _____
18. unimportant _____
19. commercial _____
20. ballerina _____

B. Write two ways in which each word may be divided at the end of a writing line.

1. imagination   imag-ination   imagina-tion
2. unexplainable _____ _____
3. tropical _____ _____
4. accomplishment _____ _____
5. encyclopedia _____ _____
6. librarian _____ _____
7. astronomic _____ _____
8. efficient _____ _____
9. cleanliness _____ _____

> ■ A **thesaurus** is a reference book that writers use to find the exact words they need. Like a dictionary, a thesaurus lists its entry words alphabetically. Each entry word has a list of **synonyms,** or words that can be used in its place. Some thesauruses also list **antonyms** for the entry word.
>
> EXAMPLE: You have just written the following sentence:
> The children **laughed** as the tiny puppy licked their faces.
> With the help of a thesaurus, you could improve the sentence by replacing laughed with its more precise synonym giggled.
> The children **giggled** as the tiny puppy licked their faces.

A. Use the thesaurus sample below to answer the questions.

> **move** *v. syn.* turn, budge, shift, retrieve, carry, transport, retreat, crawl, arouse, progress. *ant.* stay, stop, stabilize

1. Which is the entry word? _____

2. What are its synonyms? _____

   _____

3. Which word would you use in place of excite? _____

4. Which word would you use in place of rotate? _____

5. What are the antonyms of move? _____

6. Which antonym would you use in place of remain? _____

B. Use the synonyms of move to complete the sentences.

1. Sharon asked me if I would _____ the groceries in from the car.

2. Spot was able to _____ the golf ball from the lake.

3. Ryan's job is to _____ fruit from Michigan to other parts of the country.

4. The surfer had to _____ his weight from one leg to the other to keep his balance.

5. The instructor asked the students to _____ around in their chairs so they could see the map.

6. A baby has to _____ in order to get around.

7. We hope to _____ steadily up the mountain by climbing from ledge to ledge.

8. Robert wouldn't _____ from his favorite spot under the kitchen table.

Using the *Readers' Guide*

> ■ The ***Readers' Guide to Periodical Literature*** lists by author and by subject all the articles that appear in nearly two hundred magazines. Use the *Readers' Guide* when you need
> ● recent articles on a particular subject,
> ● several articles written over a period of time about the same subject,
> ● many articles written by the same author.

■ **Use the *Readers' Guide* samples to answer the questions below.**

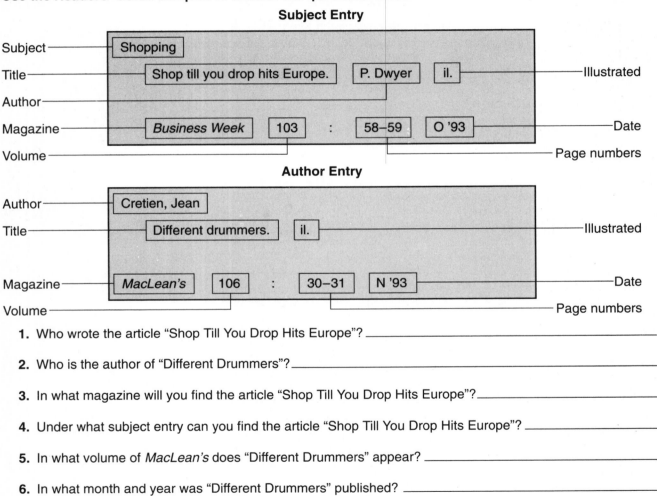

Subject Entry

Subject — Shopping
Title — Shop till you drop hits Europe.   P. Dwyer   il. — Illustrated
Author
Magazine — *Business Week*   103   :   58–59   O '93 — Date
Volume — Page numbers

Author Entry

Author — Cretien, Jean
Title — Different drummers.   il. — Illustrated
Magazine — *MacLean's*   106   :   30–31   N '93 — Date
Volume — Page numbers

1. Who wrote the article "Shop Till You Drop Hits Europe"? _____

2. Who is the author of "Different Drummers"? _____

3. In what magazine will you find the article "Shop Till You Drop Hits Europe"? _____

4. Under what subject entry can you find the article "Shop Till You Drop Hits Europe"? _____

5. In what volume of *MacLean's* does "Different Drummers" appear? _____

6. In what month and year was "Different Drummers" published? _____

7. Which article is illustrated? _____

8. In what month and year was "Shop Till You Drop Hits Europe" published? _____

9. On what pages will you find "Different Drummers"? _____

10. On what pages will you find the article "Shop Till You Drop Hits Europe"? _____

Lesson 84

Using an Atlas

> ■ An **atlas** is a reference book that uses maps to organize pertinent facts about states, provinces, countries, continents, and bodies of water. Additional maps show information on topography; resources, industry, and agriculture; vegetation; population; and climate.

A. Use the sample atlas entry to answer the questions below.

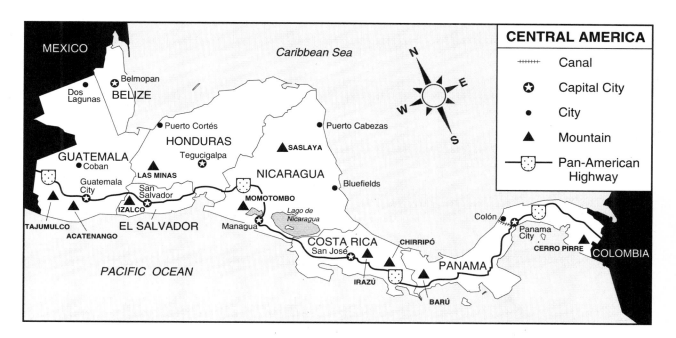

1. What part of the world is shown on this map? _____

2. How many countries make up Central America? _____

3. Which mountain is farthest west? _____

4. What major highway is shown on the map? _____

5. Which country has no mountains? _____

6. What is the capital of Nicaragua? _____

B. Answer the questions.

1. What kind of map would you use to find out where most mining occurs in a country? _____

2. Would a topographical map show you where the most people live or where the most mountains are? _____

_____

3. What kind of map would you use to decide what clothes to pack for a July trip to Japan? _____

Lesson 85

Using an Almanac

■ An **almanac** is a reference book that presents useful information on a wide variety of topics. Much of this information is in the form of tables, charts, graphs, and time lines.

■ **Use the sample almanac page to answer the questions.**

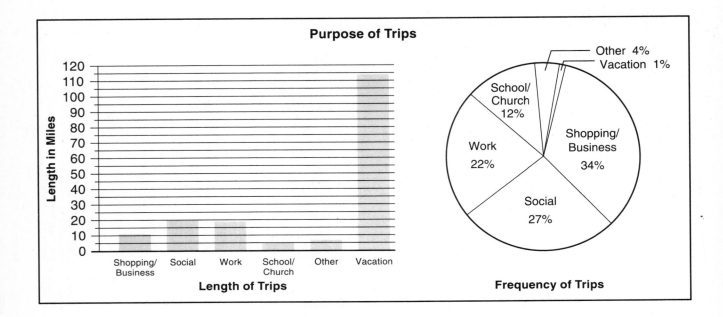

1. Which trip accounts for the most miles traveled? _____

2. What reason do most people give for taking trips? _____

3. Which three purposes together account for 60% of all trips? _____

4. Which graph shows how often people travel for a specific purpose? _____

5. Which trips are the shortest? _____

6. Do people travel farther for work or for social reasons? _____

7. Out of 100 trips, how many are made for shopping/business reasons? _____

8. What is the length of the trip least often taken? _____

9. What is the length of the trip most often taken? _____

10. Do people travel more often for school/church or for social reasons? _____

- Use a **dictionary** to find definitions of words, pronunciations of words, word usage suggestions, and etymologies, or word histories.
- Use an **encyclopedia** to find articles about many different people and things. Also use an encyclopedia to find references to related subjects.
- Use a **thesaurus** to find synonyms and antonyms.
- Use the ***Readers' Guide to Periodical Literature*** to find magazine articles on specific subjects or by particular authors.
- Use an **atlas** to find maps and other information about geographical locations.
- Use an **almanac** to find information such as population numbers, annual rainfall, election statistics, and other specific information over a period of one year.

■ Write **dictionary**, **encyclopedia**, **thesaurus**, *Readers' Guide*, **atlas**, or **almanac** to show where you would find the following information. Some information might be found in more than one source.

_____ 1. the depth of the Indian Ocean

_____ 2. the definition of the word <u>animosity</u>

_____ 3. an article on parachuting

_____ 4. the usages of the word <u>speckle</u>

_____ 5. a synonym for the word <u>build</u>

_____ 6. an article on the latest development in cancer research

_____ 7. the pronunciation of the word <u>pneumonia</u>

_____ 8. the largest lake in Louisiana

_____ 9. facts about the life of Abraham Lincoln

_____ 10. a synonym for the word <u>begin</u>

_____ 11. information about John F. Kennedy's presidency

_____ 12. the origin of the word <u>immortal</u>

_____ 13. recent articles on home fire prevention

_____ 14. the history of the French Revolution

_____ 15. the average January temperature in Santa Fe, New Mexico

_____ 16. the states through which the Mississippi River runs

_____ 17. an antonym for the word <u>answer</u>

■ Use reference sources—dictionaries, encyclopedias, the *Readers' Guide to Periodical Literature,* thesauruses, atlases, and almanacs—to find information about people, places, or things with which you are not familiar. You can also use these sources to learn more about subjects that interest you.

A. Follow the directions below.

1. Find the entry for your state in one of the reference sources. Write the exact title

   of the reference source. _____

2. Write a brief summary of the information you found about your state.

   _____

   _____

   _____

   _____

   _____

   _____

   _____

B. Follow the directions, and answer the questions.

1. Choose a famous person you would like to know more about.

   Person's name: _____

2. List two reference sources you can use to find information about this person.

   1. _____   2. _____

3. Use one of the sources you listed above to find out when the person was born.

   Write the date of birth. _____

4. Use the appropriate reference source to find the title of the most recent article written about the person. Write the title of the article.

   _____

   _____

5. Use either reference source you listed in number two. Find the entry for the person you are researching. Write a short summary of the information you found.

   _____

   _____

   _____

C. Follow the directions, and answer the questions.

1. Choose a country you would like to learn more about.

   Name of country: _____

2. List four reference sources you can use to find information about this country.

   1. _____   3. _____

   2. _____   4. _____

3. Use one reference source to find the title of the most recent article written about the country. Write the title of the article.

   _____

4. Use one reference source to find out the capital of the country. Write the name

   of the capital. _____

5. Use another reference source to find out on what continent the country is located.

   Write the name of the continent. _____

6. Find the entry for the country in any one of the reference sources you listed in number two. Write the exact title of the reference source.

   _____

7. Write a short summary of the information you found. Do not include information given in number 3, 4, or 5.

   _____

   _____

   _____

   _____

8. Find the entry for the country in one other reference source. Write

   the exact title of the reference source. _____

9. What new information did you learn about the country?

   _____

   _____

   _____

A. Use the dictionary samples to answer the questions below.

De-cem-ber (di sem′ bər) *n.* the twelfth month of the year. It has thirty-one days. [Latin *December,* which was the tenth month in the early Roman calendar, from *decem,* ten.]

den-im (den′ im) *n.* **1.** a heavy, coarse cotton cloth. **2. denims** clothing made of denim. [Short for French *(serge) de Nîmes,* a French town where the fabric was originally made.]

de-sert (dez′ ərt) *n.* a hot, dry area with few plants or animals. *-adj.* **1.** dry and barren; found in a desert: *a*

desert cactus. **2.** not inhabited: *a desert island.* [Old French *desert;* going back to Latin *desertum,* something abandoned, forsaken.]

di-et (dī′ ət) *n.* **1.** a person's or animal's usual food and drink: *A lion's diet includes meat and vegetables.* **2.** a prescribed selection of food and drink: *I hope to lose ten pounds on my diet. -v.* to eat following certain rules: *I will diet to lose weight.* [Old French *diete;* going back to Greek *diaita,* way of life.]

1. How many syllables does <u>diet</u> have? _____ desert? _____ December? _____

2. What word was named after a French town? _____

3. What part of speech is <u>December</u>? _____ denim? _____

4. From what languages did the word <u>diet</u> come? _____

5. Write the correct word for each respelling.

   a. (dez′ ərt) _____ **b.** (di sem′ bər) _____

6. Write one sentence using the second definition of <u>desert</u>. _____

   _____

7. What word originally meant "way of life"? _____

8. Through what other languages did the word <u>desert</u> come into English? _____

9. Which words can be used as more than one part of speech? _____

10. Which word comes from a word meaning "ten"? _____

B. Write <u>title page</u>, <u>copyright page</u>, <u>table of contents</u>, or <u>index</u> to tell where to find this information in a book.

_____ 1. the chapter titles

_____ 2. the page number on which a particular topic can be found

_____ 3. the name of the publisher

_____ 4. the author's name

_____ 5. the year the book was published

_____ 6. how many chapters are in the book

_____ 7. the page number on which a certain chapter begins

_____ 8. where the book was published

C. Use the graph and the chart to answer the questions below.

Pounds of Nuts Collected

Name	Percent of Total		
	Week 1	Week 2	Week 3
Sharon	10	23	10
Alberto	27	25	28
Linn	45	12	33
Ellis	18	40	29

Pounds of Nuts Collected

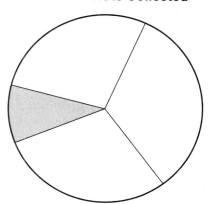

1. Which person collected the greatest percentage of nuts in Week 2? _____

2. Which person collected the total highest percentage of nuts? _____

3. Which person's total percentage is shown by the shaded portion of the graph? _____

D. Write dictionary, encyclopedia, card catalog, thesaurus, atlas, almanac, or Readers' Guide to show where you would find the following information.

_____ 1. a chart of data on the 1994 Winter Olympics

_____ 2. whether a book has illustrations

_____ 3. an article about earthworms

_____ 4. an antonym for the word charitable

_____ 5. a recent magazine article on computers

_____ 6. a map of the vegetation of Missouri

_____ 7. the author of a book

_____ 8. the origin of the word buffalo

_____ 9. cross-references for a topic

_____ 10. the most mountainous area of Argentina

A. Find the word <u>condition</u> in a dictionary. Then follow the directions, and answer the questions.

1. Write the guide words from the page on which you found the entry for <u>condition</u>.

_____

2. Write the word in syllables. _____

3. As what parts of speech can <u>condition</u> be used? _____

4. Write the history of the word. _____

_____

B. Use the sample catalog card to answer the questions.

> 808.51
> Eh
> **Ehrlich, Henry**
>   Writing effective speeches.   New York,
> Paragon House
> [1992] 214 p.

1. What type of catalog card is this? _____

2. What is the title of the book? _____

3. Who is the author of the book? _____

4. Is the book illustrated? _____

C. Find the entry for <u>apricot</u> in an encyclopedia. Then answer the questions.

1. Name three ways in which apricots are used as food. _____

2. Are the pits of apricots ever edible? _____

3. How tall can the apricot tree grow? _____

D. Use the *Readers' Guide* entry to answer the questions.

> **KERNS, LESLIE ANN**
>   The trouble with money. *Time* 68: 32–34 Je '88

1. Who wrote the article? _____

2. What is the title of the article? _____

3. In what magazine does the article appear? _____

4. Is the article illustrated? _____

E. Use the information in the chart to complete the graph. Then answer the questions below.

Average Number of Hours Spent on Sports by College Students (Per Month)

Chart

Month	Hours Spent by Students in Florida	Hours Spent by Students in Minnesota
January	40	15
March	30	25
May	25	40
July	15	35
September	20	30
November	30	15

Graph

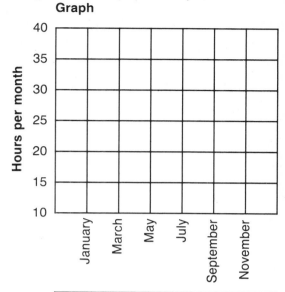

Graph Key
Students in Florida _____
Students in Minnesota _ _ _ _ _ _ _

1. In November, what is the average number of hours students in Florida spend

   participating in sports? _____ students in Minnesota? _____

2. During which two months do students in Florida spend the same average amount

   of time on sports? _____

3. During which month are students in Minnesota the most active in sports?

   _____ students in Florida? _____

4. Is there a month during which the average amount of time spent on sports is the same

   for students in Minnesota and students in Florida? _____

F. Find a resource map of Mexico in an atlas. Then answer the questions.

1. On which coast is most of the food processing done? _____

2. What mineral is mined in the Yucatan Peninsula? _____

3. What is Mexico's major crop? _____

4. What resource is found on all the coastlines of Mexico? _____

Synonyms, Antonyms, and Homonyms ▪ On the line before each pair of words, write S if they are synonyms, A if they are antonyms, and H if they are homonyms.

1. _____ aloud, allowed

2. _____ genuine, fake

3. _____ clever, smart

4. _____ threw, through

5. _____ brave, cowardly

6. _____ crave, want

7. _____ greedy, generous

8. _____ their, there

9. _____ calm, peaceful

10. _____ beech, beach

11. _____ quiet, silent

12. _____ alter, altar

13. _____ unattractive, ugly

14. _____ bloom, flower

15. _____ heard, herd

16. _____ bent, crooked

17. _____ off, on

18. _____ by, buy

Homographs ▪ Write the homograph for each pair of meanings below.

1. **a.** get down from   **b.** on fire   _____

2. **a.** from a higher to a lower place   **b.** soft feathers   _____

3. **a.** take up a weapon   **b.** part of the body   _____

4. **a.** to walk softly   **b.** a pillow   _____

5. **a.** loud noise   **b.** mesh bat used in certain sports   _____

6. **a.** to rip or pull apart   **b.** salty liquid from the eye   _____

7. **a.** belonging to me   **b.** to dig for metals or minerals   _____

8. **a.** one devoted to another   **b.** a device to stir air   _____

Prefixes, Suffixes, and Compound Words ▪ Write P if the underlined word has a prefix, write S if it has a suffix, and write C if it is a compound word.

1. _____ _____ It is time to remove the plates from the dishwasher.

2. _____ _____ Dr. Arnold is a famous doctor and research scientist.

3. _____ _____ The scouts built a campfire and planned to rearrange their tents.

4. _____ _____ They will be at a disadvantage if they mismanage the budget.

5. _____ _____ Unpleasant weather is predicted for the weekend.

6. _____ _____ Please be careful when you toss the newspaper onto the porch.

7. _____ _____ It seemed impossible that the jacket was repairable.

8. _____ _____ The dusty attic made my grandmother sneeze.

9. _____ _____ Iris and Bruce are coauthors of the newsletter.

10. _____ _____ Her impish grin made her seem more childlike than she truly was.

Contractions ▪ Write the contraction for each pair of words.

1. I have _____
2. we will _____
3. they are _____
4. could not _____
5. you have _____
6. do not _____

7. he had _____
8. I am _____
9. that is _____
10. did not _____
11. will not _____
12. there is _____

13. they will _____
14. we had _____
15. does not _____
16. it is _____
17. would not _____
18. I will _____

Connotation, Denotation, Idioms ▪ For each underlined word or words, write (–) for a negative connotation, (+) for a positive connotation, or (N) for a neutral connotation. Write I if the words make an idiom.

1. _____ The sleek horse galloped.
2. _____ She ran like the wind.
3. _____ A skinny scarecrow watched.
4. _____ An old jalopy drove by us.
5. _____ A vicious dog growled.
6. _____ I plan to drop her a line.
7. _____ The brilliant sun shone.
8. _____ It lit up the sky.

9. _____ A colorful kite flew overhead.
10. _____ An airplane carried many people.
11. _____ We stood by shooting the breeze.
12. _____ It was a relaxing afternoon.
13. _____ Two children giggled.
14. _____ Everyone gulped their lemonade.
15. _____ No one felt down in the dumps.
16. _____ Everyone got in the car and left.

Idioms ▪ For the underlined idiom in each sentence below, write the usual meaning of the words that make up the idiom.

1. You need to keep your chin up. _____

2. It really gets my goat when people litter. _____

3. I burned the midnight oil studying for that test. _____

4. She really dropped the ball on that project. _____

5. I resolved to turn over a new leaf. _____

6. I ran across some old photos in the attic. _____

7. I work two jobs to make ends meet. _____

8. I threw in the towel after trying for two hours to fix the car. _____

9. We had to eat crow when their team won the game. _____

10. Joanne spilled the beans about the surprise party. _____

Types of Sentences ■ Before each sentence, write <u>D</u> for declarative, <u>IN</u> for interrogative, <u>IM</u> for imperative, and <u>E</u> for exclamatory. Punctuate each sentence correctly.

1. _____ This dinner is delicious___

2. _____ Please pass the pepper___

3. _____ Where are the forks___

4. _____ I'm starving___

5. _____ What's in that bowl___

6. _____ Does anyone want more___

7. _____ Ouch, I burned my tongue___

8. _____ I'd like another roll___

9. _____ Eat more slowly___

10. _____ Who wants to clear the table___

Parts of a Sentence ■ Underline the word or words in each sentence that are identified in parentheses.

1. (compound predicate)   Ellen typed and proofread her report.

2. (indirect object)   Matt, lend me your black pen.

3. (simple subject)   The report is excellent.

4. (direct object)   The instructor gave the report an "A."

5. (subordinate clause)   The first draft that Ellen wrote was 12 pages long.

6. (complete predicate)   She read her notes six times.

7. (complete subject)   Everyone in the class chose a different subject.

8. (simple predicate)   All the reports were completed in two weeks.

9. (independent clause)   The reports had to be in on time, or they would lose a grade.

10. (adverb clause)   I finished before the due date.

Parts of a Sentence ■ Underline each subordinate clause. Then write <u>adjective</u> or <u>adverb</u> on the line.

_____ 1. The lawyer who defended the criminal was just doing her job.

_____ 2. The concert was over before we knew it.

_____ 3. It was the first time that Edward had been to Niagara Falls.

_____ 4. Although it was still early, Pamela left to go home.

_____ 5. Canada is a beautiful country that people like to visit.

_____ 6. When Rebecca heard that, she became very angry.

_____ 7. The horse kicked because it had never been saddled before.

_____ 8. Safety has become more important since the crime rate began to rise.

_____ 9. The people whose last names begin with "M" can enter now.

_____ 10. After the way Joe acted, I don't want to see him again.

Complex Sentences ▪ To each group of words below, add a subordinate clause or an independent clause to create a complex sentence.

1. Paul forgot the directions _____

2. After it was dark _____

3. This wasn't planned _____

4. When we took a couple of wrong turns _____

5. Before crossing the bridge _____

6. While looking for a map _____

7. When he asked for directions _____

8. No one had heard of the street _____

9. Three hours later _____

10. Before the trip home _____

Compound Sentences ▪ Create compound sentences by adding an independent clause to each group of words.

1. Walter bought a new hunting dog _____

2. She called to change her tickets _____

3. It was too late for Tom _____

4. We decided to stay at home _____

5. Leaders from several countries came _____

6. You can leave it there _____

7. It's possible that I am wrong _____

8. The wind picked up _____

Run-on Sentences ▪ Correct each run-on sentence by writing it as two sentences or as a compound sentence.

1. It was the middle of the night, the smoke alarm went off we woke up frightened.

_____

2. The reason we called you here is clear, we need to make some decisions today.

_____

Expanding Sentences ▪ Expand the sentence by adding details to answer the questions What kind? and How many? Write the expanded sentence on the line.

The butterflies migrated.

_____

Grammar and Usage ▪ **Fill in the blanks by following the directions in parentheses.**

The art of growing and _____ miniature trees is called Bonsai. The
(gerund)

Japanese word <u>bonsai</u> means "tray-planted." The Chinese first _____
(transitive verb)

bonsai over 1,000 years ago. Growing bonsai became _____ popular in
(adverb)

Japan in the 1800s. It _____ been a hobby _____
(helping verb)   (preposition)

the United States since the early 1900s and is still _____ in popularity.
(present participle)

Bonsai trees are normal trees _____ are made _____
(relative pronoun)   (preposition)

miniatures. They can be made from _____ types of trees, including
(adjective)

evergreens, pines, flowering, and fruit trees. It takes much skill, time, and _____
(abstract noun)

to make the bonsai tree look like a miniature replica of a tree in nature. Gardeners must

practice for years to _____ how to make bonsai. The bonsai
(teach or learn)

_____ are pruned and wired _____
(plural of branch)   (infinitive)

desired shapes. The dwarfed roots are kept in small containers and also pruned to stunt

_____ growth.
(possessive pronoun)

A bonsai tree ranges _____ height from two inches to two or three
(preposition)

feet. Would you _____ that a smaller tree takes much longer
(present perfect tense of <u>guess</u>)

(sometimes ten years) to achieve _____ ideal shape and size? It
(its or it's)

can grow inside _____ outside. In Japan, the healthiest and
(conjunction)

_____ bonsai are kept outside _____ are
(superlative adjective)   (conjunction)

only brought inside for viewing. _____ live for 100 years or more. In
(indefinite pronoun)

Japan, many _____ families pass them down _____
(proper adjective)   (preposition)

the next generation as a _____ heirloom.
(adjective)

Nouns ▪ Draw a line under each noun in the sentences below. Then write C or P above it to show whether it is a common or proper noun. On the line, identify each common noun as concrete, abstract, or collective.

_____ 1. Niagara Falls is on the border between the United States and Canada.

_____ 2. The citizens voted overwhelmingly for Judge Harriman.

_____ 3. Daniel showed his courage by diving into Lake Michigan.

Singular and Plural Nouns ▪ Write the plural for each singular noun.

1. volcano _____

2. painting _____

3. bench _____

4. deer _____

5. woman _____

6. mother-in-law _____

Possessive Nouns ▪ Write the possessive form of each noun below.

1. authors_____

2. men _____

3. highway_____

4. sky _____

5. envelope_____

6. Donna _____

Verbs ▪ Fill in the blank with the correct form of the verb in parentheses.

1. (show)   He has _____ his parents a great deal of respect.

2. (take)   I _____ this same route many times before.

3. (do)   Have you _____ your chores yet?

4. (speak)   She _____ more loudly than was necessary.

Pronouns ▪ Write subject, object, possessive, demonstrative, or indefinite to label each underlined pronoun.

_____ 1. Phillip gave his sister a new bicycle.

_____ 2. Do you think these are the right size?

_____ 3. They went deep-sea fishing on their vacation.

Adjectives and Adverbs ▪ Underline the correct word.

1. Roberto plays most sports very (good, well).

2. Run (quickly, quick) to the other side of the street.

3. She is the (happier, happiest) person I know.

Prepositions and Prepositional Phrases ▪ Underline each prepositional phrase. Then circle each preposition.

1. Her friend lives in the red house on the left side of the street.

2. People ran to the windows to watch the wrecking ball crash into the building.

Capitalization and End Punctuation ▪ Circle each letter that should be capitalized. Write the capital letter above it. Add the correct end punctuation to each sentence.

1. our neighborhood holds a block party every june____

2. will the organizers be mrs. hernandez and dr. altman____

3. a local restaurant, charlie's place, is donating pizzas and italian sandwiches____

4. my street will be closed off on saturday and sunday from clark st. to prairie lane____

5. mr. johnson of the store bikes for you is judging the bicycle decorating contest____

6. will the country kitchen at oakland ave. donate 100 pies for the pie-eating contest____

7. last year's champion, mark gable of rosemont, says, "i'm ready for all

   the blueberry pies you can give me____"

8. dancers and singers from the phillips school will perform scenes from

   robert louis stevenson's *treasure island*____

9. the road race begins at the corner of maple and crane streets at 8:00 A.M. on saturday____

10. there are runners entered from carlyle, rosemont, meadow grove, and newton____

Using Other Punctuation ▪ Add commas, quotation marks, and apostrophes where needed in the sentences below.

1. Why are you telling me all this now asked Cynthia.

2. You can use books encyclopedias and atlases when doing research.

3. Ive spent the last two hours waiting said Mary.

4. Scott said Youll be much happier when you get settled.

5. Lloyd Jane and Debra are all going in the same car.

6. Wont you please help me with this asked Joe.

7. Shes the one said Ellen who brought that wonderful dessert.

8. Nissans Hondas and Toyotas are Japanese automobiles.

9. My fruit salad recipe she said calls for oranges apples bananas and raisins.

10. Karen mowed the yard weeded the garden and watered the flowers.

11. Saras car was in the shop for two weeks.

12. Janet Rosa and Alicia went to Dianes dinner party.

Punctuation and Capitalization ▪ Circle each letter that should be capitalized. Add commas, quotation marks, apostrophes, periods, hyphens, and colons where needed.

1230 e. clark st.
san diego, ca 94024

mr. charles martinelli
3340 w. belden street
san diego, ca 94022

Dear mr. martinelli

on june 10 and 11, our neighborhood will be holding its fifth-anniversary summer block party____ it is a day-long event with contests performances great food and sidewalk sales____ in past years, local restaurants and businesses have donated food and prizes____ we hope your restaurant charlies place will join in and help make our block party a success____ i remember you once saying id love to pitch in next time____ please call us at 555 1270 and let us know if youll want to contribute this year____ we look forward to hearing from you soon____

Sincerely,
angela hernandez

Using Other Punctuation ▪ Add colons, semicolons, hyphens, dashes, and underlining where needed in the sentences below.

1. You mean that you said and I'm quoting you now that he was "too big for his britches"?

2. I read Lonesome Dove three times it was such a wonderful book.

3. I addressed my greeting "Dear Madam or Sir " since I didn't know whether the owner was a man or a woman.

4. The festival Saturday runs from 1000 A.M. to 500 P.M.

5. Tony bought a blue green convertible when he got his new job.

6. My sister in law writes children's stories they are also fun for adults to read.

7. My favorite show is on every Tuesday at 800 it's the best show on television.

8. The local play had parts for seventy eight people men, women, and children were invited to audition.

9. I use the money from my part time job to pay for these hobbies photography, dancing, and horseback riding.

10. Connie has seen her favorite movie, Gone With the Wind, twenty two times.

Expanding Sentences ▪ Expand the meaning of each sentence base below by adding adjectives, adverbs, and/or prepositional phrases.

1. (Airplanes flew.) _____

2. (Dogs barked.) _____

3. (Painter brushed.) _____

Topic Sentences ▪ Write a topic sentence for the paragraph below.

    Many parents encourage their children to take music lessons. Some people learn to play music immediately. Others take longer to master the skill. Practicing improves your skills and helps you learn discipline. Most adults who play instruments, whether professionally or just for fun, are thankful that they started playing as children.

Topic Sentence: _____

Supporting Details ▪ Write an <u>X</u> before the sentences that support the topic sentence.

Topic Sentence: House plants are a good addition to any home.

_____ **1.** Many house plants are easy to grow and to maintain.

_____ **2.** Plastic or clay pots are available for plants.

_____ **3.** Plants add beauty, oxygen, and humidity to a house.

_____ **4.** Studies have shown that living with plants calms people down.

_____ **5.** Some African violets have purple blooms.

Outlining ▪ Organize the following into outline form.

Topic: Painting Is Hard Work   Sand the surface until smooth

Scrape off the old paint   Preparing the surface

Painting   Spread the paint with even strokes

Stir the paint thoroughly

_____

_____

_____

_____

_____

_____

_____

Revising and Proofreading ■ Read the paragraph below. Use the proofreader's marks to revise and proofread the paragraph.

Proofreader's Marks

≡
Capitalize.

⊙
Add a period.

ⓢⓟ
Correct spelling.

/
Make a small letter.

∧
Add something.

¶
Indent for new paragraph.

∧
Add a comma.

⟋
Take something out.

⟶
Move something.

---

most people do not know that there are 48 types of eagles in the world people immediately

think of golden eagles and bald eagles two kinds that breed in North america what most

eagles halve in common are large, powerful wings and a sharp beak most eagles return the

to same nest each year and keep the same mates for life. unfortunately, both bald and

golden eagles our declining in population due to extensive hunting by man and loss of

they're natural environment. laws now Protect the eagles.

many types of eagles are the size of hawks. but the large bald eagle and the golden eagle,

with wing spans of about seven feet and body sizes from 30 to 35 inches, are smaller than

the harpy eagle of central and South America. The harpy eagles range from 30 to 37 inches

and live in jungles.

Persuasive Composition ■ Write a paragraph in which you try to convince the reader that reading throughout life is the best way to continue to learn.

_____

_____

_____

_____

_____

_____

_____

_____

Using the Dictionary ▪ Use the dictionary samples to answer the questions.

county (koun′ tē) *n.* **1.** one of the self-governing sections that a state is divided into. **2.** one of the sections that a country is divided into. **3.** the residents of a county. [French *conté,* meaning an area ruled by a count]

mark (märk) *n.* **1.** a line, scratch, or spot left by one object when it touches another object. **2.** a symbol, sign, or inscription. **3.** something, such as a line or object, used as a point of reference. *The rowers passed the half-way mark in record time.* *-v.t.* **1.** to put a mark on. **2.** to be a characteristic of. [Old English, *mearc,* meaning a boundary or sign]

1. Circle the letter of the words that could be the guide words for the above entry.

   a. corn / marine   **b.** courage / mallard   **c.** country / marlin

2. How many definitions are listed for county? _____ mark? _____

3. Write one sentence using the second definition of mark.

   _____

4. Write a sentence using mark as a verb. _____

   _____

5. What part of speech is county? _____

6. How many syllables are in county? _____ mark? _____

7. Write the respelling of county _____ mark _____

8. Which word came from the Old English word mearc? _____

9. Which word's etymology means "a territory ruled by a count"? _____

10. Which word means almost the same in Old English as it does in modern English? _____

Reference Sources ▪ Write dictionary, encyclopedia, thesaurus, *Readers' Guide,* atlas, or almanac to tell where you would find this information.

1. _____ the etymology of the word reindeer

2. _____ the history of the Better Business Bureau

3. _____ an antonym for the word hungry

4. _____ the height of Mount Rainier

5. _____ the title of an article on President Clinton

6. _____ the average rainfall in Mexico for the month of July

7. _____ the definitions of the word relate

8. _____ the life of a monarch butterfly

Charts and Graphs ▪ Use the chart and graph to answer the questions.

Movie Viewing Chart

Month	Theater	Rentals
April	53	197
May	117	133
June	201	49
July	185	65
August	178	72

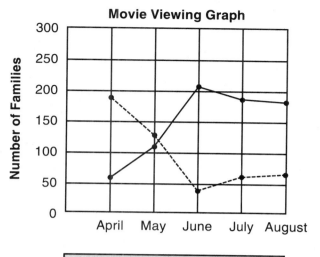

Movie Viewing Graph

Graph Key
Theater _____
Rentals -------------------------------

1. In July, did more people rent movies or go to the theater? _____

2. During which months did more people stay home than go to the theater? _____

3. Is it quicker to determine from the chart or from the graph
   the exact number of families who went to the theater each month? _____

4. Is it quicker to determine from the chart or from the graph how
   the families' movie viewing habits changed over the summer? _____

Visual Aids ▪ Use the map to answer the questions.

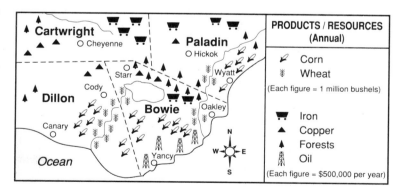

1. What is the major resource in Paladin? _____

2. What is the combined yearly value of forest products in Dillon and Cartwright? _____

3. In which state would an oil refinery most likely be found? _____

4. Which state has the widest variety of resources? _____

Index